FREEDOM
AND TABOO

DISCARD

FREEDOM AND TABOO

*Pornography and
the Politics
of a Self Divided*

RICHARD S. RANDALL

UNIVERSITY OF CALIFORNIA PRESS
BERKELEY   LOS ANGELES   LONDON

University of California Press
Berkeley and Los Angeles, California

University of California Press, Ltd.
London, England

©1989 by
The Regents of the University of California

Library of Congress Cataloging-in-Publication Data
Randall, Richard S.
    Freedom and taboo.

    Bibliography: p.
    Includes index.
    1.   Pornography—Social aspects—United States.
2. Erotica. 3. Social norms. 4. Obscenity (Law)—United States. I. Title.
HQ471.R32   1989   363.4'7   88-29629
ISBN 0-520-06379-1 (alk. paper)

Printed in the United States of America
1   2   3   4   5   6   7   8   9

For Laurie

Contents

Preface

Pornography is a familiar yet inaccessible subject, charged with stereotype and polemic, informed by ideology of one sort or another, and mined nearly everywhere with psychic defenses. It is tied to disputes about freedom, morality, privacy, gender relations, community, the Constitution, art, crime, effects of the media, and the formation of sexual attitudes. It is almost impossible to be indifferent to pornography, almost obligatory to be "for" or "against" it. On few subjects have commentators spoken past each other so often or views defied consensus so completely. Even among scholars, perspectives tend to be limited in scope. Pornography is often treated as though it were chiefly a problem in law, literature, or moral philosophy or a matter to be understood through laboratory investigation. It may be all of these, but it is also a great deal more.

My purpose in this book is not to choose one path over another or attempt to reconcile the implacably divergent, but to make new, more accurate, and larger maps of the territory. If we are to make greater sense of what has already been said and of what we already know, we need to think about pornography more inclusively, systematically, and, if possible, objectively. We need to understand why pornography has been a persistent problem for human beings everywhere and why it is almost continuously on liberal democracy's agenda of public issues.

Pornography is in the world and in the mind. It is both a universal social category that varies with cultural time and place and a psychological one, no less universal, that occupies only inner space. The transgressive themes and images of pornography confound us because they invite and repel. My analysis departs from most other studies by seeking the roots of this paradox, not in elements of rational choice and debate about freedom, morality, and censorship, important as they are, but in desideration deep within the unconscious mind.

In starting with the pornographic within, I have drawn on the insights of psychoanalysis. The obvious utility of a psychosexual theory for understanding the human capacity to be pornographic does not diminish other approaches to personality and development based on thought processes and qualitative differences in cognition or that include the wider milieu of the social world. But psychoanalytic theory is unique in stressing the power of unconscious mental processes activated and shaped initially in infancy and early childhood by sexual and aggressive drives as the latter are affected by interactive experience. Recent developments emphasizing ego autonomy and the importance of early object relations have extended the analytic focus well beyond the boundaries of Freud's classic libido theory.

One need not be uncritical of psychoanalytic theory to appreciate its explanatory scope and power. It is less a unified theory than a huge collection of parts, some of which—oedipal conflict and the dynamic unconscious itself, for example—are factually well established. Others, such as the id, ego, and superego, are metapsychological constructs that cannot be empirically weighed or put to experimental test. Like abstractions in all sciences, their value lies in being aids to conceptualization, making sense and order out of a welter of facts, and, most important, explaining the otherwise inexplicable. Wherever the psychological self is a factor in the larger study of social and political phenomena, psychodynamic insight can complement and vitally extend our traditional concerns with the formal, quantitative, and behavioral by illuminating the nonrational and showing us how often things may not be as they appear.

In examining pornography as a versatile, ubiquitous social category, the sought-after yet condemned product of mind and culture, I have departed again from most other studies. My concern is not chiefly with the securing of rights and freedom, a matter ably and exhaustively explored in innumerable serious and popular works, but with the demand and felt need for control. The analysis looks beyond the delineation of constitutional rights, important though they are, to operating freedom of speech as that freedom is determined by the social, political, and technological circumstances of a modern communications environment. In this, I have dealt with the censorship interest, its motivation, energy, and effect, not as civic pathology but as political and social force. The popularity of that interest challenges liberal society while at the same time laying claim to a petitional place in liberal democratic society.

Libertarians interested mainly in the perfection of rights may regard all this as a form of aid and comfort for the enemy. I hope thoughtful libertarians will see that the union of free speech and mass democratic societies, uneasy in the best of circumstances, is forever destined to be equivocal on transgressive sexual expression and that the constituents of each, who are of course one and the same, are often not giants of self-possession but, more than we like to admit, struggling, ambivalent human beings, in conflict with themselves and often with each other.

R. S. R.

Introduction

Few subjects in recent years have received as much attention as pornography, and few have defied public consensus or satisfactory understanding so successfully. Pornography is not new—as a form of socially unacceptable expression, it is probably as old as the human community itself. What are new are its ubiquity and pervasiveness. Individuals in modern liberal democracies are communicated with more than any humans in history and are probably more free than any previous population to produce and obtain sexual communication. Yet the modern explosion of pornography is far more entitled than in the past and occurs in societies that are socially and politically far more heterogeneous and democratic. Today in the United States pornography circulates largely free of formal control. Since the psychodynamic roots of pornography lie deep in the unresolved sexual conflicts most persons have, it is not surprising that the contemporary libertarian triumphs are accompanied by conflict and popular protests or that pornography has a continuing place on liberal democracy's table of public issues.

Conflict over pornography has produced a sizable corpus of popular and serious commentary. Yet, except for the massive research and report of the President's Commission on Obscenity and Pornography in 1970 and the somewhat lesser efforts of the Attorney General's Commission on Pornography in 1986, most studies, including some excellent scholarship, have dealt with limited aspects of the problem, and many have been works of advocacy rather than inquiry. Here, drawing on work in several disciplines, we seek a broader theoretical understanding of the nature of pornography, its place in the human condition, and its control in a modern liberal democracy. This is not a partisan work, but its conclusions will

1

challenge certain moral and policy assumptions, libertarian as well as censorial.

Censors and moralists often fail to see the inevitability of pornography in human experience and the ease with which internal stress can be projected onto social policy. Libertarians, artists, and pornographers often fail to appreciate both the anxiety produced by forbidden sexual stimuli and the consequent popular character of censorship, supposing its thrust to derive mainly from government and its agents. Neither side fully grasps the paradoxical, mutually supportive relationship between pornography and censorship.

Pornography is a product of human sexuality, but the derivation is neither simple nor direct, nor is that sexuality itself undistorted in the process. If the human sexual interest were limited to the procreation or the simple physical release that marks the animal's naturalistic sexual world, pornography and the pornographic would probably not exist at all. Human beings alone have eroticized their sexual nature and imposed on it a normative element informing both act and imagination. Eroticism is the inescapable and distinguishing psychic experience of all human beings. Its origins lie in the uniquely prolonged dependence of infancy, where the young human's remarkable cerebral capacity, not the least element of which is an ability to imagine—to "make pictures" relating to desire, fear, rage, and other emotions—far exceeds the capacity to act independently to fulfill desires or defend against threats. Inevitable restraints imposed from without, instead of simply being "learned," as they might be by the young of inferior species, act instead on an incredibly rich developing world of the imagination, creating psychic conflicts of the most complex and excruciating sort. The simple physicality of animal sexual nature is thus warped and transformed into eroticized sexuality. This "transcendence" humanizes and neuroticizes, producing, in Norman O. Brown's words, "Man, the sick animal."

It is the forbidden element in eroticism, its darker side, that makes sexual territory so often seem dangerous and that provides our chief reason for accepting regulation of it. Indeed, sexual behavior and expression are among the most thoroughly ordered aspects of our lives. Ideological claims notwithstanding, these limits cannot be understood simply as the debilitating design or by-product of Christianity, Western civilization, capitalism, "middle-class morality," sexism, or other well-established cultural forces. All known human societies—past and present, primitive and modern, Western and Eastern, theological and pagan, patriarchal and matriarchal—have sought to regulate, control, forbid, or discourage some, though not always the same, aspects of sexuality. The sexual utopianist is thus forever disappointed. Of course, restrictions may sometimes be unwise, cruel, destructive, or in their ramifications ill suited to particular persons subject to them, but sexuality incurs universal regulation because many human beings have consciously or unconsciously welcomed, even demanded, that control. External restraints in part reflect the inner police and judiciary governing each of us. No human being—libertine, "noble savage," rapist, saint, or "happily married"—has ever been completely free sexually. Complete sexual freedom is a contradiction of the human condition.

Whether imposed externally or from within, restraints are the normative element in eroticized sexuality. Yet no regulation or taboo meets with perfect or complete compliance. All are informed by ambivalence and all harbor the subordinate theme of transgression. Humankind's chief nonsexual taboo, murder, is a striking example. Though complied with much more often than not, the rule against premeditated killing is subject to a great many actual violations; countless more are committed only in wish or imagination. Here we have the paradox of all taboos: neither murder nor various other "unacceptable" acts—adultery, sodomy, incest, for example—would be the object of prohibition were they not, from time to time, very much desired.

Eroticism, then, is animal sexuality modified by psychic demands rooted in a universal human experience and by cultural prescriptions and imperfect injunctions reacting to and reflecting those demands. The result is a stupendous source of energy, far exceeding any comparable store elsewhere in the animal kingdom. As a compound of physical and psychic forces, eroticized sexuality has an extraordinary infiltrating power and makes the human being the most sexual of all animals. Nor can this erotic interest be shut off except superficially, through lack of sexual vigor, and probably not even then, for it is ontogenetically prior to genital sexuality and not limited to it. Even saints, Georges Bataille observed, have their temptations. With its injunctions on one side and desired transgressions on the other, eroticism is not only an inescapable part of the human experience but a major defining characteristic of being human.

Eroticism provides the psychological basis for both the pornographic within and pornography without. The latter is often seen as an aspect of the seemingly larger problem of sexual behavior and control. Indeed, in most societies concern about behavior does appear to be more basic than concern about mere representations of behavior. Yet the precedence is misleading; for most persons sexual expression is likely to be more troubling, consciously or unconsciously, than matters of behavior. The reason is twofold. First, the internally pornographic ontogenetically precedes regulatable behavior and persists long after issues of *conduct* are largely settled or controlled. Second, because it deals in symbols and images rather than overt acts, pornography's natural limits are the spacious ones of imagination. As repeated portrayals of inexhaustible potency, exaggerated organs, and unlikely liaisons suggest, the pornographic world is not bound by the physical limitations of the external environment or by its social probabilities. Behavior ordinarily securely inhibited or regulated by internal and external authority is common subject matter in pornography. For most persons what is "acted out" is fairly well settled, but the fantastical remains boundless. The threshold of the forbidden is more quickly reached and easily crossed in the imagination, and the delights and terrors of doing so are far richer and more improbable than anything actual behavior usually affords. Characteristically, pornographic expression is an unsettling reminder of temptations, conflicts, and tensions inhibited in behavior and possibly even denied in our conscious minds. It may thus invite and excite even as it frightens and revolts.

The cultural array of restrictions on sexual behavior, and the conventions of permissible sexuality, derive from our ability to imagine and to portray not merely "normal" and acceptable acts but also the most improbable, "perverse," and disturbing aspects of our eroticized sexual nature. This ability and our indulgence in it exist long before we are able to *act* in a truly genital mode directed at others. In the purely biological, animal world, the adult is father to the child; in the erotic, human one, matters are reversed.

We can now be more conceptually precise. The *pornographic within* is an imagistic resolution of erotic impulses or wishes to violate sexual taboos, mores, conventions, and the like. It has psychodynamic rather than material reality. *Pornography* is a material representation, portrayal, depiction, or other symbolization of the internally pornographic through a medium of expression, usually image, language, gesture, or sound. In this sense, pornography lies between the inner world of wish and impulse and the entirely external one of behavior and act, though this structural identity implies no necessary progression from wish to act.

Though they usually appear in adult dress, imagined sexual transgressions are based on erotic fantasies and conflicts of infancy. As such, they may produce sexual excitation as well as feelings of shame and revulsion. Because these wishes have a forbidden element, their material representation is, to some degree or other, objectionable, as a matter of individual perception or social consensus. In the latter case, a given representation may be objectionable in various degrees, in various circles, and at various times and places. It may be lawful or unlawful. It may be presented with artistry and insight, or partly or totally lacking in either.

Obscenity is pornography proscribed by law. We make no other distinction between the terms; they have been used so interchangeably in both serious and popular writing that separate definition would be strained. Pornography has sometimes referred to writing as opposed to other representation, or to anything deliberately designed to produce sexual excitation. Yet these distinctions between obscenity and pornography are not generally observed; in moving from the nominative to the adjectival, they break down almost completely. Because we are concerned here with eroticized representation in its broadest sense, such distinctions have little utility.

We must, however, clearly distinguish the pornographic as a psychological element from pornography as a social designation. The former describes an imagistic product of a normatively modified sexuality; the latter, a normative judgment on an expression of that product. Most commentary on pornography fails to make the distinction clearly, but focuses on one element, usually the sociological, and ignores the other, or runs the two together unawares. We hold that understanding pornography and censorship depends largely on understanding the relationship of the "two pornographies": the psychological and the sociological. Thus, for example, the anthropomorphic description of Jerusalem's corruption in the Old Testament book of Ezekiel might be functionally pornographic for some persons, yet not be pornography. Similarly, Molly Bloom's soliloquy in *Ulysses* might be designated pornography (as it once was), yet for some persons not be psychodynamically pornographic.

If the human capacity for pornography is universal, the human interest in censoring it is no less so. This is the paradox of eroticism: we cannot be characteristically human without both the pornographic and the impulse to control it. In our eroticized sexual nature many territories are forbidden; they are closed not over our protests but with our complicity. Restrictions on sexual expression exist because they address a need, though not one felt by all persons at all times. Contrary to libertarian perceptions, these regulations are not simply imposed or maintained from above, that is, by government. That is not to say that a particular regulation is desirable or its operations fair, or that regulations are not sometimes evaded or given little more than lip service. But probably no working regulation can be completely alien to those whom it governs. Regulations that operate for large numbers of persons touch something responsive in many of those persons, though the link may not be fully conscious.

The matter is complicated in a liberal society, where beyond any freedom to act lies a presumably greater freedom to express oneself through word or image. In holding to the "marketplace of ideas" as an article of civic faith, the liberal society bestows on the processes of communication an independent political standing that merits extensive protections, even to the extent of inscribing these protections in the highest law of the realm. The values of a liberal society work, in effect, to magnify the differences between behavior and image. Unacceptable sexual conduct is more easily reached and controlled than representations of that conduct. However much this distinction may be applauded, it remains true that the working freedom it aims to secure requires an unusually high, perhaps unrealistic, level of tolerance in practice. That freedom may itself produce—and make less manageable—high levels of erotically centered anxiety.

The matter is further complicated in a liberal *democratic* society, where the voice of the many is legitimate and officially sovereign. More persons and groups are likely to have a say not only in official policies, including regulatory determinations, but also in the multitude of conventions, norms, and understandings that fill the gaps between policy and the larger social environment. Modern liberal democratic societies are also communications democracies in which technological advances in representation and distribution have produced a communications-saturated environment of unparalleled diversity for an audience of unparalleled size.

During the last hundred years, the United States and Great Britain, leaders in the development of mass communications and the achievement of mass literacy, have each engaged in extensive and, at times, severe formal censorship supported by a variety of informal controls. Unexalted as it may seem, pornography as a major public issue may be one of the badges of the liberal democratic state. Far from signifying the decay or corruption of such a society, a pornography controversy may indicate that its infrastructure of individual liberties is in good working order. At the same time, continuing conflict over pornography may also signal unusual stress in the popular democratic elements of that society.

If we are to have a modern liberal democracy, the liberal society of free speech and individual rights and the mass democratic society of equality and popular rule must coexist. In the former, established civil liberties and advanced communications technology invite and facilitate various kinds of sexual expression; in the latter, large numbers of persons and groups are able to participate and be heard in policy-making and social control. The alliance has never been easy, and it is clearly strained by the question of pornography. Intelligent policy (and probably intelligent choices for each of us as individuals) depends on a clear understanding of the pornographic within as well as pornography without, and the paradoxical relationship between the latter and censorship.

Viable policy concerning sexual expression cannot rest on either of those comfortably simple, mutually exclusive ends, complete freedom for pornography or near-complete suppression of it. The seemingly more reasonable utilitarian touchstone of demonstrable harm is not satisfactory either. As an approach to policy, each of these positions rests on a valid but partial insight: the utopian, that healthy, self-possessed persons are probably less troubled by sexual expression and may possibly lead more fulfilled lives; the moralist, that images of pornography are often mean and, in particular, portray women meanly; the utilitarian, or "causalist," that protection against harm is a high and rational priority but, if no harm is shown, that freedom is an objective no less high and rational. The erotic paradox and the limited ability of human beings to remake themselves will disappoint both the utopian and the moralist; the limits on human knowledge and on its dispassionate application will disappoint the causalist.

We will begin the inquiry in Part One with the human condition: the ontogenetic fact of forbidden wishes and fantasies, and the universality and variability of social regulation of sexual words and images. We will draw on psychoanalytic insight for an understanding of the pornographic within and will examine its social appearance as pornography in various cultures and societies.

In Part Two, we will look at two quite different aspects of knowledge: what the pornographic imagination may tell us about ourselves as individuals and as a species, and what we know and do not know about the effects of pornography itself.

Part Three deals with pornography as a persistent and seemingly functional institution in the social order, its affinity with liberal society, and the difficulties that affinity poses for a liberal democratic society.

In Part Four, we examine conflict over erotic expression as a public policy issue in the American communications environment. Included here are the social and political elements that give the pornography problem its modern form: wide disagreement on substantive designation, availability of legal protections in the form of rights, an operating amalgam of formal and informal controls, and diverse responses from government itself. These elements will be dealt with in the light of changes in the technology and sociology of communications and the rise of a libertarian obscenity doctrine in American law.

Part One

_____

Condition

Chapter One

The Pornographic Animal

. . . the sexuality peculiar to man, the sexuality of a creature with the gift of tongues.

Georges Bataille

We may with advantage at times forget what we know.

Publius Syrus

Homo Sexualis

If we are to understand pornography as a human product—and it is entirely that—we must recognize that both its invitation and its offense lie in the very nature of being human. Human beings are distinguished from other animals in two profound ways, one physical, the other developmental. Our remarkable cerebral power, vastly exceeding even that of our closest relatives among the primates, has allowed us to dominate and control much of our physical environment. Yet the human infant is an unusually vulnerable creature, living in a state of dependence far longer than any other young animal. Even among the slow-developing primates, the baby lemur learns to walk within the first week, and the ape within six months. The human infant may require a year and a half to develop this skill. Other primate young are suckled for days or several weeks, but the human baby may nurse for two or more years. Intimate physical ties between mother and young last longer among humans than in any other species and are still strong when the sex impulse begins to be directed away from the self and when the mother is often still the chief and perhaps the only external presence. Young monkeys may reach social maturity in two to four months and sexual maturity in two to three years, but humans pass through many stages of social development and may not reach full sexual maturity until they have completed almost a quarter of their entire life spans.

High mental capacity and slow maturation are positively related throughout most of the animal kingdom, with humans the extreme case.

11

Although the human period of dependency varies from individual to individual and may be affected by cultural factors, prolonged infancy is a primary circumscribing biologic fact of human life. The extraordinary extended care and nurturance of the human infant shapes our psychology, our social life, all the characteristics of humanity itself.

Ascent on the evolutionary ladder is associated with changes in sexual organization. Like our closest relatives, the anthropoid apes, human beings are much less dependent on gonadal hormones and seasonal physiological changes. In the female, this is reflected in the change from an estrus, or seasonal period of "heat," to the much shorter menstrual cycle; in the male, it is reflected in a more or less constant sexual drive and, typically, a year-round sexual interest in the female. Physically, sexual behavior is largely controlled by the cortex of the brain, allowing a considerable degree of decisional and, hence, normative control.[1] The result is a highly active sexuality not directed solely or even primarily toward reproduction.

Among many, perhaps most, higher infrahuman species in the wild, little or no conflict exists between dependence of the young and sexuality. Maternal care and breeding tend to operate alternately. The sexes separate after mating, and the female bears the young alone. Dependency is over before the next breeding season, and the female's roles as protective mother and mate usually do not overlap. Indeed, the most recent offspring may actually have departed, and in many species the mother's earlier male offspring may even become potential mates on the same competitive terms as other males.[2] Such sexual/maternal role alternation does not occur in the human being. The animal that is not constrained by a breeding cycle must find a way to accommodate a more or less continuous sexual interest along with prolonged infant dependency.

In this evolutionary course we see the simple biologic underwriting of the human "family." The female's anatomical, physically gratifying relationship with the infant is a prolonged one, while the male's sexual interest in the female is noncyclical. In purely biologic terms, the female's body remains the potential battleground for divergent interests—"at once the necessary oral object of the infant and the genital object of the male."[3] Since the male lacks an anatomical or physical need that would allow him to love the child as such, the third side of the triangle of ties is more problematic. Unlike the gratifications of maternity and copulation, those of paternity are far less instinctive and must be learned more often than not.[4] Distinctive human traits that encourage development of the family as a way of ensuring the infant's survival and providing sexual gratification are the foundation for much humane and loving behavior. Yet they also saddle that institution with conflict, creating grave trials for its youngest member.

The instinctual dilemma is further affected by an extraordinary range of uniquely human mental and psychic activity: the processes we loosely call thinking—coordinating, classifying, evaluating, concluding, planning, and "making sense" of perceptions—and the ability to employ symbols, ranging from primitive surrogates for reality to the complex abstractions of language, art, and mathematics. Perceptions and other products of mental activity are retained voluntarily and involuntarily: some can be recalled at will, while others remain relatively inaccessible in the unconscious mind. These give the human animal a capacity to engage in imaginary activity or fantasy, unknown to lower species. Fantasy may serve as preparation for realistic action in the external environment, but the wishes it seeks to fulfill often remain entirely internal. Some are conscious, as in daydreams, and others arise from the unconscious and reflect forbidden desires or conflicts. Such fantasies may not correspond closely to the immediate external environment. For the young infant they may be "real" and not clearly distinguishable from external events and objects. Those derived from forbidden desires may give rise to ideas or actions aimed at gratification, usually vicarious. But they may also prompt defensive measures, such as repression or denial, to ward off the possibility or even the suggestion of fulfillment.[5]

The Sacred Rule

The physical, mental, psychological, and social characteristics that set the human being off so sharply from all other animals shape a sexuality far more convoluted, compelling, and confounding than reproduction or physical release alone could possibly require. It is not surprising that sexual behavior and expression should be among the most extensively regulated aspects of human experience. To be elaborately sexually regulated is to be human. Indeed, this constitutional fact is as conspicuous for sexual activity merely imagined or represented as it is for behavior itself.

Before we address the nature and consequences of social regulation of sexual expression, we must ask *why* the mere representation of certain sexual reality should be so troubling. We do this, in the first instance, by looking carefully at the most common regulation in the rich diversity of human sexual norms, perhaps the only one that can truly be called panhuman—the repudiation of incest.

Almost every known society, past or present, from primitive tribe to advanced civilization, has imposed taboos or restrictions on incest. Rejection of primary incest—that between mother and son, father and daughter, or brother and sister—is nearly universal. Rare exceptions can be cited: brother-sister and sometimes father-daughter relations were permitted in Pharaonic and Ptolemaic Egypt and among the Incas. But these were "privileges" of the very few, usually the ruling royalty, or were permitted only under special and ritualistic circumstances.[6] No society, however, appears to have permitted exceptions to the mother-son taboo, the most sacred restraint in human sexuality.

Social control of childhood and adolescent sexual behavior is almost always part of the larger design of incest regulation.[7] Even in societies a Westerner might consider permissive, in which heterosexual or even homosexual play and masturbation are accepted or at least tolerated, the one restraint almost sure to be found is a local variation of the incest prohibition. In almost no society is the taboo limited to the nuclear family; most, including many advanced cultures, extend it to grandparents, uncles, aunts, nieces, nephews, and first cousins.[8] In still others, it may apply to an even wider range of kin, in some instances so extensive that any given person may be precluded from marriage with half the members of the opposite sex otherwise available.[9]

It has been widely argued that human aversion to incest is natural, a trait bred into the race over thousands of generations.[10] Yet the "heredity" thesis, the key explanatory element of which is the presumed biologic harm of continued inbreeding, presents both logical and empirical difficulties. Lower species, all far more sexually programmed than humankind, offer uncertain evidence of a natural check on incest. Some minimize consanguineous mating, but it is not clear whether this avoidance is inbred or is, instead, an adaptive mechanism—such as the early inhibiting of aggression among siblings that occupy necessarily close quarters, leading in turn to lower levels of sexual curiosity and initiation—or whether it is the product of intergenerational competition for mates, in which the older, larger, and usually stronger same-sex parent drives off the sexually maturing offspring.[11] Most strikingly, complete promiscuity—indiscriminate mating with parents, siblings, and offspring—is a common mammalian pattern, observed among rats, spider monkeys, macaques, and, often to their owners' dismay, many household pets.

Genetics research itself yields inconclusive evidence of the need for outbreeding. Among many lower species, intensive or continuous inbreeding has been shown to reduce variability and thus accent maladaptive traits, such as infertility, smaller size, slower growth rate, and lower resistance to disease, as well as to affect learning ability and certain other behavioral capacities adversely.[12] Research on the effects of human inbreeding, which is not subject to experiment, is much less substantial. Although there is some evidence of a higher probability of maladaptive traits in offspring of individual consanguineous matings, these effects may be offset by a long-term gene frequency change in a population as a whole.[13] Even if biologically harmful effects of consanguineous mating are conceded, the heredity thesis must still answer the logic of natural selection; harmful consequences of inbreeding would have little phylogenetic significance if they did not lower the competitive fitness of species. Given the grinding force of natural selection, why would a maladaptive tendency toward consanguineous mating not simply breed itself out? Presumably, incestuously inclined hominids would by now have disappeared, victims of unfitness, leaving only those averse to such mating. If such has actually been the case, as the heredity thesis implies, why would a highly visible, strenuously administered, universal taboo be necessary at all?

The answer seems twofold and clear. First, the apparent widespread human aversion to incest is not inbred at all, but is an acquired preference. Second, the taboo would be illogical and its maintenance uneconomic were there not an inclination to the very end forbidden. If the aversion expressed in the taboo were biologically determined, we would expect avoidance to be unambiguous and nearly automatic. But both clinical and criminological evidence from a variety of cultures indicates that this is anything but the case. Incestuous impulses and fantasies are legion, and actual acts of incest, to judge only by the cases that have come to light, are far more common than generally supposed.[14] Without the taboo, consanguineous sexual contact, rather than being instinctively avoided, would be frequently indulged both in act and in imagination.[15]

In contrast to the heredity thesis, "environmental" theories admit, implicitly at least, that strong incestuous impulses exist, and they view the taboo as a self-imposed restraint to be explained by its biologic or social utility. Avoiding the harmful effects of inbreeding is one of those benefits.[16] Again, it is unnecessary to question the assumption about inbreeding to have doubts about its explanatory power. Awareness of a link between consanguinity and genetic harm to later generations requires a degree of biological understanding not often found in primitive societies.

Modern genetic theory itself occupies but a recent moment in historic time. In fact, if awareness of the possible harm of inbreeding were at all extensive, we would expect to find it precisely where rare exceptions to the taboo have been permitted—among certain exalted leaders and royal families concerned about the quality of heirs. Moreover, genetic utility does nothing to explain the taboo's persistent and near-universal vitality where consanguineous sexual activity is unrelated to reproduction, as in the case of postmenopausal women, or family members not bound by blood, such as step-relations, adoptees, and in-laws.

Because they require exchange of women, the taboo and its exogamous extension are seen as offering another utility—encouragement of inter-family alliances and cooperation.[17] Lévi-Strauss speculates that such transactions indirectly led to awareness of the social advantages of even larger-scale economic exchanges, collective defense, and cultural innova-tion.[18] Gains from cooperative activity are undeniable, and the link to elaborate exogamous mechanisms is easily appreciated. This utility alone, however, cannot explain the taboo's continued existence. In all complex societies and most less advanced ones, the value of interfamily alliances has diminished, and exogamy has long since been overshadowed by a host of more obviously efficient mechanisms for rewarding cooperation in social and economic endeavors and in matters of defense. Yet the incest taboo persists in all societies.

The taboo has also often been seen as a device for controlling intrafamily conflict and thus as necessary for family stability.[19] By forcing the search for sexual partners and mates outside the household, the taboo clearly works to minimize intrafamily rivalries and remove nonspousal sexual matters from the domestic arena. But this undeniable benefit fails to explain why the taboo persists even where intrafamily rivals may be dead or otherwise absent, or why incest is not accommodated, partially at least, in families blessed with low levels of conflict. This is not to suggest that the domestic environment could tolerate completely unregulated intrafamily sexual relations; but if the taboo served mainly to order and stabilize, we would expect to see many functional alternatives to outright prohibition, such as regulation within the family of time, place, and manner of access of each member to every other member, so that sexual rivalry is dealt with in the same way that many nonsexual conflicts are resolved.[20] Yet, except for rare and highly particularized circumstances, such as the Azande hunter-leader's being allowed intercourse with his daughter on the eve of an important and dangerous hunt, there is no evidence that such functional alternatives have ever been employed.[21] The spousal relationship excepted, human beings have almost always chosen to proscribe sex, rather than apportion it, within the nuclear family.

Nor does the conflict-reduction function explain why the very prospect of incest produces intense emotional reaction. We frequently read of the "dread," "horror," or "abhorrence" of incest. In a dozen or more languages, "motherfucker" is the most abusive epithet possible.[22] Actual transgression of the incest taboo brings a stronger response than almost any other sexual violation. In primitive and less advanced societies, violators are subject to public censure or punished severely, in some cases by death. In almost every modern society, including the United States, incest is a criminal offense, even when it occurs among consenting adults.[23] These would be exceptionally strong measures if the taboo's function were merely to keep family peace.

Even if there are no legal sanctions, the incest taboo appears to be strongly internalized. Violation is commonly perceived as an "unthinkable" act, subjecting the perpetrator to divine punishment or some other terrible and inexorable fate.[24] The classical transgressors, Oedipus and Jocasta, though actually unwitting participants, are mythic figures and instructive in their tragedy. Each is horrified at the discovery of their crime, and each suffers severe punishment—death or mutilation. In both cases, that punishment is self-inflicted.

We obviously feel the need to declare that we are not incestuous animals. Our fierce attempts to observe the taboo, attempts rationalized by various functional advantages, clearly earn us the right to say it. But to whom are we speaking? And why do we need to say it? For answers, we must look beyond the apparent adaptive aspects of the taboo and ask whether this universal prohibition has a less obvious yet far more compelling utility. Freud addressed precisely this question in his remarkable work *Totem and Taboo*, using insights gained in analyzing infantile conflicts to explain totemism, the near-universal practice of primitive tribes in which a "totem"—usually a species of animal or plant—is worshipped. Distinctive for each tribe or clan, the totem is regarded by members as the carrier of the spirits of dead ancestors. It is thus sacred and surrounded by many prohibitions and taboos. It may not be killed or eaten or, in some clans, even mentioned by name. Violations are often punished severely. Yet paradoxically, at certain times, such as at the death of a clan member, the totem may be treated as an enemy and consumed at a ceremonial feast. Thus the totem, which in effect identifies the clan, is holy and sacred, yet may sometimes be unclean and polluted—contradictory qualities that combine to render the object dangerous and fearful. Curiously, totemism is also associated with exogamy, the practice of forbidding marriage with members of the same clan—that is, with those who share the same totem or totemic name.

Freud was struck by the similarity between the alternating feelings of love and hate clan members expressed for the totem and the ambivalence he observed in almost all infantile wishes. The same polarity appeared in neurotic symptoms, as well as in dreams and wit; it indicated the existence of two conflicting and incompatible tendencies: a desire and a repressing moral or quasi-moral force opposed to that desire. Freud saw all taboos as characterized by ambivalence: desire and fear, love and hate, attraction and repulsion. The magical aspects of totemism reflected our exaggerated belief in the power of our own thoughts or, more precisely, our own wishes. He likened this exaggeration to the "omnipotence of thoughts" found in both adult neurotic fantasies and the mental life of young children. In *Totem and Taboo,* he tried to explain the motivation for the two chief proscriptions of totemism—against killing of the totem species and against marriage within the clan—and why these apparently unrelated rules were found together. Freud's remarkable analysis of "Little Hans" and the child's phobia of horses had shown him the significance of animals for the young, who unconsciously equated them with the father.[25] He theorized that the totem, while consciously representing dead ancestors, unconsciously represented an infantile image of each clan member's actual father.

Freud assumed, as Darwin had, that the earliest human group was some kind of "primal horde," not unlike those observed among the larger apes. Presumably, this band was led by a single, powerful, jealous male, feared and envied equally, who appropriated the females and kept weaker males at bay. The day would come, however, when the brother-sons who had been driven out joined together and killed and devoured their father. By devouring him they identified with him, each believing he had acquired a portion of the father's strength.

After they had got rid of him, had satisfied their hatred and had put into effect their wish to identify themselves with him, the affection which had all this time been pushed under was bound to make itself felt. It did so in the form of remorse. A sense of guilt made its appearance, which in this instance coincided with the remorse felt by the whole group. The dead father became stronger than the living one had been.[26]

Thus the brothers symbolically revoked their deed by forbidding the killing of the surrogate father, the totem, and by renouncing the desires that had motivated the act in the first place. They gave up their claims to women of the group, and out of a filial sense of guilt created the second taboo of totemism, the prohibition of incest.

Unfortunately, Freud believed the killing of the father-leader by the sons to be an actual event repeated many times in early human history, the psychic effects of which were genetically passed on to later generations. Genetics research has shown this Lamarckian notion of the biological transmission of acquired characteristics to be without scientific basis. But the claim, and Freud's assumption that the primal horde was the form of early human society, caused most anthropologists to receive *Totem and Taboo,* written during one of Freud's most creative periods, with skepticism. In fact, it was not until after World War II that the discipline generally came to recognize Freud's original psychological contributions in the work—what one latter-day anthropologist termed "the single most important insight into the nature of culture."[27]

Ironically, *Totem and Taboo* contains an alternate theory fully sufficient to sustain Freud's central idea of sexual rivalry between father and sons. On the next to last page he speaks of a "creative sense of guilt" observable in neurotics, which can produce new moral precepts and other internal restrictions as "atonement for crimes that have been committed and as a precaution for committing new ones." Yet any search to discover the acts that provoked such reactions would very likely prove futile.

We find no deeds, but only impulses and emotions, set upon evil ends but held back from their achievement. What lie behind the sense of guilt of neurotics are always *psychical* realities and never factual ones. . . . May not the same have been true of primitive men? We are justified in believing that, as one of the phenomena of their narcissistic organization, they overvalued their psychical acts to an extraordinary degree. Accordingly, the mere hostile *impulse* against the father, the mere existence of a wishful *fantasy* of killing and devouring him, would have been enough to produce the moral reaction that created totemism and taboo.[28]

This explanation for the persistence of totemism and the incest taboo, unlike the notion of repeated historical events in primal hordes genetically transmitted as memory, is fully tenable in the light of modern knowledge. A range of psychoanalytic and anthropological evidence suggests the rituals of primitive peoples are much more likely to have arisen from dreams and fantasies than from the performance of actual deeds.[29]

In *Totem and Taboo,* Freud did not explain why incest is consciously condemned but rather why it is unconsciously desired. As Lévi-Strauss observes, the desire for the mother or sisters, the murder of the father, and the sons' repentance, rather than corresponding to repeated actual events,

perhaps . . . symbolically express an ancient and lasting dream. The magic of this dream, its power to mould men's thoughts unbeknown to them, arises precisely from the fact that the acts it evokes have never been committed, because culture has opposed them at all times and in all places. Symbolic gratifications in which the incest urge finds its expression, according to Freud, do not therefore commemorate an actual event. They are something else, and more, the permanent expression of a desire for disorder, or rather counter-order.[30]

Humankind walks between the Scylla of instinctual forces and the Charybdis of external restrictions. Cultural defenses facilitate normative behavior but, as taboo and ritual indicate, do not end the conflict. The incest taboo stands between nature—or at least some panhuman desire —and culture, as a link between biology and social life.[31] By checking a desire that might be harmful to the species if given actual reproductive effect, the taboo helps to ensure survival of the species. Yet, tragically, the resulting inhibition wounds the individuals who must deal with eroticized consequences of the conflict all their lives. A wish met by a demand for its control is renounced but not obliterated. It lives on, although enervated, to hold each member partially within its thrall. The taboo is a universal norm imposed on nature and an alienation—at once the basis for our humanity and an invitation to neurosis.

The Impossible Dream

The repudiation of incest seeks to resolve institutionally a psychic conflict arising from the prolonged dependence of human infancy: the developing infant's erotic wish to possess one parent, a frustrating rivalry with the other, a wish to eliminate the rival, and fear of the latter's terrible retaliation. Having observed the regularity with which adults gave indication of unconsciously harboring, or once having harbored, incestuous infantile desires, Freud gave this struggle a schematic representation in the "Oedipus complex."

The oedipal struggle usually reaches its peak in the third or phallic stage of psychosexual development, when the infant's libidinal attention has typically shifted from the oral and anal erogenous zones to the genital. This shift generally occurs during or after the fourth year, when children can distinguish themselves clearly from other persons. No longer are objects of gratification merely or even mainly parts of the child's own body or those of another, such as mother's face or breast. This growing awareness makes possible a desire for a whole other being and feelings of love and hate for that person as well as jealousy, rage, and fear toward any rivals. The new focus on the genitals as a source of bodily stimulation admits vague yearnings for sexual union with the other person, even though actual physical capacity is lacking. The essential psychic elements of later sexual relationships are revealed for the first time.

In the classic oedipal experience, the young boy, whose strongest object relation is already with his mother, develops in the phallic phase a desire for her exclusive love and admiration. He wishes to possess, dominate, and monopolize her, even to be "daddy" and do what the latter does, which includes "giving" her babies, however unclearly that is understood. Rivals, especially father and siblings, must disappear. When reality fails to accommodate this design, feelings of jealousy and murderous rage ensue, and a severe and unbearable conflict arises within. Desire to remove the hated father clashes with feelings of love and admiration for him. Because he imagines that his own jealousy and rage must be reciprocated, the child fears retaliation from his rival, who may appear omnipotent. The imagined reprisal is, of course, loss of the penis, the very organ for which he has increasing esteem.

Faced with the continuing need for parental love and approval and the prospect of a terrifying mutilation, the child renounces the hopeless erotic project. The price is dear: the rivalrous sexual strivings and fantasies are banished to the unconscious, "forgotten" in a massive amnesia, to remain generally inaccessible, though not inert, for the rest of his life. With them go almost all prior sexual knowledge, including that of infantile masturbation. The child enters a "latency" period during which sexual interests are relatively dormant. In contrast to his preoccupation with hostile wishes during the oedipal conflict, the child now comes to identify himself with the parent of the same sex, striving to imitate him in non-oedipal ways. Latency ends at puberty with awakening of the reproductive system and a new thrust of sexual drive.

The oedipal complex in girls is more complicated and less well understood. The infant girl appears to enter the phallic or clitoral phase with much the same oral and anal experience as the boy. Freud believed that her attachment to the father and jealousy of the mother are a result of visual discovery of the male genitals and the conclusion that she has already been mutilated. The mother is blamed for the loss, and the child believes that the missing organs will be restored by her father in the future, or that a substitute will be received in the form of a baby. The castration concern is thus not so much a factor in resolving the oedipal conflict as a condition for shifting erotic attention from mother to father. Aspects of Freud's original formulation have been challenged, particularly the issue of whether the girl's entry into oedipal heterosexuality is a masochistic response to fantasized injury or, as in the boy's case, simply the result of development and psychologically determined genital drives.[32] Continuation of pre-oedipal attachments and the gender asymmetry of early parenting may also modify the girl's conflict.[33] No matter which view is correct, there is little doubt that the girl goes through an oedipal experience. Schematic generalizations cannot so readily be made as in the boy's case, and the conflict is probably not so often resolved by an abrupt and massive repression, but it is hardly less significant in the shaping of the child.

A vital consequence of the oedipal truce is development of the superego. With the id and ego, this agency elaborates the functional differentiation of the mind. But in contrast to the id, the source of primitive and unmediated drives, and thus the unconscious base for the erotic and hostile capital invested in the oedipal wishes, the superego corresponds in a general way to "conscience," the moral and normative components of personality. There are, of course, pre-oedipal precursors. All infants respond in some degree to moral demands made on them in various early situations—toilet training perhaps being the most significant. These demands tend to be dealt with as matters of the external environment. The infant may comply, with a view to reward or punishment, without the compulsion of an internal authority. In the oedipal period, however, the child resolves the greatest conflict of his or her life by *identifying* with the perceived moral and prohibitory demands of the parents. With development of the superego, these external constrictions become internal. Now the child may be commanded by his or her own psychic apparatus, which is likely to demand that wrongdoing—real or fantasized—be punished or repudiated. Whereas the child was previously subject to parental restriction when the parent knew about the misbehavior, there is now an omnipresent internal authority that always "knows" what the child has done or wishes to do.[34] A more effective control can hardly be imagined.

The superego's functions, like those of the id, are largely unconscious, though from time to time they may demand conscious denial of forbidden or otherwise unconscious wishes. The superego does not usually become firmly established until later in the latency period and may be modified in adolescence and adulthood by such social and cultural factors as education and religion. It is, however, always the repudiation of incestuous and parricidal wishes of the oedipal period that provides its nucleus. That heroic repression and conscious denial form the prototype for dealing with forbidden wishes throughout life.

Oedipal circumstances may differ in degree and kind from Freud's classic statement. The conflict "may come earlier or later, with sensations stronger or weaker, and may last long or end soon; and the end, the dissolution of the oedipus complex, may be sudden or long drawn out."[35] It differs according to intensity of the sexual drive, degree of frustration and aggression, amount of castration anxiety, the strength of the ego, the quality of object relations, and even who the cathected objects are.[36] Variations exist both between and within cultures. In his study of the Trobriand Islanders, Malinowski observed a different triangular pattern from that of the nuclear family. Ignorant of the father's role in procreation, Trobrianders did not consider the child's natural father to be related to him by blood. Instead, it was the mother's brother whom the child was expected to obey. Exceptional findings such as these were once thought to cast doubt on the universality of the oedipal experience.[37] Yet oedipal dynamics do not require the presence of either mother or father as the child's partners in the triangle; modal social stand-ins for these two figures are cultural variants. Globally formulated, the oedipal predicament requires only a central nurturing figure who is periodically absent, unavailable, or inattentive, and the child's perception of an interfering or competing authority which, minimally, may be simply the commonplace demands of the external world on the nurturing figure.[38] The ensuing frustrations, working on a capacious psyche, are the inevitable price of prolonged infantile dependence and the nurturance it requires.

Anthropological studies have found oedipal themes and repressed oedipal concerns in the folktales and myths of preliterate cultures as well as in dreams of individuals.[39] In mythopoesis, names and form are given to ubiquitous wishes; thus myths present "communally acceptable versions of wishes which heretofore were expressed in guilt-laden private fantasies."[40] Striking parallels have been noted between Oedipus and other mythic heroes, among them Theseus, Perseus, Zeus, Apollo, Romulus, Joseph, Moses, Elijah, Siegfried, and Arthur. Rank described the following pattern abstracted from thirty-four myths of European, North African, and Near Eastern cultures:

The hero is the child of most distinguished parents; usually the son of a king. His origin is preceded by difficulties, such as continence, or prolonged barrenness . . . of the parents, due to external prohibition or obstacles. During the pregnancy, or antedating the same, there is a prophecy in the form of a dream or oracle, cautioning against his birth, and usually threatening danger to the father, or his representative. As a rule, he is surrendered to water, in a box. He is then saved by animals, or lowly people (shepherds) and is suckled by a female animal, or by a humble woman. After he is grown up, he finds his distinguished parents in a highly versatile fashion; takes his revenge on his father, on the one hand, and is acknowledged on the other, and finally achieves rank and honors.[41]

Kluckhohn concluded that universal myths were the products of "recurrent fantasies." The persistence and resonance of these myths indicate that their images "have a special congeniality for the human mind as a consequence of the relations of children to their parents and other childhood experiences which are universal rather than culture-bound."[42] The logic and deeds of primitive myths survive into modern times. "Each of us," Joseph Campbell has said, "has his private, unrecognized, rudimentary, yet secret potent pantheon of dream. The latest incarnation of Oedipus, the continued romance of Beauty and the Beast, stand this afternoon on the corner of Forty-second Street and Fifth Avenue, waiting for the traffic light to change."[43]

In advanced societies, there is hardly an art form or medium of expression that does not suggest overt or underlying oedipal concerns in much of its social content; Sophocles' drama is hardly unique among masterworks in this regard.[44] The experience of being moved by *Oedipus Rex, Hamlet, The Brothers Karamazov, Sohrab and Rustum, Jane Eyre, Sons and Lovers,* and *Mourning Becomes Electra* may reflect, at least in part, our sense of vicarious relief from residual tensions generated by conflict long past.[45] Oedipal concerns are similarly often evident in folklore, ballads, jokes and humor, drinking songs, and graffiti.[46] Most striking of all are fairy tales—the very stories told to children during the oedipal and early latency periods. With barely disguised oedipal themes, often varying only slightly from one culture to another, these tales are told on demand, over and over again, generation after generation. Perceiving the triangular theme in such stories as "Snow White," "Jack and the Beanstalk," "Cinderella," "Goldilocks," "Little Red Riding Hood," children are able to identify closely with the struggling young protagonists, finding comfort and perhaps insight in the solutions offered, however violent or moralistic they may be.[47]

We can doubt neither the certainty of the oedipal experience nor the force of its legacy. It is the most intense love affair and conflict in many persons' lives. The riddle the Sphinx posed to Oedipus can thus be restated: "Who may love, but not love the one whom he loves?" The answer is the same: the human being. The child may love dependently but not sexually the one whom he loves. The adult man may love women sexually, but not love sexually the one whom he once loved dependently.[48] The oedipal wish, so characteristically human, may be renounced and banished but not obliterated. This prototypical sexual struggle ends with the triumph of sexual morality, but the victory is always less than complete.

Not all rebels are rounded up, and, unconsciously at least, the dream of a counterorder may never be completely abandoned. The depth of this primal struggle ensures the vitality of the sexually forbidden. In a lifetime, this bent may take many forms and serve many ends, however far removed from the conscious mind or the threshold of behavior. That his act was unwitting did not save Oedipus before the gods: that our transgressions are mere fantasy is not saving before the superego, which sees and judges all. In sex we do not allow ourselves the luxury of innocence.

Pleasure and Reality

Compared with adult genitality, infantile sexual gratification is "polymorphously perverse" or relatively unintegrated in its development through oral, anal, and phallic stages.[49] Normal healthy infants explore pleasurable activities, most of which relate to their own bodies and immediate surroundings. In the first year or eighteen months, they attempt to put everything within reach into the mouth, which, with lips and tongue, is the most readily stimulated part of the body. Later, attention turns to pleasurable sensations associated with passage of waste through the anal and urethral canals. During the fourth year, in the so-called phallic stage, the penis or clitoris becomes a chief focus of bodily gratification. In all three phases, the child's instinctual pleasures are curbed and redirected by external authority, usually parental. Distinctions are made between what is clean and dirty, acceptable and unacceptable, good and bad, and the child is expected to acquire certain skills, such as sphincter control, the prototype of motor mastery. As parental values are elaborated, the infant's broad spectrum of undisciplined instinctual adventures and delights is narrowed to a few acceptable ones through frustration and redirection. Disapproved ones are put aside or at least not indulged in front of parents. Needing parental love and approval, the infant resolves conflicts by giving up instinctual pleasures. The developing ego is the executive agency for this renunciation.

As various sexual and aggressive impulses are proscribed and inhibited, the child learns to make a general distinction between activities carried out above the waist, as it were, and those below. With genital touching during the phallic period, sexual activities are apt to gather particularly disreputable associations. Erotic aims once addressed to one's own body or parts of the mother's are now turned outward toward other persons— parents—and infantile sexuality reaches its dramatic climax in the oedipal experience. Where the conflict is largely resolved, the adolescent and adult develop a capacity for genital expression and tenderness in a nonincestuous love relationship. Erotic delights once found in the parent are available to the matured individual in loving another person. Similarly, the infant's bodily explorations in each of the earlier phases make important contributions to later organization of the sexual drive around genital primacy and the capacity for orgasm. The polymorphously perverse sexuality of infancy is retained, normally making its adult appearance in sexual foreplay: touching, looking, showing, kissing, sucking, licking, and so on. Normal sexuality, then, is not the antithesis of the perverse but the integration and synthesis of its phasic parts.[50]

Freud broadly conceptualized the lifelong struggle between unconscious instinctual drives and wishes and the various requirements of the external world—parental and cultural precepts, the needs, demands, and actions of others, rational appraisal of cause-effect relationships—as the clash of the *pleasure* and *reality* principles.[51] The behavior of infants and small children is largely under the sway of the pleasure principle and its direct, uninhibited search for satisfaction of needs and wishes and avoidance of pain and discomfort. The pleasure principle is modified by reality, and instinctual drives are increasingly tamed as the child moves through developmental phases. Search for gratification no longer takes direct routes but must make detours and suffer deferments. With the superego, many demands and expectations of the external world are internalized. In this shift from pleasure to reality we become civilized beings as well as potential neurotics—in short, uniquely human.

Yet the struggle between the poles never ends; reality's triumphs are incomplete and often transitory. Instinctual impulses, though repressed, live on in the unconscious, and regularly seek to break through to the conscious mind for fulfillment or gratification. Their reappearance and the pleasurable feelings associated with them are often threatening, since they suggest irrational urges that can be neither fathomed nor controlled.

The ego is charged with managing this tension. Anxiety, triggered by incursions of the repressed into consciousness, signals the ego to employ defenses to prevent being overrun by the impulses. The ego's capacity is affected by aspects of the external world that have become part of the psyche, including beneficial or harmful interactive experience. When the ego is successful, the pleasurable impulses are transformed enough so that some measure of gratification is secured, while the superego and external world are sufficiently appeased to limit guilt and punishment.[52] When it is less successful, repressed impulses, untransformed, achieve gratification in opposition to the superego or external reality. Pleasure is then accompanied by a sense of guilt or by external punishment. When the ego is at the mercy of severe superego demands, its defenses permit instinctual impulses little or no gratification. The censorious superego may prevent the conscious agent from coming to friendly terms with these impulses, and cause it to be hostile and incapable of enjoyment.[53] If this occurs, instinctual strivings are apt to find expression in neurotic symptoms. Extensive repression has thus been likened to the

outlawing of a revolutionary party, without any provision for integrating the rebellious forces into the life of the community, such as, e.g., measures that would tie some of the revolutionaries, particularly the leaders, to the existing system, and provision to redress at least some of the grievances of the disaffected; and without any countermeasures against a possible resurgence except police attention.[54]

It is both our bad and our good fortune that repressed pleasurable wishes can and do return to consciousness. The fantastical infantile past, in which such pleasures were known and savored, remains forever within, always partly assertable.

The Pornographic Within

Psychodynamically, the pornographic is an expression of forbidden and thus usually repressed sexual and aggressive impulses and wishes. In the adult, these infantile aims are transformed into dramas of genital sexuality and expressed in the more sophisticated language of the adult world. Though primitive strivings of the pre-oedipal period may be evident, most pornographic expression is likely to reflect the complex emotions of the oedipal experience.

Because of the ego's protective work, almost no repressed material with infantile sexual attachment returns to consciousness free of disguise. Even "hard-core" pornography, commonly thought to leave nothing to the imagination, usually employs masks provided by the structures of adult sexuality. The forbidden remains encoded, as it does in dreams, jokes, slips of the tongue, free associations, and other forms by which the repressed intrudes on the conscious mind. Some subjects, such as mother-son incest, parricide, or explicit mutilation of genitals or eyes, usually produce such keen anxiety that they are dealt with only obliquely or through manifold symbolization. Yet whatever the disguise, the pornographic retains a central characteristic of the infantile mode of thought—exclusion or distortion of the outside world wherever that world does not conform to wishes.[55] The pornographic thus remains essentially fantastical, a kind of hallucinatory realm "where everything is possible, and where we were all once originally supreme."[56] This luxurious view of things, and the immature substantive specifics, give pornographic fantasies their regressive character.

Infantile roots and regressive mechanics are strikingly evident in that most commonplace pornographic expression, the "dirty" word. Ferenczi was among the first to observe that such words had the power of forcing both normal and neurotic persons to imagine the function or organ they stand for.[57] For developing children, most words have a close and magiclike connection with actions or objects denoted. Because they cannot yet make a rigorous distinction between what is actual and what is merely imagined, all their words tend to produce hallucinatory visual imagery, a more primitive mode of thought commonly reflected in dreams. Gradually, through education and experience, words become divested of this illusional character. A capacity for abstract thought is attained, and vocabulary becomes economically suited for higher forms of intellectual activity.[58] Yet certain words denoting sexual and eliminative organs and functions come under the early influence of repressive forces, usually at the oedipal stage before a secondary sexual knowledge and vocabulary are acquired, and thus fail to become differentiated from what they signify.[59] Remaining at a developmentally more primitive stage than other vocabulary, these "dirty" words retain high levels of affect for the utterer and those hearing or reading them. The arrested character of such words is also evident in the graffiti found ubiquitously in public lavatories. The primitive power of the utterances easily returns in the setting of the public toilet, which regressively suggests the social setting of infancy.

The arrested character of dirty words also allows them to function as oaths and curses and to bear hostile feelings. As exclamations of pain, annoyance, or frustration having little or no connection with their literal meaning, they may release a variety of repressed feelings and serve as small flags of rebellion against social authority or demands of the superego. Because they can be broken so easily, verbal taboos are economical scapegoats on which hostile feelings can be displaced. If dirty words did not exist, they would "have to be invented to permit humans a psychologically suitable vehicle for the ventilation of fury and despair, the elimination of anger and aggression, the expression of rebellion, and the suppression of fears."[60]

The general affective investment of the prime dirty word in English, coupled with a mildly repressed avoidance of its literal meaning, is made clear in Wayland Young's account of a narrative reputed to be Australian, variations of which are to be found almost anywhere in the English-speaking world:

I was walking along this fucking fine morning, fucking sun shining away, little country fucking lane, and I meets up with this fucking girl. Fucking lovely she was, so we gets into converfuckingsation and I takes her over a fucking gate into a fucking field and we has sexual intercourse.[61]

The verbal interfusion of the hostile and scatological with the erotic, a characteristic of dirty words, is an active regressive residue of the more amorphous and less differentiated world of infantile sexuality.

The pornographic is inviting because its fantasies promise gratification that reality seldom affords, the infantile counterparts of which were once ardently sought. But because it is forbidden, it is also often perceived as threatening or dangerous. The suggested wishes and the fear of being overwhelmed by their instinctual impulses give rise to an intolerable anxiety that, in turn, must be warded off by defensive reactions. Not all negative or critical responses to the pornographic are so based, of course, but the conscious or unconscious stirring of forbidden desires typically produces reactive unconscious responses. In the conscious mind these are usually experienced as disgust or revulsion.

Sexual and aggressive strivings can often be sufficiently detoxified to elude the moralistic constraints of the superego as well as those of culture and education and thus receive some release without arousing great anxiety. Wit, like dreams, deals with partial and disguised reappearances of forbidden impulses from the unconscious.[62] But where the dream offers hallucinated wish-fulfillment, wit or jokes present the repressed material disguised by reactivated pleasures of exhibitionism, nonsense, and wordplay. The disguise must be good enough to protect utterer and audience from feeling shame and guilt, but not so opaque as to hide completely the forbidden sexual or aggressive desire. When wit is successful, laughter represents the sudden release of energy no longer needed for repression. Pleasure is obtained from the childish play with words and momentary undoing of inhibition.[63] The joke and the unloosening laughter provide a direct though fleeting communication with the unconscious. Jokes detoxify only when they succeed, that is, when they are witty or funny. This outcome is largely a quality of their disguise, which must balance protection from shame and guilt against ventilation of the forbidden wish. Thus a joke or witticism may succeed with some hearers while others simply "don't get it" or find it vulgar.

Repressed wishes and the conflicts attaching to them make repeated everyday appearances in other commonplace disguises. Many of these are welcomed as opportunities to return, vicariously at least, to undemanding childish ways and gain some release for anachronistic impulses. Opportunities for mild regression are offered by "entertainment" and other diversions that mask limited conscious reentry of repressed erotic or aggressive material. They are concessions of the managing ego, small triumphs for the pleasure principle having its adult moment in play, "escape," spontaneity, messiness, disorder, or simple carelessness. Many of these indulgences— double entendres, ribald songs, burlesque routines, "dirty" jokes, and less well disguised hard-core depictions—involve erotic expression. Partial disguise detoxifies the anxiety-producing aspects and permits the gratification. These occasional encounters provide most persons with important, even necessary, renewal for dealing with the "reality" burdens of work, duty, routine, rationality, conscience, deferment of pleasure, and the like. The partial gratification they supply is a psychic counterweight to external and superego expectations.[64] Tolerance for such regressive indulgences, the subject matter of which may sometimes be consciously judged objectionable or obscene by oneself or others, varies greatly among individuals. One person's amusement or diversion may be another's disgust or unsettling confrontation. This is the chief reason why popular entertainment (and functional counterparts such as swearing and writing graffiti), offered as it is to a heterogeneous audience, has inevitable margins of psychic and social unacceptability. But, typically, entertainment diverts in order to allow the gratification. Psychically at least, it owes its existence to requirements of the managing ego. If entertainment did not exist, like dirty words, it too would need to be invented.

Art and literature also provide opportunities to deal with repressed wishes and conflicts. They can engage our emotions in richer and more complex ways than commonplace amusements and diversions, without requiring any effort in the real world. As Norman Holland has persuasively argued, underlying fantasies touched or evoked by literary works receive play because they are reshaped—in effect, managed—by form and meaning. Form provides a measure of psychic distance through such devices as sequence, point of view, juxtaposition, rhythm, and omission, and thus focuses attention, controlling what we are aware of at any given moment. Meaning, on the other hand, transforms the forbidden wishes and fearful fantasies at the core of the work into social, moral, or intellectual themes, allowing otherwise rejected aspects to elude the internal censor and achieve some oblique expression and gratification.[65] Even when our response includes pain, guilt, or anxiety rather than simple pleasure, we can use form and meaning to control these feelings and transform them into satisfying experiences, perhaps in much the same way children do in their more primitive involvement with fairy tales. Pleasure is received from having the fantasy and, at the same time, feeling it to be managed. Thus we can often respond to aesthetic works in larger and more complex ways than to reality itself. Where such a work succeeds, it both "reaches 'up' toward the world of social, intellectual, moral, and religious concerns . . . [and] 'down' to the dark, chthonic, primitive, bodily part of our mental life."[66]

Nevertheless, art and literature, like wit, do not always succeed. In psychodynamic terms, the ego is not always able to effect and maintain an internal balance. The more expressly sexual the stimulus, whether or not it has aesthetic properties, the more likely the ego will be taxed in its executive task.

The ego may bend to severe superego demands and overcontrol, or, if unable to deal adequately with requirements of adult sexuality, it may permit excessive regressive indulgence. Many persons find it difficult to respond to erotic depiction without anxiety unless it is extremely well disguised or detoxified by circumstances. Such apprehension may indicate an early block in object relations that prevented normal bodily exploration or the ordering of feelings and expectations. Sexual expression may have remained connected, consciously or unconsciously, with images of violence or cruelty to oneself or others, impairing the ability to experience pleasure in later stages of sexual development. As instinctual sexual wishes and impulses thus become extensively repressed, the ego must invest great energy in an effort to maintain tight control. The awakening of repressed desires by external erotic stimuli, particularly so undisguised as pornography, may lead to conscious fantasies of which one is ashamed, or to fear of being swept away by instinctual impulses, including the wish to masturbate, as well as to intolerable feelings of guilt.[67] Regression to a more primitive level of instinctual functioning can easily be perceived as threatening personal moral values or self-control. Usually, anxiety mounts before this stage is reached. To lessen anxiety, the stimulus itself is rejected, psychically, through a sense of revulsion or disgust.[68] When actual avoidance is impossible, or education or ideology does not permit conscious rejection or suppression, laughter, drowsiness, boredom, "intellectualizing," or some other distancing may serve as surrogate for disgust. Boredom and disgust are particularly effective protections against further conscious involvement with feelings of shame and guilt. If the stimulus arousing unconscious desires takes the form of symbolic representation or expression, it may be consciously judged to be pornography.

In some cases, the very condemnation detoxifies enough to allow such expression to be explored at a safe distance on the side of "good" impulses, paradoxically affording some vicarious gratification of the unconscious desires. Though reasons to criticize pornography are many, a moralistic inveighing against it may in fact conceal an unconscious wish to explore it—reaction formation evident in the stereotypical censor.[69] Such persons may genuinely believe their suppressive efforts are designed merely to protect others from corrupting influence.

The requirements and expectations of adult genital sexuality, including the need to reconcile the oedipally split image of woman, for a man, or of man, for a woman, and thus to integrate desire and love, may produce anxiety or feelings of guilt that cannot be mastered. Where this occurs, a defensive regression to an earlier stage of psychic organization is likely. Painful feelings are avoided by avoiding the adult context, though usually not with the renunciation of conscious gratification that accompanies extensive repression.

Since normal or adult genital sexuality is not the opposite of the polymorphously perverse indulgences of infancy, but their synthesis, we can view the regression defense as a partial undoing of that synthesis, permitting a less painful (and less mature) approach to the sexual strivings and their gratification. As a retreat, regression is characterized by the mode of thought characteristic of pornography: the illusion of exclusivity and omnipotence in which unwelcome aspects of the external and adult world—demands, expectations, responsibilities, feelings about other persons, reminders of frightening struggles, and so on—are fantastically excluded or denied independent reality altogether. Objects and persons thus become mere appendages of an infantile, all-powerful, pleasure-seeking self.[70] Developmentally, such a falling back is typically a response to painful reminders of unresolved conflicts or impaired relations of the oedipal or pre-oedipal periods and the aggressive wishes associated with them. The retreat is usually to a point in the oral, anal, phallic, or oedipal phase that has remained charged with psychic energy because of earlier overindulgence or undue deprivation and survives as a weakness or fixation. A child under the stress of anal or oedipal conflict, for example, may temporarily revert to thumb sucking, a mode of the earlier oral stage.[71] The regressing adult may retain the genital mode of gratification, falling back in actual behavior only to masturbation, yet the accompanying fantasies, perhaps also genital and involving adult figures, may be of the exclusive and omnipotent sort we see in pornography. In other adult regression, such as the need to utter or hear obscene words in order to achieve coital orgasm, the falling back may be much less extensive in actual behavior or may not affect motor activity at all.[72]

Regression from demands of reality is strikingly evident in that most persistent of all pornographic images, the debased woman. Women in pornography, Peter Gay has observed,

represent, in the most extreme form, the despised half of man's split image of the first, and in some way always most important woman in his life—his mother. The small boy has not yet integrated his pictures of the cherished being who nourishes and frustrates him: the mother he wants to kill in the afternoon, he wants to marry in the evening. And his wrath at first discovering that his mother, that paragon, does *that* thing with a man, though rapidly repressed, always remains as a ground tone for disillusionment: being no angel, she must be a whore. There are adults fortunate enough to blend their images of mother into a realistic whole—neither angel nor whore, a complex, imperfect, yet lovable being. But the habitual reader of pornography, whether he consciously worships his mother or detests her, is among those who have never healed the harsh infantile division of mother into the purest and the most defiled of women. He is haunted not merely by unresolved oedipal conflicts, but also by earlier, archaic, pre-oedipal ones. And he must conjure up the grossest, most degraded of females to experience sexual pleasure and enjoy sexual consummation.[73]

Thus pornography or any thinly disguised representation of forbidden sexuality may be especially attractive to the adolescent or regressing adult. It allows avoidance of conflicts of the adult sexual world, perhaps helping to ward off more deeply forbidden impulses, while at the same time providing some motor or hallucinatory gratification of the aroused impulses. When this experience is modal rather than accessory, that is, when it regularly substitutes for more mature sexual expression, the defense mechanism, like that of extensive repression, suggests an underlying neurotic struggle.[74] In normal adults, such hallucinatory retreats may occur in dreaming, under the influence of intoxicants or drugs, or in the mild, everyday, largely conscious amusements mentioned earlier. Like so many other differences between the normal and neurotic, the matter is one of degree.

Homo Eroticus

The young child's earliest sexual design is inevitably fantastical and inappropriate in its undiscriminating, all-consuming ambition. In fantasy at least, it generates a psychic struggle resolved only by renunciation of the original goal and massive repression of its chief elements. The hopeless quest is the prototype of outward sexual purpose. Its wounding defeat leaves both a structuring of sexual transgression and anticipation of its punishment. Instinctual sexual energies are not and indeed cannot be eradicated, but the "moral" resolution of the oedipal conflict and the formation of the superego provide a lifelong psychodynamic base for conscious as well as unconscious sexual reticence and self-restraint. The simple physicality of animal sexual nature is thus warped and transformed into eroticized sexuality. We have lost animal innocence and its more or less straightforward path to reproduction and physical release, gaining in its place a richer but much less certain pursuit in which pleasure, shame, and guilt are the chief conscious considerations.

The incest proscription is an attempt externally to reinforce the repression that resolves the oedipal struggle—the heroic tribute that fear pays to impulse and wish in an eroticized world. Addressing the arch-transgression of sexual imagination, the taboo proclaims culture's sovereignty over desire and provides a groundwork for social regulation of sexual life. Though it has other utility as well, it remains our premier sexual rule.

All sexual regulations are violated in some degree; more important, all are in some measure compromises between desires, wishes, and impulses consciously and unconsciously held, and normative demands opposed to them. In the paradox of taboo, the very behavior proscribed, no matter how abhorrent, is not "naturally" rejected. If it were, the strenuous admonitions and severe sanctions attached to taboos would be unnecessary. Regulations actually hide temporizing arrangements; hence their successes are always less than complete. Tensions drawn between impulse and prohibition survive and are dramatized in myths, folk and fairy tales, jokes, and stories, as well as works of literature and art. The sexually forbidden remains a psychodynamic element in everyday life, usually in disguise but sometimes not.

Our animal sexuality is erotically bent by psychic demands rooted in a universal human interactive experience and by derivative social prescriptions and regulations. The resulting convolutions include such seemingly disparate turns as romance and disgust, object idealization and debasement, sadism and masochism, self-sacrifice and exploitation, inexplicable attractions and aversions, celibacy and unappeasable desire, nonsexual objects invested with erotic meaning and sexual ones desexualized, and so on. Human sexual pursuit and satisfaction are not merely physical release or procreative purpose, but a highly complicated psychological quest, full of allure and promise yet for most persons also shadowed by ambivalence, fear, rage, and guilt. Sublimated, they are also a source of tremendous creative energy, including the invention of culture and civilization itself.

But our concern here is with aspects less grand and less resolved. An interior sexuality of forbidden impulses, wishes, and fantasies—the pornographic within—is the psychological basis of pornography. Without it the latter would not exist. We may thus note two progressions: from within to without and from without to within. In the first, an infantile forbidden wish disguised as a pornographic fantasy finds external expression, which may or may not be socially judged to be pornography. In the second, a depiction or representation, which may or may not be sexual and may or may not be considered pornography, stimulates a pornographic fantasy that, in adult guise, satisfies a forbidden wish.

The erotic warping of sexuality is the source of a lifelong capacity for forbidden wishes and the psychological basis for an extensive sexual censorship. Pornography, the representation of forbidden desire, is a simulacrum of the forbidden sexual territory within each of us. Except in particulars, it is not the by-product of any distinctive social or economic system or other external condition. Although it is an inevitable social category, its substantive character may vary greatly from one time and place to another. Because its roots lie in a formative infantile sexual experience, it can neither be simply eradicated nor made totally acceptable. Theoretically, of course, sexual infancy is not psychologically fixed; it continues to be shaped by social and situational factors including the quality of interpersonal relations. Yet the human infant's cerebral precocity and prolonged dependence, each acting on the other, make some form of the oedipal struggle inevitable and leave many of its particulars unsettled or imperfectly settled throughout life. For the individual alone, the remedy lies in managing this dilemma through ego work, integrating its disparate elements within the personality and achieving some constructive balance among them; for the individual as social or parental actor, it lies in avoiding the pitfalls that aggravate the ordeal of the young. Our chief concern in this book, however, is with society. We must doubt, at least at this point in the inquiry, whether in politics or policy we can do much better than simply manage pornography, living with it and with our attempts to prohibit it.

Before addressing that issue directly, as we do in Parts Three and Four, we must turn to several related and possibly intervening concerns, including the cultural experience with pornography, the epistemic value of the pornographic imagination, and what we know and do not know of pornography's effects.

Chapter Two

The Social Mirror

Both read the Bible day and night,
But thou read'st black where I read white.

William Blake

I know it when I see it.

Justice Potter Stewart, *Jacobellis v. Ohio*

We have said pornography is a category of sexual expression that reflects or stimulates fantasies and impulses forbidden by internal authority, in effect, an external manifestation of the pornographic within. But pornography is also a social designation given to expression found objectionable by external authority through laws, policies, or informal standards. The distinction is critical, because external and internal evaluations may diverge or even be opposed. A given sexual representation may be pornographic for some individuals but not considered pornography by their social circle, community, or society; or may be socially designated as pornographic but not be so psychodynamically for a given person. Unrecognized or ignored, these divergences confound our thinking about sexual expression and its control. Where they hold for many persons in a community or society, as is often the case, they also create and sustain much of the social ambiguity and political conflict surrounding these matters as public issues.

As already indicated, we will avoid most terminological distinctions between "pornography" and "obscenity." The former, for example, derived from *pornographos*—"writing about harlots," possibly after the autobiographies of the Greek hetaerae, the courtesans of the Classical Age—may refer in some usage only to writing whose purpose or effect is erotic stimulation. On the other hand, obscenity, possibly derived from the Latin *ob scena*, meaning off-scene or off-stage, is sometimes applied to any expression likely to produce disgust or revulsion, and thus may involve nonsexual subjects such as eating and elimination, which do not have erotic connotations for most adults. Simplified, pornography may be seen as sexual expression that excites or invites, whereas obscenity offends or disgusts. However valid such distinctions may be etymologically, they do little to

37

advance and much to confuse our understanding of sexual expression as a psychological or social category. A given sexual expression, for example, may excite some persons but offend others. It may excite most persons in some settings but offend most persons in others. It may excite the same persons at one moment and offend them at another. When arousal is accompanied by shame or guilt, it may excite and offend the same person at the same time. Confusion lies not in having separate terms refer to different psychological responses but in using or believing those terms to signify different *kinds* of expression, as though they located and defined actual categories of independent depiction or representation.

Thus, as distinct concepts, "pornographic" and "obscene" can usually apply to the same expression. We could try to retain the distinction by referring to an expression as pornographic only when it has an arousing effect and obscene only when it has an offending one, but this is unwieldy and would require the constant qualification just mentioned. Moreover, it is precisely at the adjectival level that the terms are most interchangeable in popular usage. For these reasons, we use them here simply as synonyms, to refer to a type of sexual or erotic expression aspects of which may be inviting, offensive, or both. Our choice will usually be "pornography" and "pornographic," except where we refer, as in much of this chapter and in Chapter 8, to expression subject to legal proscription.

We consider pornography here as a social designation and examine its ubiquity in human culture and variability among and within societies, paying particular attention to the experience of two liberal democracies, Britain and the United States. Our concern is with substantive aspects of designation rather than the structure, mechanics, or politics of social control, all of which are taken up in later chapters. The examination is necessarily cursory and may cover familiar ground, but it should be sufficient to challenge and possibly lay to rest two widely held and largely contradictory assumptions, one libertarian, the other censorial. The first is that complete or near-complete freedom for sexual expression is a social possibility; the second, that objectionable or offensive expression is self-evident or has a sufficiently elemental character to allow unmistakable identification. Each has been distracting in its own way, the first, by failing to allow that pornography owes its designation as much to internal as external authority and that its invitation is often psychologically offset by its threat; the second, by failing to see that what is pornographic can never be the same for everyone at all times and places and that its threat is often offset by its fantastical promise.

Formidable problems of evidence burden any examination of erotic expression from the distant past. Such expression must be conveyed by some medium, and to be available to us, it must have survived, not merely the rigors of time and the physical environment, but also social and political upheavals. Many great ancient literate cultures—Mesopotamia, Pharaonic Egypt, and Mycenae, for example, which dominated their regions and their ages—have left few traces of writing unconnected with religion or commerce. And when sexual representation survives, how is it to be interpreted? Was it considered socially acceptable in its time or was it, in some aspect or other, objectionable or forbidden? If so, to whom? Many chroniclers of pornography seem unaware of these complications and assume that any surviving erotic expression must have been socially unobjectionable and thus reflect the norms of its bygone culture. Thus they conclude that ancient societies were much freer than those of today and the recent past. That erotic representation committed to a physically durable medium is much more likely to survive than the more fragile evidence of its social regulation is a fact largely disregarded.

One additional prefatory note is necessary. In discussing British and American experience later in the chapter, our chief examples of social designation are laws and court decisions, which provide the most readily available and sometimes the only record. They also are likely to have had great influence on other forms of control, both formal and informal. Yet we must bear in mind that laws and trials are but one measure of regulation and, as we shall note more fully in later chapters, not always the truest or most widely operating one. All societies have controlled sexual expression and representation, but not all have done so through law.

Primitive Humans

We know very little of the sexual or erotic expression of prehistoric human beings. By modern standards, representational work and communication were severely limited by physical and cultural constraints. Human capacity to make one thing stand for another was probably realized largely through behavior, in ritual and rite. Such symbolic acts could give expression to instinctual impulses or desires that would be unacceptable if acted on in daily life. As Bettelheim suggests in a study of primitive circumcision and puberty rites, symbolic acts might also serve to integrate rather than to discharge asocial instinctual tendencies and thus offer the ego social support in maintaining rational control of a personality required to deal with irrational forces within.[1]

Among the earliest known representations of any sort are the "Venus" figures unearthed in various parts of central and western Europe and the Ukraine, and the drawings of animals, hunting scenes, and apparent genitalia on the walls of caves in France and other parts of western Europe. These early works of art have been variously interpreted—they may, for example, have played a magico-religious role in fertility rites—but they were also very likely conscious or unconscious erotic expressions.[2] The figurines, made of fired clay or carved from mammoth ivory or stone, are believed to be 20,000 years old. They display outsize sexual features—breasts, buttocks, hips, and possibly pregnant bellies. The arms are commonly underdeveloped, feet often nonexistent, and the head, small and generally faceless. In this sense, they bear the exaggerated sexual features at the expense of overall realism and personality that commonly characterize stylized erotic expression, including much pornography. Although the figures suggest simple fecundity, an undefined head and face on the body of a mature woman may also reflect an unconscious erotic component, concealing or repressing the identity of the figure's real model.[3]

The cave drawings, probably Cro-Magnon, include abstract vulvae and other possible fertility tokens and suggest that sexual life had "already been endowed with magical qualities in the minds of humans."[4] There is little doubt that Paleolithic people possessed a definite system of sexual signs and must often have used them in place of more explicit representation.[5] Furthermore, the drawings were socially restricted; they tend to be found on the most deeply recessed walls, in chambers reached only with great difficulty.[6]

Even without sure evidence that prehistoric human beings experienced ambivalence or conflict about sexual expression, we may reasonably make two inferences about their lives. In view of the eroticized nature of the human sexual drive and the human capacity to symbolize fantasy externally, erotic expression must have been commonplace, much of it probably connected with magico-religious beliefs and rituals. It is also safe to assume that certain forms of sexual *behavior* were forbidden or at least extensively restricted. Indeed, no known society has been without social controls on sexual conduct, and almost none without controls on exposure of the body.[7] There is thus no reason to suppose that erotic *expression,* which inevitably dwells on bodies and behavior, was ever completely free.

Twentieth-century primitive societies whose development, until recently, was largely untouched by the great cultures of West or East, provide striking evidence of how social human beings may have dealt with sexuality and sexual expression in the distant past. Ethnographic studies of nearly 200 of these mostly nonliterate societies, representing every inhabitable continent but Europe, reveal remarkable diversity of beliefs, values, and regulations governing sexual life. Though a number of these peoples, such as the Tahitians and several others of Oceania, are relatively "free" by standards of contemporary advanced cultures, all impose restraints on sexual behavior. None are without erotic codes that convey information and set out what is "appropriate and inappropriate sexual behavior in given circumstances and how such behavior is to be rewarded and punished."[8]

Many aspects of each of these cultures focus on sexual matters, yet except for the primary incest taboo, found in all, much of the efflorescence is idiosyncratic. Thus infantile sex play, adolescent experimentation, premarital intercourse, adultery, homosexuality, masturbation, and bestiality may be subjects of extensive restriction, or entirely forbidden, or dealt with casually and even institutionally supported. Elaborate specifications of kin avoidance are found in some, whereas in others restrictions apply only to members of the immediate family. Privacy is generally preferred for intercourse but, as among the Mohave, Marquesans, and Kamano, there may be a good deal of carelessness about it. Ritual copulation for fertility (Goulbourne Islands, Kiwai, Marquesas), group trysts (Samoa, Goulbourne Islands, Mohave), and group rape (Cheyenne, Komano) often take place before bystanders. Eating and elimination are subject to a wide range of rules and customs, many of which appear to be related to sexual regulations. In several cultures, it is shameful for men and women or various other specified persons to eat together; the same may be true of simply eating in public. Some, such as the Chiricahua, Dobuans, and Manus, are prudish about bodily elimination, whereas others find urination and defecation acceptable in public. The Kurtachi of the Solomon Islands, who are not embarrassed to defecate before others, eat in private.[9] There is little doubt that many customary or casual practices in the West—kissing and other public displays of affection between friends, lovers, or husband and wife, for example—would be thought scandalous or obscene by many of these primitive peoples.

Attitudes toward clothing and nudity are particularly instructive, since display, adornment, or concealment of the body in any society is often highly sexualized, in effect a behavioral form of erotic expression. These diverse primitive cultures account for almost every conceivable combination of nakedness and body covering: the Australian aborigines are entirely naked; among the Maori, only the glans of the penis is covered; among the Thonga, the penis is covered by a sheath; and the Dobu cover the genitals but not the buttocks. Other cultures require that only the genitals and buttocks be covered, that a woman's breasts be covered in addition, that most of the body below the neck be covered, or that a woman's neck, lower face and neck, or entire head be covered. Certain garments may also be put aside on special occasions, such as the nursing of a child, athletic contests, or times of ceremonial license.[10]

Most of these primitive cultures have neither written languages nor highly developed graphic arts. The chief medium for erotic expression is the spoken word, and here, again, we find great variation between the permissible and the objectionable. Some peoples discourage sex talk, or approve only occasional euphemisms, but none restrict it completely. Some permit open and direct erotic expression and communication about sexual matters, but none appear to allow complete freedom.

Sexual language takes many forms familiar to Westerners: jokes, double entendres, storytelling, teasing, insults, and epithets. Taboos on certain profane or scatological oaths and lewd synonyms for sexual organs or intercourse—the local version of the Western "four-letter" word—yield an extensive obscene vocabulary.[11] Certain words, the equivalent of "mother-fucker" among the Muria of India, for example, may be used so commonly and indiscriminately that they lose their pornographic effect. Paradoxically, cultures with the most extensively proscribed sex talk tend to be freest about behavior and practices.[12] This pattern, confounding many Western libertarians who assume that obscenity and pornography flourish only where there is overall sexual repression, is another indication that the fascination with socially forbidden expression and the willingness to maintain its restricted status may have powerful unconscious purposes at odds with the relative simplicity of actual behavior.

These primitive and preliterate cultures permit several general observations. First, sexual behavior and expression are the subjects of an impressive array of standards, conventions, and regulations; all societies attempt to impose some regulation. Second, no society is entirely successful in realizing its governing norms, and all seem to tolerate some public behavior or expression designed, consciously or unconsciously, to be sexually arousing. Third, the cultures vary greatly both in prevailing norms and behavior and in expression considered deviant. Finally, the evidence provided by these largely insular societies leaves little doubt that anxiety about aspects of erotic expression has been part of human social and psychological life long before the evolution of advanced civilization.

The Premodern World

Although most written and graphic representation produced in societies of the distant past has been destroyed by time or social sanctions, a significant corpus of erotic expression has survived. The richness and variety of that from the ancient Mediterranean world is especially impressive. Phallic carvings and statues of Greece and Rome; lyrical and aphrodisiacal love songs in the Old Testament; erotic stories about the Greek hetaerae; double entendres and more direct sexual references in classical Greek drama; Ovid's instructional manual for Roman men, *Ars Amatoria;* Sappho's love poems; the *Satyricon* of Petronius with its details of elegant debaucheries; and the coital catalog of the Pompeian murals leave little doubt that, at least for some members of those societies, erotic representation was a significant element in sexual life.

This fact is often cited by contemporary chroniclers of pornography as evidence those societies were absent of repression compared with the later, modern West. Thus, "Among the ancients sex was unashamedly joyous, in reading as in practice. The subject carried no more taboos than food or sports, family quarrels or international wars." Or, "The truth is that the Greeks thoroughly enjoyed sex in all its sundry manifestations and felt not the slightest sense of shame about it." The ancient world was "united in an acceptance of sex not only as a fact of life but one which was in itself good and honourable."[13] Claims such as these are pure fancy and bad social science. They have become conventional libertarian wisdom, although lacking psychodynamic sophistication, ignoring social evidence we do have, and—more important—ignoring the logic of that evidence.

We cannot be sure how most surviving works were designated, or for that matter, even how representative they were of their bygone cultures. Survival alone does not signify absence of control. We cannot be sure that what alone appears to have been acceptable was not limited to certain groups, occasions, or institutional settings, or that the level of acceptability remained unchanged from one generation to the next. There is good reason to believe that much of the surviving erotic expression was created for and possessed by an elite. Greek erotic art was probably enjoyed by a more or less closed social circle of persons of cultivated habits, and orgiastic representations, like those on interior Pompeian murals, were anything but ubiquitous in the Roman world.[14] We know that a censorship debate raged for a time in early fourth-century Greece. Socrates is said by Plato to have favored expurgation of the *Odyssey,* in part because of concern that passages describing the lust of Zeus for Hera were "not conducive to self-restraint."[15] Though obscenity is said to have been merely a pretext for Ovid's banishment from Rome by Augustus, the fact that the charge was available indicates less than complete social equanimity about erotic expression, and that such representation was hardly free of control. Nor, of course, are we persuaded that the supposedly "unashamedly joyous" ancients would have found many nonobscene twentieth-century representations such as illustrations in medical books, the kissing and petting of lovers, an *apache* dance, or a burlesque striptease completely unobjectionable, to say nothing of contemporary "hard-" or "soft-core" pornography.

We also know that societies in the past took social control of sexual conduct very seriously. Rules and restrictions, often "unenlightened" by modern standards, were apt to be rigorous and wide-ranging. Violations were often punished severely. In Rome, incest, a wife's adultery, and fornication between a free woman and a slave were capital offenses. Many ancient societies punished sodomy and other homosexual acts by death or castration.[16] Even the Greeks, who are said to have been so much at ease with their sexuality, had a well-established and thoroughgoing double standard. The society that tolerated male nudity and homosexuality made extensive distinctions among women, by which the hetaerae were glorified while lawful wives were restricted and comparatively desexualized.

We also find great diversity in the sexual regulations. The ancient cultures often differed markedly in their prevailing attitudes toward virginity, infidelity, prostitution, homosexuality, and the role and social standing of sex partners. The same was true of such specific acts as masturbation, fellatio, cunnilingus, anal intercourse, voyeurism, flagellation, and bestiality. The norms of public sexuality—in its social consequences, the aspect of behavior probably closest to erotic expression—also varied, particularly on matters of nudity, exhibitionism, and sex in groups. Idealization of homosexuality among the Greeks differed from the partially institutionalized homosexuality of the Assyrians. Both approaches were rejected by the Hebrews, whose concern about masturbation and other surrogates for heterosexual intercourse was not fully shared by many other ancient civilizations. The nudity and pederasty of the Attic world was generally not acceptable in Rome and other societies where the influence of Greek civilization was otherwise strong.[17]

Well-established concerns of ancient societies about sexual conduct allows us to infer that erotic expression itself must also have come under extensive regulation. What was objectionable and not objectionable must have varied considerably, both among and within societies. Moreover, lines drawn between acceptable and deviant conduct in legal codes and religious writings indicate not only concern with actual and probable behavior but also, in their specific prohibitions, many underlying, "irrational" anxieties. It is impossible to suppose that these would not also affect expression, which, in its fantastical roots, is substantively more wide-ranging than actual behavior.

The rise of Christianity and establishment of the Church had a profound effect on sexual attitudes and norms in Europe. In its early concern with sexual morality, the Church may have been responding as much to secular conflict and social instability before and after the collapse of imperial Rome as it was to the freewheeling licentiousness of the time. Yet as it grew more and more preoccupied with "sin," its sexual doctrine became increasingly ascetic and repressive. Its code of regulations, underwritten by threats of divine punishment in this world or the next, was designed to inhibit sexual activity, discredit its pleasure, and limit its indulgence to intercourse between married persons for procreation. Church penitentials dwelt at inordinate length on sexual transgressions. Heterosexual fornication joined homosexuality, masturbation, and many other activities in being specifically prohibited. Even kissing and involuntary nocturnal "pollutions" called for penalties, as did merely thinking about sex, which in the light of the other injunctions must have been a common failing. Perhaps never have so many human beings subscribed so strenuously to norms designed to alienate them from the core of their natures. In this fear and loathing lies the hint of a "neurotic obsession with sexual matters of a truly pornographic character."[18]

Lacking good evidence about the habits of the masses we cannot be sure how extensively this sexual code affected behavior and expression. But the Church clearly succeeded in gaining nearly complete control over erotic expression in art and writing. This was made easier by a general decline of literacy and learning in the Dark Ages, when writing, art, and most other vehicles of European culture were preserved only in the monasteries. Some highly refined erotic symbolism is present in medieval Christian art, but relatively little erotic expression of the sort found in the ancient world, particularly what might have been considered pornographic, survives from the Middle Ages. Much of what does remain—manuscripts, jewelry, furnishings, and the like—were possessions of elite or wealthy segments of medieval society.[19]

The Church's censorial dominion could not obliterate sexual energy and interest, including that which might normally be expected to find some fantastical representation in external forms. The later Middle Ages are crowded with reports of sexually based hysteria and delusions connected with religious belief and superstition. Accounts of "possessions," spells, and nocturnal encounters with incubi and succubi abound. The genitalia and sexual proclivities of the Devil were matters of continuing interest and speculation.[20] Belief in witches who could impair sexual powers or work temptations through black magic was widespread in Europe for several centuries and by the late Reformation led to the trial and execution of thousands of unfortunate men and women. Acting in the name of divine authority and backed by threat of divine and temporal punishment, the repressive code provided the basis for a limited but socially sanctioned reactive "acting out" of pornographic wishes and fears, even as it succeeded in censoring expression itself.

The Middle Ages provide further evidence of the problematic character of sexual proscriptions. Christian influence, at least that of the Church, designated a range of behavior and expression with its own substantive idiosyncrasies, shaped by culturally unique beliefs and institutions.

"To Deprave and Corrupt"

The censorship experience of Great Britain and the United States shows the variability of proscriptive designation within single cultures over periods of time. The "modern" pornography problem did not begin to emerge until the Church lost its near monopoly on learning and the social forces and technological developments of the Northern Renaissance began to affect large numbers of persons. Printing provided unprecedented power to communicate. The rise of the middle class meant a corresponding increase in literacy and leisure time unimaginable in the Middle Ages. Not only were ever-larger numbers of persons reached, but they were "present" and "available" in disputes over what was or should be communicated. The size and diversity of that audience made it less likely that resolution of such conflict could be confined to a cultural elite.

Printed books were first produced in England in the 1470s; within a half-century a still small but burgeoning printing industry was subject to royal licensing. Though the initial aim of licensing was to restrict subversive religious and political expression, it established the framework used later against offensive sexual expression, the first references to which appear at the end of the sixteenth century.[21] The level of socially acceptable expression has been anything but constant in the four hundred years since.

In the age of Elizabeth I, severe political censorship contrasted sharply with a rather robust liberality in erotic expression. Judged by the popularity of books of coarse jokes, riddles, and the like, a broad humor was in vogue. Audiences were apparently unshocked by Shakespeare's erotic dialogues and ribald wit. Standards changed discernibly in the first half of the seventeenth century. A new and vocal Puritan sensibility, already evident at the end of Elizabeth's reign, attacked the licentiousness of the stage and demanded a new seriousness in literature. This zealousness reached its zenith during the Commonwealth, and met with inevitable reaction when the monarchy was restored in 1660. A cynicism and worldliness in manners and morals, at least among the intelligentsia and their aristocratic patrons at court, marked the age of Dryden and Rochester and, later, that of Congreve and Vanbrugh. The theater, banned under Cromwell, was revived; Shakespeare, who had been expurgated by the Puritans, was restored, Dryden going so far as to add risqué scenes to *The Tempest*.[22] Much of this literature would not have been tolerated half a century earlier.

Political settlements of the Revolution of 1688 and the success of a growing middle class eventually brought reaction. The early eighteenth century saw a great increase in literacy and leisure and a formidable reading public gradually replacing private patrons as arbiters of taste. As during the Commonwealth, a Puritan attitude toward literature and drama successfully vied with a more tolerant, worldly, and detached one that was often amused by the former's moral distress. It was that sensibility, foreshadowing the plenary Victorian conscience a century later, that saw literacy and literature as great socializing forces and, thus, as dangerously capable of corrupting.

The first serious attempt to control erotic publications through courts of law rather than ecclesiastical jurisdiction was made in 1708 when James Read was prosecuted for publishing *The Fifteen Plagues of a Maidenhead,* a collection of ribald poems about defloration. Judges of the Queen's Bench, unable to find injury to the government or any person, concluded that the poems may have tended to "the corruption of manners but that is not sufficient for us to punish."[23] This tolerant attitude was absent twenty years later in the prosecution and conviction of Edmund Curll for publishing

Venus in the Cloister or the Nun in Her Smock and a work on erotic flogging. The case established the common-law offense of "obscene libel" that was to become a legal mainstay of censorship battles in the nineteenth century. In the remainder of the eighteenth, however, relatively few books of any sort were prosecuted and, despite strong disapprobation in some quarters, erotic works appear to have circulated with relative freedom. *Fanny Hill* appeared in 1748 and the informative directory of London prostitutes, *Harris's List of Convent Garden Ladies*, in the 1780s. About the same time there was a brief but keen competition among entries in a new genre of periodical literature focusing on reports of sexual crimes and the sex scandals and complaints that found their way into the civil courts.[24] Other publications concentrated on erotic fiction heavy with double entendres, and on a voluminous correspondence much, if not most, of it staff-written.[25] Publications such as *The Rambler, Bon Ton,* and finally *Rangers,* which promised to outdo the others, suggest in both style and content the sex magazines of the 1960s, without, of course, photographic illustration.

In the inevitable ebb and flow of public acceptability, in the late eighteenth century, through prosecutions, publications that had circulated freely came under attack by innumerable vice societies or informal pressures exerted on proprietary interests. The revival of moral censorship saw the sentimental and "high-minded" gain at expense of the picaresque.[26]

Expurgation of the classics was well underway when Dr. Thomas Bowdler published *The Family Shakespeare* in 1818. In it he excised all that could not "with propriety be read aloud in the family," in effect, almost all sexual references and allusions, thus lending his name forever to the informal censorship of established works. During the next hundred years, many classics—*The Canterbury Tales, Gulliver's Travels, Moll Flanders,* Pepys's *Diary,* and the poems of Herrick and Dryden among them—were published only in censored editions. Inevitably, the Bible itself came under scrutiny. Excision or restatement of many of its erotic passages, including those that merely employed erotic metaphor, strikingly illustrates the variability of "obscenity" and "indecency." Episodes and passages read for hundreds of years, providing moral instruction (and perhaps no small amount of erotic excitement) for millions of readers, were no longer considered fit.

The rage to bowdlerize—Noel Perrin counted 3,000 British and American expurgated editions and estimated that there might be thousands more—was part of a textual reformation the result of which was that "three or four generations in England and America grew up with a moderately inaccurate idea of their own literature."[27]

Coarse language was a prime target. Not limited to four-letter words, this included all but the most elegant or euphemistic references to sexual behavior, elimination, and parts of the body. Even relatively elevated terms such as "prostitute" and "smock," or Latinate expressions for sexual organs or acts, invited objection. Individual words claimed magical properties. Perhaps there is no greater tribute to the supposed power of literacy and no greater literary testament to unresolved infantile conflicts than nineteenth-century bowdlerism.

More than words were changed. Double entendres and sexual allusions of various sorts were cut out or restated. In *King Lear*, the Fool's codpiece song was eliminated, as was Goneril's lament about the knights' brothel activities.[28] Pepys's faithful and literate recording of his sexual experiences, and fanciful pictures, such as the voyeuristic Lilliputian army that subdued Gulliver or Swift's classically nonerotic detailing of the Brobdignagian breast, fared no better.[29] Portrayal of sexual morality was a pressing concern. Biblical expurgators removed Lot's seduction by his daughters and Onan's sexual "deviation."[30] When Shakespeare's "Under the green-wood tree / Who loves to lie with me," became "Who loves to work with me," not only meaning but morality itself was altered.[31] Even licit relations between husband and wife might be denied. Moll Flanders, who for almost a hundred years was able to say "We supped together and we lay together that night," was forced in the nineteenth century to observe that she and her spouse merely "abided" together.[32]

Expurgation was not the isolated phenomenon of a handful of philistines temporarily in power. The reformation of literature was continuous and thoroughgoing. Ranks of the expurgators included many distinguished writers, critics, and scholars of the day: W. M. Rossetti, Robert Southey, Francis Palgrave, Lewis Carroll, and Leigh Hunt; in the United States, Noah Webster, William Cullen Bryant, and Thomas Bulfinch. They were encouraged and abetted by publishers whose business eye was sharpened by a view of what the public—at least much of the middle-class book-reading public—wanted and would tolerate.

In the first half of the nineteenth century, bowdlerism dealt successfully with the classics and contemporary works of literary merit, but it was not equal to the control of popular writing, especially what appeared in periodical form with the sole aim of satisfying or stimulating erotic interest. For these materials, largely immune from and perhaps even reactive to the cult of refinement in manners and morals, stronger measures were needed. Lines separating the acceptable and unacceptable were frequently drawn in legal actions against particular works or their publishers. In the first half of the nineteenth century, these typically were common-law prosecutions for obscene libel initiated by various private antivice societies.

Inevitably, lawmaking caught up with the growing strictness in Victorian standards of taste. In 1853, the first legislation aimed specifically at "indecent" and "obscene" expression barred importation of such material. This was followed four years later by the Obscene Publications Act, otherwise known as Lord Campbell's Act after its chief sponsor. Though it created no new criminal offenses, the act facilitated police searches and authorized magistrates to destroy confiscated items found to be obscene.[33]

The first celebrated casualty of the new law was *The Confessional Unmasked,* in 1867. Published by the Protestant Electoral Union, the work purported to show the sexual misbehavior of priests hearing confessions and contained erotic material allegedly taken from Roman Catholic devotional and theological publications.[34] That the book had been available since 1836 testifies again to the mutability of public standards. An appeal of the case, *Regina v. Hicklin,* to the Queen's Bench produced a definitive ruling by Chief Justice Sir Alexander Cockburn on the nature of proscribable erotica. The test for obscenity was whether the material tended to "deprave and corrupt those whose minds were open to such immoral influences and into whose hands a publication of this sort may fall."[35] Perhaps without intending to do so, the *Hicklin* rule, as it came to be known, recognized the personal and idiosyncratic character of the pornographic. "Whose minds are open to such influences" effectively institutionalized the variability of obscenity, while at the same time failing to provide triers of fact with guidelines to relieve their own subjectivity.

The *Hicklin* rule was perfectly suited to ever-stricter late nineteenth-century standards of taste. Under it, Victorian censorship reached its zenith. Prosecutions once almost entirely confined to coarse or licentious expression in publications of little or no literary merit now turned to serious works, striking at themes and ideas. In the 1870s, the social reformers Charles Bradlaugh and Annie Besant were indicted for publishing a pamphlet advocating birth control. A decade later, the reputable publisher Henry Vizetelly found himself in the dock for bringing out three Zola novels, *La Terre, Pot Bouille,* and *Nana,* each of which challenged aspects of conventional morality and each of which he had already expurgated. Prosecutions such as these created difficulties for other authors who sought to depict sexual and moral life radically different from what was considered proper and congenial. When their work did get published, as with Hardy's *Tess of the d'Urbervilles* and *Jude the Obscure,* abuse from critics and public was often devastating.[36] In 1898, in another celebrated prosecution, Havelock Ellis's classic *Sexual Inversion,* one of the first psychological studies of homosexuality, and already published in Germany, was found obscene.[37] These and many less well publicized cases reveal the squeamishness of a particular age and the censorious lengths to which that anxiety might be carried in reaction to countervailing intellectual, literary, and scientific values.

Another target of the law was the "underworld of Victorian literature," the sometimes flourishing trade in publications whose sole purpose was sexual stimulation. Much of this material would be tedious to readers or viewers of the eighteenth century and certainly of the late twentieth century: coy suggestions of whipping and bondage, preoccupation with underclothes, states of undress, and especially the pubic hairline, which served as an exact demarcation between unacceptable exposure and a less suspect fascination with the nude.[38] For Victorians, these publications and their depictions were pornographic.

As a social category, pornography turns conventional morality upside down. Its violation and parody of officially cherished standards is the source of both its attractiveness and its threat. Thematically, the Victorians were most outraged by debauchery in their two most exalted institutions: school and family, those pillars of righteousness and progress they believed made middle-class Victorian England unique and morally superior. But in the pornographic underworld, teachers seduce pupils, pupils seduce each other, "cousins pair off without the least inhibition; uncles exercise a sexual tyranny over nieces and nephews; fathers seduce their daughters and corrupt their sons, sons unite with mothers; brothers and sisters form homosexual or heterosexual liaisons."[39] As Donald Thomas astutely observed, "if we knew nothing of Victorian society except through its pornography, we might well guess a great deal of the rest."[40] Perhaps no less can be said of any society: repetitive pornographic themes and concerns mirror prevailing sexual and social values. In part, this explains pornography's variation with time, place, and class.

An exchange of letters between two national police officials in 1907 reflects the troublesome lack of universal accord with the Victorian view of obscenity. Attempting to persuade reluctant French authorities to act against an expatriate bookseller who had shipped a book containing pictures of nude women to England, an assistant commissioner at Scotland Yard explained that an obscene picture was one in which "the hair is clearly shown on the private parts." His French counterpart replied that pubic hair was not considered obscene in France and thus no action could be taken.[41] French standards, however, were not always more liberal than British. Social control of erotic expression had its ups and downs throughout the nineteenth century, and during more restrictive periods, enforceable standards for literary expression rivaled those of the Victorians.[42]

The late nineteenth century witnessed an explosion of erotic communication throughout western Europe, an inevitable result of a rapidly increasing audience for communications of any sort. Reaction followed in the form of private pressures and attempts by governments to impose legal control. Where official suppression succeeded, the new pornography trade was forced underground, curtailed though not eradicated. Antiobscenity laws on the Continent were generally no more precise than in Britain. This fact and the inability or unwillingness of government prosecutors and the censoring public to weigh the redemptive features of a communication meant that distinctions between ordinary commercial pornography and erotic works of literary quality, or scientific and medical treatises dealing with sexuality, were lost.[43] This undiscriminating approach should not be surprising. Sensitivity to redeeming qualities is not a "natural" part of the individual's psychodynamic response to erotic expression. It requires a certain sophistication and commitment to tolerance that had not yet found articulation in the public law of most countries.

The ebbing of Victorian censorial energy was hastened by the Great War, which was to change so many other aspects of British life. Conventions once regarded as fundamental moral canons, including many governing sexual attitudes and behavior, seemed increasingly inadequate to the disillusioned and relativistic world of the twentieth century. Sexual matters formerly ignored or treated with reticence were discussed openly. The entire period from the early twenties to the present can be seen as a retreat from Victorian standards. Yet, at the same time, the libertarian tide of the twentieth century has ebbed and flowed no less than the censorious tide of the nineteenth. The permissiveness immediately following the war led to attempts to impose more restrictive standards during the "Jix" period, in the late twenties, when home secretary Sir William Joynson-Hicks personally symbolized a new drive on erotic publications. Works such as Norah James's novel *The Sleeveless Errand,* in which characters reveal their most intimate sexual thoughts in frank language, and Radclyffe Hall's novel of lesbian romance, *The Well of Loneliness,* were suppressed. *Ulysses* and *Lady Chatterley's Lover* could not at first be published in Britain. Joyce's great work came out in London in 1936, fourteen years after it first appeared in Paris. Lawrence's novel was not published unexpurgated in his native land until the 1960s.

Renewed liberality after World War II was met by an antipornography campaign, touched off by the London appearance of Norman Mailer's *The Naked and the Dead,* which was denounced for its "foul and beastly" language. After several notable obscenity trials in the fifties, Lord Campbell's mid-nineteenth-century law was superseded by the Obscene Publications Act of 1959, amended in 1964. The new standard restated the *Hicklin* rule. A work was proscribable if, taken as a whole, its effect was "to deprave and corrupt persons who are likely, having regard to all relevant circumstances, to read, see or hear the matter contained or embodied in it,"[44] a narrower formulation than "whose minds are open to such influence." Further, the act provided a defense if publication could be "justified as being for the public good on the ground that it is in the interests of science, literature, art or learning, or of other objects of general concern."[45] In such a case, depravity and corruption could apparently be overlooked. The new law reflected a marked change in public attitudes and tolerance.

Obscenity—legally proscribed sexual expression—has changed substantially in the century since the original *Hicklin* formulation, but the central concept, "tending to deprave and corrupt," has not been abandoned. The *Hicklin* rule was one of the first attempts to define obscenity in other than tautological synonyms or descriptive categories of specific sexual acts or bodily parts. The very subjectivity invited by the vagueness of "deprave and corrupt" has allowed for changes in substance without altering the form of prohibition. Put another way, inconstancy of application has been the price for keeping the principle. The experience belies the idea that obscenity in Britain has had a fixed or near-constant meaning. It is little wonder that the Arts Council Working Party, formed to study operation of the new law, concluded in its final report: "It is impossible to devise a definition of obscenity that does not beg the question or a rational procedure for weighing depravity and corruption against artistic merit and the 'public good.' "[46] It might have added that obscenity laws, like other forms of social control, are about conformity—about what is and is not acceptable to a particular age or, more to the point, to triers of fact, makers of laws, and their constituents.

British experience is even more complicated because the "tendency to deprave and corrupt" test of the 1959 act and the common law is not the only legal measure applied to erotic expression. Materials imported, sent through the mails, or displayed in public are proscribable under other statutes if they are indecent or obscene, although these terms are not defined or amplified. In contrast to a "tendency to deprave and corrupt," which refers to a presumably injurious *effect* on an individual, "indecent" and "obscene" generally appear to be given their more commonplace meaning, essentially that of offensiveness.[47] Because "indecent" usually has a lower designative threshold than "obscene," there are actually several measures of proscribable sexual expression in British law, none of which are well defined or precisely set out.

Where the "deprave and corrupt" test applies, as it does under the 1959 act and in common-law proceedings, it is believed that many triers of fact actually decide whether a publication is obscene, in the everyday sense, that is, whether it is in accord with their own perception of what is publicly acceptable, and simply presume the existence of psychological causation.[48] Given the uncertainty surrounding the effects of erotic expression, taken up in Chapter 4, we may doubt that a literal application of the "deprave and corrupt" test has ever involved much more than guesswork or, worse, a subjective response, possibly not even entirely conscious.

In 1979, the Committee on Obscenity and Film Censorship, appointed by the Home Office to review existing laws and censorship arrangements and chaired by the philosopher Bernard Williams, concluded that vagueness and confusion about the meaning of "obscene," "indecent," and "deprave and corrupt" was so universal that the concepts should be abandoned altogether as measures of legal control. It suggested that "the principal object of the law should be to prevent certain kinds of material causing offence to reasonable people or being made available to young people." Within this framework, expression (other than the written word, which would be left free of all restraints) could be restricted—not prohibited—because of the way it portrayed "violence, cruelty or horror, or sexual, faecal or urinary functions or genital organs." These standards would also apply to films. Live performances would be prohibited if they involved "actual sexual activity of a kind which, in the circumstances in which it was given, would be offensive to reasonable people (sexual activity including the act of masturbation and forms of genital, anal or oral connection between humans and animals as well as between humans)." Though the committee's report led to public discussion and debate, it did little to change existing law.[49]

The American Grain

In contrast to Britain, the American colonies in the seventeenth and eighteenth centuries had almost no indigenous erotic literature of either a serious or popular sort. The Puritan conscience was probably even more firmly implanted on the American side of the Atlantic, and not until well into the nineteenth century did sexual expression became a persistent public issue. When it did, the nation's growing heterogeneity and widely dispersed political authority made accord on the matter even more problematic than in Britain.

Although the earliest obscenity case on appellate record dates to 1815, effective control of erotic expression throughout the first half of the nineteenth century was largely informal, relying on general social pressure, proprietary self-restraint, and the efforts of various reform groups and antivice societies. Cheap pornographic publications circulated among soldiers during the Civil War. Erotic expression increasingly became a public issue in the post-war economic prosperity and the inevitable questioning of established moral standards. Opponents of the new liberality found their leader in Anthony Comstock, the late nineteenth century's prototypical censor. Initially a self-appointed antivice crusader, Comstock worked closely with many private groups, his efforts eventually leading to a commission as "special agent" of the Post Office. He was a major force behind hundreds of prosecutions and the seizure of tens of thousands of books, magazines, photographs, engravings, and other communications. His lobbying spurred passage of a number of antiobscenity laws, including a comprehensive federal statute that came to bear his name.

Comstock led campaigns against the portrayal of female nudity and immorality. Confiscated with commercial pornography were *September Morn*, studies distributed by art students, and even Bernarr McFadden's physical culture posters showing young women clad in skintight union suits with sashes. Publication of unconventional sexual views, including advocacy of contraception, abortion, or alternatives to marriage, risked prosecution for obscenity. Bernard Shaw's play *Mrs. Warren's Profession*, attacked when it opened in New York for its discussion of prostitution, was a celebrated Comstockian target. Like many of his contemporaries, Comstock was unable, or perhaps did not care, to distinguish between a frankly pornographic book and a medical or scientific discussion or advocacy of an idea.[50] He believed, as did many judges and juries of the day, that authoritative standards must protect the most vulnerable persons in the community. In his hands, this *Hicklin*-inspired notion was as severe as it was subjective.

Though frequently lampooned, Comstock was not an unpopular figure. "Comstockery"—a term coined by Shaw himself—may have appeared ridiculous and benighted to some freethinking contemporaries, as it did to most persons of later generations, but in the late nineteenth century it came close to reflecting prevailing American standards for sexual expression.

When Comstock died in 1915, American Victorianism and the "genteel tradition" had already crested. As in Britain, decline was hastened by a war that was to be a watershed for a new sexual morality. The imperative "Back to normalcy" was stubbornly prejudicial to a temper bent on new personal freedom and a new openness in sexual matters. Conflict was dramatized in prosecutorial attacks on a number of literary works. Though representing only the front line of the phalanx of social control, appellate decisions arising from these local actions provide an illuminating catalog of the shifting designative line separating permissible from proscribed.

Early targets included Arthur Schnitzler's *Hands Around* and *Casanova's Homecoming,* Lawrence's *Women in Love,* James Branch Cabell's *Jurgen,* and Dreiser's *An American Tragedy,* which dealt with a much broader range of erotic subject matter than earlier fiction, and in which intercourse was sometimes described rather than implied. Under later attack were Faulkner's *Sanctuary,* Erskine Caldwell's *Tobacco Road* and *God's Little Acre,* and other works of sexual naturalism that used such words as "bastard," "bitch," "slut," and "whore," and in which sexual perversion or depravity was thematically central. The fiction brought to court had also moved from portrayals of isolated transgressing individuals to entire groups with permissive attitudes toward extramarital relations.[51]

In the thirties, an attempt was made to bar the importation of *Ulysses.* Joyce's frank sexual references and use of four-letter words, including the traditionally most objectionable but seldom seen "fuck," were an open invitation to censorship. In a celebrated bench trial, Judge John M. Woolsey found the novel to be not obscene: although it contained many words usually considered "dirty," nothing in it was "dirt for dirt's sake." Rather, he said, each word "contributes like a bit of a mosaic to the detail of the picture which Joyce is seeking to construct for his readers." Significantly, he departed from the *Hicklin* reference to "those whose minds are open to immoral influence," holding instead that a work must be judged by its anticipated effect on a "person of average sex instincts—what the French would call *l'homme moyen sensuel.*"[52] Affirmed on appeal, the judgment represented a significant shift in the legal concept of obscenity in the United States. It is not surprising that many literary works prosecuted in the decade that followed—Lillian Hellman's *Children's Hour*, Faulkner's *Wild Palms*, Lillian Smith's *Strange Fruit*, and James T. Farrell's *A World I Never Made*, among them—contained much blunter language than their targeted predecessors and dealt explicitly with a noticeably broader range of sexual behavior, including prostitution, homosexuality, and incest.

The liberal trend continued after World War II. As indicated by actions against Edmund Wilson's *Memoirs of Hecate County*, Calder Willingham's *End as a Man*, John O'Hara's *Ten North Frederick*, and other works depicting a wider acceptance of extramarital relations, the point at which a work might be subject to attack for its general theme or its vocabulary receded even further from the benchmarks of former proprieties. In the *Hecate County* case, in which obscenity was found at trial and on appeal, the recording of a sexual affair in frank language and detail by the novel's young narrator, represented the new, if temporary, outer limit to the steadily widening area of permissible expression. By the mid-fifties, prosecuted works "tended to depict illicit encounters as the norm for society as a whole, and as seldom raising moral questions in the minds of the characters."[53]

When the Supreme Court dealt definitively with obscenity for the first time, in 1957, it chose, significantly, two cases involving cheap pornographic books and magazines rather than works with literary claims. In the *Roth* and *Alberts* decision, it formally abandoned the *Hicklin* rule, substituting "the average person" and "contemporary community standards" for the older, more restrictive reference.[54] This decision and others that followed in the next fifteen years gradually and effectively removed virtually all restrictions on written sexual expression. Many suppressed books, such as the unexpurgated *Lady Chatterley's Lover* and nearly all of the novels of Henry Miller, became openly available. By the late sixties,

four-letter words and emetic references, which had formerly appeared once or twice in a book, suddenly became common in works of fiction involved in litigation. . . . References to the genital areas, seldom mentioned in other periods, were now frequent. Acts of heterosexual intercourse, formerly implied or described metaphorically, were now developed at length and explicitly. Deviant sexual behavior was also described in much greater detail.[55]

The movies provide even more striking illustration of the change taking place in the substantive aspects of obscenity.[56] Once under official and proprietary restraint so tight that many literary works had to be bowdlerized before they could be adapted, the movies began to catch up with the older media the 1950s. Major obscenity cases involved films such as *Game of Love, The Lovers, Lady Chatterley's Lover,* and *La Ronde,* few of which contained nudity or graphic sexuality and none four-letter words. The alleged offense was appearing to advocate behavior—usually adultery—that violated established sexual values. By the early sixties, important censorship controversies involved limited erotic nudity, such as brief glimpses of female breasts or buttocks, nonerotic nudity usually set in nudist camps, particular words in the sound track such as "shit" (as slang for heroin) in *The Connection* or "rape" and "contraceptive" in *Anatomy of a Murder,* and simulated, relatively nonexplicit sexual violence in *The Virgin Spring.* By the late sixties, controversies centered more often than not on simulated consensual sexual acts, as in the case of *A Stranger Knocks* and *491,* the latter depicting a prostitute about to have intercourse with a large dog. Cases in the seventies, including those against *Deep Throat, The Devil in Miss Jones, Behind the Green Door,* and *The Animal Lover,* involved hard-core pornographic content—usually real sexual acts, including many widely thought to be perverse. Objectionable categories of the previous decade—erotic nudity, simulated sexual acts, four-letter words, frank dialogue—came to be considered "soft-core" and thus nonactionable. The objectionable categories of the fifties—nonjudgmental portrayal of immorality and nonerotic nudity—are now rarely targets at all. In fact, it can be said that almost any cinematic content proscribed a generation ago would be undisturbed today, whereas almost any rendition fairly raising an obscenity question today would not have been produced or perhaps even considered for public commercial exhibition as late as 1965.

Abandoning the *Hicklin* approach, the Supreme Court chose not to define obscenity in *Roth* or to deal with its substantive characteristics. It offered instead the test "whether to the average person, applying contemporary community standards, the dominant theme of the material taken as a whole appeals to the prurient interest." Later it added that an expression must also be "patently offensive" and "utterly without redeeming social importance."[57] With "contemporary community standards," the test gave apparent recognition to both the temporal and geocultural variability of obscenity. Yet in decisions following *Roth* in the sixties and early seventies, in which scores of books, magazines, photographs, and movies were found to be not obscene, often without opinion, the Court gave little indication of what it would consider substantively obscene.[58] This reticence has been true of American law at all levels. No federal antiobscenity law defines the term. State statutes generally either do not define it or simply incorporate the tests set out by the Court.

The shifting cultural and legal standards applicable to erotic expression were largely responsible for Congress's establishing the President's Commission on Obscenity and Pornography in 1967 to study the problem and, among other things, to define proscribable pornography. After more than two years of work and dozens of new studies that added greatly to existing knowledge about pornography, the commission declined to formulate a definition. Application of the ramified *Roth* test to specific material, it said, required "a great deal of subjective judgment because the criteria refer to emotional and intellectual responses to the material rather than to descriptions of its content." The Commission found no consensus in public opinion about whether specific erotic portrayals were socially valuable, arousing, or sufficiently offensive to be formally proscribed. It doubted that definition was possible or desirable and recommended instead, though with less than compelling logic, that consensual distribution of sexual expression directed to adults be freed of all controls.[59]

Some of the difficulties presented by diversity of opinion and the variable nature of pornography were addressed by the Supreme Court in *Miller v. California* in 1973. Observing that the "nation is simply too big and too diverse" for standards of proscribable erotic expression to be set out in a "single formulation," the Court saw the same lack of consensus as the Commission. But its remedy was quite different. "Contemporary community standards" were not those of the nation itself, as many libertarians had assumed, but those of the state or local community. In addition, the Court tried to reduce uncertainty in both the redemptive and offensiveness elements of the obscenity test. The requirement that an expression be "utterly without redeeming social importance" was narrowed to without "serious literary, artistic, political and social value." And, for the first time, the Court set out categorical examples of what might be considered "patently offensive." These included "ultimate sexual acts, normal or perverted, actual or simulated, . . . masturbation, excretory functions, and lewd exhibition of genitals."[60]

Devolution of substantive standards to those prevailing at state and local levels increases the chances that communication will be held obscene in one jurisdiction but not in another. Although such "balkanization" is assailed by those who believe a single liberal measure can and should govern the entire nation, geopolitical variability of designative standards is one of the oldest facts of sexual expression. It reflects the heterogeneity in the social fabric and inevitable shifts in the identity of decisive groups who have the opportunity to influence or enforce social standards. This diversity and change is commonplace in most complex societies and receives formal recognition in many. For example, findings of obscenity often differ from one province to another in Canada and from one state to another in Australia. In the United States, local autonomy necessarily remains limited, since the Supreme Court has held that redemptive qualities of an expression are *not* subject to local standards but are a matter of independent finding by a court.[61]

In any event, devolution deals only with geocultural diversity and even then only on a geojurisdictional level. Lack of accord on proscriptive standards is likely to be far greater *within* states and communities than among them, since it rests more on social and psychological differences among individuals and groups than among political units.

The Attorney General's Commission on Pornography, the most recent public body to address systematically the public aspects of sexual expression and its control, did not recommend basic changes in the Supreme Court's test, nor did it develop a definition of pornography. Instead, it recognized the enormous variability and subjectivity associated with "pornography" and "obscenity" as social concepts—an unusual insight for a body favoring greater control.[62]

Diversity Abroad

The variability of proscribable sexual expression in the United States and Great Britain is part of an even larger lack of consensus among countries and cultures of the world. When representatives of forty nations met in Geneva in 1923 for the League of Nations Conference on Traffic in Obscene Publications, the delegates quickly agreed that the manufacture and trade in "obscene writings, printed matter, posters, drawings, prints, paintings, pictures, emblems, photographs, cinematograph films or articles" should be a punishable offense, but they expressly refrained from defining what they considered objectionable. Substantively, obscenity was viewed as a question of fact to be decided by the courts of each country. In the words of the French delegate, Hennequin,

The word in question has a different meaning in each language; and, what is more, it has as many meanings as there are countries, mentalities, conceptions, and temperaments. This is tantamount to admitting that it is impossible to find a solution which would gain universal support. . . . We are quite agreed that it would be better to leave the term to be defined in accordance with spirit governing the laws of each country. It would be imprudent to attempt to lift the veil which shrouds this impenetrable mystery.[63]

Although libertarians have often characterized this declaration as an admission by the delegates that they did not know what they were talking about, the position is entirely practical and realistic: objectionable sexual representation is a social category in every country and culture, but among countries and cultures there may be little or no consensus about its specifics. No universal definition of obscenity has been attempted since.

All modern countries have placed legal restrictions on sexual expression. In almost all, these extend to written and pictorial printed matter, movies, the electronic media, and the theater and other live performances, and include proscriptions on importation, shipment through the mails, and public displays. Many also have special restrictions for juveniles. When the American commission surveyed legal controls in a dozen nations in 1970, almost a half-century after the League delegates met, it found that despite statutes, court decisions, and even constitutional provisions restricting sexual expression, none of the nations had defined obscenity or given concrete substantive examples of what was proscribable.[64] The British Committee on Obscenity and Film Censorship, making a similar survey of European and Commonwealth countries a decade later, reached much the same conclusion.[65] Specific designations not only vary within countries from one period to another but often also from one city or region to another. It is not surprising, then, that administration of controls should often be erratic, contributing to the further variability of operating standards.

Actual proscriptions continue to differ widely among countries despite the global trend toward liberalization. Books banned in Australia, for example, have been freely available in Britain and New Zealand. The unexpurgated *Lady Chatterley's Lover,* obscene in Japan, was at the same time declared not so in the United States. The film *Last Tango in Paris* was found obscene in Italy but not in Britain. Simple nudity on stage has been prohibited in some Western countries but is permissible in others. *Deep*

Throat, exhibited freely in West Germany, was barred from theaters in Australia, Hong Kong, and many other jurisdictions. In an acknowledgment of cultural diversity, India has applied less restrictive standards to foreign films than to domestic productions. At one time, the latter could not depict kissing or other erotic acts considered mild and even innocuous by Western standards.

Scandinavian countries often restrict portrayals of violence rigorously, but have been much freer with erotic expression. Since 1969, Denmark has put no restrictions on printed matter, written or pictorial, for distribution to adults. Yet even Denmark, which has become a byword for permissive society, retains a number of controls. Sale of obscene pictures or objects to persons under sixteen is still a crime, and a board of movie censors conducts an authoritative prior review of all films intended for exhibition to children under sixteen. Exhibition or distribution of obscene pictures in public places, or delivery of such materials to persons who did not order them, are offenses. Live entertainment involving sexual acts was permitted for a time, but police in Copenhagen closed down such shows in the 1970s.

In recent years, Yugoslavia has moved from the Victorian reticence typical of Eastern Europe to a more moderate position. A similar transformation has been evident in democratic Spain. On the other hand, the Soviet Union and most other communist states, though also influenced to some extent by liberalization in the West, have remained generally strict and prohibitive. For many years even friendly kissing was not permitted in Soviet films, and only more recently could hand-holding between lovers be shown. In Soviet law, which makes mere possession of pornography a serious crime, the concept of "obscenity" has been called "almost infinitely elastic."[66] Such forbidden items as microfilm copies of the Kinsey Report, the *Kama Sutra,* Western sex manuals, the erotic stories of Pushkin and poems of Yesenin, as well as some contemporary pornography from the West and Soviet sources, are available on the black market, but prices are high and access is believed to be limited largely to elite circles.[67]

Instead of defining obscenity or providing examples of what is proscribed—tasks almost certain to prove futile in the long run—policies of most modern states, beginning with the *Hicklin* rule in Britain, have designated objectionable expression instrumentally, through various "tests," or left it largely undetailed, relying in effect on common understandings or on the discretion of fact finders. The tests include several measures: the presumed effect of the expression on its audience, the nature of the audience, the medium employed, the public circumstances of the expression, the intent of creator or proprietor, redemptive values, especially those of a social, aesthetic, or scientific sort, and limitations imposed by countervailing positive rights such as freedom of speech, due process of law, and privacy. Such considerations depart from the idea of obscenity as a more or less fixed category substantive aspects of which are self-evident or at least readily knowable. Each appears to "objectify" the matter and provide a basis for marking the acceptable off from the unacceptable, hence to offer a rationale for public policy. We shall examine in Part Four the role each of these measures has played in proscriptive designation and actual social control.

The notion of the pornographic or obscene is one of the oldest known to humanity and inseparable from the larger eroticization of human sexuality. No society, culture, nation, or age appears ever to have been free of a category of sexual and scatological expression considered so offensive that it must be suppressed or controlled. Determining the substance of that category is a universal task of culture, giving rise to norms, standards, rules, laws, and policies that mark off immoral, indecent, pornographic, or obscene expression and prescribe means for its social control.

The psychological underwriting is clear. In some guise or other, much sexual expression reflects forbidden fantasies that are both inviting and threatening. Insofar as these fantasies are inviting, social control of pornographic expression can never be completely successful. Insofar as they are threatening, interest in control is inevitable and persistent. Since equanimity about these underlying fantasies is rare in individuals, we are not surprised to find it lacking in groups, communities, nations, and cultures dealing with sexual expression as a social category.

The idea of pornography is so unstable in its substance and so variable in actual designation, both within and among complex societies and cultures, that we must doubt whether it can have an intrinsic character. Pornography appears to be a universal category without a universal content. Thus the claim "I know it when I see it!" is really a complex formulation, at once accurate and presumptive. Its first assertion is subjective and unarguable—each of us "knows" what is pornographic for himself or herself. But the second, projecting into the external world and implying the existence of a self-evident quality, is a matter about which there is great social disagreement. Together, they create a dilemma policymakers have been unable to resolve.

We will not digress here to the question whether there is some basal erotic expression that is universally objectionable. Infantile sexuality suggests that the roots of such a pornography exist, and we shall return to the subject at a different level in the next chapter and again in Chapter 5. But as a social category, pornography even in its hard-core form is apt to be at least partially disguised by personal defenses or by the conventions of individual cultures, and not unequivocally to bare the darkest fantasies in each of us. Much more to the point in understanding erotic expression as a diverse and discordant social category is the utter lack of universality about what is socially *un*objectionable.

In the simplest terms, pornography and obscenity are largely what decisive groups at a given time and place say they are. Changes or variations in designation of what is and is not objectionable reflect the rise and fall of their influence in response to social, political, economic, technological, and cultural factors, and as individuals members respond to their own internal environments. Thus swings between liberality and repression are, in the long run, inevitable.

Designation and social control in a modern liberal democracy are, of course, far more complex than this simple model suggests. The remainder of this book discusses how this is the case. Modern liberal democracies have witnessed and been shaped by changes so dramatic that it seems unlikely history will simply repeat itself, however the designative pendulum swings. Higher levels of education, sophistication, and self-awareness among individuals; radical and rapid changes in communications technology; establishment and elaboration of legal and constitutional rights; and a vast increase in both the number of persons and the percentages of all persons who participate, actively or passively, in the affairs of culture and state have libertarian and censorial consequences to which the past is an inexact predictor. Yet these developments must inescapably confront the hidden imperatives of an eroticized human sexuality, not so malleable as society or so adjustable as the law, that rise from the depths of the human being's unique infancy.

Part Two

Knowledge

Chapter Three

The Pornographic Imagination

Herald: If our performance causes aggravation
we hope you'll swallow down your indignation
and please remember that we show
only things which happened long ago
Remember things were very different then
of course today we're all God-fearing men

> Peter Weiss, *The Persecution and Assassination of Jean-Paul*
> *Marat as Performed by the Inmates of the Asylum of Charenton*
> *Under the Direction of the Marquis de Sade*

Holga: The same dream returned each night until I dared not go to
sleep and grew quite ill. I dreamed I had a child, and in the dream
I saw it was my life, and it was an idiot, and I ran away. But it
always crept into my lap again, clutched at my clothes. Until I
thought, if I could kiss it, whatever in it was my own, perhaps I could
sleep. And I bent down to its broken face, and it was horrible . . . but
I kissed it.

> Arthur Miller, *After the Fall*

The internally pornographic is part of the human condition. Its expressive derivative, pornography, appears in all cultures as a social category although its descriptive content varies substantially from one time and place to another. But what are the functions and consequences of pornography itself? In the next chapter, we will examine pornography's effects on the behavior, attitudes, and values of individuals, and in Chapter 5, the place of pornography in the social order. Here, we ask whether pornography has any epistemic or aesthetic worth. Can it tell us anything about ourselves as individuals or as a species? If not, the argument for control is strengthened, though not settled, since pornography can be worthless epistemically and aesthetically yet still have value as recreation. If the answer is yes, the argument for control is weakened, though not settled, since pornography can have redemptive value yet still be harmful or offensive.

Art and Value

The widely held view that intellectual or aesthetic worth and the pornographic are mutually exclusive or contradictory hinders an understanding of what pornography is and can be. Admittedly, even by the simplest critical standards, most pornographic representation, especially contemporary commercial pornography, has no aesthetic or intellectually respectable element and is not meant to have any. We cannot, however, generalize from this fact about "pornographic" as a property. In the same sense, the fact that the greater part of the world's nonpornographic expression, erotic or nonerotic, similarly lacks aesthetic or intellectual worth does not mean that all nonpornographic expression is without value. The question is not whether most pornography is worthless but the more difficult one of whether all of it is.

The law has not been of much help. In both American and British legal theory, a work having literary or artistic value cannot be obscene; likewise, one found obscene is, ipso facto, without intellectual or aesthetic worth. This categorical distinction, the libertarian prize of many hard-won battles, has kept significant works from being censored or suppressed. But in application it often finds libertarians straining to see literary or aesthetic value in pornographic works that obviously have none.

No less muddled is the tendency of some critics to use "pornography" and "pornographic" as pejoratives. Thus a work is pornography when it is poor art, and art when it is acceptable pornography. Abraham Kaplan, for example, finds the once-censored *Nana* and *Mrs. Warren's Profession* acceptable as "conventional obscenity" because they attack established sexual patterns. Works of Rabelais, Boccaccio, and Aristophanes are acceptable as "Dionysian obscenity" because their sexuality is exuberant, comedic, celebratory, and "affirming." But pornography, which is "obscenity responded to with a minimum of psychic distance," is said to have no aesthetic intent. It glorifies sexual aggression and violence or treats sex as a "disgusting necessity" and finds pleasure in that disgust. Thus Sade is clearly outside the aesthetic pale, and even the " 'realistic school' sometimes associated with the name of Hemingway" may be suspect. Pornography cannot be art, because it is "in the service of death, not life."[1]

Aesthetic judgments of erotic expression have been no more constant than the social and legal ones examined in the last chapter. Numerous works now considered literary classics were once denounced, not simply by prosecutors or members of antivice societies, but by leading segments of the intellectual community. Similarly, works once considered generally acceptable have been found objectionable by critics of later generations.[2] Such shifts raise doubts whether reliable criteria exist for separating pornography and art. When erotic works once found objectionable are no longer so, we can draw one of three conclusions: the judgment we now make about their aesthetic worth is wrong; the judgment of the past about their pornographic content was wrong; or art and pornography are not mutually exclusive at all times and places. Similarly, when erotic works once found unobjectionable are later judged obscene (difficult as it is to imagine today), either the later or the earlier view is mistaken, or, again, art and pornography are not mutually exclusive at all times and places.

When serious, complex erotic representation is disposed of by calling it obscene or pornographic, little room is left for critical consideration. We argue here that aesthetic or epistemic worth and pornographic character are independent, not necessarily contradictory properties. A work may have artistic or intellectual value without regard to whether it is pornographic, or be pornographic whether or not it has other qualities. A given representation may be art, pornography, both, or neither. The vast majority of the countless existing works, representations, or symbolizations are without either aesthetic or pornographic consequence. A relatively small number have aesthetic worth but are not pornographic, or are pornographic but have no aesthetic worth. A very small number have both aesthetic and pornographic properties.

It is the last category that interests us here. We shall use the term "pornographic imagination" to refer to a capacity of the artist, which may include perception, insight, vision, fantasy, image making, or symbolization, employed in creating a work and communicating with an audience. This capacity involves the intent—conscious, partly conscious, or unconscious—of the artist and not reactions of an audience, even though very strong responses may be evoked.

Before examining the pornographic imagination more closely, let us consider two ambitious attempts to separate works of aesthetic and epistemic worth from pornography and obscenity based on the intent or state of mind of their creators. The more systematic of these is the often-cited study of the psychologists Phyllis and Eberhard Kronhausen, *Pornography and the Law,* published in the wake of efforts by American courts and legislatures in the 1950s to revise the legal definitions of obscenity. The authors attempt to distinguish pornography from "erotic realism," described as "a historical movement in art and literature, representing in part the artist's or writer's rebellion against social pressures to deny and falsify by forcing him to exclude, minimize, and distort the sexual element in his artistic creation." Erotic realism expresses the artist's or writer's "healthy assertion" by portraying, even emphasizing, erotic aspects of life, in detail if necessary. Unlike pornography, it "limits itself strictly to the description of the realistic aspects of life. It does not aim at exciting sexual passion, nor does it act as a psychological aphrodisiac, except by the coincidence of context. Its only real goal is to depict life as it is, including man's basic biological needs."[3] Examples of such work include Mark Twain's *1601*, Poggio's *Facetiae*, Pepys's *Diary*, Casanova's *Memoirs*, Frank Harris's *My Life and Loves*, Henry Miller's *Tropic of Cancer*, and two "famous mistaken 'borderline' cases," *Lady Chatterley's Lover* and Edmund Wilson's *Memoirs of Hecate County*.

In contrast, the chief aim of pornographic writing is to stimulate an erotic response in the reader. A succession of erotic scenes must constantly be kept before the reader's mind, without "superfluous non-erotic descriptions of scenery, character portrayals, or lengthy philosophic expositions. All these are unnecessary trimmings for the writer of 'obscene' books. The idea is to focus the reader's attention on the erotic word-images and not to distract him with side issues of one kind or another." Obscene books not only have a definite structure and organization, they contain "a number of specific criteria which are based on psychological mechanisms serving the purpose of stimulating erotic fantasies and sexual arousal."[4] These include seduction, incest, the permissive-seductive parent figure, profanation of the sacred, "dirty" words, super-sexed males, nymphomaniacal females, blacks and Asians as sex symbols, homosexuality, and flagellation. To illustrate, the authors analyze and quote from ten specimens, taken mainly from the underground literature of Victorian and early twentieth-century England.

The Kronhausens' distinctions work well applied to what they choose to analyze. Their pornographic specimens are in no danger of being confused with serious literature. Their analysis of "pornography," in effect, formulates the structural and imagistic conventions of the "pornographic but not aesthetic" category distinguished earlier—the familiar staple of market-oriented hackwork. It is a systematic analogue to the appealingly simple diagnostic, "I know it when I see it." To have defined the category is no small achievement, since that category accounts for most representation labeled pornography and thus for much of the public conflict over erotic expression. The question, however, is not quantitative but qualitative: not whether *most* pornography is worthless as knowledge or art, but whether there is *any* that is not and, if so, what its worth might be.

Here, unfortunately, the Kronhausens' distinctions fall short. Neither erotic realism nor the contrasting pornographic specimens adequately comprehend the works of the most inventive of all pornographers, the Marquis de Sade. In fact, Sade appears nowhere in *Pornography and the Law,* an inexplicable omission in view of his influence on all forms of erotic writing. As we shall see, Sade's works do not fall neatly into "erotic realism" or "pornography," but have properties of both categories. The same may be said for what Peter Michelson has called "complex" pornography—serious works, Sadian in tone or subject, such as Baudelaire's *Flowers of Evil,* Georges Bataille's *Story of the Eye,* Pauline Réage's *Story of O,* or Jean de Berg's *Image.*[5] These works deal with darker elements of human sexuality and eroticism than those the Kronhausens analyze as erotic realism or as pornography, and thus present a formidable challenge to the notion that pornography and art are mutually exclusive.

In his study of late nineteenth-century British pornography, *The Other Victorians,* Steven Marcus has also attempted to distinguish pornography from literature. Though it contains some doubtful social science, the study is an intricate and elegant examination of erotic materials reflecting an age and culture. The pornographic and literary are, for Marcus, antithetical in several ways. Pornography has only one aim, that of arousing the reader erotically. Having no real beginning, middle, or end, pornography lacks literary form and can presumably go on indefinitely. A literary work is likely to have many intentions and to generate certain expectations that are carried through to completion. Since the general aim of pornography is imagery, language is a burdensome necessity. This accounts for the low quality of pornographic writing and, in a vain attempt to reach what language cannot adequately express, its heavy reliance on forbidden words. Finally, literature deals with relations among persons and with the complexity of their emotions, attitudes, and thoughts, whereas in pornography these human intricacies are embarrassments and distractions.[6]

Though Marcus's distinctions, like the Kronhausens', work reasonably well with the materials examined, they attempt to generalize from Victorian pornography to all pornography. Difficulty arises almost immediately with even a mildly challenging work such as the pre-Victorian *Fanny Hill,* which is acknowledged to contain "a number of non-pornographic elements, properties, or attributes—it may even contain these to a more substantial degree than other subsequent pornographic works of fiction."[7] Implied here is the entirely reasonable though not fully admitted understanding that the distinctions offered are those of degree, not kind. It is not difficult to show, as Morse Peckham does for the latter-day *Loon* trilogy, that claims that pornography necessarily has but one aim, or lacks a formal beginning, middle, and end, fail when applied to pornographic writing more complex and ambitious than the Victorian works Marcus examines.[8] Absence of stated feelings is not necessarily antiliterary or a failure of artistry. As Susan Sontag has observed, the emotional flatness found in most pornographic writing may actually allow readers full room for their own responses to the erotic imagery it offers. Whether a pornographic work is literature depends less on its characters' having stated emotions, or on a "consciousness more conformable to that of ordinary reality," than on the "originality, thoroughness, authenticity, and power" of the erotic imagination itself.[9] In claiming that aesthetic or epistemic value and pornography are antithetical, both Marcus and the Kronhausens apply to the entirety conclusions that are valid only about the greater part.

Underlying their analyses of form and structure is a view of psychic fitness in which literature or erotic realism is a "healthy assertion" while pornography is regressive and imagined only "by persons who have suffered extreme deprivation." The latter view needs close examination not because it is in error but because it too easily dismisses the possibility that the pornographic can say something of value. As we have defined it, pornography is always regressive, in the sense of calling up images or visions normally excluded from adult psychology. Marcus's term "pornotopia" is most apt in this regard. Pornography does create a kind of utopian fantasy in which all human experience is conceived "as a series of exclusively sexual events and conveniences." Its erotic totality is marked by "emergence of the forbidden and the systematic violation of prohibitions and taboos," offering a "culminating expression of infantile megalomania."[10]

But dismissing all pornography on these grounds is refractive thinking that distorts as it tries to illuminate. That pornography is imagistically regressive does not mean that the artist exercising the pornographic imagination has regressed in thought or act, any more than a sculptor who works with clay or other primordially symbolic material. The "health" of the artist is almost beside the point. Much of the confusion here lies in shifting the frame of reference between the creator's intent and the respondent's reaction. Neither Marcus nor the Kronhausens are consistently clear about whether pornography is regressive and bad because of what it says or is intended to say or because of the possible psychological effect of what is said. The former is relevant to appraising aesthetic worth. The latter, which we examine in the next chapter and which may be critical in formulation of public policy, is not.

Condemning pornography because it deals in regressive images discredits the very source of its power and much of what it may reveal. One result is that many works of obvious aesthetic or intellectual merit must be defended at great effort. Another is that it leaves us unable to deal analytically with more complex and challenging pornography, whose aesthetic properties may not be so readily established as, say, those of *Ulysses* or *Lady Chatterley's Lover,* and whose erotic depiction may be far more disturbing. The real question here is not whether pornography is produced by "deprived" persons or through regression, but what is the nature and quality of the "trophies" the pornographic imagination brings back from that netherworld of the unconscious and partially conscious mind.

Perhaps our difficulty with the idea that pornographic imagination can say something important lies in concern about how its message would cause us to feel about ourselves and others. Most of us would not welcome a return to the maelstrom of desire, jealousy, rage, and terror that give rise to erotic conflicts. We would prefer to let matters rest. But pornography calls us back, and the pornographic imagination may call us back a great distance. If it were simply a matter of prudery or inhibition, we might have less difficulty. But the image of sexual transgression—the hallmark of pornography—is not always simply celebratory in its emotional consequence. Violations of taboos may conjure up a Lawrentian "promised land" or other sexual utopia, but they also suggest a darker world of the mind where erotic and destructive impulses are joined. We may thus extend our argument a step further: the pornographic imagination, imagistically regressive, may have the most to say to us in exactly those areas where our resistance to exploration is understandably greatest and our defenses invested most heavily.

A Pornographic Life

To consider the pornographic imagination more directly, we must begin with Sade, the pornographer whose works for two centuries have been thought the ultimate portrayal of perversity and whose vision of humanity disturbs us even today. He is the only writer Edmund Wilson said he could not read at the breakfast table. Our squeamishness is all the keener perhaps because of what we know of his actual perversities and the extraordinary conditions under which he wrote. At least some of the terrible fantasies within, made extensively and obsessively manifest in his writing, crossed the threshold of acceptable social behavior. We learn from his eroticized life and work what we can perhaps from no other writer's.

Not all of Sade's writing can be considered pornographic. He did complete a major philosophical novel, *Aline and Valcour*, perhaps his most literary work, on which he labored three years. His reputation as a pornographer and misanthrope rests largely on three works much better known: *Justine, Juliette,* and *The 120 Days of Sodom.*

Sade wrote *Justine, or the Misfortunes of Virtue* as little more than a long short story in a two-week period in 1787. It was successively rewritten and thrice expanded, and its last, multivolume version *The New Justine,* published a decade later. With many digressions, it is the story of one of two orphaned sisters, who proceeds through life devoutly and naively adhering to Christian precepts. Her virtue goes unrewarded, sometimes gruesomely, as she moves from one frightening and cruel adventure to another. Sade greatly admired Richardson, and *Justine* is clearly modeled on the melodramatic tragedy *Clarissa.* But whereas Richardson, writing mainly for a popular audience, allowed Christian sentimentalism and bourgeois ethics to triumph over human perversity, Sade, in a parody of the form, saw no beneficent Providence at work rewarding good and punishing evil. Perversity was a natural phenomenon much more likely thrive than wither in the face of virtue. Thus, in one extraordinary incident after another, Justine falls into the hands of usurers, aristocratic lechers, a murderous and incestuous surgeon, debauched priests, and ungrateful beneficiaries of both sexes. She is threatened, abused, brutally assaulted in various pornographic episodes, and mercifully killed by a lightning bolt's striking her breast. The cultural anthropologist Geoffrey Gorer called the work one of the most depressing ever written.

In *Juliette,* the last six volumes of *The New Justine,* Sade writes of sin rewarded. Justine's sister and antipode, Juliette, progresses spectacularly through a life of crime and vice. She inhabits a brothel, revels in a lesbian orgy, poisons her husband, embarks on a rogue's tour of Italy with a wayward priest, encountering grotesque erotic figures along the way, meets and corrupts a hypocritical pope who offers to celebrate a Black Mass in return for her favors, gives her daughter to a depraved aristocrat and assists him in burning her alive, then joins him in contriving a mass atrocity, the poisoning of a town's water supply that results in 1,500 deaths. The book ends with the aristocrat becoming prime minister of France and rewarding his reprobate friends.

The vile and horrific *120 Days of Sodom* is perhaps the quintessential pornographic document. Sade wrote it in the Bastille from 1782 to 1785, in an almost microscopic hand, on a single roll of paper forty feet long. It was never actually completed and the later parts exist only in forms of notes. Unlike *Justine* and *Juliette*, it may not have been intended for publication. The manuscript was lost when the prison was sacked in 1789, but was later recovered and was held in private hands for more than a century, unpublished until 1904. It is a fantastic tale set in a remote and isolated Gothic château during the four months of its title. The chief characters are four aging libertines or "champions," their four daughters, four courtesans, four aged prostitutes, a harem of eight young girls twelve to fifteen, another of eight boys the same age, and four supervirile young men who act as sexual proxies for the libertines when necessary. The title, the cast of characters and, indeed, almost everything else in the book reflects Sade's obsession with system and arithmetic symmetry. The story is arranged in a four-part progression of "passions" from "simple" to "complex" to "criminal" to "murderous." Sade proceeds to plot 600 perversions, 150 of each category, chronicling every kind of sexual and sensual indulgence including necrophilia, bestiality, blood sucking, the exploration of vomit and excreta, cannibalism, the deflowering of babies in their cradles, murder of a sexual partner at the point of orgasm, and sexual mutilation of every conceivable sort. Gratuitous injury and criminality mount steadily until, at the end, only a handful of characters remain, the others all having met horrific and bizarre deaths. The reader is spared no physical or characterological flaw, from sores and smells to cowardice and treachery.

The revulsion and horror with which Sade's writing is usually received are all the greater because of what we know of his actual behavior and apparent character. Perhaps no other writer's work has been more affected by driving obsessions or by the circumstances under which he wrote. An extraordinary and tormented life was inseparable from his pornographic imagination.

Sade was of titled nobility, the son of a successful soldier and diplomat. The family held extensive properties in Paris and Provence and was among the leading houses of France. Sade's problematic temperament was evident as a young child. Combative and tyrannical, he was estranged from his parents and grew up in the house of his reprobate uncle, the Abbé de Sade. After youthful service in the cavalry, he entered an arranged marriage with the prudish daughter of the wealthy Montreuil family. The young libertine aristocrat was not expected to remain faithful, but a series of well-publicized "excesses" soon gained him a reputation for sexual frenzy that shocked even his rakehell circle. The most damaging was the Rose Keller affair, in 1768, in which he was arrested and imprisoned for holding captive and sexually abusing a woman he met on a street. Other misadventures followed, and for ten years Sade was either in prison or one step ahead of the police. At last his resourceful mother-in-law, Madame de Montreuil, who first tried to cover up the scandals, prevailed on Louis XVI to sign a lettre de cachet in 1788 to keep Sade in prison the rest of his life.

Conditions of confinement were severe. After a period of rage and despair, he asked for books and writing materials. His energy was gradually directed from brooding over unjust imprisonment to examining an inner world, eventually to be rendered into words on paper. Except for correspondence and an occasional play performed among friends, Sade had written very little, nor had he shown much evidence of a contemplative mind. But now, almost entirely deprived of an external world, he began to draw on a dormant literary skill and intellectual power to produce the stories, plays, and novels that make up perhaps the most disturbing work created by a single man. When prisoners held under lettres de cachet were released following the Revolution, Sade had produced fifteen volumes, in thirteen years of almost continuous solitary confinement.

Politically he became an active citizen and despite his aristocratic origins was appointed judge of a revolutionary court. Later, during the Terror, he like many others was denounced for "*modérantisme*" and condemned to the guillotine, only to be saved at the eleventh hour by the death of Robespierre. Then fifty, penniless and homeless, Sade worked in a theater and eventually succeeded in getting many of his works published, including the eleven-volume final version of the *The New Justine*. In 1801, the first Consulate of Bonaparte, reacting to libertarian excesses of the 1790s, denounced the work as pornography; Sade was again arrested and imprisoned. His sons worked out an arrangement with the new regime, and the sixty-three-year-old marquis was transferred to the lunatic asylum at Charenton, where he was housed comfortably until his death in 1814.

We must ask ourselves why Sade and his works are so disturbing. Is it simply because he wrote of things we usually reject or find revolting? Other writers have done the same. Had he merely depicted, even advocated, erotic cruelty and perversity and vice triumphant, and stopped at that, we might deal with him more easily. He was not the first to challenge the idealized images of man. Armed with alternative moral positions, we could contend with his thoroughgoing misanthropy and cynicism, his philosophy of turpitude and debauchery, as we contend with other "misguided" systems. But Sade goes further. He suggests a necessary link between the satisfaction of needs and desires and the creation of erotic pain and violence.

Kraft-Ebbing used Sade as a model for erotic cruelty, applying the term "sadism" to the complex he was thought to represent. Yet it would be a mistake to dismiss Sade as a deviate. He was indeed obsessed and tormented, but it is precisely the imaginings arising from his obsessions that cause the most distress and have the most to say. As Edmund Wilson observed, "We have never been able to shake him off, because we know that he is not entirely mad, not entirely out of touch with reality."[11]

Sade was deeply in touch with his unconscious, an awareness invited, actually forced on him, by the years of solitary imprisonment. His work is less disguised and more openly repulsive than that of other pornographers. Adult eroticism's roots in infantile sexuality and its inadmissible juncture with destructive wishes are far more exposed and detailed. In confronting Sade many of our ordinary defenses are wanting; we can neither easily explain him away nor readily distance ourselves from his images. Perversity and erotic cruelty, indescribably shocking sexual acts, repulsive tastes and pleasures are presented not merely as the facts of life but, unapologetically, as a satisfying and triumphant part of our nature. Thus Sade raged against pregnancy and motherhood, his hostility going beyond any inconvenience presented to erotic pleasure. Mothers are rejected, cursed, and abused by their children. In *Philosophy in the Bedroom,* a daughter, after participating in the torture and sodomization of her mother, in a rage sews up her vagina so she can produce no more children.

The hideous and demonic are linked to excitement and actually create it. In one of the hundreds of cruelties in *The 120 Days of Sodom,* an old woman has one of her breasts cut off. When she protests that there was no justice in this, the duke explains, "Had it been just, it would not have given us an erection." The quest for the lost primordial erotic totality, which Sade recognized so well in his proverbial remark, "Every man is a tyrant when he fornicates," is carried to a logical imagistic end by Minski, the bizarre Moscovite giant in *Juliette.* For this fairy-tale sexual ogre, bodies themselves have become completely objectified and any perspective on them as separate from the surrounding environment has broken down. In this retrogession, the very tables and chairs at a dinner feast are actually women in impossibly contorted positions. The dinner itself is "gammon of boy." The entire environment has become eroticized as only the "omnipotent" infant could have imagined or experienced it.

Sade's work disturbs us all the more for the reasons of self and circumstance that seem to have driven it. Unlike most pornographers, he was a frightening person long before he published a word. Most of his contemporaries regarded him as degenerate and dangerous, possibly even insane, and his behavior appeared to approach his later pornography. His work was not the invention of a writer seeking a living or reputation, but the product of an extraordinary self-examination under forbiddingly insular conditions. Nor was the author a predictable freak of some squalid fringe of society. He was a figure of uncommon intelligence, literacy, and charm. His background was privileged well beyond that of all but a handful of his fellows. We cannot draw moral reassurance from seeing a sinner redeemed after a long journey outside the pale. Sade remained unregenerate, his interest in and pursuit of various "perversities" slackened only with the weight of age.

That there should be attempts to redeem Sade is not surprising. Open or clandestine, his influence on Romanticism in nineteenth-century literature has been far-reaching, as Mario Praz has shown.[12] Flaubert, Baudelaire, Swinburne, and Dostoyevsky all acknowledged it. Nor is there any doubt of his link to twentieth-century surrealism. He is clearly a philosophic forefather of modern nihilism, and the moral and erotic anarchy that caused him to be perceived as a threat to state and society in his own time allow him to be appropriated by many twentieth-century revolutionaries. But matters do not rest with these established lines of effect. Sade has also been hailed as an important thinker, even if his expository efforts appear mainly to reflect the mechanistic notions of the philosopher La Mettrie. He was more intuitive than systematic or logical. In her essay "Must We Burn de Sade," Simone de Beauvoir sees him as fundamentally a great moralist. Pierre Klossowski perceives his atheism and blasphemy as a search for God. And despite his victimization of women, the novelist Angela Carter links him to the modern emancipation of women.[13] Others have discerned a "humane" Sade, making much of his being a moderate judge during the Revolution, not avenging himself on his mother-in-law when he had chance to do so, and his squeamishness about the violence meted out by the state. It is not necessary to quarrel with these interpretations to point out that they also help us deal with Sade in a hopeful way. There is perhaps no greater testament to his disturbing power. We would feel better if he had really been on our side all along, wittingly or not, as a kind of moral double agent for humanity.

Hence Donald Thomas is correct in observing, at the end of his brief biographical study, that the question whether Sade meant what he said hangs over both man and work.[14] This question, too, deflects our attention. The need to ask it deals more with our own problem in coming to terms with Sade than whether he was personally reconciled to what he advocated. This extremely complex figure remained obsessed with the polymorphous fantasies of the infantile sexual world to a far greater degree than most of his fellow humans. In that regard, he no doubt meant everything he said. The public, political, and social man may have temporized, but not the infant abiding within.

The Aberrant Heart

The pornographic imagination employs regressive, repressed infantile fantasies, reflecting the eroticization of sexual instincts curbed or reshaped by parental, and later internal, authority. Incestuous wishes and other forbidden sexual aims, mutilation terrors, parricidal rage, once put out of sight, remain in the unconscious, ever threatening to break through defenses and make themselves known again. Normally we do not "know" them because we cannot admit them. They seem to say things about ourselves and others, including those we love, that we cannot stand to hear. So they are more than simply denied; they are made to "disappear."

In pornography, these conflicts and many of the desires giving rise to them "return" as they may also do in dreams. But our defenses usually make sure that reappearance is never wholly without disguise. In pornography, the disguise often takes the form of adult sexuality with an appropriate genital component that was not available to the infant. The expression may still be imaginally fantastic and pornographic, that is, transgressive and bent toward erotic totality, but the adult shield protects against coming face to face with its terrible primordial assertions.

Artists employing the pornographic imagination provide greater insight into human eroticization and the links between adult and infantile sexualities than ordinary pornographers. They communicate with our deepest, most hidden selves. As "freelance explorer[s] of spiritual dangers," in Sontag's phrase, they have a license to move to the frontiers of consciousness and report back what they find. At times this may be at some risk to their own sanity and balance. It is as though, Goethe said, they were appointed by God to tell us how much they have suffered. The pornographic imagination sets out to explore an inner territory, a gorge in the human heart dimly reached by the lights of civilization and unserved by its moral writs. When the artists succeed nonpornographically, we are moved, touched, perhaps disconcerted or made to wonder, as children are by fairy tales or myths, or adults by a performance of *Oedipus Rex*. When they succeed pornographically, we are challenged, shocked, frightened, revolted, and perhaps also sexually aroused.

With Sade the pornographic imagination received its most systematic and imagistically inventive expression. More recent, no less pornographically challenging works, such as Georges Bataille's *Story of the Eye* and Pauline Réage's *Story of O,* offer more thoughtful and aesthetically accomplished views of human eroticization.

Bataille's novella, the surreal narrative of the obsessive sexual quest of a sixteen-year-old boy and girl, is a striking example of the artist drawing pornographically on both the memories of childhood and its conscious and unconscious fantasies. Transgressions of every sort and, at last, even death are woven into a sexual delirium. Bizarre practices and scenes alternate and ultimately coincide with sexual arousal and enactment. In a tone almost serene, infantile theater is transformed into adolescent erotomania. The "eye" is variously an egg, excreta, the gouged-out dangling organ of a bullfighter, the skinned testicles of the bull, the desocketed eye of a dead priest following his horrifying orgasmic murder in a church vestry, a fetus, and, finally, perhaps the narrator's mother. It is at once the object of the quest and, staringly ever present, its recorder and judge.

As a work of the pornographic imagination, the novella is the more remarkable for its extraordinary appended autobiographical note, "Coincidences," in which Bataille reflects on connections between events and symbols in the narrative and the memories and fantasies from a shocking childhood. They reveal the artist at the psychic frontier, crossing into the netherworld of the unconscious, a penetration of which Bataille himself was apparently no entirely aware until he completed the work.

I ventured to explain such extraordinary relations by assuming the profound region of my mind, where certain images coincide, the elementary ones, the *completely obscene* ones, i.e., the most scandalous, precisely on which the conscious floats indefinitely, unable to endure without an explosion or aberration. However upon locating this breaking point in the conscious or, if you will, the favorite place of sexual deviation, certain quite different personal memories were quickly associated with some harrowing images that had emerged during an obscene composition.[15]

He tells of his earliest memory of a syphilitic father trying to urinate. The man had already been blind when he conceived his son and was now also suffering general paralysis. As his father relieved himself, Bataille recalls his sightless eyes having "a completely stupefying expression of abandon and alienation in a world that he alone could see and that aroused his vaguely sardonic and absent laugh." Later, on the night his father finally went mad, Bataille remembers him howling at the doctor who had been called, "Let me know when you're done fucking my wife!" For Bataille, "that utterance, which in a split second annihilated the demoralizing effects of a strict upbringing, left me with something like a steady obligation, unconscious and unwilled: the necessity of finding an equivalent to that sentence in any situation I happen to be in; and this largely explains *Story of the Eye.*"[16]

When Bataille and his mother fled before the German advance in 1914, they abandoned his father, leaving him with a housekeeper. They did not go back after the Germans retreated, and his father died apart from them. Bataille concludes, "My father conceived me when blind (absolutely blind), I cannot tear out my eyes like Oedipus. Like Oedipus, I solved the riddle: no one divined it more deeply than I."[17]

In *Story of O*, the pseudonymous Réage records an erotic obsession that obliterates personality and, ultimately, the person herself. The young women of the title has been taken by her lover, René, for a brief stay at Roissy, an isolated château, at which she and several other women have only one obligation: to learn to obey. They are kept nearly naked, sometimes bound, in order to be sexually accessible at all times and in any way to the group of men, including O's lover, who maintain the château. O is sometimes blindfolded, regularly whipped, abused, and humiliated by almost every conceivable sexual practice. All is voluntary; O is free to leave at any point. But she does not. When her stay at the château is completed, she wears an iron ring signifying her status as a chattel. Her lover soon gives her to his half brother, Sir Stephen, whom she seeks to obey because it is her lover's wish. Sir Stephen humiliates her sexually, whips her, loans her to his friends, and eventually asks that she be branded with his initials and that a ring be attached to her genitalia so that she will forever be declared to belong to him. He also confesses his love for her. Toward the end, almost no longer a person, she is dressed as an owl and taken to a party on a chain that has been attached to her genital ring. Later, when Sir Stephen decides to abandon her, O prefers to die, and asks for and receives his permission to do so.

O has abandoned her freedom and her personhood. But in this annihilation of the dignities and moral agency we accord to individuality, she achieves a sexual being and a transcendence that is almost religious. After René tells her at Roissy that he loves her, she reflects on the outrages she has endured.

Daily and, so to speak, ceremoniously soiled with saliva and sperm, she felt herself literally to be the repository of impurity, the sink mentioned in the Scriptures. And yet those parts of her body most constantly offended, having become less sensitive, at the same time seemed to her to have become more beautiful and, as it were, ennobled: her mouth closed upon anonymous members, the tips of her breasts constantly fondled by hands, and between her quartered thighs, the twin, contiguous paths wantonly plowed. That she should have been ennobled and gained in dignity through being prostituted was a source of surprise, and yet dignity was indeed the right term. She was illuminated by it, as though from within, and her bearing bespoke calm, while on her face could be detected the serenity and imperceptible smile that one surmises rather than actually sees in the eyes of hermits.[18]

The mode is surrender and humiliation. With its vulnerable orifices and soft flesh to be despoiled, the body in its very limitations is the spiteful target of anger and fury at independence and the possibility of abandonment. O submits to the tortures as proof of her obedience, but with this pornographic transgression of body and personality comes a consummate and unsettling erotic identity and acquittal. At one point Sir Stephen tells her, "You love René but you're easy. Does René realize that you covet and long for all men who desire you, that by sending you to Roissy or surrendering you to others he is providing you with a string of alibis to cover your easy virtue?"[19]

Indeed, many readers find it disturbing that O is so submissive. Yet she is so at the bidding and with the blessing of her lover. He has become her accomplice. Emotionally she is faithful, physically she is wanton—a resolution of opposites that the actual world almost always denies. As Réage has said, "After all, whether at Roissy or elsewhere, O, that girl who has given herself over to her lover, is under his constant surveillance, as one is under God's, with the same faith, the same meek and trembling gentleness, the same constantly revocable certainty."[20]

In becoming a mere object, O no longer belongs to herself. She wants to be possessed utterly, ultimately, of course, to the point of death. "What does a Christian seek but to lose himself in God. To be killed by someone you love strikes me as the epitome of ecstasy. I can't bring myself to view it any other way. And I'm not alone. To take but one example, the double love suicides well known in Japan are a concrete example of the fantasy I'm referring to, which is, nonetheless, relatively widespread throughout the world."[21]

We may doubt that an erotic wish to die is as common as Réage suggests and may safely conclude that O is abnormal, clinically and statistically. But statistics are beside the point. The measure of the pornographic imagination is not whether the world is full of O's, but whether there is something of O (and Sir Stephen) in each of us.

An obsessive search to transcend the self can probably be only religious or pornographic in form. Annihilation and transcendence are as much a journey backward toward birth as forward to death. In amorphous, premoral infancy there was no separation, personhood, or individuality, no burden of genital specificity, no roles to play. For that obsessive, futile, tragic journey to the erotic headwaters, what better transport than the pornographic?

The contradiction between what we pornographically know and do not want to know is set out nonpornographically by Joseph Conrad in his psychological masterpiece *Heart of Darkness*. The story raises a question about the uses of knowledge and the possibility of unraveling the self's thin inner thread of reason and restraint, which woven together with those of other human beings forms the protective mantle of civilization.

In the compelling figure of Kurtz, who has been entrusted by the International Society for the Suppression of Savage Customs to better the lot of natives, we see how tenuous yet vital this covering may be. Gravely ill, Kurtz is rescued by Marlow, Conrad's narrator, from a remote outpost in the uncharted regions of the upper Congo, and dies during the journey back.

Marlow discovers that the idealist, of whom "all Europe contributed to the making," and who had entered the darkness to lead the natives toward light, has become totally debased. Received like a god, he found nothing to keep him from doing whatever he pleased or imagined. The primitive surroundings awakened forgotten and brutal instincts, "whispered to him things about himself which he did not know, things of which he had no conception till he took counsel with this solitude—and the whisper proved irresistibly fascinating."[22]

On the journey upriver, which Marlow likens to a return to the beginning of time, the narrator sees the reassuring cover of civilization slowly slip away. Normally inaccessible reaches of the mind are gradually exposed. Almost all the Europeans along the way have been affected. At one station, native slaves are dynamiting a mountain to make way for a railroad that will go around the mountain. A French gunboat is firing shells into the jungle to no apparent purpose, although natives are known to be in the bush. A man tries to put out a small fire, seeming not to notice that the bucket he is using has no bottom. A Swede tells Marlow of another Swede who has hanged himself.

At the same time, Marlow learns more of the man he is seeking. Kurtz has sent more ivory out of the jungle than anyone before him but has not come out himself. He started downstream once but changed his mind and went back. Marlow reads a report Kurtz had written for the Society, buoyant in its vision of the white man's powers used for good among the natives; scribbled at the bottom of the last page, apparently sometime later, is the imperative, "Exterminate all the brutes!" Within sight of Kurtz's station, Marlow trains his binoculars on Kurtz's mud hut and is struck to see, in such ruined surroundings, a number of knobbed posts placed around the house in an apparent attempt at ornamentation. But as the boat moves closer, he looks through the glasses again and realizes the depths of Kurtz's degradation. The posts are stakes and the knobs are human heads, all facing the hut.

Kurtz is unwilling to leave, but he is too weak to offer much resistance. As they depart, Marlow glimpses on the riverbank Kurtz's native mistress, a wild sexual apparition and a commanding, reproachful figure, at once stately and savage, magnificent and barbarous.

On the riverboat, Marlow witnesses the tormented Kurtz's last moments: "Anything approaching the change that came over his features I have never seen before, and hope never to see again. . . . It was as though a veil had been rent. I saw on that ivory face the expression of somber pride, of ruthless power, of craven terror—of an intense despair." At the last, Kurtz cries out, "The horror! The horror!" It is a moment of ultimate self-recognition, embracing "innumerable defeats . . . abominable ter-rors . . . abominable satisfactions."[23]

Kurtz is the complete transgressor, the more disturbing because he appeared the least likely of men. His fall—retrogression is a better word—seems to cover such a great distance. Conrad shows us someone we cannot easily dismiss. Kurtz is horrifying in the way that many of Sade's protagonists are. The journey into the jungle and the encounter with Kurtz have deeply unsettled Marlow. He sees all too clearly the lure of the primitive and why Kurtz or, for that matter, anyone might "leave the track," the conventional path bounded by surface truths obscuring darker ones, and he wonders about himself. Kurtz had "stepped over the edge, while I had been permitted to draw back my hesitating foot."[24]

Marlow has witnessed; he has not acted. But he knows that he might well have done so. Horrified by this discovery, Marlow himself falls gravely ill after Kurtz's death. He recovers and makes the journey downriver out of the darkness, a survivor as well as a more enlightened and encumbered man. Marlow cannot dislodge the image of Kurtz, not as a failed emissary of civilization, but as embodying a terrible fundamental truth.

The story of Kurtz is not finished. Marlow finds himself unable to reveal the terrible knowledge he carries. He fails to disabuse Kurtz's cousin of his belief in Kurtz's "universal genius." He gives Kurtz's report to an inquiring journalist but tears off the frightening postscript. Finally, he visits the dead man's unsuspecting fiancée, whose faith in Kurtz's goodness and humanity is the vital center of her own being. He harbors some vague intention of sharing his truth with her, but sees he cannot. What were his last words, she asks in a heartbroken whisper. He replies, "Your name."

In Marlow's abdication Conrad addresses the uses and burdens of knowledge itself. In the primitive environment Kurtz broke the most sacred rules. He returned, in fact, to a psychic time before there were rules, a time during which erotic ambitions, their frustration, and the consequent murderous rage and abject fear were all known. "The mind of man," Marlow observes, "is capable of anything, because everything is in it, all the past as well as all the future."[25] Kurtz "lacked restraint" as only a fantastical sovereign can lack restraint. After he escaped from the riverboat, the night before departure, he was found by the desperate Marlow, crawling back toward the native fires on hands and knees, like a baby.

In a sense, Kurtz and Marlow are elements of the same mind. The idealistic, European, morally informed Kurtz, presumably shaped by the conscience of the civilized world, is overcome by the primitive, instinctual Kurtz, whose desires are not simply animal, and thus satiable, but eroticized and therefore conceivably unlimited in their ambition and destructive capacity. Marlow, a more ordinary man, recognizes the temptations, but remains far more governed by himself and the constraints of the world he has known. Marlow "manages," as the ego must within the mind. He does not deny the reality of the primitive impulses, but resists and controls them and tries, if in no other way than by telling the tale, to integrate them into the self. It is at first a harrowing struggle in which he nearly dies. He survives, but we are given to understand that the burden of this struggle, which Conrad now calls "knowledge," will continue as long as Marlow lives.

Marlow narrates the story to several companions in gathering darkness on board another boat, a yacht, moored on another river, the Thames, now a busy artery to the very heart of progress but once itself one of "the dark places of the world." His listeners seem unimpressed. "Here you all are," he chides them, "each moored with two good addresses, like a hulk with two anchors, a butcher round one corner, a policeman round another, excellent appetite, and temperature normal—you hear—normal from year's end to year's end."[26] As he discovered with Kurtz's fiancée, to share troubling knowledge may be very difficult indeed.

In *Heart of Darkness,* Conrad writes of what is, at least in its darkest reaches, pornographic territory, but he does so nonpornographically. He puts distance between subject and reader, the metaphorical distance between Congo and Thames. It is, in effect, a story within a story. Marlow does not act; Kurtz does. Kurtz's acts are not dealt with in their specifics, but are left to the reader's imagination. We are allowed to reflect on the story calmly and move easily to speculation and abstraction. The pornographic imagination is much less sparing. It too deals with destruction and death, but it seeks vivid, confronting entry into that territory where our destructiveness and cruelty have their roots in the frustration of boundless desire. The pornographic imagination seeks to bring to our conscious mind ideas, images, and emotions we have, in great measure, banished to the unconscious. Such art is often difficult to receive. In inviting lust and a chaotic mixture of emotions, possibly including fear, shame, and revulsion, it touches our erotic appetite *and* alerts our defenses. In this, it is far more aggressive and cramped than the general aesthetic imagination of which it is a part.

In reading Conrad's masterpiece we have a sense of the horror of Kurtz's debasement and an appreciation of Marlow's struggle with himself. Yet it is Marlow who journeys, observes, and returns, rather than we. In *Story of the Eye* and *Story of O,* the confrontation is direct and unbuffered. We are given no "time" to gather ourselves together or "space" in which to distance ourselves. We are involved with erotic totality without much of our customary fending armor.

Nevertheless, the power of the pornographic imagination lies less in an unsettling aesthetic design than in what it may tell us about human eroticization. Where it is successful, as in *Story of the Eye, Story of O,* and many of Sade's works, the reader's own emotions, both appetitive and censoring, demand to be understood. We cannot so easily deny the dreadful affinity of the erotic and destructive, nor so easily ignore their inviting conjunction. The insight offered is necessarily personal in the first instance, but it may help us understand ourselves as a species. The horror of Kurtz—the individual's capacity for unlimited cruelty and destruction—enacted by large numbers of persons in the real world may produce horror on a monstrous scale, the social and psychic roots of which are yet to be fully understood.

The association of erotic drives with punitiveness and nightmarish destruction is effectively rendered by D. M. Thomas in *The White Hotel.* Much of this novel is a long pornographic poem and journal, written by Lisa Erdman, a woman undergoing psychoanalysis with Freud. They are an account of a fantasized seduction by Freud's son Martin and several days of sexual abandon with him at the lakeside resort of the title. The passion of the lovers is buoyant, almost celebratory. Strangely, it occurs amid continuous disasters—capsized boats, a hotel fire, an avalanche—in which many of the other guests die. The pornographic fantasy of the poem and journal are in stark contrast to Lisa's actual sexual life, which is muted and rather tentative. The fantasy is the diagnostic centerpiece not only in the treatment of her specific complaint, a hysteria manifest by recurrent pain in her pelvis and left breast, but also in a deeper, suspenseful search for rediscovery and unity with her mother and her mother's body, "the white hotel." The story explores her girlhood, marriage, success as an opera singer, remarriage, step-motherhood, and finally her tragic end in the Kiev ravine of Babi Yar.

The White Hotel is a psychoanalytic detective story in which one mystery after another is unraveled to reveal a nascent sexuality misshapen and the toll exacted. Lisa discovers what may lie at the vortex of the erotic and destructive in her own life. She is partially healed by this understanding but, like Marlow's, the knowledge is personal. The larger world neither listens nor cares to listen. The tragic outcome of the story is prefigured throughout by the association of eros with death. Lisa says of her fantasized lover at one point in the poem, "Charred bodies hung from the trees / he grew erect again—." We hear the story of Kurten, the sexually thwarted mass murderer who has killed women and children, drunk their blood, and dug up their bodies to have intercourse with them. Yet, to the rest of the world, he appeared to be quite ordinary, even "rather a nice man." After he is executed, Lisa reflects that "Somewhere—at that very moment—someone was inflicting the worst possible horror on another human being."[27]

The rounding up of the Kiev Jews by the Nazis in 1942 begins with a hopeful rumor that they are to be deported by train to Palestine and thus removed from the war. All too soon, it becomes clear that something far different is in store. No trains are waiting, the roundup becomes a march, the march a herding. The victims are relieved of their worldly valuables, then their clothes, then the last traces of dignity. The Germans and their Ukrainian collaborators, acting now like Kurtz, without restraint, proceed to commit an unimaginable mass atrocity. Lisa has a brief chance to escape but does not leave her young son who, for good measure, has been viciously kicked in the groin as a kind of wanton preliminary. Her own death is hideously pornographic. In effect, the worlds of Hitler and Freud converge, but it is the former, misshapen and so in need of the illumination and ministry of the other, that prevails.

We live anxiously in our erotic world, balancing what we must know and are tempted to know against what we dare not know. Insight provided by the artist in the pornographic imagination runs to the frontier of our consciousness. The painful awareness this encounter forces on us as individuals is also the explanatory and diagnostic power it offers to us as a species. The intuition is not merely a link between pornography and art but is also an illumination of our condition and experience as human creatures. Epistemically and aesthetically, the pornographic imagination is the redemptive property of pornography.

This recognition confers no respectability on the vast range of pornographic expression. The pornographic imagination is quantitatively insignificant within the social category pornography. Redeeming epistemic and aesthetic value is likely to be found only in rare cases and usually only on minor scale. Moreover, they deal with the insight and intent of the creator of the work and not with how that work is received. The "truth" may not make every knower freer or wiser; it may unsettle or meet with denial, projection, rationalization, or other defenses. The pornographic imagination can tell us something enormously important, but it is apt to be the insight of the few, communicated successfully to a relatively small number of persons. In a society and polity in which the voice of the many is standard and officially sovereign, recognition of the pornographic imagination by culture and policy is bound to be problematic.

Chapter Four

Cause and Effect

*Pornography collections follow the pre-existing interest of the collector.
Men make collections, collections do not make the men.*

Paul Gebhard

*More than we care to admit, our attitudes and beliefs about sexually
explicit materials are often based on little more than various
subjective impressions and assumptions.*

Edward C. Nelson

Working through the pornographic imagination, the artist may illuminate
the pornographic within and the ways it projects itself as external object
and symbol. But that illumination tells us nothing about the power of the
pornographic without or its effect on us as individuals or as a society. Much
of liberal democracy's rational debate about pornography is cast in terms of
its effects. If these are harmful, it seems reasonable that pornography
should be restricted in appropriate measure; if they are not, it seems
reasonable that freedom should prevail. If we knew whether the effects of
pornography were harmful, neutral, or beneficial, as rational citizens we
could act accordingly.

Of course the matter is not so simple. Empirical and methodological
difficulties in establishing pornography's effects are formidable. Even if we
were certain about them, the question whether a particular effect is
desirable or undesirable would remain. Sexual murder, rape, and child
molestation are universally condemned, but agreement about the harmfulness of promiscuity, the subordination of women, or masturbation, for
example, is much more problematic. And the harmfulness of still other
hypothesized effects, such as a willingness to experiment in behavior or
fantasy, remains a matter of sharp debate.[1]

Beyond the moral question of what should or should not be considered
harmful lies the political problem of weighing competing interests. If an
effect were proved and widely agreed to be harmful, we might still prefer
to realize free speech values. Conversely, even if an effect were agreed not

90

to be harmful, we might still prefer to give greater weight to considerations of privacy or decency.

Questions of consensus and priority are screens through which any knowledge of effects must pass before it can be used in social or political management of pornography. They are taken up at various points later in the book. Here, we deal only with the sufficiently difficult empirical question of pornography's effects on us as individuals; the more speculative one of macro effect is considered in the next chapter.

Conventional Wisdom

Concern about its effects is probably as old and as universal as pornography itself. Speculation has had its basis in insight, common sense, personal experience and observation, and scientific evidence, as well as in sources less rational. The views of sexual utopianists and conservative moralists—in more recent years, constitutional libertarians and antipornography feminists—may also have ideological importance in larger value systems.

Many of the viewpoints are familiar; most assume pornography to have compelling temptations as well as more subtle subversive properties. Supposed effects are behavioral, affective, or attitudinal. Thus pornography is seen as a precipitating agent of such antisocial acts as rape, child molestation, and exhibitionism and of deviant behavior generally. Its regressive, often infantile, character arrests psychosexual development, particularly in adolescence, by encouraging sexual gratification through prurient fantasy and masturbation, thus making mature sexual relationships more difficult. It is also assumed to undermine moral standards and humane values by encouraging permissiveness and callousness in one's own life and greater tolerance of such traits in others, reflected in sexual acts without love and affection, loss of respect for women, and a generally demeaning notion of the human sexual role.

Opposing views, much less widely held, see pornography as having no appreciable effect beyond immediate and rather short-lived arousal or as having actual benefit. Instead of inciting antisocial acts, pornography may redirect disturbing sexual energy into masturbation or transform it through catharsis. It may enlighten and instruct, in effect, counter excessive sexual repression and thus facilitate rather than thwart sexual adjustment and well-being.

Restrictive policies made by Congress and state legislatures, and by elected and nonelected officials in nearly every country of the world, indicate how widespread is belief in pornography's harmfulness. In the United States such policies also receive consistently high levels of public support in opinion surveys. The most extensive and systematic of these was the national probability sample of 2,486 face-to-face interviews conducted by the President's Commission on Obscenity and Pornography in 1970. Although sexual arousal was the effect mentioned most frequently by respondents, 56 percent believed that "sexual materials" (the term used in the survey instead of "pornography") led to a "breakdown of morals," 50 percent that they "lead people to commit rape," 44 percent that they cause a loss of respect for women, and 38 percent that they "make people sex crazy." Effects that might be considered beneficial were, in contrast, mentioned least frequently. These included providing "an outlet for bottled up sex impulses" (33 percent) and "affording relief to people who have sex problems" (27 percent).[2]

A more innocent picture emerged when respondents were asked which of the presumed effects they had experienced personally. Fewer than 1/2 of 1 percent mentioned "making people sex crazy" or encouraging rape. A "breakdown of morals" was mentioned by less than 2 percent and loss of respect for women by only 4 percent. Of the dozen possible effects mentioned in the survey questions, three of the four likely to be thought socially undesirable—encouragement of rape, breakdown of morals, and becoming "sex crazy"—showed the greatest disparity between perceived effect on oneself and presumed effect on others. Effects showing the least disparity were "making people bored with sex materials" and providing entertainment or information. These were also the most frequently reported as experienced personally.[3]

The Limitations of Research

Scientific knowledge of pornography's effects, though still limited, has grown substantially in recent years. More than twenty studies were sponsored by the President's Commission on Obscenity and Pornography in 1969 and 1970 alone, adding much to what was known and spurring a growing number of later studies. Taken together, these now form a sizable medical and social science literature on effects.

Before examining the findings directly, we must note general and technical problems encountered in the research. A scientific approach seeks not merely to understand and explain but also to delimit and refute. These goals require rigorous research design and procedure as well as careful interpretation and qualification of findings. Thus what is proved may be much less than what was sought or discovered. Findings that are possibly informative and even persuasive may not be conclusive. For many of pornography's presumed effects—harmful, beneficial, or neutral—actual scientific proof may still lie beyond our grasp.

The research falls generally into four categories: (1) opinions of experts and other professionals; (2) surveys based on probability samples or specific populations, employing interviews or self-administered question-naires; (3) quasi-experimental studies comparing two or more populations with similar profiles but some different characteristics, such as delinquency or convictions for sex crimes; and (4) controlled experimental research under laboratory conditions, in which particular consequences of exposure are measured in two or more groups of individuals differing in important ways or receiving different exposure to erotic material.

Isolating pornography as an independent variable from other factors shaping sexual behavior, attitudes, and impulses is a major problem. This formidable difficulty is present even when research addresses immediate or short-term effects, and is obviously greater still when longer-term effects involving broad or fundamental changes in attitudes or values are at issue.

Serious interpretative problems arise when mere association or covaria-tion is confused with causation. Many studies seek to locate links or statistical correlations between experience with pornography and various behavioral, affective, or attitudinal changes and to determine the nature and extent of covariation. Yet no matter how strong positive or negative correlation may be, it alone cannot prove a *causal* relationship between two associated variables. Many cofluctuations, even such highly correlated commonplace ones as flowers blooming in the spring and declining sales of heating fuel, are the effects not of one another but of intervening factors, which may be known or unknown, few or many in number, and major or minor in their influence. In a complex psychological development such as attitude formation or establishment of dominant sexual orientation a great many causative agents may be at work over long periods.

Where a causal relationship does exist, correlation alone does not demonstrate direction. Discovery of a strong correlation may be a key step in understanding a cause and effect; it may support inference of causation where circumstances of association logically suggest it, or may suggest the possibility of causation where none had been suspected. Yet even experienced investigators have sometimes yielded to the temptation to describe their correlative findings as though they were proof of causation.

Distortion of fact is a problem in social science research in which subject-recall and self-assessment are relied on. It is particularly severe in pornography studies, because questions about the facts of one's own sexual life or thoughts can elicit conscious and unconscious emotional responses, accompanied by distorting anxiety. Careful investigators take steps to minimize this distortion, but it is probably not completely correctable.

A question of generalizability arises in the case of surveys: To what extent do findings for those surveyed also hold for larger populations not surveyed? Generalizability is greater with large probability samples where random selection offers a good chance of capturing important characteristics of the larger population. But surveys of college students, for example, may not be generalizable to married adults, or to working-class youths whose education was attenuated.

Experimental studies under laboratory conditions provide the most rigorous test of causality, but run the risk that their findings will be trivial, or valid only in the experimental environment. Because so many of the experiments are conducted by university scientists, subjects are usually self-selected college students unrepresentative of the larger population. Findings of laboratory studies are also particularly vulnerable to distortion by the design, procedures, or instrumentation of the investigation itself.

These problems urge caution in interpreting social science findings about pornography's effects, particularly if we seek conclusive proof. Many of the studies, however, tell us things we could only have guessed at, allow us to be confident about some things we had only tentatively assumed, or cast reasonable doubt on others about which we felt sure. The illumination these studies provide differs from that we examined in the last chapter. There, insight followed dramatic, erratic explorative thrusts by an intrepid imagination, deep into the dark surrounding woods of the unknown. Knowledge provided by the scientific studies is more like a clearing in those woods, small spaces opened by small advances, gradually, unevenly enlarging the perimeter of light. Because the literature on effects of pornography is now so extensive, we can touch here only on the more important and representative studies. To examine the most significant findings, we organize the review by categories of possible effects rather than by type of study.

Sexual Arousal

It is fitting that more studies have been made of pornography's capacity to arouse sexually than of any other possible effect. Not only is most pornography so designed, but arousal of some sort would presumably precede and determine other behavioral effects. Methodologically, arousal is also probably the most readily and reliably measured of all responses, particularly in the experimental setting. In early studies, subjects were simply asked about their psychosexual reactions. Investigators recognized that such reports might not be dependable; subjects could experience affective responses masking arousal, or find it difficult to acknowledge arousal to investigators or even to themselves, or might simply lie. Attempts were made to gauge somatic responses, such as changes in respiration rate, pupillary dilation, and galvanic skin activity. These gave way to direct genital measures of penile volume and vaginal pulse rate and changes in lubricity, which now are used along with self-reporting by questionnaire. Though direct physiological measures avoid the distortions of self-reports and discriminate between sexual arousal and other emotional states, the findings produced may not be readily generalizable to larger populations, because subjects willing to submit to such intrusions often differ in sexual attitude and experience from those who are not.[4]

It is well established that pornographic depictions are sexually arousing for most persons, including many who report not being aroused. Pictorial stimuli tend to be more arousing than textual, and cinematic stimuli more arousing than still graphics.[5] Levels of arousal tend to be higher when subjects are asked to fantasize about the themes depicted. Although the more explicit the stimulus the more arousing it is likely to be, for a minority of persons this seems not to be true, possibly because such stimuli arouse defensive reactions.[6] In self-report measures, many of those who were not aroused while viewing highly explicit stimuli, became so later as a result of spontaneously thinking about the materials seen.[7]

Women were once believed to be much less interested in or aroused by pornography than men. Early studies such as the massive Kinsey survey of female sexual behavior, dependent on self-reporting, found women to be less stimulated by explicit depictions of sexuality than by more subtle ones reflected in themes of romance and affection.[8] But few gender differences are evident in more recent studies employing physiological measures as well as subjective reporting. This result suggests that earlier findings may have been influenced by cultural factors inhibiting women from acknowledging arousal, or simply by women's being less responsive to the male-oriented themes in most pornographic material.[9]

Conventional heterosexual intercourse, female nudity, heterosexual petting, oral-genital acts, and sexual acts in groups are the most arousing themes for both sexes; male masturbation and sadomasochistic acts rank among the least.[10] Women are more aroused than men by depiction of male homosexuality but less aroused than men by lesbian acts.[11] Unsurprisingly, response to themes appears closely related to dominant sexual orientation. Thus heterosexual men are most likely to be aroused by depiction of females and least likely by male homosexuality. Pedophiles tend to respond to the age of the persons depicted more than to gender. Homosexual men are more aroused by pictures of nude men and portrayal of homosexual acts.[12]

Although portrayals of violent or aggressive sexual acts are among the least arousing depictions for both sexes, contrary findings are reported when the sexual aggression was not depicted as deviant.[13] Portrayal of rape produced considerable arousal in both men and women, though most subjects also experienced negative affect. Studies conducted by Malamuth and associates show that depictions of sexual assault are less arousing than those of mutually consensual behavior; portrayal of rape in which the victim experienced involuntary orgasm was an exception. Arousal tended to be inhibited where the victim was shown as suffering pain or abhorring the assault.[14]

Personality and background and circumstances of exposure may affect arousal. Persons with more sexual experience or liberal sexual, religious, or political attitudes are more likely to report arousal than those less experienced or more conservative.[15] But "sex guilt," defined as an "expectancy for self-mediated punishment for violating internalized standards concerning sexual behavior," was found to be unrelated to levels of arousal, though associated with negative affective response.[16] Permissive, informal settings tend to be facilitating, whereas a formal atmosphere or the presence of an audience is inhibiting. Subjects told that they had consumed a quantity of alcoholic drink, when actually they had not, were more aroused, by physiological measures, than subjects not so informed.[17]

Pornography has the capacity to arouse sexually a wide range of persons, perhaps a large majority of persons, many of whom for various reasons may consciously prefer not to be aroused. Though these findings should not surprise us, they allow us to speak with greater certainty about particular associations and, as in the case of the response of women, to correct earlier misimpressions. Arousal is mediated by the circumstances of exposure, themes depicted, and the background and personality of viewers or readers. None of these intervening factors have been extensively investigated, and findings about their influence are inconclusive. Beyond these factors undoubtedly lie others relating to idiosyncratic sexual fantasies, reaching into the unconscious or well back in the psychic past, that may also affect both the incidence and qualitative variations of arousal. These are largely beyond the reach of experimental social science, though they may possibly be accessible in clinical studies of individuals.

Satiation and Habituation

The effect of repeated exposure on arousal merits special attention because, unlike single or limited exposure in most of the studies already mentioned, it raises the question of longer-term consequences. Though the conventional view is that repeated exposure is disinhibitory and addictive, a contrasting hypothesis regards it as "satiating" and thus actually lowering levels of interest and arousal. Here we consider repeated exposure only as it relates to arousal and interest; possible effects on attitudes and behavior are dealt with in sections below.

Though the relatively few experimental studies of repeated exposure yield evidence on both sides, the greater weight of it suggests that such exposure—at least to the same types of materials—is followed by lower levels of arousal.[18] Two of the most ambitious inquiries were conducted for the President's Commission on Obscenity and Pornography and provide the chief support for its confident conclusion that diminished interest in pornography was a likely long-term result of ending legal controls. In the first, twenty-three men singly viewed a variety of material for ninety minutes a day, five days a week, for three weeks, among the heaviest dosages of pornographic stimuli in the experimental literature. Arousal and cognitive interest were assessed by physiological measures, psychiatric tests and inventories, and psychiatric interviews. Though complete habituation did not occur, both arousal and cognitive interest declined markedly during the course of the experiment. When novel pornographic material was introduced, arousal increased to the initially high levels but soon returned to the lower levels.[19] In the second study, married couples were shown pornographic films weekly for a month. Arousal and interest also declined, and novel stimuli raised them only temporarily. However, when shown a pornographic film after a hiatus of two months, the subjects had physiological levels of arousal similar to those at the beginning of the experiment.[20] The "satiation" view receives some additional support from an analogous nonexperimental source. In their massive study of sexual offenders, Gebhard and his associates found that collectors of pornography reported loss of sexual interest in their material.[21]

In a later experimental study attempting to approximate a naturalistic setting by incorporating gratification as an intervening factor, repeated exposure did not result in diminished arousal for subjects permitted to masturbate following each viewing session. Levels of arousal actually increased with subsequent exposure. Though the number of subjects was too small to permit confident generalization, the findings do suggest that repeated exposure in "real life," where masturbation often follows, might be reinforcing rather than satiating. Studies of masturbatory conditioning tend to support such conclusions.[22]

The case for satiation is clearly not proved by the studies we now have. That repeated viewing of the same or like stimuli not of one's own choosing, on schedule, and in the same physical or institutional setting should result in diminished interest and arousal seems valid enough, but there is no evidence that the subjects lost interest in pornography as a long-term matter or became indifferent to pornographic stimulation. In fact, they were apt to report increased enjoyment and less sense of being offended by the pornography (though how much of this was a product of the sponsored and controlled environment of the experiment is difficult to say).[23] That pornographic bookstores and movie houses have numbers of regulars also argues against long-run indifference in naturalistic surroundings. We probably cannot make very much of apparent satiation with "old" stimuli. Gebhard's sexual offenders, and perhaps almost everyone else, might be expected to tire of the same or similar pictures. It can as easily be argued that such fare would be followed not by disinterest but by novelty-seeking or what one researcher has termed "excitation transfer."[24]

Experimenters cannot be criticized for failing to include opportunities for orgasmic relief in their laboratory procedures, but the relationships among exposure, arousal, and gratification appear so intimate and serial it is remarkable that they have not been subjects of greater speculation. Continued immediate or short-run exposure may very well result in diminished arousal, particularly in laboratory or quasi-public settings where opportunity for gratification is unavailable, inconvenient, impractical, or even illegal. But the idea that repeated long-run exposure in a naturalistic setting would have the same effect, beguiling though its policy implications may be to libertarians, must be received with skepticism. Whatever else, the effects of pornography are unlikely to be "satiated" away.

Affective Responses

It is obvious that pornography may stimulate a variety of immediate emotional responses, usually but not invariably negative or aversive. These may be experienced as anxiety, guilt, disgust, or even boredom. They may accompany arousal, though more likely they serve to inhibit or obscure it.

In the Commission on Obscenity and Pornography's national survey, "disgust" was reported more frequently than any other response, easily outranking less negative reactions such as "informed and interested," "pleased," and "amused." Between 24 and 36 percent of men and 40 to 54 percent of women, depending on the medium of presentation, experienced this reaction.[25]

Several experimental studies found that substantial numbers of subjects experienced mild emotional or mood changes, especially increased tension and uneasiness following exposure.[26] Many subjects reported feeling more "anxious," "pepped up," "jumpy," "driven," "impulsive," and "eager for contact," and less "peaceful" and "serene," after exposure. Men were likelier to report decreases and women increases in feeling "repelled," "shocked," "irritated," "disgusted," "angered," "benumbed," "depressed," "ashamed," and "embarrassed."[27] In two weeks of exposure, "mirth" and "tension," leading all other affective responses at the start, declined markedly, while "boredom" increased and became the most frequently reported response at the conclusion of the experiment.[28]

Subjects having feelings of sexual guilt before exposure were more likely to report "nervousness," "internal unrest," "guilt," and other negative emotional response, including disgust, afterward.[29] Those tending to deny or repress effects of anxiety-producing stimuli were less likely to report anxiety in response to pornography but more likely to feel anger or disgust.[30] Subjects with less sexual experience were more apt to have feelings of disgust and guilt than those with greater sexual experience. Those who were more introverted, attended church more frequently, or scored higher on authoritarianism scales were more likely to experience disgust than others.[31]

Thematically, negative reaction is closely though not exclusively related to unconventional or "deviant" sexuality. Thus heterosexual depiction resulted in less disgust, anger, shame, depression, or guilt in men than male masturbation or homosexuality did. Homosexuality depicted in members of the opposite sex produced fewer aversive responses than if depicted in members of one's own sex.[32] Similarly, fellatio, cunnilingus, bondage, flagellation, bestiality, sexual torture, and rape were strongly associated with aversive responses that included anxiety, disgust, anger, and depression.[33] Rape produced less aversive reaction when the victim was portrayed as having involuntary orgasm than when portrayed as being revolted by the experience.[34]

Affective reactions are complex, and even where predictable are mediated by content of the stimuli and the gender, sexual experience, personality, and value system of the subject. The research findings here are less satisfactory than those for arousal. Though some ingenious questionnaire scales have been developed, most of the data remain, of necessity, self-reported; there are no equivalents to the reliable physical measures of arousal. Even with careful definition, terms such as "disgust," "anger," and "boredom" retain the ambiguity of their common usage. The circumstances of "real life" exposure—the medium employed and the social, institutional, and authoritative setting of presentation or access, all of which are difficult to deal with in experimental settings—are important intervening factors that have largely been ignored.

The studies do offer two well-documented findings: a large percentage of all persons experience negative or aversive emotional responses to pornography, and, contrary to popular conceptions, these reactions do not necessarily exclude sexual arousal. Pornography can be both disturbing and exciting, repellent and attractive, for the same person at different times or at the same time. Reports of boredom, like those of satiation, must be interpreted cautiously, for that response may signal not true indifference but an ingenious defense against unwanted arousal, unwanted negative affect, or both. For an eroticized human sexuality, true indifference to pornography is probably rare.

"Normal" Sexual Behavior

Does the power of pornography to arouse sexually or stimulate cognitive sexual interest lead to changes in sexual behavior itself? Here we deal only with "nondeviant" behavior; the possibility of criminal or antisocial acts is considered in a later section.

Retrospective surveys in the United States and Sweden show a clear positive association between pornography and sexual experience. Persons who are more experienced or had their first experience at an earlier age were likely to have more experience with pornography, and more recently, than others.[35] The implications of this emphatic general finding are considered below.

Experimental studies have sought to locate and measure changes in sexual behavior occurring immediately after laboratory exposure, usually in the succeeding twenty-four hours. Married couples and single persons with coital experience were found more likely to have intercourse during this period, but less experienced subjects were not.[36] Subjects most likely to engage in intercourse or petting were those with established heterosexual relationships.[37] Men who experienced the most negative affect from exposure or who judged the stimuli most negatively reported the greatest increases in necking and petting. These changes brought them up to but not beyond the levels of those with less negative affect whose activity did not change appreciably.[38]

Exposure is associated with increased masturbation among a substantial fraction of unmarried men and a smaller fraction of unmarried women, but not among married persons or others with an available sex partner.[39] Increases were also associated with a history of frequent masturbation and relatively high levels of recent masturbation. The greater likelihood of masturbation apparently diminished within forty-eight hours of exposure.[40]

Laboratory exposure was not associated with later unconventional sexual activity—fellatio, cunnilingus, anal intercourse, sadomasochistic acts, sexual acts in groups, homosexuality, or extramarital acts including relations with prostitutes.[41] When the test period was the month preceding the experiment, the month during which regular exposure took place, and the month following, married couples inexperienced with such behavior were not likely to initiate it nor were those experienced in a particular activity more likely to reactivate it. A similar finding was obtained for unmarried college students, but the test period was limited to twenty-four hours after exposure.[42] A nonexperimental study of "swingers" found that most men who had encouraged their wives or regular partners to engage in group sex activity said they got the idea from pornographic books and films. Yet, since actual use of pornography at "swinging" parties was rare, this modeling may have been merely a trigger or a catalyst for a long-standing fantasy.[43]

Exposure is associated with increases in certain sex-related behavior and experience, including conversations about sex and sexual dreams and fantasies, although increased frequency of fantasies appeared to decline shortly after exposure.[44] For married couples, an "increased openness in discussing sex" was the most frequently reported difference when subjects were asked if participation in experimental exposure had changed their spouse's sexual behavior or attitudes.[45]

In view of pornography's power to arouse sexually, experimental findings of more frequent sexual activity—intercourse, masturbation, petting—and more frequent conversations, fantasies, and dreams about sex are hardly surprising. If anything, evidence of even greater changes might have been anticipated. Beyond this, the findings are subject to important qualifications. As with most laboratory studies, exposure was part of a socially (and academically) sanctioned experiment, conducted in a controlled environment with better-educated subjects who, for the most part, understood the nature of the experiment from the beginning. All information on behavior was self-reported and presumably vulnerable to distortion. In most instances the studies dealt only with behavior on the day following exposure, in response to a single encounter with pornography. They do not tell us anything about long-term behavioral change or what change, if any, is associated with continued regular or periodic exposure in a naturalistic setting where social relationships, established attitudes, and individual interests and needs play a much greater role. Finally, the pornography used in the studies was milder than much of that now commercially available.

At the same time, the studies clearly do not lend much support to fears that exposure leads to new or sustained higher levels of sexual activity or to marked changes in an individual's established sexual behavior. They do not prove that pornography has no such effects, but they set out to search for them and failed to establish any. They do suggest the need for further inquiry in more naturalistic settings.

Let us return to the clear association between pornography and sexual experience, evident in the retrospective survey studies and ranking as one of the strongest in the social science literature under review. One widely held interpretation is that the experience with pornography, particularly at an early age, in large dosages, or on a regular basis, is a significant agent of earlier sexual experience and experimentation and of higher levels of sexual activity overall.

Two other explanations are also possible. Cause and effect may be reversed; the earlier sexual experience and higher levels of sexual activity may account for the earlier, greater, and more regular use of pornography. Or it may be that exposure and behavior are not causally related at all, but are both products of other, underlying factors. A study of adolescents thirteen to eighteen in an urban working-class neighborhood—one of the few studies to deal with a less well educated, subadult, population—found that virtually all the boys and nearly all the girls had had some experience with pornography. Except for commercial movies, friends were the most common source of materials, and exposure tended to be in a social setting; for girls, almost entirely in mixed company. The pornography appeared to circulate largely within friendship and dating circles; in effect, a small amount of it was widely shared. The adolescents who experienced the greatest exposure were also those who were most socially active and popular, had the most friends, and dated the most frequently. The same social characteristics were evident among those with the most sexual experience, leading investigators to conclude that the high exposure and greater sexual experience were both functions of participation in normal adolescent social activities rather than cause and effect of one another.[46]

A survey of college students revealed a strong association, especially for men, between experience with pornography and "sociosexual experimentation," an index measuring the incidence of intercourse and various degrees of petting. Experience was not related to age or other social background characteristics such as class, religion, family cohesiveness, or city size. As in the case of the urban working-class adolescents, it was associated with social variables in the subject's high school experience—frequency of dating, number of persons dated or dated steadily, number of close friends, the subject's perception of his popularity among other students—and also with the academic variables of class rank and participation in a sex education course. For women, experience with pornography was strongly associated with similar social variables during the college years, especially dating frequency. Finally, the relationship between sociosexual experimentation in high school and in college was much stronger than the association between experimentation in college and experience with pornography. The investigators concluded, as they had in the study of the working-class adolescents, that both sociosexual activity and exposure to pornography were functions of a complex pattern of social participation involving dating habits, friendship networks, and other normal adolescent behavior, and especially as these factors evolved during the high school years.[47]

These surveys, undertaken when commercial pornography was less explicit and violent than it is now, do not demonstrate that pornography has no effect on patterns of sexual activity; but they do cast doubt on the belief that exposure is a prime formative agent in those patterns. It is not unreasonable to believe that the typical adolescent would find being in the presence of, talking with, touching and being touched by, another person to whom he or she was attracted (particularly when attraction is reinforced by prevailing peer standards) more sexually stimulating than mere pornographic representation of sexuality.

Attitude Formation and Change

Except for antisocial behavior, which will be considered in the next section, attitude formation and change with respect to sexual values or orientation is probably the greatest concern of articulate critics of pornography. Unfortunately, a complex psychological-cognitive entity such as attitude is far more difficult to investigate empirically than arousal, affect, or immediate behavior. A multitude of intervening and mediating factors in an individual's past and present life must be located, weighed, and disentangled from the factor under scrutiny.

With these cautionary observations, we begin by noting that the national survey conducted in 1970 revealed a strong association between "recent experience" with pornography (defined as having seen or read five or more visual or textual depictions in the previous two years) and liberal attitudes toward sexual behavior and morality. Persons with more recent experience had more tolerant views of nonprocreative aspects of sexuality, premarital intercourse, and homosexuality, and were less ready to ostracize the "deviant" behavior of others or to support legal sanctions to control that behavior.[48] A Swedish national survey taken at about the same time revealed similar positive association between greater experience with pornography and liberal views on premarital and extramarital sex, contraception, and sex education.[49]

Experimental findings are mixed. Several studies, employing a variety of attitude scale questionnaires before and after exposure, found that changes were relatively few in number and slight in magnitude. Subjects with greater sexual experience, for example, became slightly more liberal in their views of premarital intercourse, but no appreciable change was found among those less sexually experienced, and no changes were found in either group with regard to extramarital intercourse.[50] Greater tolerance of promiscuous behavior in others was accompanied by apparent reinforcement of the conservative elements in the subjects's standards for his own behavior.[51] Little evidence of attitude change was found in several studies of married couples, though in one, "desire to engage in unusual sex practices" apparently decreased for a substantial number of subjects.[52]

One matter about which attitudes changed substantially was pornography itself. Subjects tend to become less fearful about pornography, though some of this change may result from taking part in a formal, sanctioned, and "enlightened" experiment.[53] Those "massively exposed" to pornography by viewing films for forty-eight minutes once a week for six weeks later believed that both conventional and deviant behavior were more prevalent than did subjects who received far less exposure or none at all, even though the films themselves depicted only conventional sexual acts. Estimates of the prevalence of fellatio and cunnilingus made by massively exposed subjects approximated survey evidence of their actual incidence, but the popularity of more deviant practices, such as group sex, sadomasochist acts, and bestiality, was grossly overestimated. Both males and females in the massively exposed group showed lower levels of support for "the female liberation movement."[54]

Much recent experimental attention has focused on depictions of sexual assaults on women and male attitudes toward women and rape. Rape depictions showing the victim to be sexually aroused were later associated with readier acceptance of "rape myths" and the use of force against women. The association was not evident for subjects who viewed depictions showing the victim's pain or abhorrence or depictions of mutually consensual sexual acts.[55] Both males and females among the massively exposed subjects favored significantly shorter prison sentences for rapists than did other subjects. The experimenters concluded, somewhat simplistically perhaps, that massive exposure "fosters a general trivialization of rape."[56] In an earlier study, using a scale to measure agreement of males with a series of cynical, vulgar, or stereotypical statements about women, exploitative or "sex-calloused" attitudes were moderated slightly after exposure,[57] but in the massive exposure experiment, using a similar scale, males so exposed had higher scores for sex callousness than did other subjects.

A series of studies comparing reactions to three types of films— nonaggressive pornographic, aggressive pornographic, and aggressive nonpornographic—found that subjects viewing the aggressive pornography showed greater acceptance of rape myths, and greater willingness to use force against women and to rape if not caught, than those viewing the nonaggressive film. However, subjects viewing the aggressive nonpornographic film had scores on all three scales similar to or higher than subjects who viewed the aggressive pornographic film, leading the experimenters to speculate that attitudes toward rape and sexual assault might be affected more by the aggressive than the sexual content of depiction.[58]

A few studies have explored variables that may intervene in the purported relationship between pornography and attitude change and formation. Anxiety about aggression, measured by a scale questionnaire, appeared to be mediating for men viewing depiction of a violent rape, those with higher levels tending to see the victim as experiencing more pain and trauma than did those with lower levels.[59] As already noted, nonexperimental research provides some evidence that both formation of certain sexual attitudes and experience with pornography may be mediated by factors operating in the home, neighborhood, and school peer groups. A cross-sectional survey of 375 men revealed a modest negative relationship between "moral character," measured by a scale questionnaire, and experience with pornography (at least for those first exposed before age seventeen). But this link was considerably weaker statistically than that between either variable and a third—association with deviant peers. Early exposure to pornography was more strongly related to deviance in the home and association with deviant peers than to moral character, leading the investigators to conclude that early exposure might have "no impact on character over and beyond that of a generally deviant background."[60]

Research on attitudes is less extensive than research on arousal, and the findings are less satisfactory. The link of exposure, in natural or experimental settings, to somewhat more liberal views about pornography itself appears to be fairly well established. Apparent links to more liberal views about sexual behavior or to stereotypical or "calloused" views of women and a readier acceptance of sexual aggression are suggestive. Further investigation is needed to determine their strength, persistence, relation to actual behavior, and whether they are mutually consistent.

Criminal and Antisocial Behavior

Concern about a link between pornography and antisocial or illegal behavior is long-standing and ranges from simplistic fears that exposure leads to specific (and possibly immediate) criminal acts, such as rape or child molestation, to more general views that pornography is a major force in development or reinforcement of deviant, delinquent, or criminal life-styles. These concerns have always been close to the center of the public policy debate, and perhaps for that reason have received unusual attention from commentators and researchers. They have also been the subject of widely differing conclusions by several investigating bodies. As early as 1955, the U.S. Senate Subcommittee to Investigate Juvenile Delinquency declared that pornography was "one of the contributing factors in juvenile delinquency and sex crimes in the United States."[61] This emphatic conclusion was based on testimony of psychiatrists, youth workers, school authorities, clergy, police officers, customs and postal officials, and others, who offered observations based on their experience with individual cases or on inferences from statistics showing increases in crime and delinquency. In 1970, the President's Commission on Obscenity and Pornography made a comprehensive review of theoretical and empirical research on the etiology of delinquency conducted by criminologists, sociologists, and psychologists since 1915. The commission's findings differed sharply from the Senate subcommittee's. In none of more than fifty works examined, many of which expressly discussed and enumerated the causes of delinquency, was pornography mentioned as a cause or contributing agent.[62]

On the strength of such surveys and the results of several new studies it sponsored, the commission concluded that there was "no evidence to date that exposure to explicitly sexual materials plays a sizable role in the causation of delinquent or criminal behavior among youth or adults."[63] In Britain, two years later, the nongovernmental Longford Committee Investigating Pornography reached the nearly opposite conclusion that pornography was very likely a causative agent in antisocial behavior.[64] The official British Committee on Obscenity and Film Censorship (the Williams Committee), however, reporting in 1979 after examining clinical, experimental, survey, and anecdotal evidence, remained unconvinced of a causal link to crime.[65] Finally, the U.S. Attorney General's Commission on Pornography, examining the same categories of evidence in 1986, concluded that there was strong support for "the hypothesis that substantial exposure to sexually violent materials . . . bears a causal relationship to acts of sexual violence and, for some subgroups, possibly unlawful acts of sexual violence."[66] Some of the manifest disagreement between investigators may be attributable to changes in the content and availability of pornography between the late 1960s and mid-1980s, but probably a great deal of it reflects different readings of the evidence and different degrees of skepticism about what it shows. Ideological bias toward the question of pornography may also play a part.

Whatever the explanation, a growing number of empirical studies address the link to criminal and antisocial behavior directly. An early sample of more than 400 cases of delinquency, referred to the neuropsychiatric division of a large urban municipal court, concluded that pornography was "neither salient nor important enough to appear spontaneously in a probing examination of the background and circumstances of juvenile offenses."[67] Several surveys have indicated that although a high percentage of juvenile offenders have had some experience with pornography, incidence of exposure does not differ significantly from levels for adolescents generally. Nor does age at first exposure appear to differ significantly for delinquents.[68] We have already noted evidence that delinquents' experience with pornography may be influenced, if not largely determined, by social and cultural factors operating in the home and neighborhood, such as parental or sibling deviance or association with deviant peers, both of which are strongly related to early exposure.[69]

A number of studies have explored the relationship between the increasing volume and availability of pornography and incidence of known sexual offenses. Several conducted in Denmark in the late 1960s, after most restrictions on the sale of pornography ended, found an actual decline in the number of sex crimes reported to the police, including sharp drops in exhibitionism, child molestation, and homosexual offenses.[70] Though attitude change about reporting certain offenses may have been a factor, a later, closer analysis indicated that the decline in reported child molestation may have represented an actual reduction in the number of offenses.[71] Other studies indicate, however, that the incidence of rape and attempted rape may not have fallen.[72]

Several aggregate-data studies of crime statistics in Britain, Australia, South Africa, and Singapore purport to find correlation between policy changes allowing greater or lesser freedom for pornography and increases and decreases, respectively, in reported rapes.[73] Though intriguing, the findings are weakened by simplistic analysis of the policy changes that equates them with immediately higher or lower levels of pornography consumption, and by inattention to rates for other violent and nonviolent crimes, some of which changed more dramatically than did rape.[74]

These studies and the Danish ones, which reached substantially opposite conclusions, reflect characteristic problems in correlational analysis of aggregate social data: the inability to equate correlation with cause and the possibility of finding spurious correlation, that is, covariation resulting not from a causal relationship between two factors but from a link between each of them and a third or *N*-number of unknown or unexplored factors. Pornography-rape correlation studies also reveal problems with the reliability of data concerning the level of pornography consumption and the incidence of rape. For example, it is not clear to what extent changes in the apparent incidence of rape may be changes in the willingness of victims to report the crime to police. Similarly, although it is axiomatic that pornography has become increasingly explicit and violent in content as well as more available commercially, we do not know much about the rate of consumption of that pornography or the uniformity of its increase.

Aggregate-data studies have examined the relationship between rape statistics, indices of pornography, and other variables, using the fifty states as units of analysis. Though fairly strong positive correlation of .64 was found between rape rates and the combined circulation of eight adult magazines, rates were not found to be correlated with the number of either adult movie theaters or adult bookstores.[75] Factors having a positive correlation with a higher incidence of rapes included urbanization, economic inequality, unemployment, other violent crimes, and various measures of social disorganization.[76]

The experience of individual sex offenders has been the subject of survey interview study. Analyzing the sexual histories of 1,356 men convicted of sex crimes, 888 convicted of other offenses, and a smaller control group of nonoffenders, Gebhard and his associates found no significant differences in exposure to pornography, which was almost universal, or in ownership of pornography among the three groups.[77] Other studies appear to indicate that sex offenders have had substantially less experience with pornography during both adolescent and preadolescent years than either other offenders or nonoffender control subjects. Moreover, their early experience was with less explicit pornography, and they tended to have been older at the time of first exposure.[78]

Sex offenders do not appear to differ in important ways from other groups in their reported immediate responses to pornography in "real life."[79] The percentage who said they engaged in behavior depicted in pornography or in other sexual acts following exposure, or who said they wished to imitate the depicted behavior or "to try other sex," did not differ significantly from that of nonoffenders.[80] Sex offenders were far more likely to masturbate in response to pornography than nonoffenders, a tendency that appeared to be part of a larger, established masturbatory pattern typically found more frequently among sex offenders.[81] When asked directly whether pornography had anything to do with their criminal behavior, "a small but significant minority" in one study said that it was partially responsible for their offenses.[82] Such "scapegoat" questions, however, must be viewed cautiously; no such findings were obtained in two other studies making a similar inquiry.[83]

Experimental studies indicate that rapists tend to be sexually aroused by depictions both of forced or violent rape and of mutually enjoyable intercourse, while nonrapists tend to be less aroused by rape depictions. It is not clear whether the rape depiction was especially arousing for the rapists or whether the depicted force and violence failed to inhibit arousal.[84] In general, "it is not so much a case of sex offenders responding differently than normals as one of normals responding differently than sex offenders, especially to portrayals of violent sexuality; normals appear to be more responsive to inhibiting cues in such depictions."[85]

In survey interviews of several types of sexual deviates and offenders, Goldstein and associates found rapists most subject to self-generated fantasies and daydreams that disgusted them—of oral-genital acts, transvestism, and homosexuality. At the same time, the rapist was likeliest to find depictions of simple heterosexual intercourse the most stimulating pornography, leading to speculation that this thematic preference might actually serve as "a means of warding off anxiety, disgust, and guilt about his disturbing daydreams."[86] Whether this function of pornography would increase the chance of antisocial acts or would divert the disturbing sexual energy of self-generated fantasy into well-established masturbatory patterns is unclear, although the investigators lean strongly toward the latter conclusion.[87]

Experimental studies directly exploring a possible link between pornography and criminal or antisocial acts are lacking for obvious reasons. Laboratory efforts have tried to relate pornography to aggressive behavior, but the findings are unclear. Experimentally induced sexual arousal appeared not to produce aggression (as measured by a willingness to inflict unpleasant noise or what was believed to be electric shock on another subject) in subjects experimentally angered, usually through insult, or in those who were not.[88] Mildly arousing stimuli appeared to inhibit aggression in angered subjects, but more arousing stimuli resulted in aggression levels comparable to those of control subjects exposed only to nonerotic stimuli, suggesting a curvilinear relationship between arousal and experimentally induced aggression.[89] When angering did not follow viewing of movies depicting erotic, aggressive, or neutral acts, no significant differences were found in retaliatory behavior. When it did follow viewing, substantially higher retaliatory levels were evident in subjects who had seen erotic rather than the aggressive or neutral films, suggesting to investigators an "excitation transfer" phenomenon.[90]

Studies by Donnerstein and associates, referred to earlier in connection with attitudes, found that higher levels of experimentally induced aggression varied with thematic depiction. Victim-arousal rape was followed by greater likelihood of aggression. Angered subjects generally had higher levels, even in the case of victim-abhorrence rape. And though the highest levels were obtained after films juxtaposing aggressive and sexual content, exposure to films with nonerotic aggressive content was also associated with increased aggression. As noted earlier, the researchers speculated that aggressive themes might be more salient than sexual ones in determining later aggressive response.[91]

Studies purporting to discriminate, through self-report questionnaires, between male college students with high and low likelihoods of committing rape found that subjects with supposedly higher likelihood were most aroused by an audiotape describing victim-arousal rape and least by one describing mutually consensual acts. Those with low likelihood were aroused equally by the victim-arousal rape and the consensual acts but less aroused by a third tape describing victim-abhorrence rape.[92] Rape proclivity was also positively associated with higher levels of experimentally induced aggression against female subjects.[93] Intriguing as these findings are, most men, especially college students, do not commit rape, regardless of their experience with pornography. At the very least, this fact suggests some powerful inhibitory factors, hence the need for caution before equating self-reported proclivity in a general population with either the actual criminal acts or the likelihood of their commission.

The various studies examined here—retrospective surveys, aggregate-data analysis, and experimental research—supply no conclusive answer to whether pornography is causally linked to antisocial or criminal behavior. In view of the complexity of the question, the vast social and psychic territory it addresses, and methodological difficulties encountered, the failure is not surprising, nor does it mean that such links do not exist. But it should make us cautious about intuitive leaps from correlation to causality, or from arousal and attitudes to actual behavior, or from the laboratory to the natural environment, whatever assumptions we may hold about modeling effects or an inevitable progression from deviant arousal to deviant or antisocial acts.

The inconclusiveness of the evidence raises the question whether the concept of a link between rape and pornography is not too simplistic for serious inquiry into possible harmful effects of pornography. The growing body of research on the etiology of sex offenses indicates that offenders respond to a wide range of sexual stimuli, both deviant and nondeviant. In addition, nonsexual elements, including "personality characteristics, organic factors, modified inhibition due to drugs or fatigue," and circumstantial factors including the specificity of the victim, together with various facets of the offender's previous life experience, play a considerable role in commission of the offenses.[94] Studies do not reveal striking differences between sex offenders and nonoffenders in their experience with pornography or the age at which first contact occurred. They do indicate that offenders have typically experienced a greater degree of sexual repression and deprivation in their early environments. Thus sex offenders frequently report family circumstances in which there is "a low tolerance for nudity, an absence of sexual conversation, and punitive or indifferent parental responses to children's sexual curiosity and interest."[95] Histories of most offenders reveal a succession of immature and impersonal sociosexual relationships, rigid sexual attitudes, and poor occupational and interpersonal adjustment generally.[96] The magnitude and pervasiveness of these unpromising circumstances suggest that experience with pornography may merely reflect, and perhaps only in a minor way, a deprived background and general maladjustment, rather than be a trigger of antisocial or criminal acts.

Experimental studies present interesting evidence of deviant arousal in response to pornography, yet most persons aroused by deviant and even violent sexual depiction do not commit sexual offenses. The relationship between such arousal and deviant behavior is complex and affected by a wide range of inhibitory factors. Such inhibitions are also very apt to be reflected in the common reactions of boredom and disgust. Under the limitations of the laboratory, experimental studies, which examine only a small number of inhibitory and disinhibitory cues, have barely touched on this area. In short, evidence now available does not support a causal leap from deviant arousal by sexually violent pornography to the commission of sexual offenses.

Research needs to include more intensive retrospective surveys of offenders and "normals," longitudinal observation of children and adolescents, and the findings of clinical case studies. It would profit especially from the integration of behavioral and psychodynamic insight. Research needs to focus much more on the relationship of pornography to modal sexual patterns, their development, maintenance, and alteration, and perhaps less on the well-established power of pornography to effect temporary increases in sexual drive. The latter remains an important avenue of inquiry, but would profit from less preoccupation with proving or disproving links to criminal offenses.

Distinctions must also be made between exposure and use. Most contact or experience with pornography is by choice, which carries over to particular theme and imagery as well. First or early exposure, voluntary or involuntary, may be developmentally significant, but that is a very small part of total use. The pornography industry and marketplace rely on contact that is deliberately sought and choice that is made from a menu of themes and imagery. This fact also creates special difficulties for laboratory research, which typically "force feeds" stimuli chosen by the experimenters.

Research has, moreover, too often addressed the content of pornography and neglected the social context of real-life presentation. The perception of social approval or disapproval may have far more influence on reactions, long- and short-term, than specific theme or imagery. Sexual content in broadcast television programs or in R-rated films in movie theaters, for example, is no doubt perceived to have more social license than the more explicit (but usually more improbable) content of X-rated depiction. Some investigators have recognized the importance of context, but few studies have addressed it directly.[97] (Differences among the various media in the treatment of sexual themes and imagery and popular expectations about such standards—a considerable source of censorship debate—are dealt with in Chapter 7. Legal control that discriminates among circumstances is a topic of Chapter 8.)

If sexual expression is harmful at all, the harm, paradoxically, may not be to adults and adolescents from hard-core pornography, but to children in latency from the milder but far more ubiquitous expression in the highly sexualized communications environment. We know very little about the effects of a steady diet of nudity, innuendo, jokes, and other titillating references. But we believe that the child enters the massive sexual amnesia of latency to seek refuge from sexuality; earlier infantile fantasies are repressed because they are too overwhelming to be consciously managed. Conscious awareness of these fantasies may in fact be a symptom of serious emotional disturbance.[98] We also know that young children do not require hard-core pornography to be overstimulated. Pornography investigators have largely ignored this subject; others who study children and the communications media have tended to concentrate on depiction of violence even though the child may have much more difficulty unconsciously with sexual representation and suggestion.[99]

A last question may be asked about the quest for objective evidence of pornography's influence: Would clear proof on one side or the other make much difference in the perceptions of most persons or in public opinion? There is reason to believe that it would not. In the President's Commission's national survey of attitudes and opinion, taken in 1970 and still the most extensive interview study, respondents were asked whether their views on control would be modified if there were clear evidence about effects. Fewer than half indicated flexibility on this point. Forty-one percent said their views would not change, while 15 percent had no opinion or did not answer. Of those favoring restraints on pornography, fewer than a third would change their views even "if it were clearly demonstrated that materials dealing with sex had *no harmful effects.*"[100]

These findings confirm an obvious point: the views many persons have of pornography's effects may be partly irrational. Harmful effects are much more likely to be seen as experienced by others than by oneself, and even if pornography were shown to be not harmful or less harmful than commonly supposed, these views would resist change. As with the pornographic imagination and its challenging, often harrowing, insight, we face the question of the utility of knowledge itself. Scientific investigation is presumably reasoned, systematic, and empirically based, and the enlightenment it offers derives from logic, induction, and testing rather than flashes of insight, intuition, or aesthetic confrontation. But the knowledge the social scientist develops may be every bit as troubling as that offered by the artist or psychic explorer. The fantastical properties of pornography may touch disturbing residues of infantile eroticism buried in the unconscious. Troubling knowledge, whether offered by science or art, is likely to pass through an emotional and ideological screen. For many persons, belief that pornography is harmful, particularly to other persons, may be an important means of avoiding disturbing confrontations with the self while also offering apparent rational ground for supporting external controls. To be sure, opinion and beliefs are not static, but the distance between scientific findings about pornography and their utility in either public policy or private choice may often be very great.

Though we cannot be certain that pornography is harmful, we know clearly that it is disturbing. The search for evidence of harm or harmlessness needs to be carried forward. But, as we shall argue more fully later, the perceived offensiveness of pornography is not only a truer objection than concern about harm but also a sounder basis for both public and private resolutions about control.

Within and Without

In seeking to determine the effects or influence of pornography, we need to remind ourselves of both the primacy of fantasy and the transgressive nature of all pornography and pornographic imagery. Though pornography consists of deliberate sexual stimuli, there is no evidence that the pornographic within would cease to function as a source of excitation in its absence. Pornography is in fact likely to be less arousing than one's own imagination. Subjects asked to fantasize about pornographic themes to which they were exposed are usually more aroused by their own psychic efforts than by the external stimuli.[101] The capacity of the human mind to eroticize is nearly limitless, and almost any depiction, symbol, idea, or object can be transformed into a source of pornographic or near-pornographic stimulation.

Pornography may feed a prurient interest and is designed to do exactly that, but it neither creates that interest nor is vital to it. In its construction and use, pornography is an external expression or reflection of the power and primacy of an endopsychic capacity for prurient interest and transgressive sexual fantasy.

The attractiveness of pornography is precisely that it violates our taboos and norms. Such license is bound to portray the subordination and degradation of women and aggression against them. If the depictions were not transgressive, they would not be pornography and would undoubtedly be much less compelling. Our quarrel with the disturbing, mean-spirited, sometimes frightening, often infantile images of pornography is largely a quarrel with an eroticized human sexuality that creates a fantastical pornographic within, which, in turn, both invents and responds to a pornography without.

———————

Part Three

Society

Chapter Five

Pornography and the Social Order

Morality and immorality meet on the public scaffold.

Émile Durkheim

Without an elaborately cultivated transgressive sense, there can be neither aristocracies of the feeling intellect nor democracies of obedience.

Philip Rieff

All of us struggle consciously and unconsciously with forbidden fantasies of eroticized sexuality. The wish to gratify these impulses is seldom completely reconciled with the strongly felt need to control them. This ambivalence shapes much of our response to erotic expression. Societies seek to control sexual gratification and its representation, in part because individuals struggle to do this for themselves and in part because undisciplined sexual behavior and expression are believed to threaten various social ends, including the integrity of the family, the predictability of the behavior of others, the relative standing of particular groups, and the efficient accomplishment of tasks.

A representation of fantasies may both arouse sexually and call forth feelings of shame and disgust. For an individual experiencing these effects, such a representation is functionally pornographic. As an entity in the external world, however, the expression is also subject to collective perception, which may not coincide with what the individual experiences. When this collective judgment finds a representation to violate norms of acceptable erotic expression, that representation is socially pornographic. Such a designation need not be formal, in the sense of having effect in law or public policy.

For any sexual expression, then, there may be two pornographies: one in the psychic order of the individual, the other in the social order. The first is determined by the strengths and idiosyncrasies of erotic appetite in battle with the authority of conscience or superego; the second, by the balance

119

between external license and authority, based on differences in social power. Failure to distinguish between the two muddies our thinking about pornography and confuses the debate about what is and is not pornographic or obscene. A given expression can be functionally pornographic for one or even a large number of persons, yet be socially unobjectionable when measured by prevailing norms or standards. Or it may be functionally nonpornographic even for many persons, yet be socially designated as pornography.

Social designation, as the term is used here, is not limited to legal proscriptions of obscenity but includes the entire range of sexual expression found socially unacceptable or objectionable. The labeling of expression as pornography occurs in a variety of macro and micro settings, public and private, and formal and informal. These judgments may be underwritten by a range of social and economic penalties—censure, contempt, ridicule, ostracism, de-patronization, moral condemnation, and the like—in addition to the sanction of criminal law.

In purely economic terms, pornography supplies forbidden goods and services in high demand. It functions much as the internally pornographic does in the currency of imagination, or as prostitution does in sexual behavior. Though such demand can be externally stimulated, the internally pornographic can also provide its own near-perpetual wellspring of want. As the sociologist Robert Merton observed, there are few real economic differences between the provision of licit goods and the provision of illicit goods.[1] Commercial pornography is affected by many of the same production, distribution, and marketing considerations—supply and demand, competition, regulation—as other goods and services. Social judgment rather than economic determination distinguishes pornography from other erotic expression, such as pictures of nudes or figures in provocative pose, stories of romantic love, or gothic mysteries with their sublimated sexuality. In this sense, pornography resembles other deviant institutions, such as prostitution, gambling, and drug trafficking, that correct apparent flaws in distribution patterns by providing a black market for individually desired but socially denounced goods and services. In pornography, as in most deviant enterprises, organized crime is a natural broker for that which society demands and at the same time condemns.

Pornography is a compromise between normative structure and apparent asocial or antisocial gratification, in effect a remission of what Philip Rieff has called the "moral demand system."[2] Here we first consider the social reality of pornography by noting several widely held views of its supposed harmful social effect and by asking whether it may also have latent utility for the social order and the regulation of sexual life. We then look more closely at the social designation or labeling of pornography and the conflict surrounding it.

Public Morality

Many persons see pornography as subversive; its representations of sexual aberrancy are morally corrupting and pose a threat to civilization itself. Pornography ranks with crime, delinquency, drug abuse, sexual promiscuity, and other deviations associated with social disorder and disintegration. It may in fact be more dangerous, because through inurement it affects not just the libertine, misfit, underprivileged, and weak but also the average person. Pornography is thus both morally destructive and socially pathological.

Whatever its effects on immediate behavior, pornography in the long run debases character and moral standards, because it touches deep-rooted passions and base sexual inclinations. According to the political scientist Harry M. Clor, the most thoughtful and systematic spokesman for this point of view, these desires may be gratified or reinforced in a pornography-saturated environment. Higher forms of character development, never completely secure, are weakened by external factors that arouse the lower. Representations that "overemphasize sensuality and brutality, reduce love to sex, and blatantly expose to public view intimacies which have long been thought sacred or private" erode moral standards by undermining the convictions and sensitivities supporting them.

People are influenced by what they think others believe and particularly by what they think are the common standards of the community. There are few individuals among us whose basic beliefs are the result of their own reasoning and whose moral opinions do not require the support of some stable public opinion. The free circulation of obscenity can, in time, lead many to the conclusion that there is nothing wrong with the values implicit in it—since their open promulgation is tolerated by the public. They will come to the conclusion that public standards have changed—or that there are no public standards. Private standards are hard put to withstand the effects of such an opinion.[3]

Ethical beliefs and convictions also depend on an intuitive sense of right and wrong and the "finer feelings of conscience, of memory, of sympathy." Such moral sentiments are vital to the making of subtle ethical judgments.

It is by virtue of them that we feel respect for what is honorable and disgust for what is indecent—aspiring toward the former and recoiling from the latter. (When sentiments of this kind are not developed, morality tends to degenerate into a collection of abstract precepts or a calculus of self-interest.) These "finer feelings" could be blunted and eroded by steady stream of impressions which assault them. Men whose sensibilities are frequently assaulted by prurient and lurid impressions may become desensitized. . . . Obscenity promotes the grosser passions; its corroding effect is upon the higher or more refined feelings—those upon which ethical and aesthetic discrimination depend.[4]

Attitudes about what is good and bad are thus necessarily related to feelings about what is "beautiful and ugly, fitting and unfitting. . . . an ugly prurient culture contributes to the erosion of the 'finer feelings' concerning the sexual relation, the meaning of life, the worth of a human being."[5]

Others have seen pornography resulting in a loss of a "last, vital privacy," a debilitating and subversive "loss of shame," and a destruction of "empathy and mutual identification which restrains us from treating each other merely as objects or means."[6] Its fantastical and often sadistic portrayal of women "deadens feeling" and insidiously confuses these images with reality, slowly imprisoning us "in an illusion which replaces reality and leaves us devastated and despairing."[7] Several feminist writers see pornography as encouraging male hostility and brutality and helping to maintain a general environment of sexual exploitation.[8]

Ultimately, the morally corrupting and regressive aspects of pornography undermine self-government and democracy itself, for a "society of thoroughgoing hedonists, with each individual given over to self-indulgent gratification, would not generate mutual respect and the capacity for self-discipline" that a liberal democracy and constitutional system require.[9] The permissive, even nihilistic depictions of pornography are "inherently and purposively subversive of civilization and its institutions."[10] And when authorities themselves encourage the reduction of human beings to mere means, even "concentration camps become possible."[11]

The view of pornography as socially pathological and subversive appeals to common sense and is held reasonably by many persons, including many who might otherwise consider themselves opposed to any form of censorship. Yet it is anchored in shaky logic and evidence. Studies of effects examined in the last chapter, although not disproving the claims that pornography impairs ethical judgment or leads to emotional callousness, corruption of character, and aesthetic insensibility, offer little to support them. Even if there were general accord about what such complex virtues as "ethical judgment" and "character" actually are, lasting subtle or decisive effects on them from any single source such as pornography are highly questionable.

The social pathology view holds that when such effects are individually experienced by large numbers of persons they create a social and moral environment that threatens established norms and institutions governing our sexual lives and securing decent and humane sexual behavior. Even if we assume that the individual effects ascribed exist, how would they be transposed almost intact, uncountered and undiluted, to the social environment? Such a leap ignores the human tendency to unsystematic response and tolerance for dissonance both psychic and cognitive. Because of the capacity of pornography both to arouse and to disgust, it is not at all uncommon for a prurient interest to exist side by side with one supporting or reaffirming established and even highly restrictive moral standards.[12] Since most persons spend a good deal of their time effecting compromises between appetitive impulses and moral compulsions and work requirements, we cannot assume that the formidable—and psychologically useful—barrier separating the personal and private from the social and public will easily fall.

It is true that the modern pornography explosion has occurred along with an explosion in the rates of such deviancies as illegitimacy, adultery, and premarital experimentation. But at the level of macro change, where countless complex developments are coextensive and even covarying, relevant agents are numbered in the hundreds or thousands. Determining which of them may have dependent, independent, or intervening status in relation to any other is extremely difficult. Hence, causal inferences must be made with caution. The view of pornography as subversive of public morality is probably as old as pornography itself, but it can be argued that the moral course of the world has not been steadily downhill.

The claim that pornography threatens particular political arrangements or even the social order rests on all the earlier assumptions and thus is the most problematic. A causal link between sexual permissiveness and a society's decline and fall has long been a matter of speculation, but such an empirically complex proposition is almost impossible to prove or disprove.[13] Social order has coexisted with many types of sexual norms or public moralities. During the last two hundred years, self-governing nations, for example, have shown themselves capable of protecting a wide range of sexual expression, at the same time administering a wide variety of restrictions. No record exists of pornography being causally associated with the failure of any liberal or democratic government or, in fact, with the collapse of any society.[14] Indeed, as we shall argue in the next chapter, pornography and liberal democracy may actually have a strong affinity for one another.

Finally, the view of pornography as socially devitalizing assumes not only that the norms and canons on which public morality rests are unambiguous and unchanging, but that the sexual expression in question is itself largely free of multiple characterizations. Even if a society had absolute standards, it seems certain that they would not be obvious to all members in all situations and surely not to all persons outside. All societies regulate sexual expression and behavior, and in this sense all have public moralities. But variations both among and within them are legion.

That public morality exists is undeniable, but whether a particular norm or rule is essential to public morality is much less clear. Defenders of public morality in Britain and the United States over the last two hundred years have had a less than glorious record of identifying particular expressions as corrupting or subversive. They have often confused their own standards and preferences with those they believed universally unequivocal. The social pathology perspective fails to see—indeed, is almost assured of not seeing—either the conflict of values or the social struggle implicit in "public morality" and thus fails to acknowledge the vital role played by power and social standing in seeking to establish and maintain public morality. Without the advantage of hindsight, the socially pathological may sometimes be hard to distinguish from well-intentioned and perhaps intelligent demands for social change.

The view of pornography as morally subversive and corrupting holds that a pornographic interest can be suppressed or eradicated. It assumes the primacy of pornography over the internally pornographic and that the former with its explicit representations largely determines the latter. As we have seen, however, the reverse is usually the case: it is not that pornography fails to stimulate pornographic interest, but that the internally pornographic will survive the suppression of pornography. It will, in large measure, simply attach itself to new objects of interest, responding to other, ever-present stimuli—physical, behavioral, or symbolic and representational—in the external environment.

Logical and empirical difficulties notwithstanding, the social pathology perspective does tell us that a great many persons are disturbed or offended by pornography and believe it morally and socially damaging. This is an important fact and, as we shall argue in the next chapter, one that a democratic society can ill afford to ignore. But the perspective leaves unanswered, or does not satisfactorily answer, the questions why there is a public morality of erotic expression to begin with, why it varies so considerably, and why it never completely triumphs.

Alienation and Liberation

In sharp contrast to the moralist social pathology view is the perception of pornography as the product of a social environment hostile to sex and fearful of its expression. Because interest in sex is presumably normal, healthy, and desirable, the "problem" of pornography arises from the "inability or reluctance of people . . . to be open and direct in dealing with sexual matters."[15] By casting sex as a necessary evil, puritanical norms and attitudes, rooted in notions of duty, shame, and guilt, separate us from our sexual selves. They inhibit normal, healthy expression, leaving the field open to distorted forms and images. Hence a society which "represses sexual expression by social sanctions, by religious threats, and hedges it about with rituals which frustrate the natural impulse, will create the conditions necessary to make escapism both essential and glamorous."[16] Pornography is thus a flag of alienation in a sexually repressive world. Interest in it is natural, justifiable, and possibly even salutary—in any event, less socially damaging than the thwarting, inhibiting norms and attitudes that call it forth.

This view of pornography comprises two lines of thought: one progressive and ameliorative, the other radical and transforming. The former and better-established is reflected in the conclusions of the President's Commission on Obscenity and Pornography, which, despite a controversial recommendation that all legal restrictions on pornography be abolished for adults, did not regard pornography as a desirable social phenomenon. Institutions such as marriage and family rest on

healthy sex attitudes grounded in appropriate and accurate information. [This] sexual information is so important and so necessary that if people cannot obtain it openly and directly from legitimate sources and through accurate and legitimate channels, they will seek it through whatever channels and sources are available. Clandestine sources may not only be inaccurate but may also be distorted and provide a warped context.[17]

The commission proposed that a massive sex education program be undertaken to encourage "healthy attitudes and orientations to sexual relationships" and thus to counter pornography. Although the progressive view does not necessarily rely on sex education, it holds that insofar as pornography is a problem, it is the result of fear and negativism about sex. When this larger knot is untied, pornography will, in effect, wither away. Its furtive and distorted focus, like society's puritanical and repressive ones, will be replaced by an "openness and honesty" in which sex is accepted as a normal and natural part of life, and "drives can reappear as themselves and come to their own equilibrium, according to organism self-regulation."[18] As an understandable product of repressive values, pornography is thus a kind of detour on the road to a sexually healthier social order. In the long run, "a free and uninhibited flow of erotica would help demolish sexual repression and, ultimately, the need for pornography."[19]

In the radical counterpart of this view, pornography is not simply a justifiable reaction but also antidotal—a liberating end in itself, reflecting a natural element in human sexuality that is not to be grudgingly suffered but rather accepted, even celebrated. Pornography is thus recreative, a healthy escape, and a convenient surrogate sexual experience.[20] Its transgressive representations challenge the conservative moralists' idealized, romanticized picture of sexual life and their prescription of where, when, how often, and with whom the sexual interest may be indulged, all of which render sexuality stereotypical, unfulfilling, and possibly neurotic. Pornography thus attacks what is most decadent in established sexual morality, most exaggerated and estranged in its sensibilities.[21] Its moral anarchy is particularly appropriate for

the confrontation with idealism, especially in its latter-day deterioration into sentimentalism. For sentimentalism is an attempt to idealize the passions and thereby deny the natural and moral significance of their physicality altogether. By denying the passions . . . [idealism] recommends an ethos that is based on only half of human nature. The murderous chaos of contemporary world culture is evidence of how that ethos is failing us. Pornography has become, therefore, the principal rhetoric of attack on this ethos. Its physicality *is* disruptive, disruptive of the serene ignorance of moral establishmentarianism. The insistent, loin-shaking beat of its physicality refuses the human authority of sentimental idealism. As that beat urges us to dance we are forced, in our dancing, to acknowledge its viability. And, as it makes us dance *better*, we are forced to acknowledge its moral potential.[22]

Culturally, then, the pornography explosion is a positive sign, an element in much larger sexual and social change. The radical view gained new strength in the late 1960s in connection with widespread protests over the Vietnam War, civil rights, and other issues. Some thoroughgoing sexual radicals, such as Wilhelm Reich, have gone even further, arguing that in modern industrial societies sexual repression is fundamentally linked to that based on political and economic power.[23]

Both the progressive and the radical view provide some conceptual underpinning for the libertarian position on social control but make doubtful assumptions about the pornographic interest, and raise the obvious evidentiary question how pornography is connected to such complex social phenomena as norms, institutions, and attitudes. Viewing pornography as a reaction to negative social forces gives inordinate weight to cognitive factors at the expense of psychodynamic ones. Thus it is not surprising that the President's Commission, seeing pornography as providing information and satisfying curiosity, should conclude that the "problem" can be solved by better sex education. Good information will drive out bad. Although the view has a great affinity with libertarian theories of free speech, it seems a roseate analysis of pornography even if we were certain what "healthy" sex education is. Pornography does provide information about sex, which may satisfy curiosity, but this function does not explain why interest in pornography is so easily and so often renewed. Pornography satisfies fantasy, urge, or desire, which, unlike the need for information, are episodic. And, of course, when the user is an adult, as is usually the case, interest in pornography is even less likely to serve cognitive ends. The chief deficiency in the commission's formulation—and with the progressive view generally—is its almost total innocence of a conception of the internally pornographic.[24]

Though social regulations and attitudes, especially highly restrictive ones, may add to the allure of the forbidden, they do not themselves cause pornography to be produced. Social norms and rules are compromises and are interdependently related to universal internal compromises between wishes both to gratify and to control desires. Neither the progressive nor the radical view, each of which holds that external controls alienate us from our true sexual selves, sees that those controls may often be responses to the psychological and social needs of those on whom they are imposed.

In both progressive and radical views, the notions of sexual "health" and "repression" are self-evident, in much the same way as are the requirements of public morality in the social pathology view. In fact, these notions are highly subjective. Sexual health is a heavily burdened value subject to much scientific and popular debate. Even with wide agreement that much behavior and many psychic states portrayed in pornography are *not* desirable or "healthy," they cannot be equated with the actual behavior and attitudes of users of pornography. Sexual "repression" presents a similar difficulty. We may generally agree, for example, that Victorian England was a sexually repressive society, but the same cannot be said of the United States, Britain, or other Western nations in the last quarter-century.

If sexual health and repression are not reasonably self-evident or established as matters of wide accord or scientific fact, the alienating and liberating views of pornography are open to doubt. Nonetheless, they succeed in calling attention to social norms, attitudes, and controls that affect both pornography and our interest in it. They also suggest that some societies or social environments may be more restrictive or at least less wisely restrictive than others. Yet neither the progressive nor the radical view satisfactorily explains why pornography and obscenity exist in all societies or why all have been to some degree repressive, and often so by popular demand.

Pornography as a Functional Alternative

If pornography is morally corrupting, supplies disapproved sex information, or is a focus of rebellion, it would play an essentially negative or dysfunctional role in the social order. Its effect, however indirect, would be to change that order. Yet the sheer persistence of pornography in spite of massive and continuing attempts to control or eliminate it, forces us to ask whether it may not also be socially maintaining. We shall consider this possibility here and in the next section by asking, first, whether pornography may be an alternative to other sexual experience and, second, whether it may somehow contribute to the definition and clarification of established norms and thus perhaps even to a sense of solidarity among those who support them.

Control or regulation of sexual energy through repression, inhibition, channeling, and rechanneling is a task of all social systems. Although protecting the family as the primary institution of reproduction, nurturance, and early socialization of the young is usually considered its chief end, some degree of regulation is necessary simply to have reliable expectations about the behavior of others. Not least, social regulation reinforces the often precarious internal controls every person has had to place on his or her erotic energies and desires. For these reasons, institutions and patterns of behavior that accommodate and socially isolate random, impulsive, impersonal, highly eroticized, or otherwise unacceptable aspects of the sexual drive may be highly functional even though they receive no official approval and may even be stigmatized and made illegal. Though masturbation, premarital experimentation, and adultery are probably the most widely established "deviations," prostitution is the classic institutional example and the one that offers the closest social analogue to pornography.

If not actually the first profession, prostitution is one of the oldest human institutions. It is found in many primitive societies and in virtually all complex advanced ones.[25] Yet almost nowhere has it been fully legitimate. There have been educated, companionate prostitutes of special standing—the Hellenic hetaerae, the Japanese geisha, and the "temple" prostitutes of parts of the ancient world—but these women were available only to elite groups of men. Prostitution has almost never been destigmatized for a population at large. Usually it has been resolutely opposed, often in periodic morality campaigns and other concerted attempts to suppress it. Except for short periods of time, these campaigns have never themselves completely triumphed.

Prostitution has survived for compelling reasons, however morally censurable they may be. It has often been an outlet for physical release of pent-up sexual energy where regular sexual partners were absent or unavailable, especially in the case of armies in the field and isolated colonies of male workers. The sexual experience offered is available to anyone who can pay, and since all men are not equally attractive as sexual partners, this commercial impartiality has provided sexual gratification to many who might otherwise fail in the competitive pursuit of women. In rendering quick gratification of a pressing repetitive need, it is also free of the "exacting requirement of attracting and persuading a female or perhaps getting entangled with her in courtship or even marriage."[26]

If prostitution simply secured these utilities it would probably not meet with the strong condemnation it so often has. We must look further for an explanation why demand remains high in spite of such opposition. As with pornography, the answer appears to lie in the kind of sexuality it provides, and in the same forbidden sexual fantasies that are the interior counterpart of pornography. The services of the female prostitute are typically offered in sexually provocative circumstances in which transgressive desires are promised some play or gratification. The very illicitness of the transaction provides release from sexual repression and no doubt helps account for the range of "perverse" activities requested. Genet's highly detailed brothel charades in *The Balcony* and the euphemistically phrased "specialties" in ads of the *Ladies Directory* are two of the better-known examples. Transgressive fantasies may be so heavily burdened with feelings of shame or guilt that they cannot be acted on or even spoken of in socially approved relationships.[27] The prostitute with the "heart of gold" or other endearing human qualities, so often sentimentally celebrated in song and story, is an unlikely figure in transactional reality. It is precisely the impersonal, transitory sexual experience free of the inhibiting responsibilities and expectations of more complicated and involved human relations that makes the liaison so characteristically inviting.[28]

Prostitution is a remission of society's moral demands. It is a social outlet for various unacceptable sexual wishes, impulses, ambitions, and inclinations, some of which may be antisocial and most of which are pornographically informed. These impulses are alien to preferred channels such as marriage, or preferred motives such as love and procreation, and often even to preferred acts such as conventional intercourse. And because they are, they make prostitution difficult to dismiss or eliminate. "Remove prostitutes from human affairs," St. Augustine said, "and you will pollute all things with lust." For Thomas Aquinas, prostitution was the "sewer" that allowed the "palace" to remain unfouled.[29] In modern times, where the nobility and purity of marriage and family have been the most idealized, as say in Victorian England, prostitution has prospered at new levels.[30] It has served at all times as a kind of sexual lightning rod, deflecting "deviant" energy away from sanctified paths and possibly preventing other antisocial transformation of it. As the sociologist Kingsley Davis concluded,

the attempt of society to control sexual expression, to tie it to social requirements, especially the attempt to tie it to the durable relation of marriage and the rearing of children, or to attach men to celibate order, or to base sexual expression on love, creates the opportunity for prostitution. It is analogous to the black market, which is the illegal but inevitable response to an attempt fully to control the economy. The craving for sexual variety, for perverse gratification, for novel and provocative surroundings, for ready and cheap release, for intercourse free from entangling cares and civilized pretense—all can be demanded from the woman whose interest lies solely in the price.[31]

Prostitution is a compromise between the pornographic force of eroticized sexuality and established sexual norms and institutions—the moral demand system—which seek to limit or deny that energy. The limbo in which this arrangement exists—neither obliterated nor destigmatized— makes certain that social and political tension will be drawn around it. Prostitution is a triumph of sociosexual economy but, as in many great social compromises, accommodation and a tolerance for apparent hypocrisy chafe moralist and libertarian alike.

Prostitution and pornography have a strong psychological affinity. In societies with high literacy rates and mass communications technology, pornography may perform some of the functions just described.[32] Although prostitution involves sexual acts with a partner whereas pornography deals only with representations of behavior, the latter is often associated with an overt sexual act—masturbation. Even when pornography does not lead to actual physical release, it may provide a vicarious sexual experience and some relief from the psychic tensions accompanying forbidden impulses and fantasies. Such has long been a function of much erotic entertainment offered in social or public settings and occasionally found to be pornographic or obscene. Examples include "dirty" jokes, erotic folktales, drinking songs, routines of night club comics, "smoker" stag films, and the once-popular burlesque theater.

Evidence suggests that prostitution and pornography complement each other demographically. Significant differences of class and education are apparent between customers of prostitutes and the users of pornography. Images of the frolicking conventioneer or well-heeled client of the Park Avenue call girl notwithstanding, males frequenting prostitutes tend to be young, single manual laborers or semiskilled workers, less educated, and with lower incomes.[33] Patrons of adult bookstores and movie houses are more likely to be middle-aged, married, well-dressed, to have higher income and occupational status (usually white-collar, business, or professional), and to be upwardly mobile.[34] They are likely to have had their first intercourse relatively late and to have had fewer adolescent sociosexual experiences. Indeed, masturbation is likely to be a more significant source of orgasmic release than prostitution for both married and unmarried men of the middle and upper classes than for those of lower social standing.[35]

Most pornography is viewed privately, in solitude; hence most autoerotic activity associated with it falls outside a social context. But the marked increase in quasi-public viewing of pornography has, in effect, institutionalized masturbation, suggesting the organized mass accommodation of prostitution.[36] Many of the adult movie houses in seamy urban areas are, in effect, masturbation "emporiums," in which lone men observe a territorial imperative by sitting at least two seats apart.[37] In the sex arcade, where the machines and lighting are often arranged to give the viewer as much privacy as possible, masturbation is permissible, even normal, as long as it is done unobtrusively and the space used is paid for.[38]

Today pornography is more widely available than prostitution, for only a small fraction of the cost. Since it does not involve an actual partner, the near-complete commercial and social impartiality evinced in prostitution becomes total and in fact may be preferred by those who, for whatever reason, do not seek an experience with a prostitute. Whether in most cases pornography is psychically preferred to an idealized sociosexual experience has little to do with its utility as an actual outlet.

Pornography is a more economical sexual experience socially and psychically than most sociosexual acts performed with prostitutes or others. Opportunity to indulge in the sexually forbidden through fantasy and identification is much greater than in the world of actual behavior ruled by social, moral, and legal inhibitions and physical limitations. Relatively few persons have actually engaged in rape or incest, for example, but many have doubtless done so vicariously through pornographic identification. The social and legal risks involved in vicarious sexual experience through pornography are low. Even where masturbation follows, the psychic costs in anxiety, shame, and guilt may be far less than in more overt social or public deviance.

Functional utility is obviously not a complete explanation of pornography's social reality. It does not rule out consequences already considered, nor does it necessarily mean that pornography does not "feed" or otherwise stimulate sociosexual behavior. Some persons have successfully incorporated pornography's portrayals of transgressive behavior into a marital or other relationship based on love and affection. Pornography (and other erotic expression once designated as such) is now so commonplace and for many persons so integrated with other aspects of the culture that almost any generalization about its functional or dysfunctional relation to the social order must be speculative. To the extent, however, that it accommodates impersonal, transitory, and "perverse" sexual interests and inclinations and discharges some of that energy vicariously or through masturbation, pornography, like prostitution, may actually "unburden" approved modes of sexual expression and behavior.

Maintaining Boundaries

Does pornography in its ubiquity and persistence have latent social utility also for those who are not its "constituents"? The possibility lies in its very depiction of transgressive behavior. As Durkheim first suggested, deviance may keep the social order intact by giving focus to common anger and indignation, actually drawing people together in an expression of the "collective conscience" and providing a sense of solidarity. He suggested that crime (and, by extension, other forms of deviance) "brings together upright consciences and concentrates them."[39] In defying the normative standards that set limits on what is acceptable and provide patterns of constancy and stability within the larger environment, deviant behavior may have the unanticipated consequence of strengthening those standards. Thus, dialectically, "what is considered normal . . . takes place with reference to what is considered deviant, and morality is given its content through the contrast provided by that which is not moral. . . . To be 'good' makes sense only in relation to being 'bad.' "[40] The sociologist Kai T. Erikson has likened these standards or boundaries to articles of common law—decisions made by the community over long periods that retain their validity through regular use as instruments of valuation. "Each time a community censures some act of deviance, then, it sharpens the authority of the violated norm and re-establishes the boundaries of the group."[41] These manifest comparisons do not merely underwrite the reward structure that serves as an incentive for conformity; they may serve also to "purge the righteous from a sense of their own sins and unworthiness and help sustain their moral identity."[42] Social and legal confrontation of deviants and ensuing publicity about their "correction" or stigmatization "constitute our main source of information about the normative outlines of society."[43]

The boundary-maintaining possibilities of pornography seem clear enough. Depiction of forbidden or otherwise unacceptable sexual behavior may help to define that which is preferred and rewarded.[44] Thus, rather than being simply a challenge to public morality, as the social pathology view holds, pornography may also contribute to the overall stability of that morality. This reasoning is not without difficulties, but it recognizes that normative standards or boundaries may not always be clearly marked or self-maintaining. They are affected by changes in the physical, social, and economic environment, and trespassing may provoke their reassertion and clarification. Pornography, which is deviant in its depictions and often in its distribution, has sometimes had such an effect. The feminist indictment of its sadomasochistic excesses and demeaning images of women is a striking example. Though based partly on doubtful assumptions of a causal relation between representations and behavior, much of the critique has been vigorous in asserting and reasserting ideals of human sexual relations based on affection and mutual respect between the sexes. In doing so, it has informed and educated—raised the public consciousness. There also seems little doubt that common anger and indignation about pornography, whether among members of an organized group or not, may develop a keener sense of social bonds and values in common. The feminist critique and protest is an example, but not the only one.

The idea of pornography as boundary-maintaining falls short, as do other views we have examined, not in being illogical, unreasonably inferred, or without empirical substantiation, but in being at best only a partial explanation of pornography's social reality. Any latent utility of pornography for defining or sharpening preferred sexual standards appears to be a by-product of its existence rather than its chief purpose. Pornography persists despite heroic efforts to counter it, because it supplies goods and services in high demand. Sexual boundaries are, in large measure, social compromises between the erotically sought and the morally enjoined. As such, they are a complex, institutionally shaped, aggregate reflection of the internal adjustments individual members of society make between what is desired, consciously or unconsciously, and what is acceptable to the conscience or superego. Trespass may sharpen the collective sense of boundary but is probably not caused by a need to patrol that boundary. At one point, Erikson goes so far as to suggest that society may actually actively recruit deviants for this purpose, as though "society" had the kind of deliberative intelligence we associate with individual consciousness and cognition. This suggestion is unnecessary; there are far more compelling explanations why pornography exists. Boundary maintenance, which mistakes a latent by-product for a chief causal agent, has much more explanatory power for the control of pornography (which we shall consider in remaining chapters) than for its existence.

Boundary-maintenance analysis tells us that in trespassing on existing norms pornography may have latent utility and contribute in a limited way to social stability. But it provides no explanation for social change. It does not tell us when or where the volume of pornography becomes so great or restrictions on it so repressive that boundaries are obliterated rather than underwritten. Nor does it explain the enormous observable variation in normative standards or boundaries from one period or society to another. Neither functional utility we have explored here—the surrogate outlet or the latent definitional role—answers these questions. We must look further, beyond social consequences and effects, to learn how pornography is socially determined and why it is so problematic.

Conflict and Designation

In setting out what is socially acceptable and unacceptable in act, belief, and representation, norms embody standards of desirability and are a key distributive element in all cultures. Couched in terms of good and bad, beautiful and ugly, pleasant and unpleasant, appropriate and inappropriate, they allocate a wide range of material, symbolic, and purely psychic rewards and deprivations. A few sexual norms, such as the incest taboo, are so well settled as to be largely beyond dispute. But others, including many dealing with expression, are much less certain and often the object of great struggle.

These norms are given effect through various rational and instrumental concerns about public morality, psychological well-being, interpersonal decencies, and the like. But our eroticized sexuality cuts across such plausible aims and purposes to link darker recesses of the conscious and unconscious mind with external objects. The internally pornographic offers a standing invitation to indulge in forbidden wishes. Anxieties produced by these desires and the need to control them are not limited to purely personal decisions and choices but are easily displaced onto social objects, especially erotic representation, for which the internally pornographic has great affinity. Thus sexual norms, especially those governing expression, can be seen by individuals as reinforcing or as undermining personal controls. The former perception is comforting; the latter may be deeply disturbing. Judgmental responses to erotic expression are often well reasoned and articulate, but we cannot say they are entirely free of unconscious determination.

Among the purely psychic rewards and penalties distributed by sexual norms are those affecting group standing. Status anxiety is often experienced when members of a once-secure group or class perceive downward movement, or when members of a socially inferior group begin to see upward movement and possibility of further advance. As the sociologist Joseph Gusfield demonstrated in his study of the century-long conflict over temperance, members may see the group's relative standing as threatened or supported depending on the degree to which its moral or cultural standards or "style of life" prevails socially or finds recognition in public policies.[45] Status concerns are often a force in "morality" issues. They are clearly present in conflict over sexual expression for a number of groups, from fundamentalist religious sects to feminists, who also have rational and instrumental concerns. Studies of antipornography campaigns show that both activists and their opponents tend to see pornography less as a single issue than as the symbol of an alternative complex of values and norms.[46]

Disputes over sexual norms are usually more difficult to negotiate than those involving material or instrumental concerns. Emotional investment is greater, and matters at stake are not the easily quantifiable and fungible ones associated with economic issues. For the participants, conflict may involve fundamental and closely held moral principles or beliefs.

As in other conflict, discord over sexual expression involves social and political processes in which dominant groups prevail. Winners are usually those with greater social and political resources, including size, wealth, prestige, organizational efficiency, unity and commitment, access to authorities, and influence on socializing institutions. Politically, then, pornography is the social designation of unacceptable sexual expression as determined by decisive groups. In primitive or traditional cultures, dominant interests can often simply impose their preferences generally and for long periods of time. But in modern, complex, socially heterogeneous societies, especially those in which political power is widely dispersed, even victories at the highest level may be incomplete and provisional and their results in specific cases problematic.

Not all conflict over sexual expression takes the form of courtroom challenges or legislative debate. Most, in fact, is barely visible to the public eye. For every major set-piece legal battle, there have been thousands of minor, even undeclared, skirmishes in micro settings or individual encounters, in which proffered transgressions succeed or are met with socially administered corrections. Much of the struggle is not openly professed or perhaps even consciously recognized. Hence social designations that eventually emerge are not merely those embodied in laws or rules, but may be found also in informal standards, conventions, implicit understandings, as well as "instructions" submerged and diffused in socialization itself. The lines drawn may have general aim or be meant to apply selectively, in limited contexts, such as "in public," "in polite society," "while ladies are present," "in front of children," and so on.[47]

The twentieth century has witnessed radical changes in norms of sexual expression, but through history most changes have been incremental, often barely discernible. A judge's decision, highly rationalized and deliberate, may be a dramatic exception if it abruptly alters the course of earlier rules, but most changes in designation have evolved rather than broken sharply from the past.

Labeling an erotic expression objectionable or nonobjectionable—pornography or not—is different from determining its actual availability. Norm and practice are rarely in full accord, one usually being more liberal or censorious than the other. This inconsistency is only partly due to variations in patterns of conflict already mentioned. Even when wide agreement exists about a designation, as it often does in relatively homogeneous settings, the psychodynamic conflict that surrounds fanta-sized transgression and that is socially mirrored in demand for both pornographic expression and its control ensures that prevailing designations will not fit perfectly with actual practices. Libertarian evasion of censorious norms and censorious evasion of liberal ones is inevitable. Extremely permissive or extremely censorious norms may be met with wide "patterned evasions."[48]

We should not conclude that changes in designation invariably involve the "delabeling" of expression once considered pornographic. History provides almost as many examples of retreats from permissiveness as of abandoned proscriptions. It is tempting to view the changes of the last quarter-century as permanent, especially if we regard some of them as enlightened (see Figure 1). The construction "erotic realism," discussed in

FIGURE 1. Some Changes in the Social Designation of Sexual Expression Since the 1950s

Representation:	Forbidden	Disapproved	Permitted	Approved
"Erotic realism"				
Punished transgression				
Unpunished transgression				
"Four-letter" words				
"Pin-up girl"				
Full female nudity				
Explicit intercourse				
Sadistic portrayal of women				

▬▬▬▬▬ present status
————— former status

Chapter 3, is an example. But we may ask whether such representation is qualitatively different from pornography, as the Kronhausens have claimed, or whether it is merely an early (and thus, for now at least, settled) delabeled category of expression in a long swing into a more sexually permissive era. However clear the nonpornographic character of erotic realism seems now, it is not hard to imagine how some of its representations were considered socially pornographic in the past and might even be so again.

We must ask again whether pornography is the completely relative category social determinations make it appear to be. Even if most labeling is the product of conflict settled by disparities in social power, are there not some representations so clearly objectionable that they are universally proscribed? Ready possibilities come to mind: sadomasochist extremes of sexual murder, torture, and mutilation, incest, bestiality, necrophilia, and abuse of children. These representations are indeed widely proscribed and would support the idea of a self-evident pornography about which one could truly say, "I know it when I see it." Yet there are difficulties with this attractive, commonsense notion. Every society or age has had its supposedly irreducible hard-core pornography, but in fact such designations have often differed from one time and place to another. Many "ultimate" pornographies have included much more than the examples just mentioned, and others less. In our own culture, many representations— pubic hair, male genitals, the word "fuck," for example—were not long ago considered self-evidently obscene. That they are no longer so may lead us to wonder whether even some of the examples mentioned earlier in the paragraph entirely qualify. Given so many pretenders, we are tempted to conclude that there is no truly universally self-evident pornography, that all proscriptions are products of the idiosyncrasies of social disapprobation. Although it is not possible to go that far, at least on the evidence we have, it does seem clear, from the vantage point of our own permissive times, that if there is self-evident or universal pornography, it is far narrower in range than previously thought.

Even if we could find an essential pornography, proscriptions limited to it would clearly fall short of satisfying the full demand for social control of sexual expression. Thus we are led once more to the relationship between socially determined pornography and the pornographic within. As we have seen, the internally pornographic ontogenetically precedes any encounters with the socially pornographic. It may be stimulated by the latter but does not depend on it for its existence or activation. Expression or communication that has been delabeled—once designated as pornography but no longer so—may nonetheless be functionally pornographic for many individuals, including some adolescents and children. All permissive or libertarian periods—our own times a prime example—superabound in delabeled representations that still retain power to arouse or repel pornographically. Disparity between the two pornographies may be evident also in expression never designated as pornographic. The commanding example here is the Bible. Old Testament tales of lust and erotic misconduct and the compelling erotic metaphor of biblical poetry have been a source of sexual information and a focus of pornographic curiosity for generations of Christians and Jews. The Bible has probably been the Western world's most widespread and unacknowledged source of symbolically based erotic stimulation. Its relative immunity from extensive censorship, often from any control at all, has done nothing to diminish this standing.

In contrast, works or representations labeled pornography are rarely functionally pornographic for everyone. Many of the books at the center of the great censorial storms of the past provide ready examples: Elinor Glyn's *Three Weeks;* Havelock Ellis's nineteenth-century study of homosexuality, *Sexual Inversion;* Joyce's *Ulysses;* James Branch Cabell's *Jurgen;* Nabokov's *Lolita;* and Lawrence's *Lady Chatterley's Lover.* Lawrence's novel, in fact, is only one of many which were not pornographic for many persons even when labeled pornography but which remained functionally pornographic for many others long after delabeling.

The primacy of the internally pornographic means that neither the censorial nor the libertarian solution to pornography can fully triumph. Even if it were possible to designate and suppress all known erotic expression, the pornographic within would not be deactivated, as many moralists seem to believe. Very likely it would find and respond to other, seemingly innocent, external stimuli, which would then be functionally pornographic. Almost any depiction, object, idea, or person may be apprehended pornographically if circumstances are inviting. The imaginative life of children and young adolescents, relatively free of encounters with pornography, illustrate the phenomenon repeatedly. Studies of relatively repressed sexual offenders and deviants that reveal erotic responsiveness to stimuli normally nonerotic bear on the same point.[49] And in the Victorian age, the most sexually repressive period in modern times, many representations and objects—the words "bull," "smock," and "belly," an exposed female ankle, the unskirted leg of a piano—nonsexual to all appearances, became eroticized for many persons.

That delabeled representations appear to lose much of their erotic power as they become more commonplace is cited by libertarians who claim that the ready availability of pornography—in effect, extensive delabeling—has a satiating effect that will cause the pornography problem to wither away. Evidence to support this proposition, however, is hard to find.[50] Where "old" pornography has lost its novelty, the loss is less likely to result from satiation than from its not being competitive with "new" pornography—more explicit or transgressive representation that has become the focus of designation.[51] Extensive delabeling invites sexual expression to press against new frontiers. As the range of existing expression labeled pornography is narrowed, the kind of pornographic expression produced becomes more extreme (see Figure 2). Functionally, delabeling is less likely to eliminate pornography generically or as a psychoeconomic institution than to make it possible for new pornography to replace old.[52]

The transformation of the individual's repressive needs into aggregate social demands ultimately places limits on delabeling. A society may be permissive or restrictive, but it cannot be absolutely free or absolutely repressive; the eroticized tension of human sexuality prevents that. External censorial judgments may label expression but cannot eradicate the pornographic within. Social delabeling may liberate expression but cannot silence the censorial authority within.

In the long-term sociopolitical calculus, as pornography presses further into forbidden territory (following delabeling of earlier pornography), its representations become increasingly threatening and objectionable to increasing numbers of persons and decisive groups. Support for delabeling is reduced and shifts in designation begin to take place. The matter may be very complicated politically (it is one we shall focus on in much of the remainder of the book). Yet clear early signs of such reaction are evident today, even though the thrust of delabeling seems not yet spent.

Conflict over sexual expression is inevitable and continuing. The determination of what is socially acceptable and unacceptable necessarily distributes psychic benefits and privations as well as the external resource of moral propriety, informed as the latter may be by ideology or perceptions of group status. In social control it is often difficult to distinguish harm

FIGURE 2.   Social and Market Availability of Pornography

	"Nonexistent"	*Forbidden (Illegal)*	*Restricted*	*Generally Available*
"Old" (delabeled) pornography				
"New" pornography				

▬▬▬▬▬▬ present status
───────── former status

from deviance and, in a larger sense, deviance from diversity. This is not to say that pornography may not be harmful to the social order or that condemnation of departures from norms are never desirable or justified. But rational, objective assessment of macro effects cannot be conclusive, given our present knowledge and understanding.

In the conventional libertarian view, absence of conclusive evidence of harmfulness, if not equal to a claim that there are no harms, at least makes a prima facie case and thus shifts the burden of proof to those seeking social control. However unexceptionable this logic may be in a courtroom, in the study of social reality a lack of preponderant evidence, though it may cast doubt, cannot alone decide an issue.

Pornography's place in the social order cannot be understood solely in terms of possible harm. There is some evidence that pornography provides surrogate sexual experience that, like prostitution, may accommodate socially troubling sexual interest and energy. Pornography may also serve to reinforce boundaries of established norms, although such utility appears to be a by-product of pornography's existence rather than its cause. These latent functions, perhaps the mirrored "underside" of the normatively informed views on the harm question, help to explain pornography's persistence socially as the internally pornographic explains it psychically.

We have already seen that pornography is widely condemned because it is experienced as *offensive* (though the possibility of harm may sometimes provide respectable rationalization for this censorial perception). Psychologically at least, offensiveness is a far more fundamental objection than the instrumental ones we have considered here and in Chapter 4. In remaining chapters, we deal with the problems this fact creates for a modern liberal democracy attempting to resolve pornography conflict through law and policy.

Chapter Six

Liberal Society, Illiberal Majority

The will of the people . . . . practically means the will of the most numerous or the most active part of the people—the majority, or those who succeed in making themselves accepted as the majority; the people consequently, may *desire to oppress a part of their number; and precautions are as much needed against this as against any other abuse of power. . . . "The tyranny of the majority" is now generally included among the evils against which society requires to be on its guard.*

John Stuart Mill

An idea of a covenant of people not to do certain things and only to do certain other things in a certain way was well known in the formative era of our polity. . . . Shall we say then that the foundations of modern democracy were undemocratic, or shall we say that Demos, no less than Rex, may . . . rule under God and the Law?

Roscoe Pound

Liberty and equality are the two principles on which liberal democracy rests. Although they have often been mutually supportive and reinforcing in the long evolution of liberal society, their relationship on many issues has been problematic. In this chapter we depart from our primary concern with pornography to look more directly at the tension between liberty and equality—specifically, between freedom of speech and social control—which seems to be a natural condition of liberal democracy. We begin with the rise of the "many" to political and cultural sovereignty and the political contract between the many, who as the "majority" are entitled to make policy, and the "few." We then assess the nature of operating tolerance and how it often fails to accord with the free speech norm. We consider the double-edged moral authority of the majority in the American system of separate powers. Finally, we look closely at the evolution of social control of sexual expression in the United States and the modern developments that have weakened the informal control once effectively imposed by the local community. The decline of informal control has resulted in a greater popular call to government and law for restriction, at the same time that judicially developed free speech doctrine has set out unprecedented protection for the expression at issue.

Our analysis contrasts with the conventional libertarian reckoning on a number of points. The aim is not to prove the latter wrong—indeed, it has been right more often than not—but to note its constriction as it moves toward absolutism and anticipates the perfection of rights. Popular social control is a particularly troubling for libertarians who are also democrats. Conventional libertarian analysis, seeing government as the enemy, typically fails to acknowledge the historically informal character of most control of sexual expression or the psychic needs of the "average" person that give formal control its popular character. It fails to come to grips with a chief paradox of liberal democracy: personal freedoms are distributed more widely than in any other kind of society, but their limitation may be sought by the many in whose very name they are secured. Nor does conventional analysis recognize that the tolerance needed to realize prescribed liberties is often much greater than most persons are willing or able to practice, or than can be commanded by court order.

Liberty and Rule of the Many

The core of democracy's operating strength is that it deals with a dissenting minority rather than a dissenting majority. Where political choice must be made between the interests or demands of the greater number and those of the lesser, the equality principle, which confers on each member of the governed at least formal civic or participatory status, must necessarily prefer the claims of the greater number. Majority rule, in turn, derives its democratic authority from its approximation of the equality principle: it is the practical and logical alternative to improbable unanimity, on the one hand, and unacceptable rule by the few, on the other.

If majority rule allows political movement of the greater number against the preferences of the lesser (whether one person or 50 percent minus one), how, in a system based on consent of the governed, can the lesser be understood to have an obligation to consent to policies they oppose? The answer, of course, is liberty for the lesser, defeated number.

Theoretically and practically, consent is construed as given at a higher level, to the system or process by which political decisions are reached, rather than to every decision or policy. This construction is justified by guarantees to the minority that it will not be repressed by an overzealous or intolerant majority and will have opportunity, through persuasion and association, to expand its numbers—that is, to become the prevailing majority. By extension, these protections apply to the smallest of minorities, the individual.

The political contract is supported by logical and practical requirements as well. Since "consent of the governed" has little meaning unless the governed can choose between or among leaders and alternative policies, only freedom to establish positions outside those of the immediate governing majority can ensure that a choice is offered. And since no ruling group, large or small, can be considered infallible, a protected minority plays an important role in checking error—hence in the very survival of the system. Liberty cannot guarantee that the mistakes of those in power will be corrected, but it does increase the chance that the issues will be raised. Without such instrumental liberty, it is doubtful whether democracy could have long survived. Yet an inherent tension remains between the rights of the many and those of the few.

Liberty and equality were less antithetical in earlier stages of liberal democracy. "Fighting faiths" of universally stated rights were easily enlisted in struggles to widen sovereignty and open the ranks of those responsible for governance. The mobilization of nobles against monarchical power in the Middle Ages and, during the Enlightenment, of a growing middle class against an aristocratic elite were struggles of a nonruling many against a ruling few. These battles were waged in the name of both liberty and equality: liberty, because the nonruling, nonconsenting many sought fewer restraints and less interference from the ruling few; equality, because that principle implicitly favors the side with the greater numbers, even where the numbers do not include the large underclass and are actually only a small fraction of the entire population.

When the many triumphed in these struggles, government became less oligarchical and more democratic. Their voices then had more nearly equal weight with those of the few. Feudal privileges and burdensome economic requirements were eliminated or rearranged and made more congenial to the new ruling elements, who now achieved "liberty." Powerful theory supported the union of liberty and equality and generalized both ideals. The victorious many, well-armed ideologically, incorporated the liberty they had won into the constitutional structure of government as a limitation on power. In the age of mass democracy, what had earlier been an institutionalizing of a new balance of power—in effect, a securing of the gains won by the many against the former ruling few and a protection of the new ruling class—became a structural and ideological barrier against popular preferences and goals.

Liberty can, of course, also be viewed as an end in itself—a right of self-fulfillment, morally antecedent to any government, hence the very aim or purpose of the good political system. In this sense, liberty is not merely a qualified political right but a necessity of personality, and democracy is reconceived as the best political means for realizing the greatest degree of freedom. Though the instrumental version of liberty has usually prevailed in political practice, elements of the more expansive view are evident in development of the American constitutional doctrine of civil liberties over the last fifty years, particularly in the Supreme Court's interpretation of the First Amendment right of freedom of speech. The libertarian side in the contemporary conflict over sexual expression clearly reflects the concept of liberty held not simply instrumentally against government but also as an end itself.

A near-absolute idea of liberty, however, is more difficult to maintain against the government of the many than when it is the ideology of the many against government of the few. Its imposed obligations no longer fall on a privileged, withholding elite or a disconnected underclass that can be politically ignored, but on everyone, where "everyone" is not only sovereign but also an audience for communication. Failure to recognize these political, social, and psychological costs is the chief weakness of the conventional libertarian position on pornography.

A purely instrumental view of liberty implies that important distinctions can and should be made between "political" expression and expression not obviously or immediately related to decision making or the political dynamics of a democratic society.[1] In terms of democratic utility, the former would be considered qualitatively more important than the latter and thus deserving of more extensive protection. Conversely, sexual expression would be largely, if not categorically, outside the pale of legal protection. Clearly, there are differences between such nonpolitical communication and that involving public issues or candidates, but those differences are better understood as matters of degree than of kind.

It is hardly necessary to cite examples of art, literature, or entertainment that have had political meaning or political effects on their audience. Nor is it possible to predict consistently which communication or information will be found politically relevant or by whom. "One man's amusement," the Supreme Court has observed, "teaches another's doctrine."[2] Moreover, expression not normally considered political may well lead to a more informed appreciation not merely of issues but of the values implicit in them. The very entitlement to communicate, to receive communication, and to have access to diverse communications is a factor in development of the capacity to think for oneself and make discriminating choices critical to being a participating member of a democratic polity.

An even more compelling reason for hesitating to make too sharp a distinction between political and nonpolitical expression lies in the theoretical interrelation of all knowledge and information, a phenomenon especially evident in public issues. In the ontogeny of an individual's position or point of view, political issues and concerns, reflecting as they do nonpolitical matters that have progressed to a stage of public conflict, are relatively late objects of attention. Informed political positions and intelligent choices are thus apt of require scores, perhaps even thousands, of prior decisions about various nonpolitical matters—whose relation to political issues may not have been at first apparent. Almost any matter may become political, and almost every circumstance of political choice is a derivative of others that were nonpolitical. It is virtually impossible to say in advance what information or knowledge may later be relevant to political choice.

If we view the differences between political and nonpolitical expression as differences of degree rather than category, as it seems we must, we strengthen the case for protecting the nonpolitical. At the same time, since we cannot say that no utilitarian differences exist between what is immediately and critically political and what is not, or that none exist among diverse forms of nonpolitical expression, theoretically some differences may justify differences in the *degree* of protection. This matter is set out in greater detail in Chapter 8.

The Supreme Court's policy on sexual expression has been based largely on categorical distinctions between the "obscene" and the "not obscene" and thus between totally protected and totally unprotected speech. When this approach is part of an expansive free speech doctrine, the result is a very narrow category of unprotected speech and a category of protected speech that not only exceeds what popular tolerance can support but runs far beyond it. As we shall argue in Chapter 8, the obscenity doctrine would be better formulated if "obscene" were not conceived to be an intrinsic quality of expression and if the concepts of protected and unprotected sexual expression were subject to circumstantial analysis.

Ultimately, a liberal democracy must reconcile and continuously adjust the demanding philosophical and constitutional requirements of a free speech society with the political, social, and psychological needs of a mass democratic one. It must determine what is *sufficient* protection for the dissenting or self-expressive minority or individual against the possibility of repressive action by the many and their agents, and what is *too much* protection, allowing the dissenting or self-expressive minority or individual to frustrate the many in its attempt to bring power to bear on problems, establish common purposes, and realize goals sought by the greater part of society. We will consider this problem as it applies to sexual expression and its control in the remainder of this chapter and in Part IV.

The Democratization of Culture

Liberal democratic society transforms much of the sacredness of authority and hierarchy in traditional societies into the moral equality of individuals as members of society and the moral sovereignty of individuals en masse. This shift in the civic and sociological center of gravity characterizes what Daniel Lerner has called the "participant society," in which democratic governance is typically a crowning institution:

People participate in the public life of their country by having opinions about many matters which in the isolation of traditional society did not concern them . . . [and] on a variety of issues and situations which they may never have experienced directly. . . . The governed develop the habit of having opinions, and expressing them, because they expect to be heeded by their governors. The governors, who had been shaped by the expectation and share it, in turn expect the expression of *vox populi* on current issues of public policy.[3]

But the power of opinion in the participant society is not confined— indeed, could not be confined—solely to public affairs and governance. In the developed democracy, the purchasing power of the mass of the population has established a kind of popular sovereignty in the marketplace of goods and services. A vast increase in leisure time is complemented by near-universal literacy, and the extension of education generally, to produce a similar effect in the marketplace of culture. Modern society's capacity to generate and transmit information, portrayals, and representations of all sorts is virtually unlimited; the capacity of the mass of the population to consume these products is unparalleled. In expanding opportunities for both critical judgment and the sharing in decision, mass democracy is a consensual society in its moral outline and in much of its operating reality.

Before the industrial revolution, the established cultural tradition in most Western societies was formed by high, elite culture and folk culture. The latter, mainly rural and local and having its social roots in the peasantry, was reflected in such forms as folk art, handicrafts, the carnival, untranscribed ballads, dramatizations by traveling players, and the like. It was homespun, fragmented and relatively anonymous. High culture was the province of the court, aristocracy, church, and later the new merchant class, who had some education and the resources to subsidize a small number of artists and intellectuals. Their products, though addressed to a small part of the population, were recognized as *the* art or culture of the society. These distinctions between "high" and "folk" correspond closely to those in the distribution of power: in audience and standard, high culture was anything but democratic; folk culture was anything but sovereign and exclusive.

The forces of commercial and industrial revolution transformed cultural life no less than economic and political life. The presence of an educated and propertied middle class weakened aristocratic domination of high culture and partially released the artist from the mixed blessings of patronage. Relatively homogeneous and concentrated for the most part in and around cities, the new middle class formed a large cultural constituency that soon discovered its own needs and tastes and made its own demands. Formal cultural production that included "entertainment" became a profitable enterprise and industry in its own right.[4] The nineteenth century saw the general *embourgeoisement* of culture in Britain and much of the Western world. A "popular" culture distinct from both high and folk culture traditions in its sociology, aesthetics, and means of production, began to make its appearance, at the same time that the aristocratic hold on high culture weakened. Both developments were the inevitable result of the economic, political, and finally social triumphs of the middle class.

Industrialization provided the technical means for mass production of cultural goods. Nowhere was the effect more dramatic than in communication. By the late nineteenth century, inexpensive high-speed reproduction of printed words and pictures, along with improved methods of distribution, had given rise to the first modern mass media. In the twentieth, communications technology created entirely new media—sound recordings, motion pictures, and broadcasting—readily accessible to a mass audience and soon economically dependent on that audience. When these remarkable advances were complemented by a steady increase in the average person's free time and real income, they spurred the tremendous growth of a preempting popular or mass culture that marks the twentieth century's democratization of society. Folk culture was eclipsed, and high culture's former dominion as the "public" and visible culture was successfully challenged.[5]

It is through symbolic expression and representation that cultures supply information, transmit values, and project a wide variety of collective and individual aspirations and fears. These communications—art, literature, music, drama, design, news, opinion, advertising, entertainment—have much to do with how members of a society spend their free time. They reflect the underlying sociology of culture and are profoundly affected by changes in it. The products of emerging popular or mass culture were aimed at the audience of the many rather than the few. Unlike creations of high culture, which tend to be exclusive, thematically complex, and often seek new ways of recording and integrating experience, mass culture tends to offer that which is less profound or challenging. As Russel Nye observed:

[Its] standards of comprehension and achievement are received from consensus; it must be commonly approved, pervasive in the population, "popular" in the sense that the majority of people like and endorse it and will not accept marked deviations from its standards and conventions. . . . The popular artist corroborates (occasionally with great skill and intensity) values and attitudes already familiar to his audience; his aim is less to provide a new experience than to validate an older one. Predictability is important to the effectiveness of popular art; the fulfillment of expectation, the pleasant shock of recognition of the known, the verification of an experience already familiar—as in the detective story, the Western, the popular song, the Edgar Guest poem.[6]

A work of high culture is likely to have its reference in an aesthetic, literary, or scientific tradition largely independent of its audience. There is little similar autonomy in the products of mass culture. Nor can great weight be given to preferences of the individual or the few. A product of mass culture must seek the largest common denominator, and not be far off the median level of expectation. The popular artist "cannot disturb or offend any significant part of his public: though the elite artist may and should be a critic of his society, the popular artist cannot risk alienation."[7] He and the proprietor of the products of mass culture work under the same limitations as the democratic politician. The one is responsive to and ultimately controlled by votes and opinion, the other by countless decisions made at newsstands, box offices, and radio and television dials.

Transmitted representations are, in effect, cultural distributions: they say something about what is good and bad, true and untrue, appropriate and inappropriate. Thus members of the audience often make considerable social and psychological investment in them. These symbolic goods may reflect real or imagined differences in systems of belief, styles of life, the status of groups or other discriminations of social pluralism. And, since the range of substantive depiction is always greater than that of behavior, they may also touch on temptations or conflicts inhibited in the behavioral world or denied in the conscious mind.

Representations and symbols have always been objects of concern and contention, but perhaps never more so than when rendered through the power of modern communications. Cast into print on a page or images on a screen, a norm or standard acquires authority and acceptability by its very form and concreteness. Thus, for many persons, normative statements transmitted through the mass media are seen to be as much in force as laws or public policies. In this, representational differences between high and mass cultures pay an inevitable debt to underlying sociological differences. In the words of Leo Rosten:

The sheer size of an audience crucially influences the content of what is communicated to it. Taboos, in movies and television, are not simply the fruit of cowardice among producers; . . . [they] are often functions of audience size, age-range, and heterogeneity. Things can be communicated to the few which cannot be communicated (at least not in the same way) to the many.[8]

In the matter of sexual expression, mass culture is more conservative than high culture. Its audience supports a much narrower range of representation and is less tolerant of departures from it. This is especially true of pornography, which depicts the violation of established taboos that may be highly functional socially or psychologically. A few persons, by reason of personality, education, or ideology, are much less confined by these repressive barriers or, as in the pornographic imagination, may actually seek to overcome them, but as we shall see in the next chapter, much larger numbers—in fact, a vast majority—prefer not to be disturbed or confronted. As a "culture constituency," they tend to be uncomfortable with moral ambiguity or irresolvable erotic conflict, preferring representations "upholding tradition and maintaining order against irrepressible sexual impulses and other upsetting influences."[9]

The matter is not simply one of "middle-class morality" (unless that term is taken to mean the standards of mass culture itself). The supposedly greater sexual freedom and licentiousness of the working class is sometimes cited as evidence of a kind of "triple standard" in which both the upper and lower social ranks are sexually less inhibited and less censorious than the middle.[10] Such a sociology of morals may have had descriptive accuracy in earlier stages of the democratization of culture, in Britain before the mid-nineteenth century, for example, when the lower classes lacked education, free time, and even modest levels of disposable income and had not yet become constituents of a popular culture. But its general validity is doubtful for the modern working class. Although actual sexual experience may still be acquired earlier and more easily in the working class than in other social groups, it does not mean that its members are less inhibited in the face of *representations* of sexuality. Richard Hoggart observes in his study of twentieth-century British working-class culture:

The nearness to the surface accompanies, as social workers sometimes point out, a great shyness about some aspects of sex—about discussing it "sensibly," about being naked, or even about undressing for the act of sex, or about sophistications in sexual behavior. Even today few working-class parents seem to tell their children anything about sex. . . . But they are not deliberately leaving it aside because they know the street-gang will do the work for them; indeed, they are likely to be greatly upset if they find their children talking "dirty." They leave it, I think, partly because they are not good teachers, are neither competent in nor fond of exposition, prefer knowledge to come incidentally, by means of apothegm and proverb; and partly because of this shyness about bringing sex to the conscious and "sensible" level. And this will apply as much to the man who, in a suitable context, will talk sex as freely as his mates, as to his perfectly "cleanmouthed" wife.[11]

As we shall note more fully in the next section, attitudes of persons in lower ranks, as measured by income, education, occupation, and the like, are relatively censorious of sexual expression.

Democratization of culture does not mean that the resulting mass or popular culture is conservative in any absolute sense. The evolution of modern society has been accompanied, as Michel Foucault observed, by a "veritable discursive explosion" concerning sex, sexuality, and sexual life.[12] Contemporary mass culture reflects the sexual "revolution" that has overtaken all Western societies in the last two generations. These changes in attitude and behavior mark a massive underlying cultural shift, leaving mass culture today much less restricted in sexual expression than ever before. Nevertheless, however we choose to describe contemporary standards, the sexual revolution has not much changed the relative psychological and sociological differences between the culture of the many and that of the few. These differences underlie and underwrite much of the conflict surrounding the designation of what is and is not objectionable sexual expression.

In a mass democracy, the standards of the many effect social control of expression not only through the marketplace but also through popular agencies of government and private pressures brought to bear directly and informally. When basic sexual norms are in flux and communications are more pervasive than ever before, popular standards can be expected to be in almost perpetual conflict with communication rights given unparalleled libertarian interpretation.

Tolerance as an Elite Ethic

Freedom of expression—the right to communicate and be communicated with—is at the core of liberty in liberal and liberal democratic society. In a more general sense, we may call this the free speech norm, since it is a matter of attitude and ideology as well as of legal right. At its highest level, it is embodied in the compelling vision of a "free marketplace of ideas," in which truth and wisdom are believed most likely to emerge where information and competition among views and opinion are unimpeded. In effect, good ideas or expression will drive out bad—like an inverse of Gresham's law of currency dynamics. Mill explained this operation most concisely:

the peculiar evil of silencing the expression of an opinion is that it is robbing the human race, posterity as well as the existing generation—those who dissent from the opinion, still more than those who hold it. If the opinion is right, they are deprived of the opportunity of exchanging error for truth; if wrong, they lose, what is almost as great a benefit, the clearer perception and livelier impression of truth produced by its collision with error.[13]

Hyde Park is thus not merely a corner of the city but a model for the entire society. The norm and its free marketplace ideal find reference in scores of First Amendment decisions made over the last fifty years. By that measure at least, free speech is probably the centerpiece of our official liberal democratic ideology, although in actual application the Supreme Court has tended to hold back from embracing its implicit absolutism.

Our concern here is not whether the tantalizing and all but unverifiable premises of this civic faith are valid, but how the underlying norm applies as a governing rule of modern democracy. To be at all operational, a free speech norm requires a high level of practicing tolerance—a forbearance from suppression or other restriction of expression found disagreeable or threatening, in effect, a willingness to put up with what one rejects or opposes.[14]

In spite of the attractive optimism of such libertarians as Mill and Jefferson about the perfectibility of citizenship in the liberal democratic state, and in spite of the impressive gains free expression has registered, the long and continuing record of the suppression of unwanted ideas and punishment of those expressing them suggests that practicing tolerance may be not only difficult but "unnatural."

Perhaps the impulse to strike out against opponents or ideas that one finds frightening or hateful is a survival mechanism, a product of the evolutionary process. Most creatures survive by recognizing their enemies and learning how to cope with them. If one has sufficient strength and cunning to repel the enemy, one is inclined to do so unless one has discovered that, for some reason, another type of response is legally or socially required, or preferred.[15]

Tolerance exacts social and psychological costs. Granting a right—a freedom or liberty—to one person or group requires imposing an obligation on others, thus diminishing their own opportunities to act. Although a right established may arguably be available to anyone, the redistributive aspects of tolerance are often salient for most persons: the more freedom for one individual or group, the less for another. Ideas expressed by others may challenge one's own beliefs and shake whatever cognitive and psychic certainty and security those beliefs afford. Alien expression may thus be confounding or deeply disturbing, even touching elemental fears or wishes that are imperfectly understood or partly unconscious.

We learn about the value of free speech in school and through informal teaching, but the "social learning" we need to comprehend and internalize this norm also depends on factors of personality and perception that may not be widely distributed in the human population. To grasp the principles that justify tolerance, including the paradox of reciprocity and the complex and essential instrumental role tolerance plays in maintaining a liberal democratic system, requires a superior cognitive capacity and intellectual sophistication. A tolerant response is less reflexive than an intolerant one; it is more likely to depend on deliberation, a weighing of alternatives and their consequences.[16] Tolerance rests not simply on a capacity to make rational assessment of threat, but also on acceptance of one's own fallibility and life's uncertainties. This acceptance, in turn, may depend on being free from the impediments to self-esteem manifest in projection, displacement, and other psychological defenses that help an uncertain ego manage conflict within, but that invariably produce intolerant responses. This is not to say that intolerance is always the product of psychic or cognitive deficiencies or that it may never be a considered, rational response to external danger, but rather that tolerance, as a reliable operating response anticipated by the free speech norm, may require a level of "social learning" and emotional security difficult for most persons to achieve.[17]

These general observations are corroborated by a large number of opinion and attitude studies. The latter have repeatedly shown tolerance to vary with the level of abstraction at which rights are considered. Support for freedom of expression and other individual liberties is high when those rights are phrased as general principles, but falls sharply when specific application is made in concrete situations. Generally, the free speech norm is most likely to be supported by those who have been most exposed to it and are best able to comprehend it.[18] Closer examination reveals tolerance to be correlated positively with the demographic factors usually associated with social class: education, income, occupational status, and so on. Persons ranking higher in these categories, especially education, tend to be more supportive of the free speech norm in actual application than persons ranking lower. Tolerance is greater among community notables, publicly active persons, and other opinion leaders than among the general population. And though support for the norm varies with the degree of perceived threat, it is also positively related to psychological and personality variables, such as openness, self-esteem, security, flexibility, and a relative lack of dogmatism.[19]

Tolerance tends to be higher in the older and more traditional areas of free speech, involving public affairs and policies, for example, than in matters of morality, life-style, and most questions of sexual expression and behavior. When mass/elite differences are examined in this light, tolerance is highest among the elite on the older, more traditional dimensions of free speech, and lowest in the general public on the newer issues of sexual morality. A leading survey, for example, found that opinion leaders were evenly divided over whether laws should aim to "enforce the community's standards of right and wrong" rather than to "protect a citizen's right to live by any moral standards he chooses"; but more than twice as many members of the general public preferred the enforcement function to that of protection.[20]

To the question whether it would be "right for a community to adopt laws which try to stamp out sin—such as prostitution, gambling, pornography, etc.," only 18 percent of the general public answered negatively compared with 25 percent of "community leaders" and 41 percent of lawyers and judges. Similarly, half the opinion leaders, but only about a third of the general public, agreed that "censoring obscene books is an old-fashioned idea that no longer makes sense," or that movies that "use foul language or show nudity and sexual acts on the screen should have as much right to be shown as other films."[21] Mass/elite opinion differences on various questions of sexual expression and its social control are summarized in Table 1.

Evidence in the table, which is consistent with findings in other polls and surveys, discussed in Chapter 7, on the acceptability of sexual expression, reveals low levels of stated tolerance in the mass public, in absolute and relative terms. The level is lower than that for community leaders in every statement in Table 1. On none of the propositions does it reach 50 percent. Even more striking is the difference between the mass public and lawyers and judges—that segment of the elite public most likely to be involved in formulating, rationalizing, and articulating the scope and limits of the free speech norm. The average support for the tolerant response in the nine statements in Table 1 is 60 percent for the lawyers and judges and 36 percent for the mass public.

The free speech norm is, in effect, an elite prescription. Consistent voluntary observance can realistically be expected from only a relatively small number of persons who are favored in their cognitive and psychological endowments and often in their social status as well. The libertarian faith was itself formulated at a time when participants in the marketplace of ideas were a small and relatively privileged number and their effective audience a modest fraction of the entire population. We do not mean to suggest that tolerance can be expected only from members of an upper social, economic, or political stratum or that all members of such strata support the free speech norm. But most persons, perhaps a vast majority, whatever their social or economic background, may be hard pressed to be tolerant in most concrete situations. This striking fact is often denied in conventional libertarian thinking, where actual deviations from the norm are typically seen as the fault of government rather than its constituents. The elite character of the norm itself tends to be obscured by uncompromising optimism about the perfectibility of citizenship.

TABLE 1. Tolerance of the Mass Public, Community Leaders,
and Legal Elite on Matters of Sexual Expression

Tolerance Proposition	Percentage Agreeing		
	Mass Public	Community Leaders	Legal Elite
Novels describing explicit sex acts should be permitted in the library if they are worthwhile literature	42	57	73
Pornographic films are mostly harmless, even if some people find them distasteful	33	48	67
When it comes to pornographic films about sex, people should be allowed to see anything they want to, no matter how "filthy" it is	38	43	56
The Postmaster General should have no right to decide what kind of books or magazines can be sent through the mails	41	48	68
Television programs that show people actually making love should be permitted as long as they are shown in the late evening during adult viewing hours	30	31	42
Selling pornographic films, books, and magazines is really a victimless crime and should therefore be left unregulated	23	31	46
Censoring obscene books is an old-fashioned idea that no longer makes sense	29	39	54
Giving a federal board of censors the power to decide which TV programs can or cannot be shown violates the public's right to watch what it pleases	39	45	55
The movie industry should be free to make movies on any subject it chooses	46	61	81
Average for nine propositions	36	45	60

Source. Adapted from McClosky and Brill, *Dimensions of Tolerance*, pp. 60–62.

The Four Faces of Tolerance

How can a modern democracy be liberal and remain so when tolerance appears to be limited and problematic? How can the elite ethic be reconciled with strong popular misgivings about sexual expression or be sustained in the face of popular wishes for control of that expression? The free speech norm in operation falls short of its libertarian prescription, yet it is approximated far more closely than would be possible solely through the elite ethic of volitional tolerance.

To probe this paradox, we must look beyond the idea of tolerance as simply a civic posture or an attribute of personality. We do that by considering tolerance as *operating public behavior* rather than the product of ideology or attitude. As such, it is more likely to be a mirror image of popular intolerance than a phenomenon in its own right. We may think of effective tolerance then as a manifold operative restraint on the power of the censorially bent "many." Such restraint may be *self-imposed,* in which tolerance is freely accorded; *manipulated,* in which tolerance is guided; *circumstantial,* in which tolerance occurs through default; and *forced,* in which tolerance is commanded. We shall consider briefly each of these and how it relates to sexual expression.

In the light of history's many sorry episodes of popular intolerance, skeptics might dismiss majority self-restraint as mere wishful thinking. Yet no less a "realist" than Learned Hand pointed to the importance of such restraint in his celebrated reflection on liberty and the law:

Liberty lies in the hearts of men and women; when it dies there, no constitution, no laws, no court can save it; no constitution, no law, no court can even do much to help it. While it lies there it needs no constitution, no law, no court to save it.[22]

Lacking a ready measure of self-restraint, we may all too easily take its presence for granted or overlook it entirely. But liberal democracy probably could not have survived its earliest years or maintain itself today without some degree of popular self-restraint. Philosophical recognition of individual rights and glorification of them as general principles of political life are unquestionably among liberal democracy's great and necessary achievements. Widespread support for these freedoms in the abstract, repeatedly evident in contemporary tolerance studies, testifies to this fact. Optimistic developmentalists such as Jefferson, noting the close association of tolerance and education, go further and argue that proper socialization will lead to even greater tolerance for expression and other rights in everyday affairs. Yet, whatever we may concede to Learned Hand's observation at the level of general principles and however libertarian our official ideology may be, it is clear from both tolerance studies and everyday experience that the free speech norm cannot be approximated solely through popular tolerance freely accorded. This fact holds for any democracy, and especially for the heterogeneous mass society.

That the majority can be restrained by being led to tolerance finds a place in the larger notion of rule by a democratic elite.[23] For the free speech norm, it rests on the well-established finding that public leaders and politically active persons at all levels are generally more libertarian than the population at large and are much more likely to support the norm in concrete situations.[24] Thus the elite, through exhortation, reasoned argument, the power of example, or other enlistment, can appeal to and bring into play the larger population's allegiance to the abstract ideal. There is little doubt that allegiance to an ideal is an exploitable resource in the hands of skilled leadership, whose very expectation of popular tolerance may be a self-fulfilling general prophecy. This kind of influence was a factor in much of the early development of individual rights in our own nation. But optimism about the capacity or will of a political elite to inspire or otherwise manipulate the larger population to higher levels of practicing tolerance may be less justified in the democratic society of the late twentieth century. Can modern heterogeneous elites be relied on to recognize their libertarian "obligations"? And if so, will they normally be sufficiently independent to maneuver in the face of popular demands for social control?[25] Here the past provides no ready answers.

Tolerance comes about through default where the separation, dispersal, or fragmentation of power prevents a censorious majority from mobilizing effectively or being well enough positioned to turn government against a particular target. Here, in effect, the free speech norm becomes the residual beneficiary of majority frustration circumstantially induced. True, structural dispersal of power has been partially overcome by long-term centralizing trends that require power to be amassed and concentrated. But the heterogeneity and sheer size of modern democracy cause these trends to have fragmenting effects of their own, demographically and ideologically, and add to the majority's difficulty in bringing its full weight to bear on an issue. Tolerance through default is likely to be a greater factor in larger, more pluralistic cities and towns than in small, relatively homogeneous communities where intimacy, like-mindedness, and insularity serve as partial antidotes to the dispersal of power. In specific conflicts, such tolerance may have a secondary effect of providing political leadership with freedom to seek a more libertarian result than would otherwise be possible. But in the smaller community, circumstantial tolerance, less firmly established, may give way to social control imposed informally and even extralegally.

We have no gauge of the amount of tolerance that occurs through the fragmentation of power, and in fact we seldom bother to conceptualize it. Yet there can be little doubt that its silent operation underwrites much of the working applicability of the free speech norm. It may be viewed as a vital element of Madisonian or federalist democracy, but, fundamentally, it is neither liberal nor democratic. Its grudging character and inherent instability are actually discordant with our official ideology of rights and do not inspire libertarian peace of mind. Nor is the circumstantial popular frustration on which it rests conducive to a popular sense of efficacy in the enterprise of self-government.

Tolerance may be a product of command decision where the free speech norm is given legal effect through constitutional or statutory rights against government. In the traditional libertarian formulation, these rights prevail over all other interests to protect the freedom of everyone in the name of the individual. Government is seen as the major threat to free expression, while the mass of the population, loyal to the abstract ideal, are relieved to have censorious authorities checked in concrete situations. Each citizen presumably imagines that but for the grace of circumstance, he or she might be the endangered party. In casting government as the adversary, this "civics text" notion tends to obscure the underlying tension between individual rights and majority power. Protecting every person in the name of one person, a small but inspired step ideologically, is in fact a giant step in the political dynamics of democratic society. To be sure, there are many occasions in which the impetus for governmental restrictions originates entirely with authorities. But government, which often finds it easier not to act, typically censors or imposes control in morality matters because it is an agent, responding to demands of constituents who have succeeded in marshaling themselves and overcoming the barriers of dispersed power.

In concrete situations, legal or constitutional protections of the free speech norm are, in effect, forced tolerance. Government is blocked in its exercise of social control and forbidden to interfere further. To the extent that the authorities have acted as agent for a censorious majority, the majority must swallow its discontent, at times grudgingly. This is not to say that forced tolerance, whatever the residual dissatisfaction, may not be preferable to intolerance. But we should not be misled by the more idealized rationalizations on which constitutional protections often rest or about the array of forces in struggles over sexual expression.

Constitutional rights are held against government rather than against one's neighbors or the majority. Because they are both materially and psychologically costly to invoke, rights are not formally claimed with great frequency. And when they are, it is often at late stages of a conflict. Constitutional protections dramatically invoked may shine as beacons of inspiration and encouragement to those who would exercise their freedom, and may thus serve to "educate" a body politic. Yet they are not well suited to filling or monitoring the interstices of social life where, in fact, the real lines between freedom and control are drawn much more often than not. The availability of legally enforceable rights against government obscures the popular character of the censorship interest. Here, the conventional libertarian view tends to misconceive the nature not only of the enemy but of the conflict. Its formalism overestimates the efficacy of legal power in the same way that another kind of formalism often overestimates the efficacy of military power, applied to problems essentially social and political in character.

No single source of tolerance—popular support for liberties in the abstract, a political elite that tends to be more libertarian than the general public, dispersal of power, or formal constitutional guarantees—is alone sufficient to give the free speech norm wide operating effect. But taken together, they complement one another and clearly qualify the United States as a *liberal* democracy among nations. The ethos of individual rights they have underwritten as a parallel to democracy is one of the great achievements of American politics. Yet the approximation of the free speech norm they make possible ensures that conflict over what is expressed and communicated will be sustained, especially when that expression evokes a ready emotional response. Indeed, public controversy over sexual expression has been a more or less constant feature of the American political and social landscape for more than a century. Whether viewed as a struggle against repression or as a struggle to prevent offending, possibly harmful expression, the pornography issue has an unavoidable and probably permanent place on the public agenda of modern liberal mass democratic society.

We turn now to the development of the free speech norm and how it has applied to sexual expression. Our concern is chiefly with tolerance *not* freely accorded, that is, with circumstantial and enforced restraints on majority power and with what these restraints imply for majority rule and the equality principle.

Power Divided

Modern democracy evolved from early struggles of a "larger few" against a "smaller few," an aristocracy against a monarch and later a rising middle class against an aristocracy. Individual liberties have usually been by-products of the triumphs of larger groups in these struggles and, initially, have had relatively little to do with the mass of the population. Liberal democracies are almost always liberal first, at least for their dominant elite, and then democratic. No doubt many persons in the old elites saw individual liberties as the natural right of every person, but for the elite as a class, liberties were part of a larger self-interested concern to limit the power of government. Individual liberties not only afford some protection against the reassertion of oppressive policies, but also help to keep any governing group from gaining undue control over private interests and, in an age of burgeoning democracy, to keep a popular majority from using governmental power for its own ends against those vested interests.

Because there had been no feudal tradition or established aristocracy in the English colonies in America, there was no need to fear a resurgence of the ancien régime. But the various elites who made the new nation were concerned about protecting their own positions against bothersome government interference. They constructed a central government that would not threaten dominant local interests and limited all government sufficiently to prevent its capture by popular majorities, who, many believed, were disposed to a leveling of wealth.

This latter fear, of course, was ill founded. The new nation soon became the very symbol of capitalist opportunity and social mobility. Frontiers were to be explored, communities built, resources exploited, and fortunes made. Almost anyone wishing to acquire land could do so, sometimes virtually for the asking. In a country that was both spacious and socially fluid, the dissatisfied or simply unsuccessful could leave their community and seek a future elsewhere. The fruits of an ever-expanding economy and the services of a seemingly endless flow of immigrants to replace the upwardly mobile confirmed the promise of continuously improving social and material status. Economic success reduced tensions over property and material values and made such conflict manageable. In spite of the formal political restraints placed in its path, the American majority had little inclination to attack property. In Louis Hartz's apt metaphor, that majority was "an amiable shepherd dog kept forever on a lion's leash."[26]

At the same time, fear of a *national* majority that might threaten local or regional interests was natural in a heterogeneous nation founded on a multitude of localities and soon to experience the imperatives of centralization. Tension between a potential hub and the outlying parts put the question of local (and state) autonomy near the top of the American political agenda, where it has remained. In the early years, the concern of the elite about the political freedom of individuals and minority interests was overshadowed by its vested interest in protecting property and local autonomy. The entire nation waged a successful struggle in the name of liberty, and it seemed unlikely that a people who had thrown off one oppressive political yoke would reinstate another with its own hands.

In the end, it was the concerns about material opportunity and local advantages that produced a national constitutional structure that carefully and elaborately separated powers: dividing responsibilities between the central government and the states, establishing three coequal branches in the central government, and providing for indirect election of the chief executive and the upper legislative chamber and a judiciary appointed rather than elected. This structural diffusion and putative balancing of power—the Madisonian solution—superimposed on the social pluralism of a spacious and still expanding country was thought sufficient to hold the majority and any factional power in check. A majority might—and was indeed expected to—control some element of the government, but diffusion would make it difficult for a popular interest to gain all or even most power and to use it oppressively against property or against local interests.

For good measure, a list of specific liberties—the Bill of Rights—was added to the constitutional structure as a further limitation on the central government. Casting these checks as individual rights was appropriate. Real abuses of civil liberties were known, especially during the Revolution, and some individual rights had been declared in state constitutions. Moreover, individual rights occupied a key hortatory place in liberal democracy's "fighting faith"—those inalienable, individualistic goals that had philosophically sustained past struggles against oppressive power, including the American War of Independence.

In fact, the Bill of Rights was a concession by one elite, a conservative leadership seeking a stronger central government and a manufacturing economy, to other elites, well established locally, whose interests were in an agrarian economy and who, for that reason, were likely to have somewhat more popular support. One of the aims of the constitutional settlement was to keep life in a state, or locality, including relations between individuals and state and local authority, largely beyond reach of the central government. In this sense, the generously phrased Bill of Rights was as much an expression of federalism as of libertarianism. The great list of rights was not originally intended to protect individual liberty against social control by state and local government or by local majorities.

Official formulation of individual liberties in the new nation was thus largely the work of competing and cooperating elites seeking, in the first instance, to protect property and local interests by limiting governmental power. It is unclear how much actual personal freedom, including the freedom of expression, was in fact protected from state or local authority acting as an agent of social control for a dominant local elite or majority. The free speech norm was not well tested or well established as an operating principle. This state of affairs is not unusual in the evolution of a liberal democracy, nor does it preclude a genuine interest in protecting personal freedom. It does suggest that libertarian nostalgia for the past is best indulged with caution. Individual liberties were not immaculately conceived, despite the uncompromising language in which they were cast and the natural rights philosophy from which they drew much of their ideological support. They were promoted and defended with mixed motives. Their greatest statement, the Bill of Rights, applied only to government and only one government among many.

The Moral Authority of the Majority

Within fifty years of its founding, the American republic had become the world's most democratic state. Opportunities for popular participation and control widened steadily, especially in the many small communities scattered over its length and breadth. The evolving democracy was not simply one of political rights and processes; it was also a state of mind. The equality principle seemed everywhere triumphant, thrusting well beyond the polity. The observant Tocqueville focused on this remarkable and unsettling fact in *Democracy in America*. He saw democracy as the wave of the future and thought its American forerunner would lead in one of two directions. Equalitarianism could encourage independence, self-reliance, pride, political competence, and self-confidence as substitutes for the servitude and dependence that had been so often the political fate of the multitude in the past. Or it might lead instead to a breakdown of liberty, reducing men and women to the uniformity and mediocrity of the lowest common denominator. Tocqueville was not optimistic about the result. Writing when Jacksonian democracy was in full flower, he saw a somewhat different majority from the one that troubled Madison and the other founders. Property was not in danger. The typical American, encouraged by laissez-faire and by what seemed to be unlimited opportunity for gain, was too busy with material pursuits to pay much attention to unevenness of distribution. The majoritarian threat Tocqueville saw was to the mind and spirit, hence to the imperatives of moral and intellectual life and the social order informed by them. Vaunted American individualism, a natural counterweight to popular power, seemed to have spent itself entirely in material pursuit. And in the absence of the natural authority of the old European status society, America had created the only authority compatible with its ideology of equality, the authority of equal citizens en masse—the majority.

When the inhabitant of a democratic country compares himself individually with all those about him, he feels with pride that he is the equal of any one of them; but when he comes to survey the totality of his fellows and to place himself in contrast with so huge a body, he is instantly overwhelmed by the sense of his own insignificance and weakness. The same equality that renders him independent of each of his fellow citizens, taken severally, exposes him alone and unprotected to the influence of the greater number. The public, therefore, among a democratic people has a singular power, which aristocratic nations cannot conceive; for it does not persuade others to its beliefs, but it imposes them and makes them permeate the thinking of everyone by a sort of enormous pressure of the mind of all upon the individual intelligence.[27]

This situation had already come to pass in the United States, where the majority raising "formidable barriers around liberty of opinion . . . lives in the perpetual utterance of self-applause." Worse, in Tocqueville's famous warning, these circumstances provide the social and moral basis for an actual "tyranny of the majority." Pervasive conformity meant that the political structure of the country, instead of ensuring limited or balanced government, actually abetted oppression by the majority. "I do not mean to say," he wrote, "that there is a frequent use of tyranny in America at the present day; but . . . that there is no sure barrier against it." That which would "mitigate the government" was to be found not in its laws or structures but in the "circumstances and manners of the country."[28] About the latter he was not sanguine.

Tocqueville's formulation of a pretyrannical conformity of thought and habit is insightful, not for its prediction—as yet unfulfilled—of unbounded majority oppression, but for what it explains about the complexity of social control. The majority, or "many," can work its will through the agency of government by passing laws and making policies enforceable through legal penalties. The framers believed that such political power would be circumscribed and diffused through the separation of powers, making it harder even for a popular faction to coordinate overwhelming political force and to use it abusively. But interests can also be pursued informally, outside of government; most desired values and unwanted costs in life are, in fact, distributed nonauthoritatively, that is, without governmental action. Tocqueville saw that the majority would have its way as much through "public sentiment," or climate of opinion, as through law itself. Goals could be achieved and standards imposed by the force of social pressure underwritten not by legal sanctions but by the social, psychological, and even economic costs attached to criticism, scolding, ridicule, ostracism, and the like. Such social control could reach into areas that political power, dispersed or circumscribed, might find difficult to penetrate, and be all the more effective for so often being unspoken and unseen.

Conformity of this sort would not be possible if most persons did not believe that the majority—in effect, the collective opinion of one's fellows—was right. Such a belief allows the majority to prevail with an easy conscience. And even though the equality principle does not require this article of faith, it is easily misconstrued as doing so. As David Spitz observed in the 1950s:

The individual who dissents from the judgment of the majority, who refuses to adhere to the opinions of the ruling power, thereby appears to place himself in an anomalous position. As a democrat, he argues that all men are equal. But as a dissenter, he seems to insist that he knows better than the majority what is right. He implies, or seems to imply that he (or his judgment) is better than that majority, thereby seeming to affirm the very principle of inequality that he, along with the majority, had previously repudiated. His obstinacy no less than his apparent inconsistency serves only to arouse the animosity of those who are opposed to him and who command the support of the majority. Paradoxically, then, the principle of equality—which is here improperly extended to include moral and intellectual uniformity as well as political equality—enters to reinforce that terrible craving for certainty which all too often results in the efforts to suppress disconcerting differences. And it is this intolerance—of heterodoxy in belief and of nonconformity in behavior—that constitutes (for some men) the tyranny of opinion and, derivatively, of majority rule.[29]

The pervasive moral authority of the majority is a basic problem of democracy. It helps to sustain majority rule and makes its decisions more acceptable to those who have dissented. But implicit in its great ethical force is the idea that the majority is right, that it governs not simply because there is no effective alternative to realizing the equality principle, but because its policies are wise. It may be true that the majority is right more often than any other ruling agent, but this is very different from saying that the majority is right because it is the majority. What the majority is, by virtue of its greater number, is the chief constituency of government, no more and no less. Yet its operating moral authority sweeps well beyond this point, and in doing so, puts the heterodox not only in a weak political position, bad enough from a libertarian point of view, but in a weak moral one as well.

Tocqueville's analysis explains why institutional checks alone may not succeed in limiting majority power and why they are probably not themselves sufficient to maintain a liberal democracy. Before we pursue this insight further and examine the operating conditions of the free speech norm, we must look critically at Tocqueville's concept of conformity and its derivative, majority tyranny. If conformity is a product of felt pressure to comply with the wishes or standards of others and a desire for social approval, it is a fact of all human social organization and a basic element of the socialization process. It is not limited to democracies, although it may be more observable in democracies because of their ethos of equality.

But Tocqueville's analysis says little about the utility of conformity and leaves unresolved the contradiction between dispersal of power to prevent majority excesses and the majority's presumed success in effecting an all-permeating conformity. Though it may be stifling and oppressive, conformity can also provide a vital element of cohesiveness in a heterogeneous society, particularly one undergoing rapid expansion and, at the same time, subscribing to economic laissez-faire and individualism.

The competitive striving of an upwardly mobile group in a society organized around economic enterprise requires stringent discipline over expression of sexual and aggressive impulses, over patterns of consumption, over the uses of time and resources. In this respect, conformity is derivative from equality of opportunity in conjunction with success-striving. . . . Given the varied cultural backgrounds of the population and the desire that various groups should continue to live together in the same society, conformity in externals becomes sort of "social currency" making it possible to continue the society in spite of many clashes of interests and basic values. If it is gradually learned that the exhibition of cultural differences— whether they be of dress, or language, or religious faith, or political philosophy—

seems to lead to friction in interpersonal relationships or even to public disturbances, a whole series of complex adjustments are set in motion.[30]

Thus conformity may function as a counterforce to the centrifugal tendencies implicit in social heterogeneity, on the one hand, and exploitative, indulgent economic individualism, on the other. It can also provide a cushion against the personal and group insecurities that abound in a socially fluid environment. Not least, conformity may reinforce ego defenses, particularly in matters of sex and aggression, where the prospect of losing control may be especially threatening.

Conformity and the social pressures that underwrite it may also serve as a partial antidote to the structural separation and diffusion of power designed to make it hard for the majority to organize itself effectively and use governmental power. Limited government—the political hallmark of economic individualism—was particularly well suited to early nineteenth-century America, but it also meant that the ordering of many other areas of social life, having little to do with material pursuit, would be left in private hands. Thus the social control that the majority might find difficult to effect through the offices of government could be partially reclaimed through social pressure and moral authority. If hypocrisy is the tribute vice pays to virtue, then perhaps conformity is the tribute democracy's limited government pays to popular sovereignty.

The Democratic Community

The demographic patterns of the young nation and the checks placed on majority rule in the central government ensured that most governing power would remain where it had always been—in the community. At the same time, increasing vigor of the equality principle and steadily widening participatory opportunities strengthened the position of local majorities. Until well into the nineteenth century, "local communities in America ran their own affairs, by and large, and ran them by a popular political process."[31] This is not to say that ruling local majorities were stable monoliths. Often they were composed of a number of minority interests, elite and nonelite, who were able to come together on a single issue but not to form the majority on all questions. Even where dominant interests were merely shifting coalitions or pluralities, their standards could not have prevailed long in the American community of the nineteenth century without wide popular support or acquiescence, especially in matters of morality, social behavior, and expression. The ideal of equality, that every person is as good as his or her neighbor, but none is better, was too well established and real participatory opportunities too numerous for the situation to be otherwise. If not the actual cradle of democracy, the American small community was surely its nursery.

Yet Madison, the chief architect of constraints on majority power, had not been optimistic about avoiding democratic excesses in the town or village. Small scale meant fewer competing forces within, and "the fewer the distinct parties and interests, the more frequently will a majority be found in the same party; and the smaller the compass within which they are placed, the more easily will they concert and execute their plans of expression."[32] Madison feared that without benefit of the extensive pluralism he saw in the country as a whole, local democracy, all too easily embracing the moral authority of the majority, would fail to make effective provision for the protection of the few.

Nowhere was the force of the majority more likely to be felt, and to be free of interference from external powers and from nonpopular elements within, than in morality and opinion. An individual's real freedom of expression and communication was thus likely to be a coefficient of the standards of the community. Although considerable diversity of opinion could be found across the young, heterogeneous nation, there is little evidence of great tolerance of divergence within local populations. Theoretically, dissidents might find it easier to move to another community that shared their views than to maintain them uncomfortably at home.[33]

In the overwhelming intimacy of small town life, democracy's internal contradiction between the equality principle and individual freedom tended to be resolved in favor of the former. Thus American individualism, a natural counterweight to the majority, was twisted: it flourished and found its reward in economic and material pursuits. It included extraordinary self-reliance, which historians such as Frederick Jackson Turner saw as both encouraged and symbolized by the presence of the frontier, but it was stunted in matters of thought, expression, and morality. Control in these areas could usually be effected through social pressure, anticipatory self-restraint, or the socialization process—the conformity Tocqueville had observed.

The agencies of government stood ready to enact new laws and to employ such common-law instruments as those against public nuisance, breach of the peace, disorderly conduct, and obscene libel. And if government were too constricted procedurally, too weak, or simply absent, the job could be done extralegally by ad hoc "committees of safety" or other popular voluntary groups applying whatever force might be necessary.[34] There was no higher law of personal freedom or liberty to which a dissatisfied, censored, or persecuted individual or group might appeal against governmental or private power if a local or state right did not exist. In the Jacksonian era, the Supreme Court had affirmed that the Bill of Rights conferred no personal liberty claimable against state or local authority,[35] an understanding consistent with the original constitutional arrangement.

Its isolation, autonomy, and intimacy gave the local community opportunity to develop its own values and operating standards of tolerance (see Table 2). It is not surprising that range of permissible erotic expression should have been narrow. Little overt or public conflict developed over such expression until the end of the nineteenth century, a sharp contrast to the contemporary situation in Britain and France, for example, and to what was to come later in the United States. Tocqueville himself observed:

Attempts have been made by some governments to protect morality by prohibiting licentious books. In the United States no one is punished for this sort of book, but no one is induced to write them; not because all the citizens are immaculate in conduct, but because the majority of the community is decent and orderly.[36]

Human impulses toward wayward sexual expression could be contained with a minimum of government action and a minimum of opposition. In matters of expression and communication, the new democratic nation of local communities preoccupied with material development had not yet confronted the discordant implications of its own heterogeneity or the comfortably censorial ones of pervasive popular power.

In the community, democracy was joined to one of the oldest and most persistent human needs, fraternity. This elemental gratification, which "promises security, bolsters faltering egos, banishes an awful sense of loneliness, and fosters togetherness and belongingness," appeared to find its natural political embodiment in the community governed on behalf of all.[37] The affiliation and solidarity it offered, always implicit in the equality principle, supplied much of the emotional underwriting for majority rule and the unquestioning belief in the rightness of popular values. Yet, as Sherwood Anderson, the quintessential small-town expatriate, warned, "life can never be intimate enough."[38] Carried further, the fellowship of the

TABLE 2.   Comparative Operation of Tolerance

Type of Tolerance	Pre-Urban Local Community	Later Urban Environment
Voluntary	High within narrow topical range; delimited by socialized conformity	Greater topical range; well established at level of general principles, but much less certain in actual application
Manipulated	Relatively high because of homogeneity, but weakened by increasing democratization	More problematic because of diversity, but facilitated by mass media
Default	Less significant because of less extensive separation of power; partially countered by conformity	Increasingly significant because of bureaucratization, impersonality, greater heterogeneity of the city
Enforced	Relatively unimportant	Much more important; underwritten by modern libertarian legal doctrine

like-minded took on the darker face of clannishness, irrationality, and finally intolerance, the more illiberal for being backed by the weight of the majority.

The insulated, autonomous, small community has been irrevocably eclipsed, but not so the community of the mind. The social and psychological needs that the near-sovereign democratic town or village satisfied remain with us and perhaps always will.[39] Not the least of these is the security of knowing implicitly that threatening expression or behavior will be fraternally damned and subjected to social control. Yet the sense both of being able to secure one's immediate social environment and of having the moral right to do so in concert with one's fellows, so much a part of the early democratization of America, has been challenged and brought into doubt.

Toward Public Control

In the same short period, the nation's area and population expanded, and barriers of time and space were reduced. The country became more centralized politically and economically and its sections more interdependent; it became wealthier and better educated, yet more heterogeneous. Complex, large-scale economic enterprise helped to concentrate populations. An urban and bureaucratic environment brought new rationality and impersonality to commercial and social relations. The search for ever-larger markets, for a national marketplace, spurred remarkable advances in transportation and communications. The geographical barriers that had secured the autonomy of the community were largely overcome.

The absorption of millions of immigrants, though accomplished without great sacrifice of democratic forms, further challenged and modified the receiving culture. With the growth of compulsory public education, the proliferation of free libraries, and, not least, the remarkable technological advances in communications, the American population became more widely educated, literate, and informed.

Such massive, rapid, and contrasting changes were sure to increase conflict over social and moral standards. Established values of one community were challenged by those of others, including enclaves of new arrivals, and by a cosmopolitan culture that reflected the social diversity of the expanding cities. At the same time, communications media became more important as brokers of debate and value givers, sharing the socializing role that had once been the exclusive reserve of the family, school, church, and employer. Because of their representational power and popular reach, media such as the movies and, later, broadcasting were thought by many to have an almost irresistible power over minds.

Early efforts to impose control on communications often did not involve use of government power, relying instead on internalized standards, tacit understandings, or overt social or economic pressures on local agents of the media. Regulative influence could also be exercised by advertisers, who were usually cautious in their sponsorship and attentive to popular interests.

Informal control was much less effective in the rapidly growing cities. The law was called on more frequently, complemented by a new institution of social regulation, the antivice society. One of the first of these groups, the New York Society for the Suppression of Vice, founded in 1872 by the intrepid moral crusader Anthony Comstock, became the prototype for censorial groups in other cities, including Boston's puritanical Watch and Ward Society. Chartered by the state legislature and generously financed by wealthy contributors, the New York group brought a variety of social pressures to bear on publishers, bookstore owners, and others with a proprietary interest in communications deemed obscene or otherwise offensive because of their sexual content. If these pressures failed, the society initiated prosecutions by legal complaint.

Although Comstock and the vice societies are now ridiculed as zealots, they commanded wide public support and esteem in their early years. They pursued mainly cheap, low-quality erotic books and magazines that often circulated clandestinely. Many of these groups were considered to be philanthropies, and most identified themselves with the larger reformist spirit of Progressivism and its concerns for child welfare, social hygiene, and other problems of an industrializing civilization. Comstock, himself a career crusader, was also an indefatigable popular exposer of a variety of sharp practices, including illegal gambling schemes and fraudulent advertising.[40]

That the societies should have been an early and important regulatory mechanism in the cities is not surprising. With their quasi-official status and heavy reliance on social pressure, they were a small-town mode of control adapted to a growing cosmopolitan urban environment. Like the informal control the homogeneous community so effectively imposed, their efforts were most successful where they had the backing of dominant interests and the public in general, as they often did before the turn of the century, when a local urban value consensus was easier to discern. As the cities became even more socially and culturally diverse and general standards of tolerance for sexual expression grew more liberal, these nonelected societies found it harder to discover, much less to represent, commonly held standards. They remained stationary while the moral ground around them shifted. Their own excesses in the years following World War I, including well-publicized attempts to suppress such literary works as *An American Tragedy, Lady Chatterley's Lover, Jurgen,* and issues of H. L. Mencken's *American Mercury,* divided the elite and aroused formidable opposition, hastening their decline.

The rise of large-scale, centrally run media with unprecedented distributive capacities, and great technical power both to communicate ideas and to portray behavior, greatly weakened informal control (see Table 3). Increasingly, the threat of objectionable sexual expression was met formally, through government, by declarations of policy and by

TABLE 3.   Comparative Control of Sexual Expression

Type of Control	Pre-Urban Local Community	Later Urban Environment
Informal, unorganized (e.g., "public sentiment")	Permeating, major control	Less significant because of greater heterogeneity of the city
Informal, organized (e.g., pressure groups)	Major auxiliary control	Important in transition between rural and urban demography, but later less effective
Proprietary self-restraint (organized and individual)	Considerable self-censorship, anticipatory, largely unorganized	More differentiated; "maverick" exceptions; large-scale, industry-wide organization
Government, other than the criminal process	Secondary, backup; infrequently used	Major instrument; increased and greatly ramified; used with other controls
Government, criminal process	Very infrequent use	Vast increase in incidence, variety, and secondary effect

regulatory instruments that could be effective beyond the single community. The first national action was an 1842 customs statute barring importation of pictorially obscene matter. In 1865, partly in response to the circulation of many cheap erotic novels during the Civil War, Congress forbade the mailing of obscene materials. Largely through the lobbying of Comstock, the scope of the statute was soon expanded and penalties augmented. The revised law, known as the Comstock Act, survives with few changes to the present day as the chief source of federal power over obscene matter in the mails. Comstock himself was made a special agent of the Post Office, charged with enforcing the act. Still later, in 1897, Congress made it a criminal offense to ship obscene material across state lines for commercial purposes.[41]

Legal control was sought increasingly at the state level as well. A handful of states had anti-obscenity statutes before the Civil War; the oldest, Vermont's, dated only to 1821. By the turn of the century thirty states had such laws, and by the 1920s, every state but New Mexico, which delegated responsibility to municipalities, had instituted some form of regulation. Significantly, early demands at both state and national levels for legislation and other authoritative action came mainly from the cities, where social and cultural diversity was greatest and informal controls least effective.[42] Prosecutions under these new statutes or under older common-law provisions have increased steadily from the nineteenth century to the present. Only two appellate obscenity cases were reported in the entire country before the Civil War, but between 1870 and 1890, the highest courts in at least thirteen states heard such actions. In the twentieth century, obscenity cases have been regularly on the appellate dockets in almost every state.[43]

Libertarian observers writing from a legal or literary perspective have often attributed growing public concern about sexual expression to a Victorian morality, a return to Puritan standards, or some other shift in sexual anxieties. These attributions, difficult to substantiate or impeach without survey evidence, ignore the social context in which control or suppression is sought and the tension between individual liberty and popular preferences that characterizes a democratic order. Growing demands for censorship and control are much more likely to be the product of qualitative and quantitative changes in unwanted expression and the diminishing effectiveness of established controls. Indeed, the volume of textual and pictorial communication with erotic or sexual meaning has grown rapidly and substantially since the last third of the nineteenth century.

Advances in photography and the appearance of such media as moving pictures provided artists, proprietors, and exploiters of various sorts with unparalleled opportunities. Popular tolerance was challenged directly and repeatedly when this communication took aim at ever wider audiences. Values established in earlier isolation were confronted by the diverse values of a heterogeneous culture, and by others emerging from a netherworld of heterodoxy. Growing public anxiety about sexual expression cannot be attributed simply, if at all, to a new sexual conservatism. In fact, attitudes toward sexuality and sexual expression became more liberal, as they have in our own time, only to be outpaced again by changes in the communications environment.

Twentieth-century social control of erotic material has been a complex amalgam of governmental actions, media self-regulation, and informal checks, running the gamut from mild conformist pressures to unlawful coercion. This pattern, examined more closely in the next chapter, was relatively stable until after World War II. Though not nearly as effective as the informal control practiced a century earlier in small communities, new laws and a growing number of prosecutions of proprietary interests reflected the responsiveness of popular agencies of government to censorship interest. In turn, action by government encouraged preventive self-regulation within the media and thus had a restrictive effect considerably beyond its visible lines in legislative chambers, courtrooms, and police stations. When a popular censorship interest was unable to employ government, a grudging de facto tolerance usually resulted, occasionally punctuated by resort to informal means.

Judicial Libertarianism

Legal protection for the free speech norm, though prescriptively stated in the Bill of Rights and in many state constitutions, did not develop in doctrine or operation until well into the twentieth century. Appellate decisions were few, and almost none of those involving sexual expression had a libertarian result. Constitutional rights protect against government action rather than social regulation; in the era of informal control, they were seldom invoked. The separation of power designed to make some agencies—the courts in particular—more responsive to nonmajoritarian interests, or, at least, less likely to be swayed by numbers, was partly overcome by the homogeneity and smallness of scale that produced value consensus and conformity. Courts and judges, immersed in the prevailing ideology of laissez-faire and economic individualism, stood ready to protect property and enterprise against popular interference, but were less independent on questions of expression, morality, and social behavior generally.

Yet, as conflict over expression became more public and formal, the basic structural diffusion of power made divergence of response from agencies of government on morality issues as inevitable as on those involving property and enterprise. The great libertarian turn in the law that was to recast the balance between free speech and popular control awaited structural, proprietary, and ideological changes not fully realized until the period between the two world wars.

Starting with the freedoms of speech and press, the Supreme Court began to apply rights in the Bill of Rights as checks on state and local power through the Fourteenth Amendment, which forbade any state to deprive any person of "life, liberty, or property without due process of law."[44] This nationalizing of rights radically altered the federal system's balance, not simply between central and local power, but also between liberty and majority. It meant that in controlling expression, states, cities, and local communities could themselves be limited by prescriptive, legally enforceable standards originating from without. Rather than choose between conformity and exile, a losing dissident in a local dispute might now appeal to authority outside the community.

Moreover, those who controlled the external media could utilize the authority of national rights against local restriction. Proprietary developments—technical, marketing, and creative changes within media—produced a powerful vested interest in the free speech norm, particularly against local interference. Circumstances of conflict were thus very different from those in which a village dissident or local entrepreneur was the libertarian party. Media interests with formidable financial means and an external base were far better situated to defend the free speech interest and resist local authority and pressures.

These structural and proprietary requisites for a major shift in the operational life of the free speech norm, which were in place by the 1930s, would have been of little use without an appropriate libertarian legal doctrine. Formulating the latter required a major ideological shift among the justices of the Supreme Court, an unlikely prospect in the early thirties but exactly what was underway by the end of the decade as a by-product of the Court's unsuccessful attempt to veto the New Deal economic recovery program. President Roosevelt was able to make seven new appointments in four years, including those of Justices Black and Douglas, who were to be leaders in shaping a libertarian freedom of speech. As the new Court began to divest itself of much of its economic policy-making role, it turned to issues of individual rights. Within ten years, civil liberties cases, once rare on the Court's docket, made up nearly half its workload, and the proportion has not changed since.

Social control by state and local government was now reviewable by a national body whenever the action was alleged to interfere with constitutionally protected rights; but at the same time, the scope of those rights was rapidly expanding. In policy-making responsibility, this was a major shift from the executive and legislative agencies to judicial. As the anti–New Deal Supreme Court had sought to retain a constitutional veto over economic policy, the Roosevelt Court established one over policies affecting expression and other personal liberties. Although intragovernmental conflict was inherent in a political design that separated power widely, such conflict had not generally characterized disputes over the free speech norm. But by the 1940s a new pattern had been established: free speech conflict escalated to the level of governmental action typically opposed state or local executive or legislative policy against that formulated by the national judiciary.

The Court applied the expanding libertarian doctrine to sexual expression in the 1950s, first by scrutinizing procedural aspects of prior censorship of movies by states and municipalities, then by reformulating the substantive test for proscribable obscenity and applying it to both federal and state prosecutions.[45] These decisions, in turn, gave rise to two lines of cases: one, essentially procedural, held government to more rigorous standards of due process in the means employed to control sexual expression, and the other, largely substantive, narrowed the range of sexual expression that could be legally proscribed as obscene.

From a libertarian point of view, it would be tempting to say that these struggles have arrayed an enlightened national majority against narrow censorial local interests. But that is not typically the case. Opinion polls and other survey data, as we shall note more fully in the next chapter, show not only wide public support for vigorous social control of sexual expression but also the unpopularity of the permissive communications environment and several of the Supreme Court's rulings associated with it. In many of these libertarian decisions, the Court and the judicial branch have, in effect, applied essentially elite standards of tolerance to the entire country.

In a system of separated powers and divergent government response, the courts have become the chief architects of libertarian policy and thus the major institutional check on popular social control. Elite and cosmopolitan values have fared particularly well in the federal courts, where the chief policymakers are not popularly chosen and have life tenure, circumstances that make for relative independence and weaker constituency ties than those of legislators and elected executives. State judges, though typically less insulated from popular pressures than their federal counterparts, are still far more protected than state policymakers in executive and legislative branches. Many state judges are elected, but they serve relatively long terms, and incumbents have unusual advantage in subsequent elections. These hurdles to popular influence and control are reinforced by public and professional expectations that judges will be nonpartisan and that their carefully rationalized decisions will reflect the deductive integrity of the law. They are not free agents politically, but they are far freer than other policymakers to respond to nonpopular demands and to interests from outside the community. In this sense, judicial independence is the condition less of an objective, detached judiciary ready to administer clear legal or constitutional requirements than of the relative insulation of judges from constituent pressures and, consequently, of the greater range of value choice available to them as policymakers.

Different degrees of independence are observable within the judiciary. Trial courts have the least, and the free speech norm is less apt to prevail at trial than at any other stage of the judicial process. Hence it is not surprising that nonlibertarian outcomes at trial are far more likely to be appealed than libertarian ones, and that the former are more likely to be overturned than the latter. One of the chief functions of appellate courts in free speech cases appears to be the "correction" of nonlibertarian decisions below.[46] Conversely, a libertarian decision by an appellate court may be "modified" or even ignored, and the elite tolerance values it may contain checked or filtered out in remanded proceedings or in closely related cases later brought to trial. In both appeals from lower courts and instructions from higher, there is a clear positive relationship between level of decision and the likelihood of a libertarian result.

Within the trial courts themselves, the free speech norm is less apt to prevail in cases heard by juries than in bench trials. Though juries are seldom truly representative of their communities, they are likely to be far more representative than the average trial judge and far less heedful of such legal considerations as impartiality, consistency, and logic. Because their decisions are less open to review on appeal, local or popular values contained in them are less likely to be modified than in bench decisions. Once hailed as a libertarian agency in obscenity cases, the jury is evaluated more critically today.[47] The failure of jurors to reach libertarian decisions as often as judges is another indication of the elite character of tolerance demanded by the modern obscenity doctrine.

The rules and traditions of the judicial process tend to equalize the parties to a conflict and thus appear to favor the less popular or numerically weaker side. Voir dire examination of jurors, venue changes, jury sequestration, restriction of media coverage, procedural equality within the courtroom, rules of evidence, and jury instruction all serve as checks against local or popular influence on the proceedings. Unsurprisingly, those who challenge government policy in civil actions often stand outside the dominant majority and are sometimes even rather isolated in their communities.[48] Even where the state brings the action, as in obscenity prosecutions, it is the defendant libertarian who has often chosen to use the courts—more accurately, forced them to be used against him—by resisting previous formal or informal attempts to impose community values, since a prosecution in a free speech case almost always indicates the failure of other efforts to obtain a censorial result.[49]

The relative independence of the judicial branch creates a bias that allows individual or minority interests asserted in its chambers to stand taller against popular forces than they might elsewhere. The power of courts to review constitutionally the acts of other agencies of government renders them ultimate makers of policy on civil liberties. This fact and the Supreme Court's own libertarian free speech doctrine, nearly fifty years in the making, have shaped the present libertarian era and made possible the explosion of sexual expression within it.

A liberal democracy must reconcile liberty of the individual or the few with the will and preferences of the many and must continue to adjust them in the face of constant, and sometimes rapid, changes in social, political, and economic environment. The task admits to no final solution. To idealize and exhort liberty is a vital part of our civic socialization. But liberty as an absolute value negates the legitimacy and prudence of all opposing interests and obscures the actual probabilities and necessities of liberal democracy.

In our preoccupation with government control we often forget that it is the many in whose name and on whose behalf government generally acts, and that the many are not naturally tolerant. The highly rational, frequently self-denying tolerance demanded by the free speech norm requires personality traits and demographic circumstances shared by a relatively small number of persons even in a modern "enlightened" population. Nowhere is this more evident than with sexual expression, where the threshold of perceived threat and offense is relatively low and unconscious factors are readily activated. Operating tolerance for such expression is likely to fall short of the civic response assumed by idealized liberty. Weighed against this are formal protections, the fragmentation of regulating authority, and the not infrequent libertarian preferences of leadership, all of which render operating tolerance greater than what would be popularly and willingly accorded without them.

However long individual rights and liberties have been established in ideology or as matters of philosophical speculation, the past was not liberal, save perhaps for a privileged few. Historically, for most persons, both personal and civic freedoms have been substantially constricted by formal authority and informal pressure. Extensive operating freedom for large numbers of persons or entire populations is an evolutionary development of modern liberal democracy. Many freedoms, old and new, acquired their present scope only in our own time. The observation of a contemporary civil libertarian, that we have never had more freedom, is strikingly accurate.[50] This, of course, is not to say we should not aspire to and work for still more freedom, but we should be somewhat skeptical of libertarian alarms that any new restriction of speech would betray a glorious past or, worse, cause the house of liberty itself to fall. The experience of liberal democracy clearly shows that restrictions may themselves be restricted.

From separated, often opposed, authorities, the divergent policies that have so frequently marked free speech controversies emerge and compete with one other. This uncertain, untidy, sometimes arduous process is how liberal democracy represents its disparate elements and attempts to strike some balance among them. The issue is not judicial independence or the role of higher courts as overseers of liberty, but the quality of specific policies and decisions. The chief evaluative question in every case is not whether freedom has been maximized, but whether the best balance has been struck between its protection and countervailing interests that often have popular support—ultimately, whether the imperatives of a free speech society have been reconciled with those of a mass democratic one.

We turn now to how those countervailing interests have made themselves felt formally and informally against sexual expression in a rapidly changing communications environment and how a libertarian legal and constitutional policy has tried to deal with them.

Part Four

———

Policy

Chapter Seven

The Communications Environment

The public expression of things sexual is entirely unlike what it was a few years back, and it is challenging one's credulity to assert that this public expression is not the consequence of other changes in the social order and does not have consequences of its own for man—the doer and actor.

Edward Sagarin

For many people, pornography is not only offensive, but deeply offensive.

Bernard Williams

Conflict over pornography ebbs and flows as the content and availability of sexual expression are adjusted or not adjusted to demand for control. Even in simpler times, operating freedom and operating control were far more complex and qualified than simple prescribed rights or obligations would have them. In modern liberal democracy, a continuing communications revolution allows nearly all expression to reach vast numbers of persons—in many cases without their choosing—and do so with unprecedented representational power. At the same time, established social control has been weakened by new legal protections for speech, or simply overwhelmed by demographic change. The resulting explosion of pornography has produced wide popular resentment. Conflict over sexual expression has increased notwithstanding a liberalization in sexual attitudes and some gains in tolerance. As in the past, much of the conflict has to do with the distributive context of sexual communications, particularly with differences among the communications media.

The Democracy of Communications

Communications revolutions are not new. Almost every powerful new medium—the printing press, telegraph, photograph, radio, telephone, motion picture, and television—has changed the social, economic, and political status quo. New opportunities and combinations of interests are created and older established ones threatened. Technical advances in the power to portray reality and fantasy and to make that representation widely available arouse concerns about status and moral propriety. Conflict is aggravated where, as in liberal democratic societies, communications advances bring about rapid and extensive changes in audience sociology.

Printing, of course, is the most striking example. Compared with the slow, tedious copying of texts by scribes, the early crude press was a means of mass production. It opened the door to a much wider dissemination of the written word and, with it, the possibility that large number of persons would be reached, not simply by learned argument and discourse, but also by general information and the representation of both real and imaginary experience. No matter that these persons, who would have to be at least rudimentarily literate, were but a small fraction of the population. To widen the audience for the written word from 1 or 2 percent of the population to 5 or 6 percent was a huge change and, like the later expansion of the electorate, easily seen to have great consequence for established institutions and beliefs. It was not surprising that the printing press and the fledgling industry of publishing quickly became objects of conflict, that attempts were made to control them, or that restriction was resisted in the name of profit and, eventually, liberty.

Political democracy in both its early bourgeois and later mass working-class stages grew coextensively with communications technology that increased the power of media to represent reality and focus information and to distribute its products quickly to ever-larger numbers of persons. It is hard to imagine liberal democracy, which views virtually all adults as members of a competent participating citizenry, without the "permanent revolution" in communications.

Twentieth-century mass media are the complex product of earlier technical advances and the consequent democratization of the communications audience. The American prototype was the New York *Sun*, founded in the 1830s by the printer Benjamin Day. Its appearance coincided with the invention of the steam-driven press and manufacture of cheap wood pulp newsprint, two developments that would prove vital to the mass production of newspapers. It took direct aim at the newly literate working classes, who had been largely unreached by the press. Its pages were filled with reports of crime, disasters, indiscretions, and occasional hoaxes, as news was redefined to fit the "tastes, interests, and reading skills of the less-educated level of society."[1] Newsboys hawked the *Sun* on the streets for a penny a copy, a sixth of the price of its competition. Within four years, daily circulation reached a dizzying 30,000, more than the combined total for all newspapers in the city only a short time before. Its success was not lost on retailers and manufacturers who saw daily mass circulation as a means of bringing their products and services to the attention of large numbers of prospective customers. The marriage of extensive commercial advertising to an established organ of communication transformed newspapers and set a pattern for many of the media to come. The highly profitable three-way relationship of proprietor, advertiser, and reader-listener-viewer-consumer was also to have major consequence for social control.

The American daily and Sunday press became the first modern mass medium. It blanketed the country with a communications quilt of hundreds of individual papers of wide local circulation. By 1910, with new high-speed presses and more rapid delivery, circulation averaged 1.36 copies per household; few families were left untouched. The cheap, easy-to-read, ubiquitous publications may also have been the most important single factor in a rapid assimiliation of millions of immigrants to an "American way of life." When the nation entered World War I, more than 2,000 papers virtually saturated a population of nearly 100,000,000 with daily communication, an achievement without parallel in the diffusion of information and a giant step in the democratization of culture.

The last quarter of the nineteenth century saw the development of photoengraving, the first telephone message by overhead wire, the invention of the phonograph, Mergenthaler's introduction of the linotype, the perfection of the motion picture projector and the first public showing of "movies," and Marconi's transmission of wireless messages. Published communication now embraced accurate pictorial representation, electrical signals, images that moved, the recording and reproduction of sounds including the human voice, and the broadcasting of these representations over the air waves.

Movies were the first of the new media to achieve mass diffusion. By 1930, a little more than a quarter-century after their primitive commercial debut in a Broadway kinetoscope parlor, more than 23,000 movie theaters were operating and weekly attendance exceeded 90,000,000—an average of more than three admissions for each American household. The rise of radio broadcasting was no less spectacular. There were only five commercial stations in 1922, more than 1,000 after World War II, and more than 8,000 in the 1980s. Over the same period, radio sets in use increased from fewer than 400,000 to 60,000,000, then to nearly a half-billion. By 1965, 99 percent of households and 80 percent of automobiles had receivers. Commercial television broadcasting, technologically feasible in the late 1930s but delayed by World War II, grew as rapidly as radio a generation earlier. In 1946, the nation had six television stations, and about 8,000 homes had receiving sets. Within a decade, 35,000,000 homes were receiving programs from 357 stations. By 1966, more than 90 percent of all homes had sets, and in the 1980s less than 2 percent were without them. The number of weekly viewing hours per household, increasing almost yearly since the 1950s, grew to a remarkable 49.7 in 1984.[2] Broadcasting now reaches virtually every man, woman, and child to form a communications blanket even bigger than that of daily newspapers a century earlier.

Other media have grown almost as dramatically. Annual sales of books, reaching 200,000,000 in 1925, declined by almost half during the Depression, but grew rapidly again after World War II. After paperbacks were introduced, sales reached one billion in 1958 and doubled by 1983. Nonschool libraries with holdings of 10,000 volumes or more have grown almost annually for over a century and now number more than 30,000. By 1962, aggregate per issue sales of general circulation and farm magazines reached 200,000,000, a tenfold increase in less than fifty years. Per issue circulation grew in the same period from 26.5 to 157.1 for every hundred adults and has continued to increase almost yearly. Annual sales of recordings, first in cylinder form and later as disks and tapes, numbered fewer than 3,000 in 1899 and grew to 107,000,000 by 1919, to one billion by 1973, and to nearly five billion by 1984.

Communications growth in the last hundred years is without precedent. Never have so many persons or so great a percentage of all persons been communicated with by so many means, so often, about so many things as at this moment.

Freedom's Division of Labor

The communications revolution directly challenged the insularity of the small community and the isolation of individuals within it. Demographic changes in the nineteenth century had already weakened a once effective, largely informal, local system of control. A new and more complex pattern of regulation followed; its accommodation to the new communications environment is strikingly shown in the contrasting paths taken by the two earliest mass media—newspapers and movies.

Of all the media, newspapers lay claim to the greatest freedom from formal restraint. They were "the press" the drafters of the First Amendment had in mind. Freedom of newspapers from governmental prior restraint is as close to an absolute right as any medium has ever had in the United States. Generally, newspapers have been formally restricted only by the proscriptions of libel, obscenity, and incitement to disorder placed on all media. Despite this favored and protected status, however, they have had the *least* operating freedom for sexual representation. The paradox is instructive. Before they became a mass medium in the late nineteenth century, newspapers addressed the literate middle and upper classes with reports of political, social, and commercial events and opinion about them. They sought to inform and persuade more than entertain or divert. Being of the community, their manifest restraint in sexual matters and moral issues was largely self-imposed; their proprietors wished to avoid giving offense or had themselves internalized prevailing community standards.

Mass circulation weakened but did not destroy these local and informal controls. As a village or community institution, the local newspaper became a more broadly based vehicle of socialization, subject to the same public opinion and other normative pressures, subtle and not so subtle, that set informal limits for the political, social, and intellectual life of the community. Mass circulation meant addressing an undifferentiated audience with a content appealing to a wide range of readers, without alienating or greatly disturbing any large number of them. It also brought a new, albeit indirect, form of control—advertising. Hoping to stimulate demand for a product by informing and persuading, advertisers were especially wary of offending prospective customers. The increasing dependence of newspapers on income from advertising gave these commercial buyers of space—frequently themselves part of the community establishment—regulative influence on the press, particularly in matters of sexual expression and moral propriety.

In the scramble for the lion's share of readers, the sensationalism of Day's *Sun* was a model for yellow journalism. But such excesses, upsetting to the industry itself, were eventually countered, though never completely eradicated, by codes and norms of professional responsibility. The sensationalist press, titillating and vulgar though it might be, seldom reached pornographic levels. Lurid content was usually combined with reportage of actual events, rather than being a product of the imagination.

Pictorial matter was strictly confined and "four-letter words" forbidden. Even today, full nudity and four-letter words almost never appear in mass circulation newspapers.

The movies, in contrast, were the first medium without roots in either elite or folk culture. Their appeal to an undifferentiated mass public was untempered by any tradition of providing news and opinion. From the outset their tremendous representational power was used almost exclusively to entertain and divert. Where the mass circulation newspaper reached new *readers,* the movies reached new audiences of the literate and nonliterate alike. They were exclusively a public medium, not to be wrapped up, taken home, and savored in private. They came from outside the community and were not indebted to it. With few exceptions, no advertisers influenced their content; financially they depended almost entirely on those who paid to see them.

The movies were thus able to establish a direct relationship with their viewers, free of the mediating forces that restrained newspapers. They did not report events but dramatized works of imagination, and the temptation to emphasize the erotic was irresistible. The medium's public character and unique representational power meant that many of these portrayals, though profitable, would be socially objectionable. Informal community pressures were limited and proprietary and advertiser restraint largely absent. Social control of movies was forced to seek more formal means. After the medium's stormy infancy, control was imposed through a unique combination of government censorship boards, organized religious pressure, and formal industry-wide self-regulation.[3]

By the early 1920s, more than a score of states and large cities had established licensing authorities empowered to view films before exhibition and to withhold permits from or require deletions in those found offensive. The Roman Catholic church's reviewing and rating body, the Legion of Decency, formed in the 1930s, threatened producers with parish boycotts of objectionable films. To meet these and other private pressures and quiet a rising call for federal censorship, the major studios established the Production Code Administration—the "Hays Office"—to review and edit films before release. This self-regulation, which depended on the domination of the industry by a handful of large studios—the "majors"—who controlled production and, in large measure, distribution and exhibition as well, was effective. The triad of government boards, organized private pressure, and formal self-regulation, aided by the profitable economics of the "family" film, brought a measure of censorial stability until the movies were unseated as the nation's prime source of entertainment by television following World War II.

Differences in sexual representation between the daily press and movies are part of an even larger pattern. Operating freedom has been narrowest in the mass media—newspapers, movies, general circulation periodicals, recordings, radio, and television—all of which are cheap and accessible. Freedom is much greater in the "elite" media—books, specialized periodicals, the theater, and the other performing arts—which usually address smaller, more intellectually sophisticated audiences. The "price of admission" to elite media is usually higher, and they typically require greater cognitive effort from the audience. Operating freedom in the mass media has almost always been less than that allowed by law or protected by constitutional right; in the elite media it has sometimes been greater.

The elite and mass media each have clandestine segments, access to which has normally been highly restricted. These under-the-counter, relatively high-priced communications have usually been directed at very small and typically homogeneous audiences. Their operating freedom has always been greater than that of the elite media and, of course, always more than the law allows.

This triadic division of the media, reflected in all major categories of sexual representation, is policed in many ways, which we shall consider in a later section. Though not deliberate, the division is, in effect, a compromise in a marketplace and polity that have become increasingly democratized. In the past, at least, this compromise has allowed the revolution in communications technology to be adjusted to inevitable changes in communications sociology.

Operating freedom in a medium varies inversely with size of audience, accessibility, technical power of representation, and decentralization of production. Tables 4 and 5 show this relationship during a more stable period before the contemporary pornography explosion.

The larger and more heterogeneous the audience, the more content is likely to reflect popular values and tastes and hence general standards of acceptability. The presence of children and youths in the mass undifferentiated audience reinforces this bent and increases the censorial interest of many persons both in and outside that audience. Mass media proprietors recognize these facts, and the "common denominator" products they so frequently offer tend to be "safe," compared with those of other media.

TABLE 4. The Communications Environment and Operating Freedom, Circa 1960

Medium	Locus of "Consumption"[a]	Locus of Content Determination[b]	Cost of Access[c]
Newspapers	Semi-public	Largely local	Very low
Movies	Public	Nonlocal	Moderate
Radio and television	Largely private	Mixed but more nonlocal	Free
Recordings	Private	Nonlocal	Moderate
General circulation magazines	Semi-public	Nonlocal	Low
Specialized periodicals	Semi-public	Nonlocal	Low
Books, paperbound	Semi-public[d]	Nonlocal	Moderate
Books, hardcover	Semi-public[d]	Nonlocal	High
Stage	Public	Mixed but more nonlocal[e]	High
"Underground"	Private, furtive[f]	Nonlocal	Very high

Medium	Type of Audience	Youth in Audience	Degree of Operating Freedom
Newspapers	General, local	Some	Low
Movies	General	Many	Low
Radio and television	General, local and national	Many	Low
Recordings	General	Some	Low
General circulation magazines	General	Some	Low
Specialized periodicals	Limited, specialized	Few[g]	Low to moderate
Books, paperbound	Mostly limited	Few	Moderate to high
Books, hardcover	Very limited	Very few	High
Stage	Very limited	Very few	High
"Underground"	Very limited	Very few	Very high

Table 4, *continued*

[a]Refers to both the point of access and the place where most of the communication takes place or is consumed.

[b]Refers to the relationship of proprietary decision making to the local community with regard to content. "Nonlocal" refers to decisions that are usually national or bureaucratically centralized.

[c]Refers to the "price of admission" or cost of purchase; excludes initial cost of "receiving" equipment.

[d]Includes libraries.

[e]Although most decisions are local, most legitimate theaters are in atypical localities, mainly a few big cities.

[f]Some consumption is social though nonpublic.

[g]Excluding comic books and a few other publications directed mainly or specifically at youth.

TABLE 5. Social Control of Media, Circa 1960

Medium	Formal: Federal Government[a]	Formal: State/Local Government[b]	Informal
Newspapers	Almost none	Almost none	Some
Movies	Customs review	Several censor boards, few prosecutions	Considerable
Radio and television	FCC "traffic" regulation, otherwise none	None	Some, nonlocal
Recordings	None	Almost none	Little
General circulation magazines	Almost none	Almost none	Little
Specialized periodicals	Customs seizure, postal exclusion	Infrequent prosecution	Little
Books, paperbound	Customs seizure, postal exclusion	Occasional prosecution	Some, local
Books, hardcover	Customs seizure, postal exclusion	Occasional prosecution	Little
Stage	None	Infrequent prosecution	Little[c]
"Underground"	None by definition	None by definition	Little[d]

Table 5, *continued*

Medium	Advertiser Influence	Institution-alized Self-Restraint	Informal Self-Restraint[c]	Degree of Operating Freedom
Newspapers	Great	None	Very great	Low
Movies	None	Code authority	Great	Low
Radio and television	Great	Code authority	Very great	Low
Recordings	None	None	Very great	Low
General circulation magazines	Consider-able	None	Very great	Low
Specialized periodicals	Some	None[f]	Great	Low to moderate
Books, paperbound	None	None	Moderate	Moderate to high
Books, hardcover	None	None	Little	High
Stage	None	None	Little	High
"Underground"	None	None	None in production, very great in distribution[g]	Very high

[a]Criminal prosecution, business licensing, etc.

[b]Private pressures through complaints, boycotts, harassment; extra-legal action by public authorities through threats and other coercion.

[c]Largely because theaters are located in a few large cities.

[d]Although there was enormous potential for informal control, it was largely anticipated and headed off. The same was true of governmental control through criminal prosecution.

[e]Through calculation or internalization.

[f]There were some exceptions, such as the comic book publishers' code.

[g]In distribution, as opposed to content, there was considerable proprietary self-restraint in anticipation of governmental and informal control. In this sense, the latter controls were effective in keeping distribution furtive.

The investment risk and profit potential involved in addressing a mass audience are huge and dictate caution. The Hollywood "family" film that was the movie industry's staple for more than a generation, and the bland fare that came to dominate television screens represented the apex of popular inoffensiveness. Proprietary self-restraint, whether a response to the box office or simply a tactic to avoid other regulation, varies directly with the degree to which a medium deals with a mass undifferentiated audience.

The mass media are characteristically accessible to juveniles. Radio and television are ubiquitous and newspapers nearly so. In contrast, books, especially hardcovers, are much less accessible. Movies, where the industry's rating system is enforced, are now the least accessible, with X-rated films presumably entirely off limits to juveniles, and R-rated limited to admission with a parent. The cost of admission follows the mass/elite division. Radio and broadcast television are free to anyone with receiving equipment. Newspapers have a nominal price, and general circulation magazines are still relatively inexpensive; specialized periodicals invariably cost more. These are followed by the movies, paperbound books, hardcovers, and, finally, by the performing arts.

Significantly, when the "underground" media were more clearly segregated than they are today, their limited and clandestine access was a chief rationale for their defense. Sometimes sold literally from under the counter, they were available only to those who knew of their existence and asked for them. The price of "dirty" books or "stag" films was much higher than that of nonpornographic works of comparable length and technical quality.

Operating freedom is less where the technical power to portray fantasy and behavioral reality is greater, but more where the cognitive or intellectual effort required to comprehend that representation is greater. Movies and television, for example, stand in sharp contrast to books. Almost anything materially manifest in three-dimensional space can be convincingly simulated by the pictorial media and, in the case of the movies, projected several times larger than life. Words on paper are not faithful reproductions of reality but abstract encoded symbols of it, requiring a degree of education and age maturity to comprehend. Though some four-letter words may have a direct visceral impact, words generally distance the audience from reality. The relative passivity of movie and television audiences, however, is seldom a bar to successful communication.

The theater might at first appear to be an exception to the general rule. It is a comparatively free medium, and its use of actual persons seemingly gives it even greater representational power than movies or television. The advantage of live actors, however, is offset by technical barriers: the distance of the audience from the performers, physical confinement of the stage, and more limited opportunities to focus or calibrate audience attention. For the pictorial media there is no stage, no limitations on juxtaposition or directing of attention. The perceptual distance between audience and representation can be reduced by the camera to a fraction of an inch.

Other things equal, operating freedom is greater where major decisions about content are made extra-locally, as they are in book and magazine publishing, network broadcasting, and the movies. Most production work in these media is centrally or nationally organized and directed, and need not give great weight to standards of communities generally or individually. These media provide an expansive role for the writer, artist, or other creative personnel. The elite media's distance from the audience permits their cosmopolitan values and standards of tolerance to intrude and challenge local and popular ones. In the mass media this freedom may be partly countered by local segments the proprietors of which tend to be sensitive to popular standards of acceptability. Differences between hub and rim are particularly sharp in movies and broadcasting. Such conflict sometimes exists in the elite media, as, for example, when certain books are not stocked by bookstores or acquired by libraries, but this retail-level influence on production is generally less common and less extensive than in the mass media.

Although operating freedom has grown steadily for all communications, the relative differences among mass, elite, and underground media remain. In all aspects of sexual representation—theme, language, nudity, and portrayed behavior—mass media lag behind elite. Broadcast television has only recently dealt with prostitution, abortion, incest, and homosexuality, although these subjects had long been in the elite media. A broadcasting executive in the mid-eighties doubted that nudity would ever be permitted on network television: "Only within the past year have we begun to allow a man to lie on top of a woman. We are reaching the point of physical motion under the covers of a bed."[4] Such tepid profanity as "hell" and "damn" may be used cautiously, but sterner epithets with sexual connotations, such as "son-of-a-bitch" and "bastard," are rarely heard in the broadcast media or, for that matter, seen in the daily press, and four-letter words almost never.

Nowhere are differences more sharply drawn than when a work from an elite medium is adapted for, or reviewed or advertised in, a mass medium. Four-letter words, nudity, and scenes of explicit sexual behavior are routinely cut from R-rated movies before they appear on the major television networks; the X-rated type are not shown at all. Newspapers frequently censor movie ads, altering provocative titles, eliminating descriptive phrases, and even doctoring pictorial matter. In one notable instance, the New York *Daily News,* at the time the paper with the largest circulation in the country, actually changed the name of a theater from "Tomcat" to "Thom." Producers of the film *Sexual Perversity in Chicago,* based on David Mamet's play and not about sexual deviance at all, changed its title to *About Last Night . . .* after national television networks and several daily newspapers refused ads under its original title.[5]

Theatrical productions and books may also create difficulties. Reviewing the opening of Michael McClure's play *The Beard,* New York City dailies were deliberately oblique about a fanciful portrayal of cunnilingus, describing it as "a highly publicized sexual act" (a reference to the play's controversial opening earlier in San Francisco), "an unorthodox sex act," and "a sexual act that can't be described in a family newspaper." When the Yale Drama School advertised its production of John Ford's seventeenth-century *'Tis Pity She's a Whore,* the New Haven *Register* changed the title to " 'Tis Pity She's Bad" and the Hartford *Courant,* adding a touch of mystery, substituted " 'Tis Pity She's." Two of the country's largest newspapers had second thoughts about a Sunday supplement review of Desmond Morris's work of popular anthropology, *The Naked Ape,* which discussed the sexual capacities of the human male. The Chicago *Tribune* recalled more than a million copies of the supplement *Book World* at a cost of perhaps $100,000, and the Washington *Post,* though it did not recall its half-million copies, struck out lines referring to the human penis.[6]

Nor is news reporting unaffected. When the distributor of *The Connection* took the now defunct New York state movie censors to court over denial of an exhibition permit because the word "shit" was used (as slang for heroin), New York City newspapers treated the word almost as though it had magical qualities, substituting a variety of euphemisms even in reporting the decision of the highest court of the state, where the word was the main point in overturning the censors' action.[7]

After many towns and cities redrew their obscenity laws in an attempt to conform to the Supreme Court's narrowing of proscribability to "hard-core pornography," the new provisions were often so specific in describing anatomical features and sexual acts that local newspapers, including in one instance the Miami *Herald,* refused to print their texts. This created an impasse when other laws required new ordinances to be printed in a local newspaper of general circulation in order to take effect.[8]

When President Ford's secretary of Agriculture, Earl Butz, claimed in a *Rolling Stone* interview that the reason Republicans could not attract more black voters was that blacks wanted only three things: "a tight pussy, loose shoes, and a warm place to shit," the remarks caused a storm of protest and led to his resignation. In reporting the matter, the daily press, almost without exception, deleted words from the remark or paraphrased it altogether. The broadcast media were even more restrained. The CBS Evening News said the report was so vulgar that "it's not being repeated in most news accounts, including this one." NBC called it "the kind of language you could replay for certain people. But on this broadcast, where the company is mixed and unknown, we cannot do it. If you want to know the exact words, see the October seventh edition of *Rolling Stone* magazine."[9] Clearer acknowledgment of mass/elite differences in operating freedom would be hard to find.

Differences also exist between elite and underground media. Since the latter's restricted availability makes its greater freedom of content possible as a commercial fact, specific demarcation has depended a great deal on the obscenity law of the day. Thus substantive boundaries have often been defined and redefined by well-publicized government prosecutions or seizures, such as those of Mary Ware Dennett's work on sexual education, *The Sex Side of Life,* in the 1920s, for its descriptions of sexual organs, Joyce's *Ulysses* in the thirties, and Lawrence's *Lady Chatterley's Lover* in the sixties, because of objections to theme and four-letter words. Although each of these actions ultimately failed, some serious works, such as Henry Miller's *Tropic* books, which would have been discussed and disseminated in elite media, remained underground. More to the point, however, thousands of stag or "smoker" films, "dirty" books, comic books, and photographs, with their deviant themes, four-letter words, and portrayal of nudity and explicit sexual acts, were also off limits to both elite and mass media. Their appearance in either would have guaranteed quick formal or informal censorship.

Changes in the substantive and procedural aspects of the obscenity doctrine have elevated much of what was once underground and obliterated many of the old lines that applied to theme, language, and nudity. Elite/underground differences remaining today mainly involve explicit sexual behavior. Hard-core pornography—"lewd" pictorial representation of genitals, masturbation, or "ultimate" sex acts—are still not generally part of the operating freedom of the elite media. But the lines are blurred, and their operating force is less certain than that of boundaries of the past. The same rapid changes in the obscenity doctrine and in communications technology and sociology that have destabilized the mass/elite division have done no less to the elite/underground.

The movies, once a highly regulated mass medium, now a much less regulated one having characteristics of both mass and elite media, provide the most striking example of boundary change. For fifty years, the medium had addressed an undifferentiated mass audience—virtually the entire population. Its chief product, the enormously profitable "family" film, was the country's major source of media entertainment. When the rise of television ended this golden age, the movies were forced to search for a new audience. Television sets in American homes increased more than tenfold during the 1950s, while movie theater admissions fell by 50 percent. At the same time, the older medium acquired a new status in the law: once considered simply a "business," the Supreme Court in its celebrated *Miracle* case held it to be an organ of speech and press entitled to protection of the First Amendment. Other rulings followed, limiting the powers of the government censor boards. These legal and economic changes also undermined the medium's code and self-regulatory office and weakened individual proprietary restraint.

A radical increase in sex and violence followed in Hollywood productions and in the new exploitation genre—first the "nudie" and nudist camp features, then the more explicit and explorative "X-rated" film. In effect, the medium breached almost every functional distinction that had governed operating freedom among the mass, elite, and underground media. Movies were still aimed at a largely undifferentiated mass audience and were shown in the same theaters and advertised in the same ways as before, but now they exercised a freedom in sexual portrayal that had largely been reserved to the elite media. With the appearance of the X-rated film, they also crossed the line separating elite from underground media.

The new, ambiguous identity led to wide censorial reaction. The decline of censor boards and the industry's code meant that objectors sought satisfaction through other social controls: obscenity prosecutions, various civil actions and business regulations by local government, and private and extralegal pressures on local exhibitors. The industry responded by restructuring its code and self-regulatory apparatus, introducing the four letter ratings—G, GP, R, and X—aimed at relieving censorial pressures, especially at the local level, and heading off more rigorous, nonproprietary, control. The rating system was the industry's attempt to impose within its own ranks a counterpart of freedom's general division of labor among the media, an implicit acknowledgment that it had violated important demarcations of operating freedom. By singling out mass, elite, and underground segments, the movies have tried to observe, or to appear to observe, the older distinctions.

Similar destabilization has occured in television because of market shifts brought about by extensive technological changes. Television is no longer a single medium effectively dominated by commercial, network broadcasting, but now includes public television, with a much smaller and more select audience, and rapidly growing cable systems. The last are not subject to the same range of Federal Communications Commission (FCC) regulations as the broadcast sector, and neither they nor public television are bound by the formal self-regulatory guidelines and proprietary policing of the National Association of Broadcasters and its code of standards. As a result, cable television, which often shows R- and X-rated films unedited, exercises an operating freedom much closer to that of the movies. Moreover, cable operators are often required by law to set aside one or more "public access" channels, the programming time on which must be leased to applicants on a first-come, first-served basis and the content of which is not subject to the operator's editorial control. The television screen, which in the past was governed by the informal restraints of a mass medium, may now carry a content otherwise associated with the elite or underground media.

Conflict over sexual content today is caused as much by the weakening of established differences among the media as by radical changes in the content of that expression. Differences in operating freedom are thus a key to managing the modern pornography problem. Prescriptive freedom, which in liberal democracies knows few media distinctions in law or ideology, has never been fully realized as operating freedom, however libertarian or censorious times may be. Judges and other policymakers face the difficult practical task of adjusting prescriptive freedom to popular demands for social control in a communications environment shaped by almost constant social, economic, and technological change. We turn now to the rise of that censorial demand and to mechanisms by which control is imposed. Doctrinal aspects of prescriptive freedom and control are taken up in the following chapter.

Pornography Arrived

Today's explosion of sexual representation is, of course, part of the larger "sexual revolution." It is not the first shift in sexual standards and probably not the last, but the rise in sexual expression is different from any occurring before. Advances in communications technology and increases in income and leisure time have made it far more pervasive and enveloping, so that the present American generation is probably the most sexually stimulated and confronted in history. Levels of tolerance too have changed; much representation considered objectionable or pornographic merely fifteen or twenty years ago is no longer so. But, as we shall note more fully in the next section, tolerance has clearly not kept up.

Sexual themes, language, and pictorial representation have been a source of entertainment or diversion in all human cultures. For many persons in liberal societies today, sexual themes and imagery in communications are a means, perhaps a chief one, of participating in the sexual revolution. The observable increase in conscious and overt interest in sexuality has brought with it greater willingness to indulge in sexual representation, including that designated as pornography by social judgment or as obscene by law. The constituency for pornography, though a small fraction of the total population, is sizable in absolute terms and no doubt larger than any similar group in the past. It does not appear to be a cross section, but neither can it be dismissed as a deviant fringe of society. Consumers of pornography today include many persons of above-average income, education, and occupational status.

Although pornography has become more explicit, it is doubtful whether deeply transgressive sexual themes and imagery have changed much. Themes and images that include genitalia, intercourse, and such deviant sexual acts as incest, sadomasochism, pedophilia, urolagnia, coprophagia, and bestiality have always been part of human fantasy life. Even when standards of public acceptability and obscenity have been relatively strict, extreme representation existed; it was merely harder to find. The modern pornography problem has less to do with new themes and imagery than with wider and readier availability of the "old" in a highly fluid communications environment.

This holds for representations in the established mass and elite media as well as for products of the pornography industry. For example, the number of "mainstream" sexually explicit magazines sold at most news outlets has grown to more than a dozen since appearance of the prototype, *Playboy,* in November 1953. Movies with R and sometimes X ratings are produced by major companies and exhibited in established theaters. Since the letter rating system was introduced in 1968, more than half the nearly 8,000 films rated have received an R or X, a fact that is even more striking when we realize that the rating standards themselves have been relaxed. Though broadcast television has rarely shown explicit sexual activity or even frontal nudity on camera, sexual reference and innuendo are now commonplace. Films with R and X ratings are shown on cable television, while public access channels may be leased for sexually explicit programming, such as the well-publicized *Midnight Blue* in New York. Sexually explicit videocassettes are stocked for rental or purchase by perhaps two-thirds of the country's 20,000 video outlets.[10] Sexually explicit lyrics are part of many rock music albums and videos marketed routinely by the established recording industry. Most of the sexual themes and imagery in mainstream distribution are not legally obscene today, but many are offensive and socially unacceptable to a large majority of the population.

The pornography industry has itself been a leading area of economic growth for the last quarter-century. Though it corresponds roughly to what was once the under-the-counter segment of the established media, its contemporary products are more explicit and far more available, privately and publicly. The industry was estimated to have sales of more than $500 million in the late 1960s, $4 billion in the mid-1970s, more than $5 billion in 1980, more than $7 billion in the early 1980s, and "multi-billions" in 1986.[11] It produces theatrical films, eight millimeter films, video- and audiocassettes, paperback books, photomagazines, photo sets, and accessories, including bondage devices and other sadomasochistic paraphernalia, aphrodisiacs, dildos, penis rings, and life-size inflatable dolls. About 100,000 persons are believed to be employed in the legal parts of the industry and perhaps tens of thousands more in illegal or fringe sectors.[12]

As many as twenty production companies turn out about 100 full-length sixteen and thirty-five millimeter films a year, which play in nearly 700 "adult" theaters, and produce an estimated $500 million in box office receipts.[13] A few of these films, such as *Deep Throat, The Devil in Miss Jones,* and *Behind the Green Door,* break out of this pattern into limited general distribution. *Deep Throat,* which has generated gross receipts of more than $50 million since its release in 1972, has become the most profitable motion picture ever made.[14] Fifty or more companies produce pornographic videocassettes. Some have recorded existing theatrical films, but most now make full-length features specifically for cassette distribution. An estimated 1,700 new titles were released in the mid-eighties. Sales and rentals of cassettes are believed to be as high as $750 million a year.[15]

Sales of photomagazines and paperback books, long the staple of adult retail outlets, have also risen. A survey of sixteen stores in several eastern cities revealed 2,325 magazine and 725 book titles. As many as 5,000 new book titles are published annually and hundreds of new magazine titles monthly. More than 60,000 magazine titles are believed to be currently available.[16] Half the sales are through the adult retail outlets, the remainder by mail order. Pornographic photo sets and audiocassettes are also available in the outlets or by mail. Sexually explicit telephone messages— "Dial-A-Porn"—became available following federal deregulation of "Dial It" service in 1982. One type of call provides a brief recorded message after a 976 number is dialed. Another offers a live conversation with a performer, which may last up to forty-five minutes and be paid for by credit card. Calls to the recorded messages, numbering in the hundreds of millions a year, represent a large fraction of all "Dial It" calls in the United States.[17]

Adult retail establishments can be found in every metropolitan area and in many smaller cities and towns. They are typically storefronts in downtown business districts, often on rundown blocks, but in some communities they may be in or near residential areas. Although it is illegal in most states to admit underage persons—usually those younger than seventeen or eighteen—proprietary enforcement is often lax.[18] The outlets are very different from the adults only bookstore of a generation ago, which stocked mainly photomagazines and paperback books. Today's shop carries a variety of media products and paraphernalia, often arranged by sexual interest or taste. Large establishments may also house "peep show booths"—four-sided cubicles of wood or plastic, typically three by five feet, containing a coin-operated movie peep show machine and a bench. These booths may have "glory holes" in side walls connecting them with adjacent booths to permit anonymous manual, oral, or anal sexual contact. Although small, the booths can be occupied by two persons. Deposits of semen, urine, feces, and saliva may create public health and sanitation problems even with periodic disinfecting. The booths may also facilitate the transmission of acquired immune deficiency syndrome (AIDS). Booths cost $20,000 to $30,000 each to install and are believed to be the most profitable segment of the pornography industry, producing estimated annual net profits of $2 billion.[19]

The industry's videocassettes, photomagazines, and paperback books may also be handled by many convenience stores, video stores, general bookstores, and newsstands, whose merchandise is mostly nonsexual and whose clientele is under no age restriction.

Sexually explicit portrayals of children—"child pornography"—which has also burgeoned, does not fall completely into the production and marketing patterns described. Most appears to be created noncommercially, through the photographic work of the child abusers themselves, or is of foreign origin. Much of it is sold or exchanged by mail. Rigorous enforcement of antiobscenity laws often results in its being unavailable, at least openly, even in adult retail outlets.[20]

It is not the steadily growing sales alone that make the pornography business profitable. Measured against nonsexual or less explicitly sexual products of comparable length and technical quality in the established media, the industry's production, distribution, and retailing costs are low and its markups high. A sixty- or ninety-minute feature recorded directly on videotape, for example, can often be completed in a matter of days or weeks on a budget of $4,000 to $20,000. Typically, the producer sells the tape to a distributor for twice the production costs. After preparing the individual cassettes and the advertising and promotional material, the distributor sells the product to a wholesaler at a 100 to 400 percent markup. The wholesaler adds another 10 to 20 percent in distributing the cassettes to the adult outlets. Where they are offered for sale (rather than rental), an additional 70 to 75 percent may be added.[21]

Its status on the fringe of law and respectability leaves the industry largely untouched by labor, health, safety, or other workplace rules. Exploitation of employees, including the performers, and illegal marketing practices are not uncommon and work to reduce costs, eliminate competition, and allow evasion of taxes. As one proprietary figure put it, "It is a very hard business to lose money in."[22] Extraordinary profits have allowed the industry to become better organized and more sophisticated in almost every facet of operation. The industry has set up national distribution networks, constructed buildings and made other large capital investments, published "trade" newsletters and arranged for systematic exchange of information, and, not least, hired highly skilled attorneys to defend against legal controls.

High profits and an operation at the edge of the law or in violation of it invite organized crime. Illegal or stigmatized goods and services for which there is high steady demand, such as prostitution, narcotics, and gambling, probably cannot be supplied on a large scale without the involvement of organized crime. The extent to which organized crime controls pornography is difficult to assess, though it appears greater in distribution and retailing than in production. In 1970, the President's Commission on Obscenity and Pornography found "insufficient evidence at present" of major control, but a 1978 report of the Federal Bureau of Investigation concluded that involvement was "significant" and that there was "obvious national control directly and indirectly by organized crime figures."[23] In 1986, the Attorney General's Commission on Pornography, which considered the question more extensively than the 1970 commission, concluded that organized crime not only was a major force in the industry but was linked to other criminal activity, including prostitution, narcotics distribution, money laundering, and murder.[24]

Pornography Opposed

So rapidly has the public availability of pornography changed, we can almost say that any expression that was at the center of a pornography conflict a generation ago would now be free of legal proscription, whereas almost any sexual expression proscribable today would, a generation ago, have had only the most clandestine distribution if it were commercially produced at all. Libertarian reformulation of obscenity law has allowed the content and availability of sexual expression to run far ahead of changes in tolerance. The difference in pace of these parallel developments—a major source of the public conflict over pornography—is unlikely to be relieved by voluntary tolerance's catching up. Despite the greater willingness of many persons to acknowledge interest in it, pornography remains widely unpopular and, for many, deeply disturbing.

Concern about availability and content is clearly documented in surveys of attitudes and opinion. Here the Commission on Obscenity and Pornography's 1970 national survey, based on interviews of a probability sample of 2,486 persons, twenty-one or older, is still the most thoroughgoing. Though the commission in its final report struck an optimistic note about tolerance and the growing ease with which sexual expression would be accepted, its own survey reveals a quite different picture. A degree of tolerance was indeed manifest, but most persons believed much sexual expression to be harmful and in need of restriction. Two-thirds agreed that "some people should not be allowed to read or see some things," and well over half of these thought restrictions should apply to adults as well as juveniles. Ninety-four percent of the entire sample felt that "sexual scenes" serving merely to entertain should not be allowed on television and 88 percent that they should not be allowed in movies. Even as "part of the story," such scenes were disapproved of on television by 85 percent and in movies by 69 percent. Availability of "sexual materials" in bookstores was opposed by 54 percent. Fifty-six percent did not wish to receive mailed advertisements of sexual materials, and one-third un-qualifiedly believed it "not all right" to have sexual materials available for adults for reading or viewing in their own homes. As for legal control, 91 percent believed distribution should be barred to persons under seventeen, 73 percent to persons under twenty-one, and 44 percent to "everybody." Very large percentages also favored other social control: "parents teaching children what is good for them" (96 percent), "librarians keeping objectionable materials off the shelves" (76 percent), "instruction in school that teaches children what is good for them" (76 percent), "having companies that produce sexual materials get together and agree not to print certain things" (72 percent), and "local boards of citizens from different walks of life keeping objectionable things out of the community" (72 percent).[25]

In a survey of attitudes and opinion of 1,061 randomly selected members of seventy organizations in the Detroit metropolitan area, also conducted by the commission, 43 percent of the respondents did not think that sexual materials should be available in bookstores even to persons who wanted to buy them. Of 86 percent of respondents having an opinion, almost two-thirds disagreed with the statement "erotic materials should be permitted to be sold; they should just be more difficult to obtain." Eighty-three percent believed "unsolicited advertisements for sexual materials are an invasion of privacy" and of 88 percent having an opinion, more than a fifth opposed public availability of studies of sexual behavior such as the Kinsey reports. Almost half would not allow a sexual scene in a movie even if it "helps tell the story."[26]

These findings of concern about sexual expression and low tolerance for its circulation are confirmed in almost every survey conducted since 1970. A nationwide Gallup poll in 1973 indicated that 55 percent of the respondents found pictures of nudes in magazines objectionable and 65 percent objected to actors or actresses appearing nude in Broadway plays.[27]

In a survey of views on sexual representation in movies conducted in five counties in Maryland in the early seventies, 90 percent of the 340 respondents said they would prohibit films depicting sexual acts with exposure of genitals from being viewed by juveniles, and more than a third would have barred them entirely; a quarter would have barred such films even where genitals were not shown. More than a quarter would have barred films in which "a large number of vulgar, obscene or four-letter words were used" and 16 percent where such language was used only occasionally. Eighty percent thought such films unsuitable for juveniles. Nineteen percent would have barred films where "female breasts were fully exposed and sex activity is implied but not shown" and 12 percent those in which sexual activity was merely implied rather than shown, even if there was little or no nudity.[28]

In a poll of 600 Minnesotans in 1973, in which respondents were asked to assume that they were serving on a commission to set standards in their community, 87 percent found depiction of "abnormal sexual relations" to be pornographic; 71 percent, "normal sexual relations"; 60 percent, a completely nude human body, male or female; 46 percent, the use of four-letter words; 40 percent, a "half-naked" female body; and 22 percent, a "half-naked" male body. Overall, a third of the respondents favored banning pornography completely. A Minnesota poll of 1,000 adults in 1977 indicated that of 93 percent having an opinion, two-thirds favored "more strict censorship" of adult bookstores and theaters that showed X-rated films. Only one in twelve favored less censorship.[29]

Though 35 percent of respondents in a nationwide Gallup poll in 1977 favored keeping local standards of availability of "sexually explicit material . . . as they are now," eight out of nine who were dissatisfied with standards believed stricter ones should be imposed.[30] The same question, put to 1,020 adults in a 1985 Gallup poll for *Newsweek*, indicated that 48 percent were willing to see standards remain the same; but of those who were dissatisfied, 91 percent favored stricter controls.[31] Since neither poll indicated whether "community standards" referred to enforced legal policy or, as is more likely, a set of prevailing norms, it is unclear what those who *were* satisfied were satisfied *with*.

In a 1977 Roper poll, based on a nationwide sample of 2,000, 40 percent believed X-rated movies should be banned completely. A nationwide Gallup poll in 1978 found that of respondents having an opinion on future trends, two-thirds would not welcome "more acceptance of sexual freedom." Seventy-three percent opposed such a development in response to the same question in 1981.[32]

A national survey of 1,500 adults by the National Opinion Research Center (NORC) in 1973, found that 89 percent of the respondents favored laws against the "distribution of pornography to persons under eighteen," while 42 percent thought "pornography" should be banned entirely. The same question asked in similar NORC polls in 1975, 1976, 1978, 1980, and 1983 yielded remarkably similar results: between 40 and 43 percent would ban pornography for everyone, between 88 and 94 percent for persons under eighteen. The percentage who opposed laws "forbidding the distribution of pornography" dropped from a 9–11 percent range in the early and mid-1970s to a 5–6 percent range in the 1980s.[33]

In the 1985 *Newsweek* poll, 73 percent said they would "totally ban" magazines depicting sexual violence and 93 percent would permit "no public display" of such publications. Similarly, 68 percent would bar theaters from showing movies that portrayed sexual violence and 63 percent the sale or rental of videocassettes that did so. An additional 21 and 23 percent, respectively, would place restrictions on movies and videos showing sexual violence. Large majorities would ban or in some other way restrict magazines showing adults having sexual relations (87 percent), X-rated movies in theaters (77 percent), and X-rated movies on videocassettes sold or rented for home viewing (71 percent). Even magazines merely showing nudity would be banned by a fifth of the respondents, while an additional one in two would bar their public display. Only for these magazines and for X-rated videocassettes for home viewing did tolerance levels (favoring no restrictions) reach 25 percent, and only in the case of the magazines showing nudity did the percentage who would tolerate them exceed the percentage who would ban them totally.[34]

The same poll showed a majority of respondents offended by the "sexual content" in the mainstream mass media: "top TV shows," "advertising," and "top Hollywood movies." But only one in four found such content offensive in the elite medium of "contemporary novels," another indication of the relatively greater salience of context over content.

One searches in vain for a single survey or poll of national, state, or community opinion attesting to popular support for pornography or "sexually explicit material" at its present level of availability or content.[35] The public opinion data confirm what is widely known intuitively and anecdotally: much sexual expression in the media is objectionable to large numbers of persons. Depending on the specific representation and the medium being used, very large majorities favor censorship. The surveys and polls reveal another striking fact: large numbers of persons, sometimes a majority, would prohibit, rather than simply restrict, a great range of sexual expression—nudity, four-letter words, for example—in fairly common circulation today and not legally proscribable by current standards. Overwhelming majorities favor restricting, if not entirely prohibiting, most erotic expression for young persons.

The marked objection to pornography cannot be attributed to some return to puritanism or a general sexual squeamishness. In fact, certain other problematic sexual communication receives strong affirmation. The six NORC polls, for example, consistently show support of 90 percent or more for making birth control information "available to anyone who wants it," and 76 to 80 percent for "sex education in the public schools."[36]

Sexual violence, "abnormal" or less conventional sexual acts, and homosexuality are more likely to be objected to than other depiction. In the national survey by the President's Commission, sexual activities involving whips, belts, spanking, "mouth–organ contact between a man and a woman," and "sexual activities between people of the same sex" were more objectionable than heterosexual intercourse, which was, in turn, more objectionable than mere depictions of sexual organs.[37] When asked to view a series of sixty erotic pictures, members of community organizations in a large metropolitan area found those of homosexual fellatio and cunnilingus the most offensive. Other portrayals ranking high were those of group sexual activity, heterosexual fellatio and cunnilingus, male masturbation, and intercourse. Least offensive were pictures of clothed persons, brassiere advertisements, *Playboy* nudes, and heterosexual nudist groups. Unsurprisingly, pictorial representation is more often objectionable than description through language, though four-letter words are often an exception.[38]

Large numbers of persons believe that the sexual expression they find objectionable is also harmful, at least to other persons. In the national survey, 56 percent thought such expression led to a breakdown of morals, 49 percent, to the commission of rape, 44 percent, to a loss of respect for women, and 38 percent, to making persons "sex crazy." Many of the remaining respondents were unsure of the effects.[39] These findings are largely confirmed by the six NORC surveys between 1973 and 1983. The percentage of respondents believing that "sexual materials" (which, subjectively, might include much more than socially designated pornography) "lead to a breakdown of morals" ranged from 51 percent to more than

60 percent. Fifty to 58 percent thought such communication "leads people to commit rape." For both sets of belief, the percentages increased slightly from the earlier to the later polls.[40]

Despite these findings of utilitarian concern, evidence indicates that objections may also have a less rational, perhaps even a less conscious, base. Percentages of persons believing that pornography should be restricted or prohibited, for example, are generally higher than those believing it to be harmful. This holds even though substantial numbers recognize that pornography may also have some beneficial or at least socially neutral effects, such as providing entertainment or information, improving sexual relations in marriage, or "giving relief to persons with sex problems."[41] Moreover, of those believing pornography to be harmful, strikingly few believe they themselves have been injured. In the 1970 President's Commission survey, only 2.5 percent of those believing that pornography led to a breakdown of morals (1.5 percent of the entire sample) said that they personally experienced that effect. Fewer than one half of 1 percent said the same about their belief that pornography led to rape or made persons "sex crazy." And only 5 percent said that they themselves had experienced a loss of respect for women. But where positive or socially neutral effects were perceived, much higher percentages reported being personally affected.

Who, then, is seen as being injured by pornography? About a quarter of those believing pornography to be harmful said it was to "someone they knew personally." For the remainder, it was to no one in particular.[42] Something is obviously askew when large numbers of persons believe pornography to be harmful yet almost none believe themselves to be harmed, especially as respondents were carefully selected to be representative of a general population. Reality cannot possibly confirm both perceptions. Large numbers must be mistaken either about pornography's being harmful to others or about its not being harmful to themselves. Directors of the survey, though not addressing this conundrum directly, thought the perception of harmful effects to be based on "hearsay" and a "part of the conversational currency about erotic materials" rather than on actual events.[43]

This explanation may be valid in part, but there also are compelling psychodynamic reasons why pornography would be seen almost exclusively as harmful to others (including persons unknown) rather than to oneself, especially where very large numbers of the same respondents also support restrictions on pornography. Normal psychosexual development produces a need to repress many sexual fantasies. These may be touched or stirred by pornography's forbidden images, producing sexual arousal or feelings of disgust or both. For many persons, perception of pornography as harmful mainly to others may be a vital projection, that is, a defense, not to be understood simply as hearsay or unfounded cognition.

Our conclusion draws additional support from the tenacity with which censorial views are often held and their resistance to rational appeal. In the national survey, more than half of those favoring some restriction of pornography—two-thirds of the entire sample—would not change their view even if pornography were clearly shown not to be harmful. Only a third would be persuaded, while the remainder had no opinion. This pattern is all the more striking when we realize that interview respondents who expressly reject hypothesized conclusive evidence of harmlessless may be forced to confront not merely their own irrationality on the question but also their abandonment of the socially approved posture of rational citizens ready to give weight to considerations of utility. We may assume, then, the actual number of those who would hold to their censorial views even if pornography were clearly shown not harmful is even greater than the already high percentages suggested by the survey. The same persistent belief in the face of contrary evidence is evident in the large numbers of persons in the survey and large numbers in the later NORC studies who believe pornography leads to rape. Of all hypothesized effects of pornography offered to respondents in the surveys, the one for which there is the least evidence or scientific support is the arousal to antisocial acts.

Rational concerns about harm do exist and may be intelligently held, especially in the absence of conclusive opposing evidence, and may be particularly well reasoned about the exposure of juveniles. Yet clearly they cannot account for all or even most censorial energy; and, alone, they provide a narrow base for formulation of public policy, even when well reasoned. As we shall argue more fully later, effective political management of pornography requires a weighing of all objections, not just those that seem to be rationally held.

Objections to pornography are not evenly distributed through the population. Though demographic differences are not great, they are consistent and stable and confirm the mass/elite distinctions we have come to expect on questions of tolerance. For example, Gallup polls asking whether local standards should be made more strict for nudity in magazines and on stage found objections to pornography to vary inversely with levels of education, income (except sometimes for the lowest group), and occupational status (except sometimes for manual laborers).[44] Clear gender, age, and marital status differences exist: women, older persons, and married persons are more censorious. Attitudes vary with size of community: persons in smaller cities and towns tend to be more censorious than those in larger cities, except in those of a million or more, whose residents tend to be more censorious than in mid-sized big cities. Smaller differences exist for race, religion, region, and party identification, with whites, Protestants, Republicans, and persons in the Midwest and South being slightly more censorious than others.[45] Persons who attend church more frequently or have less experience with pornography tend to have more restrictive beliefs than those who attend less often or have more experience. [46] In one community study, members of church groups with lower average education than members of other community organizations were more restrictive than members of community service organizations, who in turn were more restrictive than members of professional groups with higher average education.[47] Demographic differences are less pronounced where consensus is greater on the offensiveness of a particular expression.[48]

Censorial activists—those who participate actively in community antipornography drives—tend to have middle- and upper-middle-level incomes, white-collar jobs, and some college education, are somewhat more conservative in their general beliefs, more active in civic, community, and church organizations, and more likely to come from small towns.[49] In contrast, anticensorship activists tend to be "better educated, younger, less family and religiously oriented, reared in larger cities, in professional or technical occupations . . . less authoritarian, dogmatic, and politically intolerant . . . less traditional in their view of sexual behavior, and . . . to oppose censorship for any purpose."[50] They are more frequent users of the mass media, and their views appeared to be part of a general liberal ideology extending to other issues such as racial integration and pollution of the environment.[51] They tend to speak of pornography "less as a single issue than as a symbolic representation of an alternative value/norm/role complex"—one opposed to that of censorial activists.[52]

These manifest demographic and attitudinal differences are not surprising. Many of the sharper ones—in education and income levels, occupational status, and size of community—confirm what we have come to expect in a modern liberal mass democracy that is increasingly centralized and homogeneous in its political and cultural life. The chief modal characteristics of that society—a high school education, middle and lower-middle incomes, low- and middle-level white-collar employment, being white, Protestant, church-attending, and married—are also the characteristics of those tending to be more censorious rather than less. These characteristics parallel objections to theme and image already noted, where perceived offensiveness varied with the degree of explicitness or deviancy in behavior portrayed. In the aggregate, neither these substantive objections to pornography nor the objectors themselves appear idiosyncratic or in any way exceptional; quite the opposite.

Whether the objections are wise or persuasive, two things are clear: opposition to pornography has a popular element (not based simply on rational fear of harm), and those who favor greater control are more representative of their society or community than those who do not.

The Anatomy of Control

Social regulation of pornography is not simply a legal or governmental matter. It is true that official policy prevails where conflict has escalated and may also set a general tone even where conflict has been contained or resolved at lower levels. But control of sexual expression is a vast patchwork of unpredictable and sometimes ungeneralizable actions, tactics, and strategies that are both public and private, legal and extralegal, deliberate and spontaneous, discriminating and heavy-handed, measured and overzealous, rational and irrational. Its boundaries, affected by the types of tolerance noted earlier, define the operating rather than the prescribed freedom of the media. Thus what is actually restricted in content or distribution is usually more than the law requires and less than preferred by most members of most communities. Standards of popular acceptability, though more permissive today than in the past, are more conservative and restrictive than the libertarian standards that prevail in highest policy.

Changes in communications technology, sexual attitudes, and the Supreme Court's obscenity doctrine have destabilized former patterns of control without finding a new equilibrium. Though a balance between freedom and control constantly shifts, there are periods of stability and instability. We have been in one of the latter for at least the last twenty-five years. If a new equilibrium is established, it will very likely be at a level more libertarian than in the distant past but less libertarian than that now prescribed in highest policy. In the remainder of the chapter we consider how social control has been imposed on unacceptable sexual expression, the instruments used, their effectiveness, and their relation to one another.

The Marketplace

For many libertarians, decisions in the communications marketplace by individual members of the audience provide all the control of sexual expression that is necessary. Many proprietors cite the "voice" of the marketplace to explain their own production or distribution decisions about sexually explicit communication: they merely provide what is demanded and do not offer what is not. It is true enough that any consumer of communication can register an individual judgment simply by turning a dial or not buying a ticket or making a purchase. Multiplied thousands or millions of times, these "box office" votes, theoretically at least, serve as a kind of social control, since they can make unwanted communication unprofitable or less profitable than the acceptable.

Yet viewed more closely, the marketplace is a much less effective control than might be assumed. First, though the box office is not silent, it does not explain its verdict. Proprietors can never be sure of the specific grounds for the box office result or even whether the nature of sexual portrayal was a factor. Second, where a communication has become the object of a publicized censorship struggle, that attention may itself produce a box office triumph, thus defeating the marketplace altogether as an instrument of control. Third, the effectiveness of the marketplace as a functioning control varies with proprietary costs, and is greatest with big-budget productions such as Hollywood movies, network television programs, and mass circulation magazines. Yet many commercial communications, including those involved in disputes, are cheaply produced and can often show significant profits from relatively small audiences. In the case of the typical low-budget X-rated movie, for example, even massive rejection by the marketplace may not be as effective as social control. Finally, where communications are not offered for profit, box office sanctions are largely irrelevant.

For the marketplace to function as effective control it must be clear and exact in its message, severe enough in its penalty to threaten profitability, and not beaten to the censorial mark by other controls. Except perhaps for an organized boycott, this combination of circumstances is extremely improbable. A communication about which the box office message was clear and the sanction sharp would already very likely have been the target of other objections, pressures, and regulative action. Finally the individual viewer, reader, or listener cannot be meaningfully "enfranchised" without advance information or warning about the communication. Unwanted or offensive communication that takes its viewer, listener, or reader by surprise—a scene in a movie or television drama, for example—may reduce the marketplace decision to walking out or turning away, choices that come too late either to impose direct economic sanction or to avoid the experience.

Proprietary Restraint

Self-regulation functions in all media and at every level. Much of it is unseen, unarticulated, and in some instances no doubt unconscious. Although often not even perceived as social control, it is probably the most effective kind of all when applied, because the potentially offending communication may not reach its full audience or even be produced. Proprietary restraint is usually greatest where audience and local interests have greatest access to proprietors. Small and medium-size newspapers, local radio and television stations, local newsstands, bookstores, libraries, and movie theaters are examples. Such restriction usually reflects purely personal values or those of the community; in the latter case, values may be internalized or simply accepted, for tactical purposes, sometimes after pressures have been applied.

Physical or organizational distance between production and retailing sectors of a medium may produce sharply contrasting degrees of operating self-restraint and an absence of accord among proprietary groups. Clashes between movie exhibitors' groups and production studios, between local television stations and networks over programming, or between newsstand dealers and distributors or publishers are not uncommon. The most effective self-regulation outside the community is likely to be in policies developed by major national corporate proprietors—a television network, for example—and enforced within their proprietary domains. Often developed as a response to diverse censorial pressures, such policies are subject to erosion or reversal when pressures abate or when continuing the policy would impose substantial economic costs, especially loss of a competitive advantage to a corporate rival.

In several media with production far removed from local reaction, self-regulation has been organized formally to satisfy retail-level proprietary interests or to head off legal action or other external controls. It is most highly developed in the movies, where it has had continuous life since the Hays Office was established in 1930 and is part of the internal government of the medium. In broadcasting, network radio and television maintain codes for programming and advertising, and both have code boards and a code authority director who may monitor programs, attempt to reconcile complaints, and actually enforce code provisions on broadcasters. Although direct sanctions, limited to forbidding display of the "Seal of Good Practice" and the removal of a station's call letters from the Code Register, are relatively weak, voluntary observance is usually high.

Institutionalized self-regulation functions as a highly visible organized defense against external threats and pressures and, as such, has a cosmetic as well as a regulatory purpose. Antitrust laws and corporate rivalry require that observance be largely voluntary. Effectiveness depends on the strength of continuing censorial pressures, the threat of other governmental controls, and the degree of economic concentration within a medium.

Though not technically a proprietary restraint, the influence of advertisers and patron sponsors is integrated with production and sometimes retailing, and is typically felt before communication reaches its audience. In "riding" a primary communication to carry their own message, advertisers hope of course to induce members of the audience to make a favorable decision about their products. The goal is jeopardized, if not defeated, by negative box office decisions, and much more by retaliatory responses. Advertisers may thus try to anticipate strong reaction and head it off. Active influence is probably greatest in broadcasting and mass circulation magazines. Interest in not offending may be even greater in newspapers, but proprietary restraint in that medium is typically so well established and effective that advertiser concerns are less apt to require articulation.

Advertiser influence is virtually nonexistent in the elite media, though patron sponsorship may occasionally have regulatory effect. Nor is it a factor in the movies—another reason why that medium has had the most highly developed formal proprietary regulation.

Informal Action

No society or community is without regulative standards imposed informally through private acts of individuals and groups in everyday encounters. These may be low-level, inconspicuous, even subtle. They may involve not much more than a raised eyebrow or simple articulation of values, and thus be part of socialization itself. They fill the interstices of social control in all cultures. Our concern here is with action that is more deliberate, specifically purposeful, and aggressive. It may be limited to the acts of a single person or be well organized and have hundreds, even thousands, of participants. It may involve only private persons and groups or be carried out extralegally by governmental authorities or by combinations of authorities and private persons. It may often precede such formal controls as inspection, arrest, or prosecution. Unsuccessful attempts to impose informal control may spur demand for formal action. On the other hand, where legal controls are hard to impose or authorities are reluctant to take formal action, private pressures may be escalated.

Because informal control takes a variety of forms and often leaves no public trace, we know little for certain about its incidence. Yet there is reason to believe that its more deliberate and aggressive form may increase as the gap between what is legally proscribable and what is socially acceptable widens. The number of censorial incidents reported by American librarians, for example, grew tenfold during the 1970s, and the 1,000 or more incidents reported in 1981 are believed to represent only about 20 percent of those actually occurring.[53] More than a third of high school librarians in a 1982 national survey reported having books censorially challenged and more than a sixth, periodicals or films. These figures were higher than those in similar surveys in the 1960s and 1970s. Seventeen percent reported contact with organized groups of critics compared with only 1 percent so reporting five years earlier.[54]

Informal action is not confined to small communities. Perhaps because the range of sexual communication available tends to be greater in cities, almost every metropolitan area, including New York, has experienced periodic and sometimes large-scale protests and campaigns. Most often such pressures are directed at adult movie houses and retail outlets whose stock is pornographic publications and paraphernalia. Conventional movie theaters and bookstores are sometimes targets in the case of a particular film or book. In recent years, pressures have also been directed at local cable television systems over programming, particularly that on public access channels.

Pressures may focus on legally proscribable expression—obscenity—and serve to bring it to the attention of authorities. But most targets of informal censorship are representations the law would protect however, unacceptable they may otherwise be. The aim is often restriction of public display or availability, rather than outright prohibition.

Organized efforts have diverse sponsorship. Local associations of ministers and other church-connected groups, social and fraternal orders, feminists, education-minded groups such as the PTA, business associations, and local chapters of such established censorship organizations as the Citizens for Decent Literature have all been active in informal control.[55] In some communities, ad hoc local groups have led campaigns.

Most organized efforts employ one or more of three basic strategies: seeking publicity to generate wider public pressure, direct confrontation of proprietary interests, and persuading public officials to take legal or extralegal action.[56] Addressing the community at large serves both to agitate and to educate. Tactics include letter-to-the-editor campaigns, talks to local groups, organization of public forums or seminars, designation of "decency weeks," distribution of leaflets, spot announcements on local radio and television stations, and lobbying the media for interviews, editorial support, and refusal of ads from adult movie theaters. General campaigns almost always try to capture public attention. In a three-day "Stamp Out Smut" rally in New York, 8,000 persons, led by a number of stage actors and other celebrities, marched through Times Square.[57] Often, however, antipornography groups have chosen to work quietly and minimize publicity, either because members were reluctant to give undue attention, free advertising, to the object of complaint or because they did not want to risk being labeled censors. Usually in such cases, the group has been seeking specific and limited regulative ends rather than full-scale censorship.

Direct action against local proprietors may begin with polite requests and reasoned attempts at persuasion or with threats, implied or express.[58] If these approaches fail and conflict escalates, picketing, boycotts, or other disruptive action may be organized. In extreme cases, movie ticket lines have been infiltrated by persons buying tickets with $100 bills or pennies painstakingly counted. Patrons entering or leaving theaters or bookstores have been shouted at or photographed. Proprietors have had leases canceled by landlords themselves under pressure, been subjected to citizen's arrests, expelled from church congregations, and otherwise socially ostracized.[59]

Occasionally, in the hands of zealots or unstable individuals, direct action has taken tragic and even criminal turns, including the theft or destruction of library card catalogs, early-morning rifle shots through storefront windows, stink bombs in theaters, and even theater arson. Supreme Court Justice Byron White was struck in the face after addressing a bar association meeting by a man from the audience shouting "You brought us pornography and four-letter words!" In Minneapolis, a woman who had been handing out antipornography leaflets in front of an adult bookstore entered the store and, drenching herself with gasoline, set herself aflame.[60]

Much energy is spent lobbying police chiefs and prosecutors to crack down or on convincing local and state legislators to enact new laws or invigorate old ones. Local officials are frequently sympathetic, but see the matter as futile from a legal standpoint. If they act, it is usually late in a conflict, when private actions have failed and dissatisfaction remains high. Initially, they may apply pressure of their own or take extralegal action rather than begin formal proceedings. Such tactics are often seen as necessary steps in the evolution of formal action, and as far more efficient if they succeed.[61] A formal action in the case of an obscenity prosecution is likely to be costly, time-consuming, and risky because of the high failure rate under the libertarian obscenity doctrine.

Face-to-face efforts at persuasion are the most common official action. The assignment usually falls to a police officer or member of the prosecutor's office, who may make a request, offer "advice," or threaten a raid and arrest. When threats are carried out, the aim is often to escalate pressure as much as to prepare for an indictment. Police "overkill" is not uncommon. Employees may be arrested with proprietors and the "fruits" and "instrumentalities" of the allegedly illegal activity confiscated. In periodic actions against Times Square adult movie houses, New York City police routinely arrested projectionists—not to bring charges against them, which might not hold up in court, but in the hope that a night in jail would provoke the militant projectionists union to bring pressure of its own against theater owners. Since most adult movie houses and storefronts are rented, landlords may be pressured to evict, break leases, or harass their tenants. "Routine"—really ad hoc—inspections by fire marshals or health wardens can uncover violations of detailed and sometimes archaic codes. Police or prosecutors may capriciously enforce curfew ordinances or blue laws. In the case of public or school libraries, funds for acquisitions or other operations may be reduced.[62]

We cannot know for certain how effective private or official pressures are. Without large-scale, systematic surveys, we cannot even be sure how often they are employed. Despite occasional well-publicized incidents of the sort already mentioned, most encounters leave little or no public trace and are meant to leave none. Since pornography has continued to become more explicit and grow in volume, it would be easy to say that local pressures, like most other controls, are largely ineffective. Yet there is reason to believe that the explicitness and availability of pornography would be greater still without informal pressures against it.[63]

There is some evidence that censorship campaigns against newsstands and newsdealers meet with short-run success, with offending publications removed from sale.[64] Once censorship pressures abate, as they invariably do, the magazines are often restocked, in some instances bringing renewed pressure. Campaigns fail in the short run where proprietors believe that they can defend themselves in court or that cooperation with complainants would only bring more demands. If public authorities refuse to support a campaign, it is easier for wholesalers and retailers to resist pressures. Short-run failures are also likely if leaders of the campaign themselves become convinced that prevailing obscenity doctrine would prevent legal sanctions from succeeding. In the long run, most local campaigns fail, chiefly because of the substantial profits from the offending publications, sales of which may be increased by the publicity of the campaigns. Publishers, well aware of the Supreme Court's decisions widening protection of sexual expression, often pressure wholesalers and retailers to restock. The reluctance of many censorial activists to be labeled censors may also have a long-term effect on campaigns.

Of nearly 1,000 censorship incidents reported by public and school librarians in a ten-year period, offending books or periodicals were removed from shelves and circulation in 58 percent of the cases, and in 10 percent the holdings were retained but placed on restricted shelves and parental permission required before they could be viewed or borrowed.[65] More than half the complaints reported by high school librarians in a period in the early eighties resulted in the challenged work's removal from the shelves or curriculum.[66]

Reports of censorship pressures appear in the press and media trade publications almost weekly. These conflicts have left traces, but many others—in the case of public and school libraries, an estimated four times as many—do not. No doubt the pressures in the unreported incidents often fail, but it may equally be the case that they are unpublicized when they achieve their ends.

Whatever their immediate effects, many censorial incidents have longer-run effects on proprietary self-restraint. A bookstore owner, movie exhibitor, or librarian feeling the edge of social control confrontationally or merely hearing about such conflict may silently, perhaps even unconsciously, alter his or her future policy. More than half the wholesale and retail newsdealers in small and middle-size cities reported censoring their inventory and were more likely to do so when they had been subjected to pressure. A prior censorship is practiced by many librarians when they do not purchase books because they believe they might be the object of future complaint. Though personal values may be involved, anticipation of what the community will tolerate and uncertainty about the legal status of the publications appear to be more decisive considerations.[67] Where proprietors are members of the community and value that status, informal pressure is more likely to succeed and anticipatory self-censorship to follow as a secondary result.[68]

On the other hand, proprietors of adult bookstores, movie houses, and peep show parlors, who are usually the chief adversaries of informal censors, are often not members of the local community and may have ties to organized crime. They usually are less intimidated by censorship pressure, considering it simply a cost of doing business. Against them, informal censorship is least effective both immediately and in the long run. The resistance of these proprietors, reinforced by new constitutional rights, is a chief factor in the losing battle to impose social control on commercial pornography at the local level.

Although all efforts at informal control are intended to be coercive, relatively few are of the overzealous, unlawful, even violent sort noted earlier. The occasional bizarre or dramatic tactic tends to obscure unexceptional requests, complaints, or demands that are far more numerous. The picture of the informal censor as irrational and belligerent is a stereotype. In most cases, a complainant, knowledgeable or not, is apt to be a "concerned parent or citizen sincerely interested in the future well-being of the community."[69] That most would recoil from being labeled censors, even from thinking of themselves as such, is also a tribute to the underlying ethos of liberty and the esteem in which freedom of speech is held, at least as an abstract principle.

Social control in a pluralist society is sometimes sought by small or unrepresentative groups. Informal censorship, however, often emerges from popular elements in the community, and its aims, if not always tactics, have wide support. For this reason, local executive and legislative authorities are seldom on the proprietor's side in a conflict, and it is not unusual for them, and sometimes local judges as well, to be sympathetic to the censorship interest and eventually to ally themselves with it. Though generally viewed with misgiving by libertarians, responsiveness of local nonjudicial officials to strong and persistent complaints from large numbers of persons is part of the political logic of a democratic society.

The Criminal Process

Prosecution for unlawful possession, sale, distribution, or exhibition of sexual expression defined as obscene is the traditional formal means for controlling pornography. Though the remedy is now almost entirely statutory, its roots are well established in Anglo-American common law. From a libertarian perspective, it is probably the preferred mode of formal social control. The defendant proprietor is entitled to a trial with its procedural safeguards, including the presumption of innocence and the heavier burden of proof borne by the government. The conflict is resolved by an open, deliberate process governed by rigorous standards of proof, with each side presenting its case to a presumably impartial third party. Unless and until a conviction is obtained, the offending book, periodical, film, or other expression, theoretically at least, may continue to circulate in the marketplace of ideas, in a sense also being presumed innocent. Yet, despite these libertarian advantages, the criminal process can impose heavy burdens on a proprietor, including risk of fine or imprisonment if convicted. And even a defendant who wins may have major legal expenses, the more if an appeal is necessary.

The number of actions in the United States ranges between 2,000 and 3,000 a year, but criminal prosecution remains a relatively little-used means of social control.[70] The reasons are several. Prosecution is almost always a later stage or escalation of an existing conflict, in effect, a set-piece battle fought only after efforts at compromise have failed. It is not surprising to find that prosecutors in larger cities, where informal control is less effective, are more likely to bring actions, or at least to see the need for doing so, than those in smaller communities.[71]

A trial may last several days or a week and requires considerable advance preparation. Thus it is costly and time-consuming for a prosecutor's office, typically understaffed and geared to avoiding trials where possible. Moreover, the prevailing obscenity doctrine makes cases difficult to win at trial and overturns many convictions on appeal. Because obscenity cases are only a small fraction of all criminal actions, many prosecutors have limited experience with them and find themselves overmatched in court, where a defendant's counsel may be a specialist in obscenity. Rare is the state's attorney who does not understand "the difference between prosecuting a mugger represented by a young public defender with too many cases and too little time and resources . . . and prosecuting a pornography distributor who has a team of senior trial lawyers at his disposal and who will probably receive only a minimal sentence even if convicted."[72] Where cases are disposed of through plea bargaining, the modest fines are easily absorbed by the proprietor as a cost of doing business. Finally, the Supreme Court's requirement of "scienter"—that proprietary interests must have specific knowledge of the proscribably obscene nature of the material sold or displayed to be held criminally liable for its circulation— has often meant that absentee owners of adult establishments, the big fish of the pornography industry, cannot be successfully prosecuted even where local jurisdiction is obtained.[73]

For these reasons, many prosecutors, although generally sympathetic to complaints about pornography, give relatively low priority to obscenity cases. The criminal prosecution today is likely to be used sparingly, only against the most explicit hard-core pornography, and, even then, only against organized proprietary interests. The sorts of books, magazines, and films involved in censorship causes célèbres of the past, or that arguably have artistic, literary, or informational status, are unlikely to be targets of criminal indictment now.

A successful prosecution, of course, like successful pressure, may have censorial effect well beyond the communication at issue. In view of the difficulties of winning obscenity cases, it is probably this "power of example" that lies behind most prosecutions today, rather than punishment of particular persons for specific wrongdoing. The threat of successful prosecution has no doubt effected far more control than the action itself.

Most obscenity actions allege violations of state or local laws, and the persons indicted are usually involved in local distribution or sale. Federal prosecution is now limited largely to child pornography or cases growing out of large Justice Department police operations such as MIPORN, in Miami, directed against large-scale pornography production and distribution networks linked to organized crime. Relatively few federal actions arise from the thousands of investigations by postal authorities of allegedly obscene material every year or from the thousands of seizures of imported material by the Customs Service. Customs and postal agents commonly perceive federal prosecutors as reluctant to bring obscenity cases.[74]

On the other hand, a few U.S. attorneys, encouraged by the Supreme

Court's emphasis on the use of local rather than national standards to determine obscenity, have invoked federal statutes that make it unlawful to transport or conspire to transport such materials in interstate commerce. Usually these actions are aimed at publishers and other nonlocal parties involved in production. In a well-publicized case in Memphis growing out of shipment of the film *Deep Throat* into Tennessee, these "outsiders" included several of the film's performers and members of a New York advertising agency that had prepared copy for it. Libertarians have been critical of bringing publishers and other producers to trial in local communities where materials have been shipped or sold rather than in communities of origin, calling the practice "forum shopping." Though these prosecutions provide the community with one of its few avenues of immediate attack on outside or absent proprietary interests, it seems clear they are also often aimed at a long-run intimidation of those interests.

Other Official Action

In view of the high costs and uncertain results of obscenity actions, many cities and towns have sought to control pornography through residual municipal powers (see Table 6). Since Boston's initiative in the early 1970s, local zoning laws have increasingly been used to regulate the location of adult bookstores, movie houses, and peep show parlors. Focusing on restriction rather than outright suppression of pornography, they are designed either to concentrate the adult establishments or to disperse them. In Boston's case, a two-and-a-half-block downtown area, already the site of many such outlets, was designated an "adult entertainment district," and opening new adult enterprises in other parts of the city was barred. For better or worse, the "Combat Zone," as the area has come to be known, is a tourist attraction contributing to the economy of the city.

Dispersal is more often the course. Several large cities, including Detroit, Los Angeles, and Kansas City, and many smaller ones, have used zoning powers to bar adult establishments within a certain distance— 1,000 feet, for example—of any other adult business or of schools and churches. These laws, which are not retroactive, aim at new establishments and are often seen as fighting neighborhood deterioration as well as imposing social control. The Supreme Court's denial of a First Amendment challenge to Detroit's regulations in *Young v. American Mini Theatres,* in 1976, spurred zoning efforts in other cities.[75] Because these regulations represent an effort to "live with" pornography, although limiting its location, the Court held that they avoided the constitutional objections that community-wide suppression would raise. Though the laws sidestep the difficult question what is or is not proscribable obscenity, they do present definitional problems about what is or is not a regulated use, that is, an adult establishment.

In many communities, officials have used public nuisance laws and other civil statutes to enjoin sale or exhibition of proscribably obscene materials, and have sometimes succeeded in closing adult establishments. Obscenity must still be proved, but the state carries a lesser burden of proof about the defendant proprietor's conduct than it would in a criminal action. Absence of criminal penalties may increase the chance of a censorial verdict.[76]

A few cities still employ boards of censors to review and license movies before exhibition. Typically, the agencies are empowered to refuse permits to obscene films. However, the Supreme Court has required that any film found objectionable must be promptly taken to court and its obscenity proved before local exhibition can be finally denied.[77] Though the Court has never held prior censorship of the medium to be unconstitutional, procedural requirements on the boards are cumbersome and costly. Few still operate, and most that do deal only with age classification—review and regulation for juveniles. There is little doubt that governmental prior restraint would be unconstitutional if imposed on the printed media.

In response to feminist censorial efforts, a number of cities have considered ordinances attacking pornography as a violation of women's rights. Typically, these measures would bar any depiction of women sexually enjoying pain or humiliation or simply being an object of sexual domination or conquest. A woman who felt aggrieved by such portrayal could bring a civil action against a proprietor or file a complaint with a local equal opportunity office, which, in turn, would be empowered to seek a "cease and desist" order.[78] Constitutionally, such laws pose equal protection rights against free speech rights. The Supreme Court has affirmed lower court decisions that the laws discriminate unconstitutionally against the content of speech by seeking to establish an approved view of women and to silence nonconforming expression.[79]

Social control of pornography is a complex phenomenon variously determined by consumer decisions, proprietary self-restraint, and manifold informal pressures, as well as by law and official policy. Neither regulative standards nor actual operating freedom is ever constant. In the last

TABLE 6. Contextual Analysis of Selected Controls on Sexual Expression

Type of Regulation	Protected Interest	Availability of Target Expression	Perceived Offensiveness	Redemptive Value
Prohibition	General population	None, except "underground"	"Patent"	None, supposedly
Restriction: Audience	Juveniles	For adults only	"Patent" in re juveniles	Variable
Restriction: Location	Neighborhood, "unwilling audience"	At designated locations	Very high	Variable
Restriction: Display	Juveniles, "unwilling audience"	Retail segregation, concealment	High, very high	Variable
Restriction: Media	Juveniles, "unwilling audience"	Confined to certain media	High, very high	Variable, possibly great

Type of Regulation	Nomen-clature	Major Focus of Control	Effectiveness	Operating Freedom
Prohibition	"Hard-core pornography"	Criminal law, informal	Direct: slight; indirect: considerable	Narrow but greater than law allows
Restriction: Audience	"Obscene" (for juveniles)	Proprietary, informal, law	Uncertain	High for adults
Restriction: Location	"Adult"	Zoning law	Great, but not retroactive	Geographic limitation only
Restriction: Display	"Adult"	Informal, proprietary	Uncertain, probably mixed	Display limitation only
Restriction: Media	"Indecent"	Proprietary, informal	Generally high	Variable but less than law allows

twenty-five years expanded constitutional protection of free speech has weakened authoritative and proprietary control and, with major changes in communications technology, has destabilized many distinctions in operating freedom among the mass, elite, and underground media. The resulting pornography explosion, breaking all previous barriers, has generated great popular discontent not stilled even by more liberal sexual attitudes.

Disparities between formal, official standards and informal, popular ones are not new. The one measure is almost always certain to be more restrictive or more permissive than the other. Continuing high levels of popular resentment in a mass democracy are another matter; they indicate that a new equilibrium between free speech values and concerns about pornography is in order but yet to be established.

Chapter Eight

Pornography and Law

We have been unable to provide "sensitive tools" to separate obscenity from other sexually oriented but constitutionally protected speech, so that efforts to suppress the former do not spill over into the suppression of the latter. [I] am reluctantly forced to the conclusion that none of the available formulas . . . can reduce the vagueness . . . to a tolerable level.

Justice William Brennan, dissenting,
Paris Adult Theatre I v. Slaton

Even though we recognize that the First Amendment will not tolerate the total suppression of erotic materials that have some arguably artistic value, it is manifest that society's interest in protecting this type of expression is of a wholly different and lesser magnitude than the interest in untrammeled political debate.

Justice John Paul Stevens, *Young v. American Mini Theatres*

Although law is but one instrument in social control of sexual expression, it is society's ultimate sanction. Its standards, narrow or broad, and its procedures, solicitous or repressive, carry well beyond the formal writ and set the tone for an entire communications environment. Legal determination of obscenity is made by legislative enactment, and by judicial interpretation of such law and its application to specific cases. Here we deal with highest legal and public policy, the Supreme Court's doctrine of obscenity, which governs both statute and case law.

In its extraordinary constitutional protection of sexual expression, the Court has opened new First Amendment territory but has also formulated a proscriptive test that ignores much of the social context of communications. It has failed to say why obscenity is bad, that is, why it should be controlled at all, and appears, in some measure, to have misconceived both the psychodynamics of pornography and demand for its control. In all of this, the Court has lacked a sure consensus on many theoretical elements of the obscenity doctrine and has left, as a result, far more than the usual number of inconsistencies and uncertainties to be expected when law changes.

227

Difficult as proscriptive rationalization may be in a libertarian age, complete legal freedom for sexual expression is unlikely now or in the future. It is a path no modern society has taken. At the same time, constitutional protection for sexual expression, particularly for the redemptive free speech values in the obscenity test itself, are certain to remain a vital check on legal control. The remarkable development of First Amendment doctrine in the last half-century and the nation's commitment to maintain itself as a free speech society, the general principles of which command strong and wide public support, are too firmly established for any significant retreat on sexual expression, libertarian fears notwithstanding.

For these reasons, our analysis here will differ from most writing on obscenity law. We deal with pornography less as a problem of constitutional rights than one of social control. This choice reflects no preference for proscription over protection, but rather seeks to avoid the uncritical exaltation of rights that orients and often distorts so much legal writing on pornography. If the pornography problem is to be understood as more than simply an impediment to the perfection of rights, and thus be managed politically as effectively as it might, we need to amend our doctrinaire notions of intrinsic categories of "protected" and "unprotected" speech. We need also to question the often tightly held idea that any incremental increase of control must sweep on irresistibly, like a social contagion, to infect all other free speech. This has not been the lesson of our history; indeed, if freedom of speech were so fragile, pornography would not now be an issue on a liberal society's public agenda.

The Supreme Court has constructed a libertarian obscenity doctrine where none existed before. The Court has the same freedom to modify that doctrine without doing violence to the Constitution that it had to discover that the Constitution "required" certain amplified protection for sexual expression. The First Amendment itself actually requires very little, because it says very little. It is through interpretation and embellishment by five or more of nine justices that the amendment has come to mean so much. Five or more justices may also say what the amendment and the Constitution do not require. The point, of course, is that in doing either, the Court determines the relative weights accorded to the government's power to act for ends of social control and to the countervailing redemptive interests of free expression, reflected in constitutional recognition that control must be limited. Arguments abound over where to draw the lines for sexual expression: hence so many dissenting opinions. There are also many arguments about how those lines are best rationalized: hence so many concurring opinions. Constitutional requirements are what a majority of the justices say they are, no more and no less.

The Formulaic Labyrinth

In Anglo-American experience, legal control of pornography has closely followed the democratization of culture and the technological advances that allowed larger and larger numbers of persons to be reached by communications. Not until the late seventeenth century did sexual expression unconnected with religious belief or political views become an object of appreciable public demand for legal control. Yet it cannot be supposed, as many libertarian writers have done, that sexual expression qua sexual expression was previously of little or no concern or that there was great tolerance of it. Law and government are never the only means of limiting sexual expression; as in most areas of social life, most control has been administered informally. It is when powerful, decisive, and (in democracies) popular groups or forces perceive these controls to be ineffective, as they often do in the face of major political, social, economic, or technological change, that the formal, symbolic, but sometimes less efficient restrictions of government are sought.

Early legal sanctions against sexual expression bear witness to this relationship. Neither the common-law offense of obscene libel, nor the Vagrancy Act of 1824 and Lord Campbell's Act of 1857 in England, nor the various American state laws, beginning with Vermont's in 1821, defined exactly what was to be proscribed—an unusual degree of vagueness, considering that legal punishment followed conviction. The terms "obscene," "indecent," "immoral," and the like were thought self-evident or at least sufficiently clear for most persons including the juries of peers who would decide the cases. This failure to elaborate did not reflect a liberal social or intellectual environment or one indifferent to control, but rather a wide consensus associated with control by informal means. Official offenses assumed to be self-evident could only have been built on earlier informal ones.

Under early common-law and statutory controls, offending expression—that considered unsuitable for public utterance or circulation—most often involved profanity or "indelicate" language dealing with sexual matters, or "ideological obscenity," *themes* of transgression against established morality, especially where the wrongdoing was portrayed favorably or unpunished. The first attempt at definition emerged from the English case of *Regina v. Hicklin*,[1] in 1868, involving a pamphlet purporting to describe sexual depravity and immorality in the Roman Catholic clergy. Legal proscription depended on "whether the tendency of the matter charged as obscenity is to deprave and corrupt those whose minds are open to such immoral influences and into whose hands a publication of this sort may fall."[2] Such a finding could be based, not on the effect of the entirety, but on isolated passages. Intent and countervailing literary or social values did not matter. The *Hicklin* rule, as it came to be called, tied legal designation of obscenity to *effects* the expression *might* have on persons who were particularly susceptible, discounted by the improbability of exposure. Though skewed and imprecise by modern standards and altogether lacking in concern for the values implicit in freedom of speech, the rule did begin to move the law away from assumed self-evidence to a standard of utility. Sexual expression was proscribable for the high public good of protecting the individual (and, by implication, society) from harm. True, the reference group was the most vulnerable in the population, and the uncertain, unspecified harms of "depravity" and "corruption" might not be clear enough barriers to prevent the assertion of essentially moralistic concerns. Yet such concerns were no more than the law had already allowed and certainly no more than that on which most informal control rested.

The *Hicklin* rule prevailed in both English and American law for nearly a hundred years, and its deficiencies grew ever more clear. It did little to prevent prosecution of many nineteenth- and early twentieth-century works of literary merit. Nor could it be easily accommodated to growing constitutional interest in the value of speech. Vague terms such as "those whose minds are open to such immoral influences" were increasingly ill suited to an age in which social and moral pluralism undermined a comfortable consensus about particular sexual expression, and in which, for those very reasons, the law was asked to play an ever larger role in social control.

Although American courts had heard hundreds, even thousands, of obscenity cases by the 1950s, the Supreme Court had given almost no attention to the doctrinal or theoretical aspects of designation before its *Roth* decision in 1957.[3] In the few cases even remotely connected with sexual expression, the Court dealt with procedural questions rather than those of substance or definition. In *Roth,* it abandoned the *Hicklin* rule and recast legal designation of sexual expression.[4] Affirming the active role of law in social control, the Court said that obscenity, like libel and "fighting words," was one of the few categories of speech outside the First Amendment. Such expression was "utterly without redeeming social importance."[5] Put another way, sexual expression determined to be obscene could be legally proscribed simply as expression, without showing of a clear and present danger of harmful effect or any other proof normally associated with restriction of communication. In this "two-tier" categorical approach, the key question is whether an expression is "obscene" or not; sexual speech found obscene is proscribable, that not so found remains constitutionally protected.[6]

Answers are determined by "whether to the average person, applying contemporary community standards, the dominant theme of the material taken as a whole appeals to the prurient interest," a succinct formulation that became known as the *Roth* test.[7] This was a major departure from the *Hicklin* rule. First, the hypothetical referent was not the most vulnerable individual in the population but the "average person." Second, that person must be of the "contemporary community," not that of another day, a matter the older rule had left open. Third, the communication must be judged not by isolated or selected parts but by "its dominant theme . . . taken as a whole." Finally, its effect or design must be the stimulation of "prurient interest" rather than a tendency to "deprave or corrupt."

Although the Court in fact upheld the conviction in *Roth,* the new formulation was immediately recognized for what it was—a libertarian test that would narrow the scope of proscribable sexual expression. Like many reformulations, it raised almost as many questions as it answered. What, for example, was "prurient interest"? In a footnote, the Court equated it with "lustful thoughts," then cited the definition of "prurient" given in *Webster's Second Unabridged:* "Itching; longing; uneasy with desire or longing; of persons, having itching, morbid, or lascivious longing; of desire, curiosity, or propensity, lewd."[8] Though the Court said "obscenity and sex are not synonymous," it did not attempt to deal with the logical problem of defining "prurient," "obscene," "lewd," and "lascivious" as synonyms of one another. Was obscenity's being "utterly without redeeming social importance" simply a conclusion issuing from the fact of proscription, or was it another requirement of designation? Finally, the Court did not say whether the "community" whose "contemporary" standards were to be applied was the nation, the state, or the locality. Later decisions would clarify some but not all of these questions.

Although it was a major departure from *Hicklin,* the *Roth* test was equally one of utility. Sexual expression was proscribable because it had a particular effect—an appeal to prurient interest. Without this effect there could be no proscription. Yet like all utility tests it must rest not only on a certain clear effect—here, prurient arousal—and agreement about its being wrong, but also on a demonstrable link between that effect and the agent at hand, that is, the particular expression under attack.

The years following *Roth* saw a surge in sexual expression of all sorts and a much greater explicitness in what was portrayed. Obscenity prosecutions in response to popular demands for control increased as well. When convictions were obtained, as they frequently were, the new obscenity test encouraged appeals. As a result, much sexual or erotic representation—mainly in books, limited-circulation periodicals, and movies—came under designative scrutiny in the higher courts, in several cases the Supreme Court itself. Yet not until *Miller v. California*, in 1973, were a majority of justices able to agree on a definitional elaboration.[9] So lacking was a doctrinal consensus that Justice Harlan could observe a decade after *Roth* that "the subject of obscenity has produced a variety of views among members of the Court unmatched in any other course of Constitutional adjudication." In thirteen cases with signed opinions between 1957 and 1967, the nine justices filed fifty-five separate statements of their views.[10]

The Court was much more of one mind in application. The initial libertarian thrust of *Roth* was given full effect in a steady narrowing of the range of expression designated as obscene. In one six-year period alone, 1967–1973, thirty-one convictions were reversed. Many were disposed of per curiam, that is, through decisions without opinions or with short, sometimes cryptic, unsigned opinions.[11] In all, the Court's obscenity work in the sixteen years between *Roth* and *Miller* put it at odds with popular agencies of government—legislatures, local prosecutors, and juries.

Despite its fractionalization, the Court made several important doctrinal alterations in the basic *Roth* test. The most important were the "patent offensiveness" and "without redeeming social importance" requirements. The former meant that proscribable sexual expression, in additon to having prurient appeal, would need to affront "contemporary community standards relating to the description or representation of sexual matters."[12] Though it did not elaborate much further, the Court appeared to mean expression going "substantially beyond customary limits of candor."[13] Standing alone, of course, patent offensiveness would constitute a fairly restrictive test, but as an added element, its effect, as intended, was to narrow further the scope of designation.

A plurality opinion suggested that sexual expression could not be obscene unless it were also "utterly without redeeming social value," a matter mentioned but left in doubt in *Roth*.[14] This interpretation made the redemptive element a requirement of the test rather than merely a description of proscribed sexual expression. Although a clear majority of the justices did not endorse this addition or that of patent offensiveness, two justices who did not, Black and Douglas, found it easy to apply the requirements to reach libertarian decisions, since they opposed any regulation of sexual expression without evidence of a causal link to criminal or other harmful behavior.

Shortly after *Roth*, the Court removed so-called thematic or ideological obscenity from proscriptive designation. The New York State Board of Film Censors had refused to license *Lady Chatterley's Lover* because it portrayed adultery as a "desirable, acceptable, and proper pattern of behavior." Observing that the state had, in effect, tried to control advocacy of an idea, the Court held that portrayal of immoral behavior alone was not obscene even if shown in a favorable light.[15] The decision was something of a milestone, since depiction of immoral behavior, along with profanity and nudity, had historically been a prime target of social control. More flagrant depiction had not generally been at issue, because it was not widely produced or circulated.

This decision and the apparently additional requirements that designated expression be both patently offensive and without redeeming social importance led many observers and lower courts to conclude that the obscenity test was now so rigorous that only hard-core pornography would be proscribable.[16] Even so, exactly what expression would be included in this residual category was unsettled. In its several reversals of lower court findings of obscenity, the Court had declined to offer any definitive examples of what might be considered hard-core pornography or proscribable expression.

Justice Stewart, who had earlier and memorably claimed "I know it when I see it" in reference to hard-core pornography, offered some illumination in *Ginzberg v. United States:*

Such materials include photographs, both still and motion picture, with no pretense of artistic value, graphically depicting acts of sexual intercourse, including various acts of sodomy and sadism, and sometimes involving several participants in scenes of orgy-like character. They also include strips of drawings in comic-book format grossly depicting similar activities in an exaggerated fashion. There are, in addition, pamphlets and booklets, sometimes with photographic illustrations, verbally describing such activities in a bizarre manner with no attempt whatsoever to afford portrayals of character or situation and with no pretense to literary value.[17]

At odds with the hard-core pornography interpretation were several other cases in which the Court seemed to say that obscenity might vary with the circumstances of the communication and the nature of its audience. The issue emerged dramatically in *Ginzberg,* in which the defendant publisher was convicted under an antiobscenity postal statute for mailing issues of two periodicals, *Eros* and *Liaison,* and a book, *The Housewife's Handbook on Selective Promiscuity.* The Court upheld the conviction, not because the materials were shown to be obscene under the *Roth* test, but because they were presented to the public in a way the Court described as "the sordid business of pandering."[18] Justice Brennan spoke for the Court:

Where an exploitation of interests in titillation of pornography is shown with respect to material lending itself to such exploitation, through pervasive treatment or description of sexual matters, such evidence may support the determination that the material is obscene *even though in other contexts the material would escape such condemnation.*[19]

He took note of advertisements stressing lewd rather than redeeming literary aspects of the publications and the attempt to get them postmarked in such places as Intercourse and Blue Ball, Pennsylvania, and Middlesex, New Jersey.

As a conditional step back from the hard-core interpretation, the ruling incorporated the idea of "variable" obscenity, which had been urged on the Court by some leading commentators.[20] The Court refrained from developing the "pandering" criterion more fully in later cases, though it has not abandoned the idea that evidence of such presentation may be relevant in determining whether an expression has redeeming value.[21]

The Court has been willing to apply the variable concept to sexual expression directed at deviant groups. In *Mishkin v. New York,* it rejected a claim that publications depicting homosexuality, fetishism, bondage, and other sadomasochistic acts were not obscene under the *Roth* test because they did not have prurient appeal for the "average person." Speaking for the majority, Justice Brennan acknowledged that the Court was adjusting the prurient appeal requirement:

Where the material is designed for and primarily disseminated to a clearly defined deviant sexual group, rather than the public at large, the prurient appeal requirement of the *Roth* test is satisfied if the dominant theme of the material taken as a whole appeals to the prurient interest in sex of the members of that group.[22]

This recognition of "social realities," as the Court termed it, left open the questions of who constituted a deviant group and what was an appeal to its members.[23] A variable notion of prurient appeal could theoretically narrow designation as well as broaden it. Though the Court has not directly held on the matter, expression with prurient appeal for the average person might not be obscene if used, say, by social scientists in scholarly analysis or medical doctors and other therapists for clinical or diagnostic purpose.[24] As we will argue presently, the entire concept of prurient appeal becomes vague and empirically difficult when it is expected to serve as a guide for meting out criminal penalties or defining First Amendment limits.

Juveniles are another and far larger audience for whom the "average person" standard does not apply. Though very little pornography is aimed directly at them, shielding young persons is one of the chief aims and conscious motivations for legal control of sexual expression. Under the *Hicklin* rule, juveniles could themselves be a reference group for general proscription, but with the inclusion of "average persons" in the *Roth* reformulation, they may no longer be.

Further, though the Court had long recognized that a special social interest in the well-being of juveniles might justify some narrowing of their freedom, it had held emphatically that communication could not be kept from adults simply because it might be harmful to minors.[25] When the Court finally addressed the problem of sexual expression and juveniles directly in *Ginsberg v. New York*, it again gave the obscenity test a variable interpretation.[26] Under a statute prohibiting distribution of materials "harmful to minors," defined as persons under seventeen, the defendant had been convicted of selling underage persons "girlie" magazines that in earlier cases had been found not obscene for general distribution. Using the approach adopted in *Mishkin*, the Court held that obscenity "might vary according to the group to which the questionable material is directed or from whom it is quarantined." When sexual material is distributed to minors, the prurient appeal to be shown is not to the "average person" but to minors.[27]

Later, again emphasizing separate applicability of the test, the Court held that children could not be considered part of the demographic pool from which the hypothetical "average person" is derived, lest triers of fact find prurient appeal more readily than when the pool is limited to adults.

"Sensitive persons" and members of deviant groups, however, could be included in deriving the hypothetical average person.[28]

In still another variation, involving regulative structure, the Court was willing to delabel entirely sexual expression possessed in the privacy of the home. Possession of a hard-core eight millimeter film seized in an otherwise lawful police search of a house was held not to be a punishable offense, because of a countervailing right of privacy. "A state has no business," the Court said, "telling a man, sitting alone in his house, what books he may read or films he may watch."[29] In later cases, however, it refused to extend this principle to obscene films in an adult movie theater, obscene material imported in one's luggage for private personal use, the willing reception of such material through the mails, or interstate transportation of it solely for the private use of the person transporting.[30]

The Court approved a sharply contrasting variation in regulatory structure on privacy grounds when it upheld a federal postal statute allowing authorities to order a mailer to stop sending unsolicited advertisements to an addressee who "at his own discretion" believed them to be obscene, even though they were not otherwise legally proscribable.[31]

In the decade and a half following *Roth,* the formulaic aspects of the obscenity test, and the inherent tension between its apparent hard-core designation and the "variable" exceptions, offered uncertain guidance to lower courts and to legislators and prosecutors faced with growing censorial pressures from constituents. The Court's underlying determination to narrow the scope of proscribable obscenity left it little choice but to review almost every conviction appealed to it. To many, the Court seemed ever more to resemble the Supreme Board of Censors Justice Black feared it would become.[32] The nation, as a consequence, was unsure whether a given expression was or was not obscene until the Court ruled on it.

In 1973, in *Miller v. California,* the Burger Court, able at last to marshal a majority on certain theoretical aspects, attempted to both clarify and revise major elements of the test. It began by reaffirming the inclusion of patent offensiveness, equating it with hard-core pornography. Such representations included "ultimate sexual acts, normal or perverted, actual or simulated, . . . masturbation, excretory functions, and lewd exhibition of genitals."[33]

The Court went on to revise the redemptive element, expressly abandoning "utterly without redeeming social importance" for the formulation "whether the work, taken as a whole, lacks serious artistic, literary, political, or scientific value."[34] Since prurient interest, patent offensiveness, and the redemptive element were each a necessary rather than sufficient part of the designative test, the revision meant that prurient, patently offensive depiction could be obscene only if it were also lacking in "serious artistic, literary, political, or scientific value." The new redemptive measure did not so much broaden the scope of obscenity designation as save it. "Utterly without redeeming social importance" had to be abandoned if legal regulation were to be maintained at all, since any sexual expression, including hard-core pornography, could probably be claimed to have *some* ideological, educational, psychological, or recreational value.

The Court also clarified "community" in the original *Roth* test. Before *Miller* most lower courts, in the absence of a definitive statement, held that the community was the nation itself.[35] This idea was now emphatically rejected. Prurient appeal and patent offensiveness were "essentially questions of fact, and our nation is simply too big and too diverse for the Court to reasonably expect that such standard could be articulated for all 50 States in a single formulation, even assuming the prerequisite consensus exists."[36] The "community standards" to be applied were those of the state or possibly a more locally defined jurisdiction.[37] But variant state or local standards would not apply to the redemptive element, which as a question involving constitutional fact—here interests protected by the First Amendment—must be governed by national uniform standards.

By clarifying designative obscenity and devolving controlling standards to the community, the Court also tried to shift some of the burden of obscenity cases from its own chambers to the lower courts and, in doing so, to strengthen the role of the fact-finding jury in the designation process.[38] That different juries might reach different conclusions about the same material was "one of the consequences we accept under our jury system."[39] Juries were better able to assess state or local standards of prurient interest or patent offensiveness than national ones (if, in fact, the latter could be found). Yet there would be limits to this division of labor. Because nonobscene speech is constitutionally protected unless it offers a clear and present danger of, or some other close link to, actual behavior that government may ordinarily regulate, no factual finding of obscenity could be entirely immune from appellate review.[40]

Devolution of the sort intended by *Miller* works well where doctrinal requirements are understood and adhered to by actors at lower levels. Just how problematic this might be in obscenity designation was evident in *Jenkins v. Georgia*, just one year later, when a jury applying local community standards found the Hollywood film *Carnal Knowledge* obscene even though it fell far short of hard-core pornography.[41] When the state supreme court upheld the finding, the Court was forced to intervene. On its own viewing, it found the work not patently offensive and concluded that juries did not have "unbridled discretion" to determine patent offensiveness (or, presumably, any other element) in the obscenity test.

By affirming the hard-core limitation, *Miller* did little to resolve the doctrinal tension between this essentialist approach and the "variable" obscenity the Court had embraced in several earlier decisions. The latter was used again in several later cases to avoid the libertarian results of a strict application of the *Roth-Miller* test. A major departure came in *F.C.C. v. Pacifica Foundation,* in which the Court reviewed the threat of Federal Communications Commission (FCC) sanctions against a New York City radio station that had broadcast a twelve-minute segment of a recorded satire on "dirty" words, including "shit," "piss," "fuck," "motherfucker," "cocksucker," "cunt," and "tits." Conceding the words themselves were not obscene, the Court nonetheless found them "indecent" under a federal statute barring use of either "obscene" or "indecent" language in broadcasting. Citing "the ease with which children may obtain access to broadcast material" and the medium's inherent intrusiveness into the home, the Court found the words "patently offensive." Vulgar, offensive, and shocking language was not entitled to "absolute constitutional protection under all circumstances."[42]

In another departure, the Court held that a state might legally proscribe photographic or cinematic depiction of "sexual conduct"—actual or simulated intercourse, masturbation, bestiality, sadomasochistic acts, or "lewd exhibition of genitals"—of persons under sixteen, even though such expression might not be obscene under the *Roth-Miller* test.[43] In this step it widened the area of proscribable sexual expression without formally altering the obscenity test. The Court's distaste for child pornography is reflected not merely in its unanimity but also in its willingness to apply regulation to the *sale* of such material, and thus to abridge free speech rights of persons not themselves involved in exploiting children. Presumably this new exception to the obscenity test would not apply to depiction of the sexual acts of children if children were not involved in creation of the material itself.

In still another variation, perhaps one of even greater consequence in overall legal control, the Court upheld Detroit's "Anti-Skid-Row" ordinance that prohibited adult bookstores and movie houses within 500 feet of any area zoned for residential use or 1,000 feet of any two other "regulated" uses. It thus approved use of municipal zoning power to regulate the *availability* of sexual communications.[44] The ordinance defined an adult movie theater as one emphasizing films depicting certain sexual activities or "anatomical areas." Since such content was not limited to hard-core pornography under the *Roth-Miller* test, the Court had again upheld limited regulation of sexual expression falling short of proscribable obscenity.

The Need for Revision

The obscenity test lacks the flexibility in theory and application that a pluralist democracy in a complex communications environment needs from its highest public policy on pornography. In commendably expanding constitutional protection for sexual expression, the Court has said very little about why any sexual expression should be regulated by law.[45] It has offered an excessively convoluted test for distinguishing between two categories of speech, rather than providing criteria for dealing with a social problem that also has important free speech dimensions. Unsurprisingly, it has had to abandon its formula at various turns. In important ways, the doctrine also fails to comprehend the psychodynamics of pornography itself. In this section we examine several elements in or related to the obscenity test—prurient interest, harm, redeeming value, hard-core pornography, and patent offensiveness—and suggest that a comprehensive notion of offensiveness should serve as its chief rationale and operating edge. In the next section, we shall argue for a flexible application of the test, based not only on the content of expression but also on the circumstances of availability.

Prurient Interest

Though the Supreme Court has placed prurient stimulation at the verbal center of the obscenity test, it has done little to explain what it means or what designative purpose it serves. Whether conceived of as "lustful thoughts" or as a "shameful or morbid interest in nudity, sex, or excretion"—two descriptions offered in *Roth*—it is not clear whether a stimulated prurient interest is a harm and thus to be prevented, or the characteristic effect of proscribable sexual expression and therefore essentially a measure for identifying that expression.[46] In other words, does prurient interest describe why or what? If the latter, prurience seems almost redundant today, since most sexual expression the Court has labeled hard-core pornography would probably also in some measure appeal to the prurient interest of the average person. On the other hand, if prurient stimulation is thought to be so seriously harmful that it should be prevented by law, the harm appears at least exaggerated, if not psychodynamically misconceived. Evidence of the effects of pornography, considered in Chapter 4, offers little support for the idea that prurient appeal is harmful per se to those experiencing it or to others associated with them.

Nor is it clear whether appeal to prurient interest refers simply to a response of the reader, viewer, or listener or whether it may also refer to proprietary purpose. Occasionally the Court has spoken of it as though it were the latter to uphold findings of obscenity.[47] Yet unless this meaning of prurient appeal is limited strictly to examination of intent rather than the actual attempt to make such an appeal, the question unavoidably returns to one of response.

As an inducible psychic response, prurient interest is a near-universal quality of eroticized sexuality and subject to great individual variation. Arousal is not limited to obvious sexual objects. A great many "nonsexual" objects, symbols, and events have been known to awaken or excite "lustful thoughts" or "morbid interest in sex." Large segments of the advertising and entertainment industries work hard to stimulate such a response, subtly or not so subtly. Obviously, it is not totally unsought or, especially if partially disguised, unwelcome. Yet prurient interest is unquestionably disturbing to many persons and, at certain levels, perhaps to a vast majority of all persons. It may be met with feelings of disgust and revulsion and thus the external sources of it perceived to be offensive. As already noted, many persons are also made uneasy by the thought of prurient interest being widely stimulated in others.[48] This may reflect entirely rational concerns about where such interest may lead, or less rational, perhaps entirely unconscious, ones having roots in exclusion or other fantasies of infantile sexuality.

Prurient appeal has a further defect as a central element in the obscenity test: the subjectivity inherent in its "factual" determination. Because it is a rousable response accompanied by strong positive or negative feelings, perhaps not totally conscious, prurient interest and what appeals to it are not readily disclosed by most persons, however self-aware. Prurient interest is far more private and concealed than the cognitive components of most public policy issues. Nevertheless, in court, the trier of fact—judge or jury—is necessarily asked to determine whether a given expression appeals to a prurient interest, not his or her own but that of the "average person." It is likely that the trier's own reaction will be substituted for evaluation of an external condition. Nor is prurient interest apt to have much utility in the "community standards" part of the test. Except where very well-defined subcultures are present, prurient interest of the hypothetical average person is not likely to vary greatly from one contemporary community to another.

If prurient appeal or arousal is objectionable as a social or personal matter and is to be considered so in law or policy, it is more straightforwardly understood as being offensive rather than harmful. Intentionally or unintentionally, the Supreme Court may recently have moved in this direction by holding, almost as a caricature of its previous decisions, that "prurient" could include incitement of "lust," so long as "lust" was not taken to mean "*normal* interest in sex."[49] Thus "prurient" necessarily comes to mean an interest in sex that is other than "normal." The Court did not elaborate. If by "normal" it meant healthy, it is fortunate the Court did not say more, since there is a marked lack of consensus among scientists, therapists, and moralists about what sexual health is, particularly with regard to exposure to erotic representation. If "normal" means what is generally acceptable, however, then "prurient" comes close to the notion of offensiveness, which is already part of the obscenity test and, as we shall argue below, is a much sounder and more workable element for policy, both in and out of court.

The Element of Harm

Prevention of harm is clearly the most rational and intellectually respectable basis for a policy of social control. For John Stuart Mill it was the one acceptable purpose a state could have in limiting individual freedom, a view that remains at the center of libertarian theory of free speech. But law and policy have never been clear about whether proscribable expression—obscenity—is harmful or, if it is, why it is. Under the *Hicklin* rule, based expressly on harm, the preventable injuries were the morally and empirically ambiguous ones of "depravity" and "corruption." In the *Roth* reformulation there was no mention of harm (unless prurient stimulation was assumed to be harmful). In fact, the Court has said very little about whether obscenity is injurious at all, at least to adults. It obliquely referred to a "social interest in order and morality" in *Roth*.[50] Later, but again in passing, it said that "empirical uncertainties" about the effects of obscenity would not make it unreasonable for a legislature to regulate public availability in the interest of preventing "antisocial behavior" or to conclude that it had a tendency to "injure the community as a whole, to endanger the public safety, or to jeopardize . . . the right to maintain a decent society."[51]

If the Court has not expressly included the element of harm in the test, it may be for good reason. Short of finding obscenity categorically harmful as a matter of law, including a harm element would require proof of specific cause and effect before proscription could be imposed in an individual case. As we have seen, "empirical uncertainties" about cause and effect are formidable indeed. Though the evidence does not conclusively demonstrate the absence of harmful effects, it gives little or no indication of them for adults. Further, when harmful effects are conceived so broadly as the endangering of "decent society" or the "community as a whole," conclusive scientific or courtroom proof of cause and effect may never be forthcoming. The Court has chosen wisely not to require a showing of harm. Moreover, in decisions such as *Stanley v. Georgia,* in which possession even of hard-core pornography within the home was not punishable, the Court itself cast doubt on the relative importance of harm.[52] If obscenity were so harmful to individuals or society that its public consumption by consenting adults in an adult theater, for example, should be proscribed, why is it less so in the home, particularly since most persons who believe pornography to be socially damaging believe that its effects are indirect and long-term? It is true that the additional countervailing interest in privacy was present in *Stanley,* but this is merely another way of saying the Court concluded that whatever the harmful effects, they were not so great or prevention so compelling as to be decisive in such circumstances. A more persuasive distinction between hard-core pornography in the home and in limited-admission adult theaters is that the latter is far more *offensive* than the former.

As we have seen, survey evidence indicates that large numbers of persons believe pornography to be harmful to individuals, but only a small fraction believe that they themselves have been harmed. The mutually contradictory nature of those two beliefs is apparent. Moreover, fewer persons believe pornography to be harmful than believe that it should be restricted or prohibited. And about one person in three would still favor restriction or prohibition of pornography even if pornography were clearly shown to have no harmful effects.[53] Clearly there are important and widely held objections to pornography on grounds other than harm. In hinting strongly at less conscious censorial motivations, these objections beg for a broader doctrinal understanding of the censorial response.

We have been speaking here only of harm to adults. The harm to juveniles is less uncertain. Both scientific data and intuition support this impression. Prudent legal theory and public policy would need to include age distinctions, a possibility discussed more fully below.

Our point here is that for adults—that is, for *general* control of unacceptable sexual expression—harm is both too ambiguous and too problematic to be proved in a courtroom or made the express aim of proscriptive public policy. Actual concern about harm to individual adults—oneself and others—like concern about prurient interest, to which it may be closely related, can be better subsumed under a rule of offensiveness.

That society itself may be harmed is a different matter but one no more satisfactory for legal probate or as a rationale for policy. Even if there were general agreement about what was and was not injury to the social order, the dangers posed by expression or representation, unlike those of action or behavior, would very likely be indirect and their effects long-term rather than immediate. And even if pornography's association with social harm were to be shown, a formidable empirical task would remain. Correlation alone cannot satisfy causation even when the suspect social phenomenon is conspicuous and provocative.

In an ideal world, in which we had the necessary facts and could approach things calmly and objectively, the criterion of harm would be a logical and practical basis for drawing the lines between freedom and control. But we do not have the facts, and we are not calm and objective. We cannot afford to wait; policy needs to be made and conflict dealt with here and now. Without the proof, which may always be elusive, strict empirical application of the harm criterion would likely result in little or no formal social control—a libertarian result but also a politically unacceptable one. On the other hand, because the harm question evokes very strong feelings, relaxed application of the proof requirement would all too easily transform a factual inquiry into an assertion of moral preferences about the good society and good persons in it—a conservative but constitutionally unacceptable result.

We do not suggest that ascendancy of moral preferences results simply from factual uncertainty. Yet even where moral preferences rest carefully on facts or on knowledgeable insight, they are apt to be far more sweeping and exclusive than empirical evaluations of social phenomena. On issues of great emotional valence, moral assertions may substitute for empirical fact—may at times even withstand fact.

Moral preferences, at least those of decisive groups, are very likely to be reflected in social control, both informal and effected through the agencies of law and policy. But it is important in a liberal pluralist democracy that these preferences fly under their own colors. Debate about the good life and the good society is desirable and even necessary to social vitality and direction. But policy must take care to keep differences between preference and fact as sharp as possible, for only then can it keep itself open to new facts and the challenge of new preferences.

Concern that pornography may be harmful cannot be dismissed simply as moralistic or irrational. Nor is it without valid place in the demand for social control through law and policy. Our point is simply that the question of harm, difficult to isolate and put to empirical test, tends to be expressed in assertion and is thus both distracting and misleading as a criterion for social control. We will argue more fully below that offensiveness, rather than the possibility of harm, provides the best psychological understanding of the antipornography position and its formidable censorial energy, as well as serving as the most certain and inclusive criterion for social control.

Redeeming Value

The established redemptive elements in the obscenity test need not be affected by clarification and revision of the restrictive elements. Whatever force is given to patent offensiveness, for example, no general suppression is possible unless a work or expression is also without serious literary, artistic, political, or scientific value. These countervailing considerations are not merely weights on a scale but are, in effect, constitutional vetoes of formal social control, at least as that control seeks total proscription. Expression having redeeming value is protected "regardless of whether the government or a majority of the people approve of the ideas these works represent."[54]

The determination of value is not to be left to the standards of the community or those of the "average" person within it.

Just as the ideas a work represents need not obtain majority approval to merit protection, neither . . . does the value of the work vary from community to community based on the degree of local acceptance it has won. . . . The proper inquiry is not whether an ordinary member of any given community would find serious literary, artistic, political, or scientific value in allegedly obscene material, but whether a reasonable person would find such value in the material, taken as a whole.[55]

Though the Justices do not appear to agree about the competence of a properly instructed jury to make such a finding of fact, there is little doubt that, in the end, the question of redeeming value is subject to an independent finding by an appellate court.[56]

Hard-Core Pornography

As applied, the obscenity test gives constitutional protection to a great range of sexual expression that in the past was scarce, hidden, or not produced at all. Proscribable expression is largely limited to hard-core pornography, but this designation is surely applicable only to adults and, although the Court has not yet actually said so, probably only to movies and some print media. In fact, the Court has had to abandon or modify the obscenity test several times because of its reduction to hard-core pornography, and to embrace notions of variable obscenity.

Before considering these departures, we need to examine the ambiguity in the hard-core concept. The Court has not made it clear whether hard-core pornography is simply a descriptive label applied to expression that meets the obscenity test or whether it is, in effect, an independent criterion by which to determine if the test has been correctly met. In the first case, "hard-core pornography" is convenient nomenclature but conceptually redundant, referring to patently offensive, prurient sexual expression without serious literary, aesthetic, political, or scientific value. In the second, it is not coterminous with proscribable obscenity but rather an additional requirement. Presumably, then, sexual expression might be prurient, patently offensive, lacking redemptive elements, and yet not be hard-core pornography and thus not obscene. Unfortunately, the Court appears to have used the term in both ways.[57]

Hard-core pornography seems to be sexual expression about which there is the greatest and widest disapprobation. For this reason, it may seem readily identifiable, as Justice Stewart suggested when he said "I know it when I see it." Yet the idea of a self-evident hard-core pornography presents many difficulties. Whether there is an irreducible, intrinsic, universal pornography is a profound sociosexual question for which, as we saw in Chapter 2, there is no clear answer. As with the question of harm, it depends on facts and knowledge not now available and that may never be conclusively available. Even if there were an essential hard-core pornography, it is not clear that the Supreme Court, using contemporary community standards and the redemptive veto, would be able to locate its boundaries.[58]

As the concept has actually been applied, hard-core pornography is distinguished from other sexual expression in degree rather than kind. Its content has not been historically constant. Many depictions that might today be met with a shrug—exposure of genitals, complete nudity, provocative poses, certain four-letter words, for example—would have struck our Victorian or Edwardian forebears as leaving nothing to the imagination or as going as far as one can go. Rather than a distinctive category with identifiable substantive characteristics, hard-core pornography is more usefully conceived of as continuous with other sexual expression—an area on a scale of disapprobation whose boundaries and content change with the standards of the day. Its constant in any age is likely to be its designation of sexual expression for which there is the greatest consensus about need for social control.

The relatively narrow character of the Court's current hard-core designation is both its strength and its weakness as a legal category and an element of policy. Actual proscriptions tend to be more predictable and to meet with fewer libertarian objections than those of almost any other sexual expression. On the other hand, their designation obviously does not cover a vast range of sexual expression considered objectionable and for which there is widespread demand for control. As the chief proscriptive standard in obscenity law today, the narrow hard-core designation requires a level of tolerance for other sexual expression well beyond that freely given by most persons in most settings. Its narrowness has been the major factor in the increase in the volume and explicit nature of sexual expression commercially available. As we have seen, whatever proscriptive standard is legally in force, a semi-underground industry dealing in forbidden images is certain to offer the very type of pornography that lies on and just over the boundaries.

The Supreme Court appears to have recognized some of these problems. As we have seen in the cases of "pandering," appeal to deviant groups, and exposure of juveniles, it has departed from the hard-core notion and embraced one of variable obscenity to proscribe pornography that would not be obscene under a strict application of the *Roth* test. A similar variation was embraced in *Miller* for differences among community standards of offensiveness. In these departures, the Court retained the basic obscenity test but modified elements to suit exceptional circumstances.

Where the test could not be modified without undermining its integrity, the Court has simply worked outside it, proscribing, in limited contexts, objectionable sexual expression that was not hard-core pornography: that contained, for example, in unsolicited mail entering the home or in an afternoon broadcast over a radio station, or portraying juveniles photographically. In addition, the Court has allowed communities to restrict the location of adult bookstores and movie theaters.

Conceptual difficulties with hard-core pornography could be overcome and the term made less categorical were it to refer to sexual expression that is extremely offensive rather than a category having substantive characteristics of its own.

Offensiveness

Offensiveness—"patent offensiveness," in the obscenity test—provides a more inclusive and fundamental understanding of why pornography is objectionable and a surer, more flexible measure for social control than prurient interest, harmfulness, or conceptions of the "good society." It has been adopted as the standard for the control of pornography in France and Denmark and is a key element of regulation in Britain and West Germany.[59]

Being offended is an unmistakable, conscious, expressible, socially measurable defensive response to pornography. In portraying forbidden sexual wishes and acts, pornography challenges not only everyday conventions but far deeper taboos imposed early in psychosexual life. Sexual arousal may be consciously acknowledged and experienced as prurient interest, which in turn may be pleasurable or disturbing or both, at the same time or in succession. But for many persons in many situations, and perhaps most persons in some situations, the deep stirrings do not break through well-constructed defenses and thus do not enter fully into conscious awareness. Feelings of disgust and revulsion are experienced instead, and the stimulus expression is, in evaluative and cognitive terms, "offensive." This may sometimes be the end response even when prurient arousal is consciously acknowledged and indulged.

These personal responses or evaluations may be aggregated as "patent offensiveness," reflecting something so widely, commonly, and emphatically held or experienced that it composes a social standard—designating, in effect, that which goes substantially "beyond customary limits of candor." As an operating social criterion, offensiveness can also encompass objections to pornography based on concerns about harm, whether these are merely rationalizations of the deeper psychodynamic responses just discussed, rest essentially on moral preferences, or are simply rational assessments of objective evidence.

Informal operating control, through organized crusade, private complaint, or simply the proverbial raised eyebrow, has usually asked little more than whether or not an expression was offensive. As for formal control, most laws in the past were actually phrased in those terms—the common-law standard of "indecency," for example, was and is simply a conceptualization of objection based on offensiveness. Thus even Justice Stewart's simple identifying criterion can be given its full and unspoken measure: "I don't like it when I see it, and I don't want myself or others to see any more of it!"

Although a sense of being offended is obviously subjective, "patent offensiveness"—which the Court has described as going beyond the *customary* limits of candor—is objectively measurable, and a trier of fact need not be thrown back on his or her own responses. Whether circumstantial availability of a particular representation is offensive to a community's hypothetical average person is an inherently easier factual question than whether it has prurient appeal to or is likely to harm that person. As a measurable social aggregate, clear or patent offensiveness is particularly well suited to the "contemporary community standards" requirement. Standards of offensiveness are much more likely to vary from one community to another than are those of prurient stimulation or degree of harmfulness.

Almost any community can supply evidence of what is patently offensive. We are not speaking here of public opinion polls, which do not exist in most communities and would probably not be the best indicator of community standards in any case. More to the point are actual communications. The chief evidence of existing community standards on any matter is what has actually been done or practiced and what the community's response has been to departures from the customary. What sorts of sexual material have been openly available? Covertly available or available only on a restricted basis? Or not available at all? To whom, from whom, when, and where have they been available? Was there protest or complaint, indifference, or approval? If so, by whom and in what numbers?

These are factual questions on which factual evidence can be presented. They do not rely on intuitive knowledge that a trier of fact may or may not have about a community, or on his or her personal view of prevailing standards, or on questionnaire responses, or even on expert testimony. An average local trier of fact can be reasonably expected to have some knowledge of manifest community standards or, at very least, be able reasonably to evaluate evidence of such standards when it is formally presented.

But the Court has not said clearly how much empirical room it would give local triers of fact. A year after it emphasized local appraisal of community standards in *Miller*, it reversed a finding by a Georgia jury that the film *Carnal Knowledge* was obscene, saying that local juries did not have "unbridled discretion" to determine patent offensiveness. The Court may have set some unfortunate categorical limits on patent offensiveness when it observed that although "the subject matter of the picture is, in a broader sense, sex, and there are scenes in which sexual conduct including 'ultimate sexual acts' is to be understood to be taking place, the camera does not focus on the bodies of the actors at such time. There is no exhibition whatever of the actors' genitals, lewd or otherwise, during these scenes."[60] It might have reached the same conclusion of nonproscribability simply by finding that the film had redemptive qualities—in this case, obvious artistic value—a matter never intended to be left to community standards.

Because levels of acceptability and tolerance vary with the context of communication—the medium and the nature of the audience—offensiveness also provides a flexible measure for designations that fall short of outright proscription. In other words, offensiveness follows well-established operative distinctions present in informal control. Differences in operating freedom among the media, discussed in the preceding chapter, are differences in an offensiveness standard applied, rather than differences in prurient stimulation or proved harm. Offensiveness also offers a ready basis for discriminating between a willing audience and an unwilling audience, to whom prurient interest, harm, and moral preference criteria barely apply.

Not least, the measure provides a thread of doctrinal consistency where the Supreme Court has departed from strict application of the obscenity test. In *Mishkin v. New York*, for example, expression aimed at homosexuals was probably offensive but not pruriently stimulating to the average person in the community. In *Stanley v. Georgia*, materials probably having prurient appeal to the average person, since they were hard-core pornography, were not proscriptively offensive, because they were in the home and subject only to private viewing. In contrast, in *Ginzberg v. United States,* the manner of public presentation—"pandering"—was patently offensive, but the publications themselves were not. In *New York v. Ferber,* where the Court's decision rested expressly on harmfulness (though not for the audience), the sexual portrayal of children, probably not pruriently appealing to the average person, was clearly patently offensive.[61] A phonograph record satirizing the use of four-letter words, which probably had little prurient appeal for the average adult and probably would not have been considered offensive by most audiences of adults in most listening contexts, was offensive when broadcast on a radio station in the afternoon.[62] In each of these decisions, the Court was forced to depart from its obscenity test, because of the compelling nature of the communications context and because the prurient interest criterion failed. Yet if offensiveness had been the chief measure, acknowledged or not, the decisions would not be inconsistent with each other or with most others the Court has made.

Would patent offensiveness freeze present standards, since, theoretically at least, anything breaching them would be subject to regulation? Such immobility is unlikely, and it clearly has not obtained in the past even though offensiveness has generally been the touchstone of social control. In any event, the redemptive element in the current legal formulation would prevent proscription of any new (or old) expression having serious literary, artistic, political, or scientific value. Changes in standards of acceptability for sexual expression probably depend less on changes in expression itself than on changes in sexual attitudes, behavior, customs, ideology (both sexual and nonsexual), and general levels of tolerance.

Offensiveness addresses the censorial complaint as most persons experience it psychologically; patent offensiveness does so as most communities experience it socially and politically. In its relative simplicity, patent offensiveness allows for an important designative flexibility that a modern demographically and technologically complex society needs in dealing with conflict about sexual expression.

From Content to Context

Placing offensiveness at the center of the obscenity test clarifies the aims of formal control of pornography. More important, it facilitates a shift from a categorical approach in which a sexual expression is "obscene" or "not obscene"—totally protected or totally unprotected—toward regulation in which actual control can vary with the context of expression. A single test for obscenity or standard of designation, whether libertarian or censorial, is ill suited to a complex communications environment. The distinction between juveniles and adults—one of the oldest in social policy and social life—should alone preclude uniform legal treatment of sexual expression. The Court appears to have recognized the problem here in its forced departures from the obscenity test, but its use of a variable designation has been unpredictable and unsystematic.

Among its sanctions, a coherent legal doctrine or policy would need to include limited restriction rather than to rely simply on outright proscription. Discrimination among the circumstances of communication, particularly in time, place, and manner, is vital. Differences in operating freedom already existing among the media also merit greater formal recognition.

Distinctions of time, place, and manner acknowledge that objection often has less to do with content than with indiscriminate availability. Expression not offensive for adults, for example, may be offensive if made available to juveniles; that not offensive in private or in limited public settings may become so if displayed on the street or to unwilling viewers; and that generally not offensive in substance may become so if pandered. Controls might include zoning and age classification, both of which the Court has approved; restrictions on public displays; limited or separate access to premises offering sexual materials; advance notice to those not seeking an encounter with sexual expression or materials; or segregation of sexual materials within retail establishments that do other business.

Sustaining a degree of restriction, rather than complete suppression, also, of course, means sustaining a degree of protection. Courts would need to find that the patent offensiveness of an expression that resulted from much wider availability could outweigh whatever redemptive value it might have. The obverse of this finding would be that within the limited availability no amount of offensiveness short of hard-core pornography, and perhaps not even that, would support outright prohibition.

As we have seen, well-established differences exist among the media in informal and proprietary control as well as in social standards of acceptability and in audience expectations. Although many of these have become blurred in recent years, no single operating standard exists for all media, nor is one likely. What is not considered offensive in print, for example, may be so in photographs. What is not offensive in a periodical of limited circulation and specialized readership may be in a mass circulation magazine; what is not on a commercial movie screen or home videocassette may be on a network television program; what is not on a sound recording may be if the recording is aired.

With a handful of exceptions, such as *Pacifica* and earlier cases upholding prior censorship of movies, the Supreme Court has heard few disputes in which comparative media freedom was an issue.[63] Informal controls and distinctions in operating freedom saved the Court this task. But as the *Pacifica* case indicates, industry-maintained distinctions are much less reliable now. The problem is complex, because as informal distinctions in operating freedom erode, demand for entry of the law increases. Moreover, technological advances have radically changed not only the structure of the media but also their sociology. It is much more difficult now, for example, to speak of the "television industry" or "the movies" as single entities or to generalize about their audiences. Movies have entered the home and radio and television are in it more intimately than ever before.

As with time, place, and manner retail restrictions, formal censorial distinctions among the media mean that some sexual expression falling short of hard-core pornography and having redemptive value would be restricted in some but not all media. The matter is analogous to zoning restrictions on adult bookstores and movie theaters. In a given community these outlets can be regulated but not eliminated. Thus some types of explicit sexual expression might be limited in some media, or at least in some circumstances, but not in all.

The Court's leader in seeking a more flexible approach has been Justice Stevens, who wrote the majority opinions in *Young* and *Pacifica*. He has criticized the categorical approach of *Roth* as resting on

the assumed premise that all communications within the protected area are equally immune from government restraint, whereas those outside that area are utterly without social value and, hence, deserving no protection. . . . As long as the government does not totally suppress protected speech and is faithful to its paramount obligation of complete neutrality with respect to the point of view expressed in a protected communication, I see no reason why regulation of certain types of communication may not take into account obvious differences in subject matter. It seems ridiculous to assume that no regulation of the display of sexually oriented material is permissible unless the same regulation could be applied to political comment.[64]

Placing limited restriction on certain sexual expression according to time, place, manner, or medium, when that expression would not be proscribable for its content alone, is a formidable censorial step. Yet in the long run it could easily have a libertarian effect as well. Addressing clear and strong popular demand for control in certain circumstances could substantially reduce demand for outright prohibition, and thus very possibly allow a broadening of protection overall.

Variability in obscenity control would require a restatement of the basic test for proscription and a test for limited restriction. Informally, the restatement might be something like the following: An erotic work or expression is obscene when, taken as a whole, it is patently offensive in its communications context to the average person, applying contemporary community standards, and is otherwise without serious literary, artistic, political, or scientific value. Here, "communications context" would refer to the time, place, and manner of the communication, including the medium employed, the social setting in which it takes place, and the nature of the audience addressed.

A test for limited restriction might be roughly stated as follows: An erotic work or expression, not otherwise obscene, may be reasonably restricted (but not altogether prohibited) in time, place, manner, or medium, where it is patently offensive in its communications context for the average person, applying contemporary community standards. Here "reasonably" would mean no more than necessary where the interest in preventing patently offensive availability outweighs redeeming literary, artistic, political, or scientific value.

The prospect that the Supreme Court and the appellate judiciary can reduce their role in public management of pornography does not appear promising despite the Court's clear desire to that end. Interest in pornography or objectionable sexual expression, entrepreneurial or creative motives for offering such expression, and popular antipathy to pornography and demand for its control are not likely to disappear. A modern pornography controversy is one of the troubled offspring of the union of a free speech society with a mass democratic one, an alliance itself requiring continual reconciliation and adjustment. In the management of pornography conflict only the appellate judiciary can adequately ensure that redemptive elements in expression receive their due weight against popular interest in social control.

Neither we nor the justices should complain that the Court must be ultimate reviewer or even, in Justice Black's pejorative phrase, a "Supreme Board of Censors." Designative lines will be drawn, if not by the courts and ultimately the Supreme Court, then by other decisive agencies or groups, responding to their own perceptions and using their own criteria. We might prefer the courts because of their presumed greater wisdom or greater objectivity. We should certainly prefer them for their greater deliberation and visibility. We may disagree with some of the lines they have drawn, and clearly large numbers believe the courts have moved too far too quickly, in effect imposing objectionable communication of dubious redemptive value on unwilling communities and the general population, setting themselves at odds with most other, more popular policy-making institutions.

Chapter Nine

Between Libertarian
and Censor

Pornography is one of the oldest continuing issues in human social life. Though its specification may vary with societies and cultures and from one age to another, it remains the product of a human psyche whose ambivalence about transgressive sexual fantasy has probably not changed much in thousands of generations. In representing such fantasy through word and image, pornography is part of the nature of being human—the inevitable price of an eroticized sexuality subject to psychic injunction within and social regulation without. There is no indication that human beings ever lived in community without imposing controls on transgressive sexual representation. Individuals of course may vary sharply in their need or capacity to indulge in such expression and their need to reject or deny it. Societies, however, are lumbering aggregates whose majorities overwhelm the wayward individuals. That there are more Comstocks than Marlows among their members may seem a poor bargain; that there are more Comstocks than Sades may not.

Liberal Society and Liberal Democracy

In liberal society, established personal freedoms and the sway of individualism permit various redemptive values to be asserted against social control. For most persons, this liberty provides the most hospitable political environment for the expression of transgressive fantasies, and for those fantasies to be touched by external representation. Our "natural interest" in pornographic expression finds a powerful external ally in hallowed freedoms to speak and publish. Although these freedoms owe their development and early rationalization to considerations far removed from sexual life, their priority irretrievably alters the balance between sexual expression and social control and gives liberal society its underlying affinity for pornography.

Law varies inversely with other control. As informal local controls and proprietary self-restraint lose much of their force, the authority of law is increasingly called on to regulate and restrict. Yet as government intrusion increases, law is also called on, in countermeasure, to permit and protect. Policy-making is thus inevitably at odds with itself: libertarian interests are more effective in the courts, which are less subject to popular control and less responsive to majoritarian values, whereas desire for social control has greater force in the legislature and executive, and in local policy-making, where the heterodox is less welcome and the intelligentsia and "outside" proprietary interests have less weight. Liberal democracy has an affinity for pornography because it is liberal; it has an affinity for conflict over pornography because it is democratic.

Increasingly judicialized and nationalized, pornography policy runs well ahead of advances in popular tolerance of sexual expression over the last twenty-five years and is far more libertarian than the opinions of the general population and most interested groups. Much sexual expression that is still psychodynamically or socially pornographic has become legally nonpornographic. Politically, this represents an unprecedented advance in freedom of expression for limited interests and a considerable frustration of popular will.

Liberal democracy rests on the uneasy union of a free speech society with a mass democratic one. Individual liberties must coexist with the equality principle and its operating agent, majority rule. This complicated arrangement involves considerably more than simple demarcation of constitutional or legal rights. Vital as those protections are, they are never the equivalent of actual operating freedom. In theory, a free speech society works because its members are wise enough, mature enough, or simply self-controlled enough to check their natural inclination to silence troubling views and disagreeable expression. Supposedly we recognize the longer-term political and social benefits to be gained from allowing expression to enter a free marketplace of ideas in which error is exposed and better representations drive out worse. Yet few members of any society can consistently reach such heights of political wisdom and temperance. A votive free speech norm is an elite prescription, probably workable only for a select minority. For the rest of us, a modified intolerance is a more natural and likely voluntary response to alien and objectionable expression.

Fortunately, a free speech society does not depend solely, or even mainly, on tolerance freely given. If it did, there would be much less communication as we know it and surely much less sexual expression. Because political and social leaders tend to be more tolerant than the population at large, the latter can be guided to higher levels of practicing tolerance than it would otherwise be willing to accord. Social pluralism and dispersal of power often prevent a censorious many from marshaling itself into a politically effective majority favoring greater social control; in such cases, grudging de facto tolerance may emerge from popular intolerance circumstantially frustrated. Though we usually do not think of it as such, tolerance can also be coerced by command decisions creating and enforcing legal and constitutional rights. Some combination of all four kinds of tolerance is probably required for a free speech society to survive its union with a mass democratic one. For that union to be felicitous, each of the four probably needs to be in good working order. That freedom for pornography has come to rely so heavily on enforcement of rights indicates considerable resistance elsewhere in the tolerance system and much less than optimum management of the controversy itself.

In liberal democracy, operating freedom will always be less than prescribed in rights but more than popularly preferred; actual tolerance is less than the elite standard requires but more than the popular one accords. This "slippage"—in effect, compromise—is vital to the confederacy of free speech and mass democratic elements of modern liberal democracy. Shaped by several kinds of tolerance (and by a variety of other factors), operating standards are always in flux. In a libertarian period, all standards—prescriptive, operative, and popular—are much less restrictive. But in a libertarian period such as our own, marked by high levels of conflict, the distance between operating standards and those officially prescribed is less than between operating standards and those popularly preferred. Today, in the United States as well as in most other Western democracies, operating standards for sexual expression are more libertarian than at any time in the past. Though still falling some distance short, they are also far closer to approximating idealized elite standards constitutionally prescribed. The social and political space between operating standards and those popularly preferred has correspondingly increased and finds reflection in heightened popular dissatisfaction.

Popular standards can be more permissive than official ones set by a morally repressive elite, but this is an improbable disparity in a modern liberal mass democracy. So demanding socially, politically, and psychologically is the established free speech ethic of liberal democracy that it will almost always be found more congenial and less threatening to the few than the many (at least until we learn much more than we now know about restructuring our patterns of sexual development).

Thoughtful libertarians may recognize the implicit danger in calling reflexively for ever greater liberty without regard to the consequences of such absolutism for other values. The question is not whether freedom of speech should submit to popular preferences and majority will—a question that probably has no final answer—but whether the inevitable and continuing conflict between these two vital elements of liberal democracy has been managed as well as it might be and whether public policy has adequately performed its task of reconciliation: protecting necessary freedom and preventing unnecessary reaction.

The Task of Policy

A libertarian obscenity policy progressively narrowing proscribability to hard-core pornography makes most distinctions of content irrelevant. This reduction may seem to have much to recommend it in view of the endless traps that await a content-based test. Yet such a policy assumes either that sexual expression has within it a discoverable category inherently different from other content or that "hard-core" simply refers to whatever is objectionable to almost everyone. We have argued that both concepts are flawed. The first, which appears to be without psychodynamic basis, ignores the variability of pornography. The second, which brings policy one step short of no legal control at all, ignores most conflict over sexual expression and the popular dissatisfaction with the ready availability of pornography. Neither recognizes why sexual expression is objectionable, where it is objected to, or allows any calibration of legal control. The simple two-tier policy that makes sexual expression categorically "obscene" or "nonobscene," the latter totally protected as "speech" and the former totally unprotected as "nonspeech," if it ever had merit, has little or none in a complex, fluid, saturated communications environment in which informal control has become problematic.

We argued in the previous chapter that proscribable obscenity should vary circumstantially and have offensiveness as its central measure, rather than have as it does now an essentialist hard-core content based on prurient appeal. The obscenity test would show fewer psychodynamic contradictions and be more straightforward politically if its restrictive element corresponded to most persons' perceptions of their negative response to pornography—that it is offensive. This awareness, as the Court's own construction, "beyond customary limits of candor," suggests, is far more objectifiable than prurient appeal, which places legal control in the unenviable position of scrutinizing invitation rather than threat. As a recipient's perception rather than a presumed inherent characteristic of expression itself, offensiveness is a matter of social judgment and designation, depending on context as well as content.

Transgressive sexual expression differs from other protected speech enough to justify differences in *degree* of applied legal control. In providing a psychosexual experience, its chief function is aphrodisiacal; it would not be economically viable on any other ground. This places almost all of today's commercial pornography far from the madding crowd of ideas, opinions, views, and information that a liberal society must leave nearly totally unrestricted for its own maintenance and survival. Speech may also have value and be protected simply as self-expression even when it contributes little or nothing to intelligence and discourse. But even here, pornography differs markedly from other communication. Of all expression, sexual representation is probably the least rational, least consciously accessible, most distracting, and most potentially threatening. Even depictions of extreme violence and aggression, disturbing as they are, may not arouse or preoccupy in the same way. Such differences from other expression and "self-expression" do not justify removal of protection, but they do support some amending and tailoring of that protection circumstantially.

The Supreme Court has made two important exceptions to the hardcore standard—narrowing protection for materials directed at juveniles and broadening it for those held in the privacy of the home—but it needs to go much further in circumstantial analysis. Theoretically, any pornography falling short of rarefied legal obscenity can now be made available (at least to adults) anywhere, including the same stores, movie theaters, showcases, racks, or shelves in which other erotic and noneroric expression is offered. Such wide and undiscriminating accessibility works to subvert policies that distinguish between adults and juveniles and invades the privacy of the unwilling audience. In the past these problems were avoided by furtive and sometimes literally under-the-counter distribution. Today, formal distinctions of time, place, and presentation may be in order, at least where traffic seems likely to involve the general public. The matter is one of segregation rather than suppression. Clearly, the right to publish, distribute, or have access to pornography need not include the right to have it available everywhere at all times.

The Court needs also formally to recognize and rationalize differences among the communications media and perhaps also within segments of individual media. Technology has eroded the old functional division of labor among the media. Nevertheless, important differences based on relative accessibility, representational power, cognitive effort demanded, and the social makeup of the audience all continue to exist, as do corresponding long-standing, widely relied-on expectations that some media have less license for sexual representation than others.

Circumstantial variation of control does not alter the preemptive role of free speech values. Serious literary, political, or scientific value, not dependent on community standards or those of the many, remains a constitutional veto of outright proscription no matter how offensive a representation may be. That ultimate determination is correctly placed in the hands of the appellate judiciary.

It is difficult to take seriously the libertarian claim that any retreat from the farthest outposts of pornography freedom is a first step in a censorial retrogression that will threaten the very foundation of free speech society. A modestly more discriminating social control in a highest policy that is itself at its libertarian zenith would not signal a return to orthodoxy or the more restrictive standards of the past, or even mean less diversity. Two hundred years of the Bill of Rights, a half-century of expansive First Amendment development, and thirty years of steadily growing freedom for sexual expression speak powerfully to the contrary. A free speech policy-making that can move only in one direction or that is unable to weigh countervailing values and interests, admit and correct its own mistakes, or adapt itself to a complex, changing communications environment ultimately risks both its political capital and its credibility.

An Erotic Legacy and Its Social Probate

All known societies have had to deal with sexual expression judged to be objectionable. None has succeeded in eradicating transgressive representation. The invitation of forbidden fantasy to external play through symbol is far too strong ever to be completely suppressed by external authority.

The function of pornography socially, like that of pornographic wishes, is precisely to trade in the forbidden.

In the pornographic within, transgressive wishes are mediated by our capacity for thought and imagination and by our ability to create and use representation. Transgressive images, words, and ideas give symbolic form to these forbidden impulses and desires and serve as external attachments for them. Disturbing as they may sometimes be, neither the fantasies nor their external manifestation in pornographic expression can be considered alien. As the legacy of an ontogenetically eroticized sexuality, they mark us as a species as much as does falling in love, worshipping God, or making war.

Without them and the incompletely resolved psychic conflicts from which they spring, we would have no pornography and no pornographic response to other sexual and nonsexual expression. Without them there would be no reaction of disgust or revulsion and, thus, no determined efforts to censor. The human animal is, in effect, psychodynamically programmed by nurturance rather than birth to be pornographic—to have transgressive fantasies, to represent them and respond to their representation, and to try, sometimes desperately, to suppress or otherwise restrict them. These basic yet simple facts are typically ignored by libertarian and censor alike. The former does not see why pornography must be censored; the latter, why it can never completely be so.

Many erotic representations—a double entendre, risqué joke, "cheese-cake" photo, burlesque routine, nude study, or even a performance of *Oedipus Rex*—are actually quasi-pornographic, serving to focus or discharge the energy of conscious and unconscious transgressive fantasy without triggering the aversive defensive reaction that lies in wait for expression insufficiently cloaked or encoded. In the same way, particular sexual words, images, or ideas may be acceptable and even attractive to some persons yet be objectionable to others, or be acceptable in some contexts but not in others. Hard-core pornography is not a qualitatively different sexual expression but simply a less disguised surrogate indulgence.

Censors and moralists do not see the enormous marginal variability of pornography among cultures, or within their own cultures among individuals or social and intellectual circles. This explains in part the heavy-handedness with which social control has so often been sought and imposed. To the censor, the matter always seems simpler than it is; concurrence on specific objects of regulation is assumed or vastly overestimated. Libertarians, by contrast, tend to focus on variability alone, dismissing the matter of control as culturally relative and individually subjective. Variability is proof that control is bound to be idiosyncratic and ultimately capricious: one person's vulgarity is another's lyric. Libertarians tend not to see these diverse conceptions and regulations of pornography for what they really are—variations of an underlying and troubling universal theme.

Nor does it follow, as some libertarians and utopianists have claimed, that delabeling or freeing all erotic expression would remove its forbidden invitation and thus eliminate pornography. Where legal restrictions have been relaxed, neither pornography nor the pornography business has flagged. Instead, for many persons, much delabeled expression has remained functionally pornographic, and "new" pornography has pressed on in word and image further into forbidden territory. In effect, pornography seeks to remain forbidden even where it has been designated not so. Rather than eliminating pornography as an institution, delabeling tends to shift its boundaries.

We have suggested that pornography's analogue in sexual behavior is prostitution. Both institutions are functional alternatives to preferred sexual avenues, their very deviancy perhaps underscoring and even helping to define those avenues. Both are, in effect, compromises—remissions of the moral demand system in which unwanted sexual interest and energy are accommodated, while conflicting psychodynamic demands not completely acknowledged or understood find limited reconciliation.

A deeper functionality lies in the ontogenetic utility of pornographic fantasies themselves. When primitive infantile attempts to possess or consume the original love object meet with frustration or denial, desire is fatefully diverted from behavior to fantasy—a giant individual step toward membership in a civilized community. Transgressive aspects may later be repressed but they are no eradicated. They survive to return and attach themselves to external objects: to "deviating" behavior, in the case of prostitution, or to mere representations of such behavior—pornography. In this sense, pornography and our indulgence in it are themselves conforming, parts of an even larger process of self- and social policing in which forbidden desire, having renounced its original objects, accepts surrogates and symbols.

Most pornographic indulgence remains at least partially camouflaged. Even sexual utopianists may, at some point, prefer a degree of distance to conscious confrontation with repressed conflict. It is no accident that relatively little pornographic expression has directly involved mother-son incest, necrophilia, bestiality, coprophilia, or extremes of sadistic behavior, especially genital or eye mutilation. These images and subjects too closely approach desperately repressed erotic dramas and conflicts for most persons to avoid the pronounced aversive reaction that serves as the readiest defense of the self against itself. Even in liberal societies, most pornography controversies—at least in the past—have dealt with erotic expression far more disguised: four-letter words, degrees of nudity, stories of adulterous behavior, suggested or simulated intercourse, and the like. Psychodynamically, these marginally transgressive representations are several levels removed from the starker elements of primitive erotic fantasies.

Our composure is challenged by the artist using the pornographic imagination. The disguise and baggage of self-deception are cast aside, giving access to a part of our nature we have tried to shut away. That aggressive and unsparing vision is deeply disturbing; its revelations may be most profound exactly where we have greatest difficulty confronting them. The reader-witness is like Marlow in *Heart of Darkness,* whose long journey to the forbidding and nearly uncharted waters of the upper Congo to rescue the depraved Kurtz is, in its darkest reaches, a passage into pornographic territory. His horrifying discoveries about the fallen hero are, in effect, self-discoveries. They are unwelcome because they show how thin is the fabric of reason and restraint that holds our ontogenetically more primitive selves at bay and on which our self-possession and even sanity may depend. When the pornographic imagination is successful, as it is in Bataille, Réage, and much of Sade, the reader, like Marlow, is troubled for an understanding of his own emotions, both appetitive and censoring. In that imagination, the erotic and destructive converge to demand recognition and acknowledgment.

Though most pornography has no such diagnostic or epistemic worth, most succeeds in touching erotic conflict within. Our fascination with transgressive sexual expression and our need to censor it may seem to be opposite ends politically or socially, but they are scarcely so psychodynamically. As long as we are eroticized creatures, we will have sexually transgressive fantasies, and they will seek or be responsive to their material representation—pornography—whether we like it or not. Pornography will continue to make us anxious, and we will often be consciously offended by it.

The Question of Harm

Functional utility does not mean that pornography is without harm. Yet there is little conclusive evidence of harmful effect, and in particular no confirmation of a causal link between sexual expression and any sort of antisocial behavior. The only act demonstrably associated with pornography—masturbation—is a sexual release that may actually reduce the likelihood of other sexual acts, including the antisocial. Nor is there any clear proof of an effect, harmful or otherwise, on emotional development or attitude formation.

The inconclusiveness of the research is not surprising. Even if it were possible to establish a consensus about what a harm is—the complexity of which is often ignored by censors—the difficulty of isolating pornography (or any sexual expression) from hundreds of other possibly relevant factors in the internal and external environments is probably insurmountable. Formation of sexual attitudes is a complicated matter involving both sexual and nonsexual factors, many of which are at work long before any exposure to pornography. An effect attributable to pornography would also need to be separated from those of the pornographic appeal of a great range of external objects, circumstances, and actual persons encountered in everyday life. And even if effects were discoverable, their result might not be harmful in all or even most instances. Lack of conclusive evidence hardly proves an opposite case, but it does require skepticism.

Concern about harm is rational, and inquiry should be carried forward. But the direction of cause and effect deserves more attention, particularly the possibility that pornography may be a *dependent* factor in the individual's tangled experience of establishing a social and psychological identity. Until now, such inquiry has been of much less interest to researchers and their sponsors than that seeking to establish pornography's agency. Attention has also probably focused too much on what is most offensive—hardcore pornography—and its chief consumers, adults and adolescents. Too little attention has been given to the possible overstimulating effect of less explicit expression on the latency-age child in a highly sexualized communications environment.

Harmfulness must be distinguished from offensiveness. Inconclusive findings about the former contrast sharply with wide-ranging evidence of the latter. Perceived offensiveness is also likely to withstand almost any empirical findings of harmlessness or of functional utility. Censors and moralists fail to appreciate this or the social and psychodynamics on which it is based. Hence they often fail to distinguish fact and preference, tending to see the former in the latter.

As a salient censorial position, the feminist indictment of pornography, descriptively accurate and eloquent in calling attention to the demeaning and often sadistic portrayal of women, also misses the diagnostic mark. It does not follow that pornography's negative images are models merely because they exist. As stigmatized expression, pornography may actually serve to sharpen or reinforce what is acceptable or favored. The call for eradication of the imagery is futile, though the urging of greater control of its expression—in effect, a renewed and reinvigorated stigmatization—may be a well-aimed thrust in the larger, never-ending struggle to denounce and limit disturbing representation while at the same time asserting preferred sexual values.

The Politics of a Self Divided

Forbidden sexual fantasies—the pornographic within—tempt us with their promise of delight and impossible gratification and disturb us by their trespass and perversity. No external liberty can completely free us from anxiety about the latter, and no social censorship is so complete that it can obliterate the seductive invitation of the former. We try to come to terms by indulging without fully admitting that we do so and by keeping the imagery, internal and external, in disguise. The compromise is bared by the pornographic imagination working through art. Its disturbing revelations may not themselves free us from the tyranny of the erotic paradox, but the illumination they provide may make us wiser and less innocent. Marlow sees both the temptations of Kurtz and the denials of Kurtz's betrothed. In the end, he is able to tell the full tale to his shipboard friends with a certain equanimity. Unlike Comstock, a more ordinary man whose energies were spent stilling the inner erotic voice heard in myriad external representations, Marlow has journeyed and come upon valuable self-knowledge. Although this heroic path is theoretically open to anyone through art, insight, or therapies of the mind, it is, as Conrad observed, closed not to but *by* most persons. In some distant and favored future perhaps it may be more commonly taken.

In revealing what the censor in us most fears, the pornographic imagination renders censorship itself suspect. Yet we cannot forget that a society must be run. Most of its members, including Marlow's shipboard friends, are neither artists nor giants of self-possession; they are bound to seek help outside for what they perceive to be outside. The darkest truths may thus also favor, at times at least, a compassionate censorship.

We live in a free speech society and a mass democratic one that coexist uneasily much of the time. The former—perhaps the bravest political arrangement ever conceived—would solve our problem by welcoming not only the knowledge and insight but also the great accumulation of dross found in pornography. Yet to work as prescribed, that society requires a very high level of practicing tolerance that, in the matter of sexual expression, is probably beyond the capacity of its average constituent. In providing license for the representation of forbidden fantasies, it asks for a suspension of many of our chief defenses, psychic and institutional, against such ideas and images. In a society in which the voice of the many is not only legitimate but sovereign, operating freedom will always depend heavily on a diffusion of tolerance.

For these reasons, pornography is an issue in which all triumphs, libertarian and censorial, are likely to be partial and short-lived. A human nature that seeks to indulge in forbidden wishes, at the same time rejecting and seeking to control them, defies any complete resolution of the conflict. At best, perhaps, we can only manage the problem in incomplete and often untidy steps many of which will be resisted by libertarian or censor. Management is essentially a political task, and, like the psychic ministry of it in that first commonwealth, the human mind, it may be performed either skillfully or unskillfully.

In the mind, the ego executive must try to balance forbidden images that promise pleasure and delight against the anxiety those images inevitably arouse. In the external world, the policymaker must arrange a set of compromises for the substantive and distributive aspects of the representation of those images. He or she must measure speech and expression as constitutional right but also majority preferences as legitimate and entitled power. The sought-after must be weighed against the tabooed, indulgence of the few against reaction of the many, risk of alienation against the comfort of conformity, recreational regression against the possibility of harm, art against dross, and the epistemically valid against the meaningless. The policymaker must also take into account the organization and technology of the media of communication, the sociology of their audiences, and the character of policing procedures, none of which is constant. Successful management will rarely be credited, but poor management will be denounced under some other name, by one side or the other. Yet the policymaker must not be diverted either by the libertarian ideologue lacking compassion or the censoring zealot lacking tolerance. The ideologue is unable to see that censorship is inevitable, the zealot that it is inevitably ambivalent and porous.

The images of forbidden desires and their public control have shaped our individual and collective lives and will continue to do so. The images may yield pleasure, revulsion, perhaps insight; the censorship may be moderated and fitted. The first will challenge our courage; the second, our craft.

Notes

References cited in abbreviated form in the notes may be found in full in the bibliography.

Chapter 1

1. Frank A. Beach, "Cross-Species Comparisons and the Human Heritage," p. 301.

2. Weston La Barre, *The Human Animal,* p. 209.

3. Ibid., p. 123.

4. We have come to appreciate that "mothering" may also be, in part, socially determined. Since a disproportionate amount of early nurturance is provided by women in almost all cultures, mothering by women may help to create women who will be mothering and men who will resist the impulse to mother. To a degree, mothering may thus "reproduce" itself. Such social determination, though qualifying our understanding of the asymmetry of early parenting, does not deny gender-related differences based on anatomy and instinct. See Nancy Chodorow, *The Reproduction of Mothering.*

5. Though endopsychic dynamics come to have a salience of their own, parents and children participate together in early psychosexual development. Conscious and unconscious fantasies may be powerfully and idiosyncratically affected by the quality of the child's external environment, especially by parental personality and behavior and, indirectly through it, by social and cultural norms.

6. See, for example, Russell Middleton, "Brother-Sister and Father-Daughter Marriage in Ancient Egypt"; Keith Hopkins, "Brother-Sister Marriage in Roman Egypt"; and Pierre L. Van den Berghe and Gene M. Mesher, "Royal Incest and Inclusive Fitness."

Even as ritual or royal prerogative, incest may have carried a price. The periodic killing of kings or leaders in some primitive cultures may have been linked to their license to commit father-daughter or brother-sister incest. See Geza Roheim, "The Psychoanalytic Interpretation of Culture," in *Man and His Culture,* ed. Warner Muensterberger, p. 33.

7. Clellan S. Ford, "Sex Offenses: An Anthropological Perspective," pp. 226–235.

8. David Aberle et al., "The Incest Taboo and the Mating Patterns of Animals," p. 261. More than a dozen consanguineous relations—"uncovering the nakedness of" proscribed family members—were enumerated and biblically enjoined for the ancient Hebrews and the later Judeo-Christian world in the laws of Moses. See Leviticus 18:6–18.

9. Ford, "Sex Offenses," p. 232; La Barre, *Human Animal,* p. 129. See also George P. Murdock, *Social Structure,* pp. 284–313.

10. Among recent studies, see, for example, Norbert Bischof, "The Biological Foundations of the Incest Taboo"; Melvin Ember, "On the Origin and Extension of the Incest Taboo"; R. D. Murray, "The Evolution and Functional Significance of Incest Avoidance"; and Seymour Parker, "The Pre-Cultural Basis of the Incest Taboo: Toward a Biosocial Theory."

11. Parker, "Pre-Cultural Basis," pp. 291–295. See also K. Kortmulder, "An Ethological Theory of the Incest Taboo and Exogamy." Intergenerational competition is discussed in Aberle et al., "Incest Taboo," p. 261.

12. See, for example, studies summarized by Gardner Lindzey in "Some Remarks Concerning Incest, the Incest Taboo, and Psychoanalytic Theory," pp. 1052–1054.

13. Lindzey, "Some Remarks Concerning Incest," p. 1054. See also Newton E. Morton, "Morbidity of Children from Consanguineous Marriages," in *Progress in Medical Genetics,* ed. Arthur G. Steinberg; and William J. Schull and James V. Neel, *The Effects of Inbreeding on Japanese Children.* For discussion of possible adaptive changes, see, for example, Frank B. Livingston, "Genetics, Ecology, and the Origins of Incest and Exogamy"; and David Lester, "Incest." Some writers have speculated that under certain conditions inbreeding might produce a superior strain. See, for example, Aberle et al., "Incest Taboo," pp. 256–257; Murdock, *Social Structure,* p. 290.

14. Among recent studies, see John Crewdson, *By Silence Betrayed;* Susan Forward and Craig Buck, *Betrayal of Innocence;* Blair Justice and Rita Justice, *The Broken Taboo;* Linda Muldoon, ed., *Incest: Confronting the Silent Crime;* C. Georgia Simari and David Baskin, *Incest: No Longer a Family Affair;* David Finkelhor, "Sex Among Siblings: A Survey of Prevalence, Variety, and Effects"; Judith Lewis Herman, "Father-Daughter Incest"; and Joyce Spencer, "Father-Daughter Incest: A Clinical View from the Corrections Field."

15. Lindzey, "Some Remarks Concerning Incest," p. 1056.

16. See, for example, Ray H. Bixler, "The Incest Controversy."

17. See, for example, Talcott Parsons, "Social Structure and Development of Personality: Freud's Contribution to the Integration of Psychology and Sociology"; and Leslie A. White, *The Evolution of Culture.*

18. Claude Lévi-Strauss, *The Elementary Structures of Kinship,* pp. 3–11.

19. See, for example, Talcott Parsons, "The Incest Taboo in Relation to Social Structure"; and Brenda Z. Seligman, "The Problem of Incest and Exogamy."

20. Aberle et al., "Incest Taboo," pp. 257–258.

21. La Barre, *Human Animal,* pp. 122–123. Polygamous and polyandrous

societies provide further evidence that the conflict-reduction function is less than universally compelling. In the former, mothers and daughters may sometimes share the same husband, though it is not the daughter's father. In the latter, fathers and sons may share the same wife, though it is not the son's mother. Brothers may share a wife, though it is not their sister; sisters may share a husband, though it is not their brother. See Aberle et al., "Incest Taboo," p. 257.

22. Charles William Wahl, "Psychodynamics of Consummated Maternal Incest," p. 188.

23. For primitive sanctions, see Ford, "Sex Offenses," p. 230; Murdock, *Social Structure*, p. 288. In the United States, consanguineous relationships are legally proscribed in every state. The typical law forbids marriage with a parent, offspring, sibling, grandparent, aunt, uncle, niece, or nephew. Fifteen other consanguineous relations are proscribed in the various states. See Karl G. Heider, "Anthropological Models of Incest Laws in the United States."

24. Murdock, *Social Structure*, p. 288.

25. Ernest Jones, *The Life and Work of Freud*, vol. 2, p. 351.

26. Freud, *Totem and Taboo*, p. 143.

27. See Edwin R. Wallace, *Freud and Anthropology*, esp. pp. 129–162; see also Weston La Barre, "The Influence of Freud on Anthropology," p. 291.

28. Freud, *Totem and Taboo*, pp. 159–160.

29. Derek Freeman, "Totem and Taboo: A Reappraisal," in *Man and His Culture*, ed. Warner Muensterberger, p. 75; Lévi-Strauss, *Elementary Structures of Kinship*, p. 491.

30. Lévi-Strauss, *Elementary Structures of Kinship*, p. 491.

31. Ibid., pp. 24–25.

32. See, for example, Henri Parens et al., "On the Girl's Entry into the Oedipus Complex," in *Female Psychology*, ed. Harold P. Blum.

33. "The organization of parenting generates a relational situation in a girl's oedipus complex in which she does not need to repress her oedipal attachments so thoroughly as a boy does. Her attachment to her father in particular is more idealized and less intense than a boy's to his mother. Given this less charged attachment, and given her ongoing relation to her mother, she is less likely to fear maternal retaliation, and maternal retaliation fantasies are less likely than paternal retaliation fantasies toward a son" (Chodorow, *Reproduction of Mothering*, p. 133). For a concise discussion of the various controversies that have arisen as well as a psychoanalytically oriented critique of Freud's classic theory as it applies to girls, see Chodorow, *Reproduction of Mothering*, chaps. 6–9.

34. Through the superego, Freud wrote, "civilization obtains mastery over the individual's dangerous desire for aggression by weakening and disarming it and by setting up an agency within him to watch over it like a garrison in a conquered city" (Sigmund Freud, *Civilization and Its Discontents*, pp. 123–124).

35. Robert Waelder, *Basic Theory of Psychoanalysis*, p. 113. It has been claimed, most notably by Melanie Klein and her associates, that an earlier oedipal-like phase, transient and less intense, occurs before the age of two. Melanie Klein, *The Psycho-analysis of Children*.

36. Wallace, *Freud and Anthropology*, p. 209. Negative variations are observable

when attachment is to the parent of the same sex, and rivalry for his or her affections is with the parent of the opposite sex. See Sigmund Freud, *The Ego and the Id*, pp. 32–33. In practice, a whole range of hybrid cases extends between the positive and negative forms of the complex. See J. Laplanche and J.-B. Pontalis, *The Language of Psychoanalysis*, p. 284.

37. Bronislaw Malinowski, *Sex and Repression in Savage Society*, p. 44. See Francis H. Bartlett, "The Limitations of Freud"; see also Geza Roheim, *Psychoanalysis and Anthropology;* and Alfred Kroeber, " 'Totem and Taboo' in Retrospect," in *Psychoanalysis and History*, ed. Bruce Mazlish, pp. 45–49. Ernest Jones argued that the "ignorance" was actually a form of denial, that is, a defense mechanism alleviating the guilt of infantile sexuality by deflecting hostility normally directed at the father onto the maternal uncle ("Mother-Right and the Sexual Ignorance of Savages," in *Psycho-Myth, Psycho-History*, vol. 2, pp. 45–173).

38. Laplanche and Pontalis, *Language of Psychoanalysis*, p. 286.

39. For example, William M. Stephens, *The Oedipus Complex;* Roheim, *Psychoanalysis and Anthropology;* George Devereux, *Reality and Dream* and *Ethnopsychoanalysis;* W. Sachs, *Black Hamlet;* and Warner Muensterberger, "Biopsychological Determinants of Social Life." L. B. Boyer has summarized current findings in "Mutual Influences Between Anthropology and Psychoanalysis." See also discussion in Paul Kline, *Fact and Fantasy in Freudian Theory*, pp. 130–159.

40. Jacob Arlow, "Ego Psychology and the Study of Mythology," p. 378.

41. Otto Rank, *The Myth and the Birth of the Hero*, p. 61; see also Lord Raglan, *The Hero: A Study in Tradition, Myth, and Drama*, pp. 177–185.

42. Clyde Kluckhohn, "Recurrent Themes in Myth and Mythmaking," p. 270.

43. Joseph Campbell, *The Hero with a Thousand Faces*, p. 4.

44. In his psychoanalytic analysis of the literary response, Norman N. Holland concluded that almost all of the "greatest literature builds from an oedipal fantasy" (*The Dynamics of Literary Response*, p. 47).

45. Ernest Jones, "The Oedipus Complex as an Explanation of Hamlet's Mystery: A Study in Motive."

46. On folklore, see Gershon Legman, *The Horn Book;* Weston La Barre, "Kiowa Folk Sciences" and "Obscenity: An Anthropological Appraisal." A summary of works on the psychoanalytic study of folklore published before 1948 may be found in Weston La Barre, "Folklore and Psychology."

One of the most strikingly explicit ballads is the anonymous "Edward" widely popular in the British Isles in the Middle Ages. See Helen Child Sargent and George L. Kittridge, *English and Scottish Popular Ballads*, p. 25. See also Martin Kallich et al., eds., *Oedipus: Myth and Drama*, pp. 389–391.

On jokes and humor, see Sigmund Freud, *Jokes and Their Relation to the Unconscious;* Maurice Grotjahn, *Beyond Laughter;* and Gershon Legman, *Rationale of the Dirty Joke*. On oedipal concerns in drinking songs, see Weston La Barre, "The Psychopathology of Drinking Songs," and for graffiti, see Robert Reisner, *Graffiti*.

47. See generally Bruno Bettelheim, *The Uses of Enchantment*.

48. La Barre, *Human Animal*, pp. 209, 214.

49. Sigmund Freud, "Infantile Sexuality," in *Three Essays on Sexuality*, pp. 173–206.

50. Sigmund Freud, "The Transformations of Puberty," in *Three Essays on Sexuality*, pp. 207–230.

51. Sigmund Freud, "Formulations on the Two Principles of Mental Functioning," p. 215.

52. In such situations, the id, superego, and forces of the outside world are in relative harmony. See Anna Freud, *The Ego and the Mechanisms of Defense*, pp. 175–176.

53. Ibid., pp. 55, 60–61.

54. Waelder, *Basic Theory of Psychoanalysis*, pp. 184–185.

55. Robert Gosling, untitled article in *Does Pornography Matter?* ed. C. H. Rolph, p. 72.

56. Steven Marcus, *The Other Victorians*, p. 241.

57. Sandor Ferenczi, *Sex and Psychoanalysis*, pp. 112–130. See also Edmund Bergler, "Obscene Words."

58. Ferenczi, *Sex and Psychoanalysis*, pp. 118, 123. See also Jean Piaget and Barbel Inhelder, *The Psychology of the Child*, pp. 68–91; and Heinz Werner and Bernard Kaplan, *Symbol Formation*, pp. 40–62.

59. Leo Stone, "On the Principal Obscene Word in the English Language," p. 30.

60. Renatus Hartogs with Hans Fantel, *Four-Letter Word Games*, p. 152. See also David Paletz and William F. Harris, "Four-Letter Threats to Authority."

61. Wayland Young, *Eros Denied*, p. 19.

62. See generally Freud, *Jokes and the Unconscious*. See also D. W. Abse, "Psychodynamic Aspects of the Problem of Definition of Obscenity," p. 580.

63. Grotjahn, *Beyond Laughter*, pp. 10–16.

64. The psychodynamic functions of entertainment, particularly to serve fantasy needs, are often overlooked in the massive scholarly effort to discover the effects of the mass media on behavior. Nor do they receive much attention in the extensive and inexhaustible debate over the intellectual quality of mass entertainment. For a brief but cogent treatment of psychodynamic aspects, see Harold Mendelsohn, *Mass Entertainment*, pp. 100–136. See also, generally, William Stephenson, *The Play Theory of Mass Communication*. "Gratifications" research has similarly touched on psychodynamic functions. See, for example, Jay G. Blumler and Elihu Katz, eds., *The Uses of Mass Communications*; and Heinz-Dietrich Fischer and Stefan R. Melnick, eds., *Entertainment: A Cross-Cultural Examination*. On the role of popular culture, see, for example, Norman F. Cantor and Michael B. Werthman, eds., *The History of Popular Culture*.

65. Holland, *Dynamics of Literary Response*, p. 189. See also, generally, Simon O. Lesser, *Fiction and the Unconscious*.

66. Holland, *Dynamics of Literary Response*, p. 310.

67. Gosling, untitled, pp. 68–70.

68. Abse, "Psychodynamic Aspects," pp. 582–583; Ernest van den Haag, "Quia Ineptum," in *"To Deprave and Corrupt . . ."* ed. John Chandos, pp. 121–123.

69. Gosling, untitled, pp. 64–65; van den Haag, "Quia Ineptum," pp. 121–122.

70. Gosling, untitled, pp. 71–72; Abse, "Psychodynamic Aspects," pp. 575–577.

71. Charles Brenner, *An Elementary Textbook of Psychoanalysis,* pp. 198–209.

72. Bergler, "Obscene Words," pp. 236–241.

73. Peter Gay, *The Bourgeois Experience: Victoria to Freud,* vol. 1, *The Education of the Senses,* p. 376.

74. Gosling, untitled, pp. 70–76; Willard Gaylin, "Obscenity Is More Than a Four-Letter Word," in *Censorship and Freedom of Expression,* ed. Harry M. Clor, p. 161.

Chapter 2

1. Bruno Bettelheim, *Symbolic Wounds,* pp. 21–32.

2. For a brief summary of these, see Reay Tannahill, *Sex in History,* pp. 33–37.

3. Max Kohen, "The Venus of Willendorf."

4. Norman Sussman, "Sex and Sexuality in History," in *The Sexual Experience,* ed. Benjamin J. Sadock, Harold I. Kaplan, and Alfred M. Freedman, p. 8.

5. Arlette Leroi-Gourhan, *Treasures of Prehistoric Art,* p. 144.

6. Gertrude R. Levy, *The Gate of Horn,* pp. 11–12.

7. William H. Davenport, "Sex in Cross-Cultural Perspective," in *Human Sexuality in Four Perspectives,* ed. Frank A. Beach. See also, generally, Vern L. Bullough, *Sexual Variance in Society and History.* For systematic examples with regard to behavior, see Clellan S. Ford, "Sex Offenses: An Anthropological Perspective"; with regard to nudity, see William N. Stephens, "A Cross-Cultural Study of Modesty and Obscenity," pp. 411–412.

8. Davenport, "Sex in Cross-Cultural Perspective," p. 118.

9. Stephens, "Cross-Cultural Study of Modesty and Obscenity," pp. 405–410.

10. Ibid., pp. 411–412.

11. Alan Read, "An Obscene Symbol."

12. Stephens, "Cross-Cultural Study of Modesty and Obscenity," pp. 415–416.

13. Passages from, respectively, David Loth, *The Erotic in Literature,* p. 46; H. Montgomery Hyde, *A History of Pornography,* p. 51; and D. F. Barber, *Pornography and Society,* p. 47.

14. See Otto J. Brendel, "The Scope and Temperament of Erotic Art in the Greco-Roman World," in *Studies in Erotic Art,* ed. Theodore Bowie and Cornelia V. Christenson, pp. 34–35; Albert Ellis, "Art and Sex," in *Encyclopedia of Sexual Behavior,* ed. Albert Ellis and Albert Abarbanel, vol. 1, p. 161.

15. Plato, *The Republic,* Book III, 390A.

16. Edgar Gregersen, *Sexual Practices,* pp. 23–24.

17. See generally Bullough, *Sexual Variance;* and Gregersen, *Sexual Practices.*

18. G. Rattray Taylor, *Sex in History,* p. 70.

19. Peter Webb, *The Erotic Arts,* pp. 104–105.

20. Taylor, *Sex in History,* pp. 120–123.

21. Norman St. John-Stevas, *Obscenity and the Law,* p. 10.

22. Noel Perrin, *Dr. Bowdler's Legacy,* p. 89.

23. Quoted in Donald Thomas, *A Long Time Burning,* p. 78.

24. Peter Wagner, "Pornography in the Courtroom: Trial Reports About Cases of Sexual Crimes and Delinquencies as a Genre of Eighteenth-Century Erotica," in *Sexuality in Eighteenth-Century Britain,* ed. Paul-Gabriel Bouce, pp. 128–130.

25. Thomas, *Long Time Burning,* p. 117.

26. St. John-Stevas, *Obscenity and the Law,* pp. 25–26.

27. Perrin, *Dr. Bowdler's Legacy,* pp. viii, xv.

28. Ibid., p. 96.

29. Ibid., pp. 225, 227.

30. Ibid., p. 126.

31. St. John-Stevas, *Obscenity and the Law,* p. 33.

32. Perrin, *Dr. Bowdler's Legacy,* p. 241.

33. Thomas, *Long Time Burning,* pp. 261–262.

34. Ibid., p. 264.

35. Regina v. Hicklin [1868] L.R. 3 Q.B. 360, 371.

36. St. John-Stevas, *Obscenity and the Law,* pp. 76–77.

37. Thomas, *Long Time Burning,* p. 270.

38. On Victorian preferences in popular erotic writing and public displays, see Ronald Pearsall, *The Worm in the Bud,* pp. 58–71, 102–109.

39. Thomas, *Long Time Burning,* p. 273.

40. Ibid., p. 290. "The twentieth-century reader, though disapproving of incest, is less likely than his Victorian predecessor to be either stimulated or outraged by jibes against the 'happy family,' but much more likely to be affected by later and perhaps more ingeniously perverse writing whose effect is to ridicule faith in racial tolerance and the equality or emancipation of women. 'Votes for women' in reality prepare the way for *Histoire d'O* in fantasy" (p. 274).

41. *Joint Select Committee Report on Lotteries and Indecent Advertisements* (1908), p. 40, quoted in Thomas, *Long Time Burning,* p. 289.

42. Alec Craig, *Suppressed Books,* pp. 176–188.

43. Peter Gay, *The Bourgeois Experience: Victoria to Freud,* vol. 1, *The Education of the Senses,* pp. 362–365. See also Herman Musaph, "Introduction," in *Handbook of Sexology,* ed. John Money and Herman Musaph, p. 9.

44. Obscene Publications Act of 1959, 7 & 8 Eliz. 2, c. 66, section 1.1.

45. Paul O'Higgins, *Censorship in Britain,* p. 69.

46. Ibid.

47. Bernard Williams, ed., *Obscenity and Film Censorship,* p. 10.

48. Ibid., pp. 10–12. The development and application of the myriad laws governing "obscenity" and "indecency" are summarized in United Kingdom, Parliament, *Report of the Committee on Obscenity and Film Censorship,* app. 1, pp. 167–185.

49. Ibid., pp. 162, 164. One result of the committee's work was the Indecent Displays (Control) Act of 1981, prohibiting display of any indecent matter in a "public place." The act does not define "indecent," a term presumably of broader scope than "obscene" (Indecent Displays [Control] Act 1981, c. 42). For a concise

description of the response to the Williams Report and the uncertain state of British obscenity doctrine since, see A. W. B. Simpson, *Pornography and Politics: A Look Back to the Williams Committee.*

50. Heywood Broun and Margaret Leech, *Anthony Comstock: Roundsman of the Lord,* pp. 184–189.

51. Felice Flannery Lewis, *Literature, Obscenity, and the Law,* p. 132.

52. United States v. One Book Called "Ulysses," 5 F. Supp. 182, 184 (S.D.N.Y. 1933).

53. Lewis, *Literature, Obscenity, and the Law,* p. 183.

54. Roth v. United States and Alberts v. California, 354 U.S. 476 (1957).

55. Lewis, *Literature, Obscenity, and the Law,* p. 223.

56. See generally Richard S. Randall, *Censorship of the Movies;* Ira H. Carmen, *Movies, Censorship, and the Law;* and Edward de Grazia and Roger K. Newman, *Banned Films.*

57. Manual Enterprises v. Day, 370 U.S. 478 (1962); and "Memoirs of a Woman of Pleasure" v. Massachusetts, 383 U.S. 418 (1966).

58. For a summary of substantive aspects of material found not obscene, see President's Commission on Obscenity and Pornography, *Report of the Commission on Obscenity and Pornography,* pp. 371–372.

59. Ibid., pp. 45, 47–48.

60. Miller v. California, 413 U.S. 15, 25 (1973).

61. Smith v. United States, 431 U.S. 291, 301, 305 (1977).

62. U.S. Department of Justice, Attorney General's Commission on Pornography, *Final Report,* pp. 228–232.

63. League of Nations, *Records of the International Conference for the Suppression of the Circulation of Traffic in Obscene Publications,* chap. 4, pp. 21, 22.

64. See generally "Comparative Perspectives," in *Technical Report of the Commission on Obscenity and Pornography,* vol. 2, pp. 91–241. These findings are summarized in the Commission's *Report,* pp. 394–410.

65. United Kingdom, *Report of the Committee on Obscenity,* app. 3, pp. 196–219.

66. Mikhail Stern with August Stern, *Sex in the U.S.S.R.,* p. 185.

67. Ibid., p. 189.

Chapter 3

1. Abraham Kaplan, "Obscenity as an Esthetic Category." For another important statement from a similar point of view, see George Steiner, "Night Words: High Pornography and Human Privacy."

2. See generally, for example, Paul S. Boyer, *Purity in Print;* Noel Perrin, *Dr. Bowdler's Legacy;* and Donald Thomas, *A Long Time Burning.*

3. Eberhard Kronhausen and Phyllis Kronhausen, *Pornography and the Law,* pp. 26, 28.

4. Ibid., pp. 178, 243.

5. Peter Michelson, *The Aesthetics of Pornography,* pp. 24–25.

6. Steven Marcus, *The Other Victorians,* pp. 277–281.

7. Ibid., p. 281n.

8. Morse Peckham, *Art and Pornography,* pp. 29–31.

9. Susan Sontag, "On Pornography," pp. 197, 191.

10. Marcus, *Other Victorians,* pp. 273, 216, 195.

11. Edmund Wilson, "The Vogue of the Marquis de Sade," in *Eight Essays,* p. 179.

12. Mario Praz, *The Romantic Agony,* esp. pp. 95–195.

13. See Simone de Beauvoir, "Must We Burn de Sade?" pp. 3–64; Pierre Klossowski, "Nature as Destructive Principle," pp. 65–86; and Angela Carter, *The Sadeian Woman.*

14. Donald Thomas, *The Marquis de Sade,* pp. 206–207.

15. Georges Bataille, *Story of the Eye,* p. 105.

16. Ibid., p. 108.

17. Ibid., p. 116.

18. Pauline Réage, *Story of O,* p. 44.

19. Ibid., p. 84.

20. Régine Deforges, *Confessions of O: Conversations with Pauline Réage,* p. 145.

21. Ibid., p. 94.

22. Joseph Conrad, *Heart of Darkness,* p. 86.

23. Ibid., pp. 96–98.

24. Ibid., p. 98.

25. Ibid., p. 65.

26. Ibid., p. 76.

27. D. M. Thomas, *The White Hotel,* p. 179.

Chapter 4

1. Sexual deviation alone is a matter of considerable dispute. Just how complex the idea of deviancy can be is suggested by Murray S. Davis, "Periodic Table of Sexual Perversions," in *Smut: Erotic Reality/Obscene Ideology,* pp. 157–159.

2. President's Commission on Obscenity and Pornography, *Technical Report,* vol. 6, pp. 54–55.

3. Ibid., pp. 56–59.

4. See, for example, Sharlene A. Wolchik, Sanford L. Braver, and Karen Jensen, "Volunteer Bias in Erotica Research: Effects of Intrusiveness of Measure and Sexual Background," p. 93; and Sharlene A. Wolchik, S. Lee Spencer, and Iris S. Lisi, "Volunteer Bias in Research Employing Vaginal Measures of Sexual Arousal," p. 399.

5. See President's Commission on Obscenity and Pornography, *Report of the Commission on Obscenity and Pornography,* p. 202. See also William Griffitt, "Sexual Stimulation and Sociosexual Behaviors," in *Love and Attraction,* ed. M. Cook and G. Wilson; William Griffitt, James May, and Russell Veitch, "Sexual Stimulation and Interpersonal Behavior: Heterosexual Evaluative Responses, Visual Behavior, and Physical Proximity"; and John Money, "Pornography in the Home: A Topic

in Medical Education," in *Contemporary Sexual Behavior: Critical Issues in the 1970's,* ed. Joseph Zubin and John Money.

6. See Donn Byrne and John Lamberth, "The Effect of Erotic Stimuli on Sex Arousal, Evaluative Responses, and Subsequent Behavior," p. 62; Jay Mann, "Experimental Induction of Human Sexual Arousal," p. 39; Marvin Brown, Donald M. Amoroso, and Edward E. Ware, "Behavioral Effects of Viewing Pornography"; and Marvin Brown et al., "Factors Affecting Viewing Time of Pornography."

7. Brown, Amoroso, and Ware, "Behavioral Effects of Viewing Pornography," p. 235.

8. Robert B. Cairns, J. C. N. Paul, and J. Wishner, "Psychological Assumptions in Sex Censorship: An Evaluative Review of Recent Research," pp. 5–21.

9. See, for example, William A. Fisher and Donn Byrne, "Sex Differences in Response to Erotica? Love Versus Lust"; J. R. Heiman, "A Psychophysiological Exploration of Sexual Arousal Patterns in Females and Males"; and Gunter Schmidt, "Male-Female Differences in Sexual Arousal and Behavior During and After Exposure to Sexually Explicit Stimuli."

10. President's Commission, *Report,* pp. 208–209.

11. D. Turnbull and Marvin Brown, "Attitudes Toward Homosexuality and Male and Female Reactions to Homosexual and Heterosexual Slides."

12. President's Commission, *Report,* p. 211.

13. For the finding that aggression is least arousing, see Robert A. Baron and Donn Byrne, *Social Psychology: Understanding Human Interaction.* See also H. E. Barbaree, W. L. Marshall, and R. D. Lanthier, "Deviant Sexual Arousal in Rapists"; and Gene G. Abel et al., "The Components of Rapists' Sexual Arousal." For contrary findings, see Schmidt, "Male-Female Differences," p. 353.

14. Neil M. Malamuth, "Rape Fantasies as a Function of Exposure to Violent Sexual Stimuli"; Neil M. Malamuth and James V. P. Check, "Sexual Arousal to Rape and Consenting Depictions: The Importance of the Woman's Arousal," and "Penile Tumescence and Perceptual Responses to Rape as a Function of the Victim's Perceived Reactions"; Neil M. Malamuth, Scott Haber, and Seymour Feshbach, "Testing Hypotheses Regarding Rape: Exposure to Sexual Violence, Sex Differences, and the 'Normality' of Rapists"; and Neil M. Malamuth, Maggie Heim, and Seymour Feshbach, "Sexual Responsiveness of College Students to Rape Depictions: Inhibitory and Disinhibitory Effects."

15. President's Commission, *Report,* pp. 211–212.

16. Rose E. Ray and C. Eugene Walker, "Biographical and Self-Report Correlates of Female Guilt Responses to Visual Erotic Stimuli"; Donald L. Mosher and I. Greenberg, "Females' Affective Responses to Reading Erotic Literature."

17. D. W. Briddell et al., "Effects of Alcohol and Cognitive Set on Deviant Stimuli"; see also Mann, "Experimental Deduction," p. 56.

18. Dolf Zillman and Jennings Bryant, "Effects of Massive Exposure to Pornography," in *Pornography and Sexual Aggression,* ed. Neil M. Malamuth and Edward Donnerstein; Kathryn Kelley, "Variety Is the Spice of Erotica: Repeated Exposure, Novelty, and Sexual Attitudes"; Helmuth H. Schaefer, G. J. Tregerthan,

and Aloma H. Colgan, "Measured and Self-Estimated Penile Erection"; Gavin Tennent, John H. J. Bancroft, and James Cass, "The Control of Deviant Sexual Behavior by Drugs: A Double-Blind Controlled Study of Benperidol, Chlorpromazine, and Placebo"; Jay Mann et al., "Satiation of the Transient Stimulating Effect of Erotic Films"; Clifford B. Reifler et al., "Pornography: An Experimental Study of Effects"; James L. Howard, Clifford B. Reifler, and Myron B. Liptzin, "Effects of Exposure to Pornography"; D. R. Laws and H. B. Rubin, "Instructional Control of an Autonomic Sexual Response."

19. Howard, Reifler, and Liptzin, "Effects of Exposure to Pornography."

20. Mann et al., "Satiation of the Transient Stimulating Effect," p. 729.

21. Paul H. Gebhard et al., *Sex Offenders: An Analysis of Types,* pp. 670–678.

22. Helmuth H. Schaefer and Aloma H. Colgan, "The Effect of Pornography on Penile Tumescence as a Function of Reinforcement and Novelty." See also, for example, D. R. Laws and J. A. O'Neil, "Variations on Masturbatory Conditioning"; D. A. Kantorowicz, "Personality and Conditioning of Tumescence and Detumescence"; and Gene G. Abel and Edward B. Blanchard, "The Measurement and Generation of Sexual Arousal in Male Sexual Deviation," in *Progress in Behavior Modification,* vol. 2, ed. M. Herson, R. M. Eisler, and P. M. Miller; and "The Role of Fantasy in the Treatment of Sexual Deviation."

23. Zillman and Bryant, "Effects of Massive Exposure," p. 129.

24. Reactions to most stimuli tend to lessen with repeated exposure, particularly when conditions do not require an overt response to the stimulus. See W. W. Grings and M. E. Dawson, *Emotions and Bodily Responses: A Psychophysiological Approach;* Thomas J. Tighe and Robert N. Leaton, eds., *Habituation: Perspectives from Child Development, Animal Behavior, and Neurophysiology.* For a discussion of excitation transfer, see Dolf Zillman, *Connections Between Sex and Aggression,* pp. 153–156.

25. President's Commission, *Technical Report,* vol. 6, pp. 63–67.

26. Keith E. Davis and George N. Braucht, "Reactions to Viewing Films of Realistic Heterosexual Behavior"; Donald L. Mosher, "Psychological Reactions to Pornographic Films"; Gunter Schmidt and Volkmar Sigusch, "Sex Differences in Response to Psychosexual Stimulation by Films and Slides."

27. Mosher, "Psychological Reactions," p. 255.

28. Berl Kutchinsky, "Effect of Pornography," pp. 143–144.

29. Mosher, "Psychological Reactions," p. 255. See also Thomas Schill, Mark Van Tuinen, and Don Doty, "Repeated Exposure to Pornography and Arousal Levels of Subjects Varying in Guilt"; William Griffitt and Donn L. Kaiser, "Affect, Sex-Guilt, Gender, and the Rewarding-Punishing Effects of Erotic Stimuli"; and Frederick X. Gibbons, "Sexual Standards and Reactions to Pornography: Enhancing Behavioral Consistency Through Self-Focused Attention."

30. Donn Byrne and John Sheffield, "Response to Sexually Arousing Stimuli as a Function of Repressing and Sensitizing Defenses."

31. Byrne and Lamberth, "Effect of Erotic Stimuli," p. 41; Mosher, "Psychological Reactions," p. 255; Donald L. Mosher, "Sex Callousness Toward Women." See also Byrne, "Social Psychology and the Study of Sexual Behavior"; Byrne et al., "Evaluations of Erotica: Facts or Feelings?"

32. Byrne and Lamberth, "Effect of Erotic Stimuli," p. 41. See also Donald L. Mosher and Kevin O'Grady, "Homosexual Threat, Negative Attitudes Toward Masturbation, Sex Guilt, and Males' Sexual and Affective Reactions to Explicit Sexual Films."

33. Dolf Zillman, Jennings Bryant, and R. A. Carveth, "The Effect of Erotica Featuring Sado-Masochism and Bestiality on Motivated Intermale Aggression"; Zillman et al., "Excitation and Hedonic Valence in the Effect of Erotica on Motivated Intermale Aggression"; Leonard A. White, "Erotica and Aggression: The Influence of Sexual Arousal, Positive Affect, and Negative Affect on Aggressive Behavior"; Mann et al., "Satiation of the Transient Stimulating Effect," p. 729.

34. Malamuth, Heim, and Feshbach, "Sexual Responsiveness of College Students," p. 399.

35. Keith E. Davis and George N. Braucht, "Exposure to Pornography, Character, and Sexual Deviance: A Retrospective Survey"; Alan S. Berger, John H. Gagnon, and William Simon, "Pornography: High School and College Years," and "Urban Working Class Adolescents and Sexually Explicit Media"; Hans L. Zetterberg, "The Consumers of Pornography Where It Is Easily Available: The Swedish Experience."

36. For inexperienced subjects, see Donald M. Amoroso et al., "An Investigation of Behavioral, Psychological, and Physiological Reactions to Pornographic Stimuli"; and Mosher, "Psychological Reactions," p. 255. Kutchinsky, "Effect of Pornography," p. 133; and Mann, "Experimental Induction," p. 39, discuss married subjects; Schmidt and Sigusch, "Sex Differences," p. 268, discuss experienced single subjects.

37. Davis and Braucht, "Reactions to Viewing Films," p. 173. For a tabular summary of earlier studies, see President's Commission, *Report,* p. 223.

38. William A. Fisher and Donn Byrne, "Individual Differences in Affective, Evaluative, and Behavioral Responses to an Erotic Film."

39. E. Heiby and J. D. Becker, "Effect of Filmed Modeling on Self-Reported Frequency of Masturbation"; Brown, Amoroso, and Ware, "Behavioral Effects of Viewing Pornography," p. 235; President's Commission, *Report*, p. 222. Effects on unmarried subjects are discussed in Byrne and Lamberth, "Effect of Erotic Stimuli," p. 41; and Kutchinsky, "Effect of Pornography," p. 133. See also President's Commission, *Report,* summary table, p. 221.

40. Davis and Braucht, "Exposure to Pornography," 173; Brown, Amoroso, and Ware, "Behavioral Effects of Viewing Pornography," p. 235; Kutchinsky, "Effect of Pornography," p. 133; Mosher, "Psychological Reactions," p. 255.

41. Mann et al., "Satiation of the Transient Stimulating Effect," p. 729.

42. Mosher, "Psychological Reactions," p. 255.

43. Gilbert D. Bartell, "Group Sex Among Mid-Americans," p. 113.

44. Howard, Reifler, and Liptzin, "Effects of Exposure to Pornography," p. 97.

45. Mann et al., "Satiation of the Transient Stimulating Effect," p. 729.

46. Berger, Gagnon, and Simon, "Urban Working Class Adolescents," p. 209.

47. Berger, Gagnon, and Simon, "Pornography," p. 165.

48. President's Commission, *Technical Report,* vol. 6, pp. 50–51.

49. Zetterberg, "Consumers of Pornography," p. 453.

50. Mosher, "Psychological Reactions," p. 255.

51. Howard, Reifler, and Liptzin, "Effects of Exposure to Pornography," p. 97.

52. Kutchinsky, "Effect of Pornography," p. 133. See also Mann et al., "Satiation of the Transient Stimulating Effect," p. 729; and Byrne and Lamberth, "Effect of Erotic Stimuli," p. 41.

53. Davis and Braucht, "Exposure to Pornography," p. 143; Howard, Reifler, and Liptzin, "Effects of Exposure to Pornography," p. 97; Mann, "Experimental Induction," p. 39.

54. Zillman and Bryant, "Effects of Massive Exposure."

55. Neil M. Malamuth and James V. P. Check, "Effects of Aggressive Pornography on Beliefs in Rape Myths: Individual Differences," "Effects of Mass Media Exposure on Acceptance of Violence Against Women: A Field Experiment," and "Penile Tumescence," p. 528; Malamuth, Haber, and Feshbach, "Testing Hypotheses," p. 121; Malamuth, Heim, and Feshbach, "Sexual Responsiveness of College Students," p. 399.

56. Zillman and Bryant, "Effects of Massive Exposure," p. 134.

57. Mosher, "Psychological Reactions," p. 255.

58. Edward Donnerstein, "Erotica and Human Aggression," in *Aggression: Theoretical and Empirical Views,* ed. Russell G. Geen and Edward Donnerstein; Edward Donnerstein and Leonard Berkowitz, "Victim Reactions in Aggressive Erotic Films as a Factor in Violence Against Women"; Edward Donnerstein, "Aggressive Erotica and Violence Against Women." These studies are coordinated in Donnerstein, "Pornography: Its Effect on Violence Against Women," in *Pornography and Sexual Aggression,* ed. Neil M. Malamuth and Edward Donnerstein.

59. Malamuth, Haber, and Feshbach, "Testing Hypotheses," p. 121.

60. Davis and Braucht, "Exposure to Pornography," p. 173.

61. U.S. Congress, Senate, Subcommittee of the Committee on the Judiciary, *Hearings, Juvenile Delinquency: Obscene and Pornographic Materials,* p. 313.

62. Lenore Kupperstein, "The Role of Pornography in the Etiology of Juvenile Delinquency: A Review of the Research Literature."

63. President's Commission, *Report,* p. 32.

64. Longford Committee Investigating Pornography, *Pornography: The Longford Report,* p. 413.

65. Bernard Williams, ed., *Obscenity and Film Censorship,* pp. 62–86.

66. U.S. Department of Justice, Attorney General's Commission on Pornography, *Final Report,* p. 326.

67. Terrence P. Thornberry and Robert A. Silverman, "Exposure to Pornography and Juvenile Delinquency: The Relationship as Indicated by Juvenile Court Records."

68. President's Commission, *Report,* pp. 263–264.

69. Davis and Braucht, "Exposure to Pornography," p. 173.

70. Richard Ben-Veniste, "Pornography and Sex Crime—the Danish Experi-

ence," p. 245; Berl Kutchinsky, "Towards an Explanation of the Decrease in Registered Sex Crimes in Copenhagen."

71. Berl Kutchinsky, "The Effect of Easy Availability of Pornography on the Incidence of Sex Crimes: The Danish Experience."

72. John H. Court, "Pornography and Sex Crimes: A Reevaluation in the Light of Recent Trends Around the World"; Victor Bachy, "Danish 'Permissiveness' Revisited."

73. John H. Court, "Sex and Violence: A Ripple Effect," in *Pornography and Sexual Aggression*, ed. Neil M. Malamuth and Edward Donnerstein, pp. 143–172, "Rape Trends in New South Wales: A Discussion of Conflicting Evidence," "Pornography Update," and "Pornography and Sex Crimes."

74. See criticism of Court's studies in Williams, *Obscenity*, pp. 69–86.

75. For the positive correlation, see Larry Baron and Murray A. Straus, "Sexual Stratification, Pornography, and Rape in the United States," in *Pornography and Sexual Aggression*, ed. Neil M. Malamuth and Edward Donnerstein. The magazines were *Chic, Club, Gallery, Genesis, Hustler, Oui, Penthouse,* and *Playboy*. No correlation was found by Joseph E. Scott, "An Updated Longitudinal Content Analysis of Sex References in Mass Circulation Magazines."

76. Baron and Straus, "Sexual Stratification," p. 185.

77. Gebhard et al., "Sex Offenders," pp. 670–678.

78. C. Eugene Walker, "Erotic Stimuli and the Aggressive Offender"; Robert F. Cook and Robert H. Fosen, "Pornography and the Sex Offender: Patterns of Exposure and Immediate Arousal Effects of Pornographic Stimuli."

79. President's Commission, *Report,* pp. 281–283. See also Cairns, Paul, and Wishner, "Psychological Assumptions in Sex Censorship," p. 5.

80. Michael J. Goldstein et al., "Exposure to Pornography and Sexual Behavior in Deviant and Normal Groups"; Walker, "Erotic Stimuli," p. 91.

81. Michael J. Goldstein and Harold S. Kant, *Pornography and Sexual Deviance,* p. 135.

82. Walker, "Erotic Stimuli," p. 91.

83. Weldon T. Johnson, Lenore R. Kupperstein, and Joseph J. Peters, "Sex Offenders' Experience with Erotica"; Cook and Fosen, "Pornography and the Sex Offender," p. 149.

84. Barbaree, Marshall, and Lanthier, "Deviant Sexual Arousal," p. 215; Abel et al., "Components of Rapists' Sexual Arousal," p. 895.

85. Edward C. Nelson, "Pornography and Sexual Aggression," in *The Influence of Pornography on Behavior,* ed. Maurice Yaffe and Edward C. Nelson, p. 221.

86. Goldstein and Kant, *Pornography and Sexual Deviance,* p. 138.

87. Ibid., pp. 133–138.

88. Ann Frodi, "Sexual Arousal, Situational Restrictiveness, and Aggressive Behavior"; Robert A. Baron, "The Aggression-Inhibiting Influence of Heightened Sexual Arousal," and "Sexual Arousal and Physical Aggression: The Inhibiting Influence of 'Cheesecake' and Nudes"; Robert A. Baron and Paul A. Bell, "Effects of Heightened Sexual Arousal on Physical Aggression."

89. Edward Donnerstein, Marcia Donnerstein, and Ronald Evans, "Erotic

Stimuli and Aggression: Facilitation or Inhibition"; Robert A. Baron and Paul A. Bell, "Sexual Arousal and Aggression by Males: Effects of Type of Erotic Stimuli and Prior Provocation."

90. Joanne Cantor, Dolf Zillman, and Edna F. Einsiedel, "Female Responses to Provocation After Exposure to Aggressive and Erotic Films." See also Neil M. Malamuth, Seymour Feshbach, and Yoram Jaffe, "Sexual Arousal and Aggression: Recent Experiments and Theoretical Issues."

91. Donnerstein, "Pornography," p. 78.

92. Neil M. Malamuth and James V. P. Check, "Sexual Arousal in Rape Depictions: Individual Differences."

93. Neil M. Malamuth, "Aggression Against Women: Cultural and Individual Causes," in *Pornography and Sexual Aggression,* ed. Neil M. Malamuth and Edward Donnerstein.

94. M. Cox, "Dynamic Psychotherapy with Sex-Offenders," in *Sexual Deviation,* ed. Ismond Rosen, p. 308.

95. President's Commission, *Report,* p. 285.

96. Goldstein and Kant, *Pornography and Sexual Deviance,* p. 152.

97. See, for example, Malamuth, "Aggression Against Women," pp. 42, 54; Donnerstein, "Pornography," pp. 79–80.

98. Charles Sarnoff, *Latency,* pp. 71–75, app. C. See also Joseph H. Di Leo, *Children's Drawings as Diagnostic Aids,* pp. 51–55.

99. See, for example, National Institute of Mental Health, *Television and Behavior,* vol. 1, *Summary Report.*

100. President's Commission, *Technical Report,* vol. 6, pp. 91–92 (emphasis in survey question).

101. See, for example, Nelson, "Pornography and Sexual Aggression," pp. 183, 185.

Chapter 5

1. Robert Merton, *Social Theory and Social Structure,* p. 78.

2. Phillip Rieff, *The Triumph of the Therapeutic,* p. 237.

3. Harry M. Clor, *Obscenity and Public Morality,* pp. 168, 170.

4. Ibid., p. 171.

5. Harry M. Clor, "Obscenity and Freedom of Expression," in *Censorship and Freedom of Expression,* ed. Harry M. Clor, pp. 106–107.

6. Respectively, George Steiner, *Language and Silence,* pp. 75–76; Walter Berns, "Pornography vs. Democracy: The Case for Censorship," p. 13; and Ernest van den Haag, "Democracy and Pornography," in *Where Do You Draw the Line?* ed. Victor B. Cline, p. 259.

7. Susan Griffin, *Pornography and Silence,* pp. 93, 127.

8. Ibid.; in addition see, for example, Laura Lederer, ed., *Take Back the Night;* and Andrea Dworkin, *Pornography: Men Processing Women.*

9. Clor, "Obscenity and Freedom of Expression," p. 109. See also Berns, "Democracy vs. Pornography," p. 15.

10. Irving Kristol, "The Case for Liberal Censorship," p. 113. See also, gener-

ally, David L. Paletz and William F. Harris, "Four-Letter Threats to Authority."

11. van den Haag, "Democracy and Pornography," p. 260.

12. See, for example, Charles A. Sundholm, "The Pornographic Arcade: Ethnographic Notes on Moral Men in Immoral Places"; Lyle Knowles and Houshong Poorkaj, "Attitudes and Behavior on Viewing Sexual Activities in Public Places," p. 130; and Don J. Lewittes and William L. Simmons, "Impression Management of Sexually Motivated Behavior," p. 39. On the capacity of juvenile delinquents to remain committed to dominant norms that they have violated in their behavior, see Gresham M. Sykes and Donald Matza, "Techniques of Neutralization: A Theory of Delinquency."

13. See, for example, J. D. Unwin, *Sex and Culture;* and Pitirim Sorokin, *The American Sex Revolution.*

14. As a radical critic of modern liberal society, Herbert Marcuse has argued that permissive sexual ideologies are distracting—stealing energy and motivation required for transformation or overthrow of the social order; see *One Dimensional Man,* pp. 72–85.

15. President's Commission on Obscenity and Pornography, *Report of the Commission on Obscenity and Pornography,* p. 53.

16. D. F. Barber, *Pornography and Society,* p. 85.

17. President's Commission, *Report,* p. 54.

18. Paul Goodman, *Utopian Essays and Practical Proposals,* p. 55. The sociologist Murray S. Davis systematically elaborates this general view as the ideal type, "Naturalism," in contrast to "Jehovanism" and "Gnosticism"—rough counterparts of the public morality and radical views described here. The three are seen as constituting phenomenologically the major ideologies of sexuality. See generally Murray S. Davis, *Smut: Erotic Reality/Obscene Ideology.*

19. Murray Hausknecht, "The Problem of Pornography," p. 195. Describing the complex, evolutionary "deployment of sexuality" of the modern and early modern world, Michel Foucault has argued that the liberating humanist optimism in pursuit of the "truth of sex" has had its own regulating mechanisms and its own controlling sexual ideology (*History of Sexuality,* vol. 1). Concern with appropriate sex education has a well-established history. See Walter Kendrick's discussion of "The Young Person," whose welfare has been a continuing but modifiable object of social control, in *The Secret Museum: Pornography in Modern Culture.*

20. Kenneth Tynan, "Dirty Books Can Stay," in *Perspectives on Pornography,* ed. Douglas A. Hughes.

21. Donald Thomas, *A Long Time Burning,* pp. 314–318. See also Fred R. Berger, "Pornography, Sex, and Censorship," pp. 190–193.

22. Peter Michelson, *The Aesthetics of Pornography,* pp. 178–179.

23. See Wilhelm Reich, *The Mass Psychology of Fascism,* and *The Sexual Revolution.*

24. This is in contrast to many of the studies it commissioned. Yet there were no psychoanalysts on the commission itself, neither among staff and presidential appointees nor among the many independent contractors it hired, a remarkable omission considering the nature of the subject under study.

25. We deal here with only one of four types of prostitution, heterosexual, where the female is the prostitute. This is not only the relationship to which the term commonly refers but also the most institutionalized and socially significant type. Cf. Alfred C. Kinsey, Wardell B. Pomeroy, and Clyde E. Martin, *Sexual Behavior in the Human Male,* p. 596.

26. Kingsley Davis, "Sexual Behavior," in *Contemporary Social Problems,* ed. Robert K. Merton and Robert A. Nisbet, p. 359.

27. John H. Gagnon and William Simon, eds., *Sexual Deviance,* pp. 105–106. Cf. Charles Winnick, "Clients' Perceptions of Prostitutes and of Themselves"; John Murtagh and Sara Harris, *Cast the First Stone,* pp. 180–186; and James Bryan, "Apprenticeships in Prostitution."

28. Cf. Kinsey et al., *Sexual Behavior,* pp. 606–608; and Davis, "Sexual Behavior," pp. 356–360.

29. Quoted in Reay Tannahill, *Sex in History,* pp. 278–279.

30. As a leading historian put it in the language of his day: "Herself the supreme type of vice, she is ultimately the most efficient guardian of virtue. But for her, the unchallenged purity of countless happy homes could be polluted, and not a few who, in the pride of their untempted chastity, think of her with an indignant shudder, would have known the agony of remorse and despair. On that one degraded and ignoble form are concentrated the passions that might have filled the world with shame. She remains, while creeds and civilizations rise and fall, the eternal priestess of humanity, blasted for the sins of the people" (W. H. Lecky, *History of European Morals,* pp. 282–283).

31. Davis, "Sexual Behavior," p. 360.

32. Ned Polsky, *Hustlers, Beats, and Others,* pp. 184–192.

33. Kinsey, Pomeroy, and Martin, *Sexual Behavior,* pp. 351–355, 598, 601.

34. See, for example, Morris E. Massey, "A Marketing Analysis of Sex-Oriented Materials in Denver"; Harold Nawy, "The San Francisco Erotic Marketplace"; and Charles Winnick, "Some Observations of Characteristics of Patrons of Adult Bookstores," pp. 3–98, 155–244. These findings are summarized in the President's Commission, *Report,* pp. 157–166. See also Sundholm, "Pornographic Arcade"; Knowles and Poorkaj, "Viewing Sexual Activities."

35. Kinsey, Pomeroy, and Martin, *Sexual Behavior,* pp. 488–493.

36. The modern massage parlor where women staff masturbate male clients, usually in a pornographic context, stands between the masturbatory accommodations of quasi-public viewing of pornography and conventional prostitution, in effect completing a behavioral chain between the two sexual institutions.

37. Joseph P. Slade, "Pornographic Theaters Off Times Square," pp. 35–43. See also Peter Donnelly, "Running the Gauntlet: The Moral Order of Pornographic Movie Theaters."

38. Sundholm, "Pornographic Arcade," p. 51.

39. Émile Durkheim, *The Division of Labor in Society,* p. 102. George Herbert Mead later made a similar point: "The attitude of hostility toward the lawbreaker has the unique advantage of uniting all members of the community" ("The Psychology of Punitive Justice," p. 59).

40. Lewis Coser, "Some Functions of Deviant Behavior and Normative Flexibility," p. 174.

41. Kai T. Erikson, "Notes on the Sociology of Deviance," p. 310. See also the application of this theory to crime rates in seventeeth-century colonial Massachusetts, in Kai T. Erikson, *Wayward Puritans*.

42. Coser ("Some Functions of Deviant Behavior," p. 174) goes on to suggest a psychodynamic link: "Such indignation may well serve as a reaction-formation, securing the ego against the repressed impulse to identify with the criminal." See also Robert A. Dentler and Kai T. Erikson, "The Functions of Deviance in Groups"; and Anna Freud, *The Ego and the Mechanisms of Defense*, pp. 117–121.

43. Erikson, "Notes on the Sociology of Deviance," p. 310.

44. See, for example, Gary Fine, "Obscene Joking Across Cultures"; Allen Walker Read, "An Obscenity Symbol," p. 267; and, generally, Weston La Barre, "The Psychopathology of Drinking Songs"; and Renatus Hartogs with Hans Fantel, *Four-Letter Word Games*.

45. Joseph Gusfield, *Symbolic Crusade*.

46. Louis A. Zurcher and R. George Kirkpatrick, *Citizens for Decency*, p. 265.

47. Though our analysis of pornography as a product of social designation shares much of the labeling or social-reaction perspective of the sociology of deviance, it also departs from that point of view in important ways. "Labeling" and "designation" refer to deviant expression rather than to persons, groups, careers, subcultures, and the like, which are the central concern of the labeling perspective. More important, we view deviant or transgressive sexual expression as deriving from erotic fantasies. Thus "deviation" first occurs in psychodynamic lapses in the *internal* control system. Typically, some prior psychological labeling or designation has taken place. Labeling theorists, emphasizing deviant behavior as a product of social designation rather than an essentially objective phenomenon, usually limit their analysis to the social context and seldom venture into psychodynamic territory to ask about the prior role of individual controls (except as they are believed to be determined or influenced by the labeling process itself), or why these may lapse earlier, more easily, or more completely in some persons than in others. Indeed, one of the difficulties with the labeling or social-reaction perspective generally is that it tends to be primarily sociological. For a recent review of the labeling perspective, its limitations and its utility, see Edwin M. Schur, *The Politics of Deviance*, esp. pp. 17–21.

48. See, for example, Robin Williams, *American Society*, chap. 10.

49. For example, Michael J. Goldstein and Harold S. Kant, *Pornography and Sexual Deviance*, pp. 31, 108–109. See also Earl Finbar Murphy, "The Value of Pornography," pp. 668–669.

50. Berl Kutchinsky's is one of the few systematic studies of the surge and decline in the production and reading of pornographic books in Denmark following abolition of legal restrictions on pornography in the 1960s. His study shows a decline only to prior levels of consumption—very different from a satiation effect. More important, no account was taken of the probability that diminishing interest was due entirely to pictorial pornography, on which legal restrictions had just been dropped, and which then became easy to obtain. See Berl Kutchinsky, "Eroticism Without Censorship."

51. As experimental studies examined in Chapter 4 indicate, satiation with the genre of pornography is unlikely except in the very short run or where contact has been highly routinized, as in some of the studies themselves.

52. For a schematic representation of a circular "feeding" effect between the perceptions of authors, publishers, and producers on the one hand and censoring authority on the other, see Christie Davies, "How Our Rulers Argue About Censorship," in *Censorship and Obscenity,* ed. Rajeev Dhavan and Christie Davies, p. 16.

Chapter 6

1. The point has probably been made most forcefully by Alexander Meiklejohn; see esp. *Political Freedom,* pp. 25–29, and chap. 15. For general discussion of the instrumental view of freedom of speech, see Frederick Schauer, *Free Speech: A Philosophical Inquiry,* pp. 35–46; and D. F. B. Tucker, *Law, Liberalism, and Free Speech,* pp. 11–30.

2. Winters v. New York, 333 U.S. 507, 510 (1948) (Justice Reed for the Court). One student of the cultural effects of entertainment has observed that entertainment is less a result of the aims of the communicator than of the recipient's interpretation of the communication. "Psychological predispositions, physical condition, level of education, group membership and situative factors . . . play the decisive role in determining what is perceived as entertainment." For the communicator, entertainment is the "manifold attempt to free the recipient from the constraints of his work environment, using various forms of mass communications. On the other hand, the recipient can perceive almost anything as entertainment" (Heinz-Dietrich Fischer, "Entertainment—an Underestimated Central Function of Communication," in *Entertainment: A Cross-Cultural Examination,* ed. Heinz-Dietrich Fischer and Stefan R. Melnik, pp. 15–16).

3. Daniel Lerner, "Toward a Communication Theory of Modernization: A Set of Considerations," in *Communications and Political Development,* ed. Lucien W. Pye, pp. 342–343.

4. See Raymond Williams, *The Long Revolution,* pp. 173–176.

5. On the latter point, see, for example, Stuart Hall and Paddy Whannel, *The Popular Arts,* pp. 51–56.

6. Russel Nye, *The Unembarrassed Muse,* p. 4.

7. Ibid., p. 6.

8. Leo Rosten, "The Intellectual and the Mass Media," p. 337.

9. Herbert J. Gans, *Popular Culture and High Culture,* pp. 85–86.

10. Milton Rugoff, *Prudery and Passion,* pp. 30–32.

11. Richard Hoggart, *Uses of Literacy,* p. 83. Conservative values of the middle class no doubt also performed a socializing role, both in terms of their domination of the general culture and through assimilation as the ranks of the lower middle class were permeated. See, for example, Edward J. Bristow, *Vice and Vigilance: Purity Movements in Britain,* p. 31; and Jeffrey Weeks, *Sex, Politics, and Society,* p. 75.

12. Michel Foucault, *The History of Sexuality,* vol. 1, p. 17.

13. John Stuart Mill, *On Liberty*, p. 21.

14. John L. Sullivan, James Piereson, and George E. Marcus, "An Alternative Conceptualization of Political Tolerance: Illusory Increases, 1950s–1970s," p. 784.

15. Herbert McClosky and Alida Brill, *Dimensions of Tolerance: What Americans Believe About Civil Liberties*, p. 13.

16. Ibid., pp. 17–18.

17. The cognitive and personality requirements of tolerance are similar to those required by the "individualistic" society. See Robert Lane, "Individualism and the Market Society," pp. 379–381.

18. McClosky and Brill, *Dimensions of Tolerance*, pp. 30–31.

19. See generally John L. Sullivan, James Piereson, and George E. Marcus, *Political Tolerance and American Democracy*, chaps. 6 and 8; McClosky and Brill, *Dimensions of Tolerance*, chap. 8; Michael Corbett, *Political Tolerance in America*, pp. 175–184.

20. Adopted from *Washington Post* survey, November 1979. McClosky and Brill, *Dimensions of Tolerance*, p. 197–198, table 5.5.

21. McClosky and Brill, *Dimensions of Tolerance*, p. 197–198, table 5.5; pp. 60–61, figure 2.2.

22. Learned Hand, *The Spirit of Liberty*, p. 144.

23. Two general but contrasting statements of the role of an elite in the American democratic system may be found in Peter Bachrach, *The Theory of Democratic Elitism*, and Thomas R. Dye and L. Harmon Zeigler, *The Irony of Democracy*.

24. See, for example, Herbert McClosky, "Consensus and Ideology in American Politics"; McClosky and Brill, *Dimensions of Tolerance*, pp. 240–242, 370–387.

25. See, for example, William Kornhauser, *The Politics of Mass Society;* Dye and Zeigler, *Irony of Democracy*, pp. 139–144.

26. Louis Hartz, *The Liberal Tradition in America*, p. 129.

27. Alexis de Tocqueville, *Democracy in America*, vol. 2, p. 11.

28. Ibid., pp. 274–275; see also p. 272.

29. David Spitz, *Democracy and the Challenge of Power*, p. 20.

30. Robin M. Williams, *The American Society*, pp. 453–454. See also David M. Potter, "Changing Patterns of Social Cohesion and the Crisis of Law Under a System of Government by Consent," in *Is Law Dead?* ed. Eugene V. Rostow, pp. 273–279.

31. Robert C. Wood, *Suburbia*, p. 23. See also, generally, Richard Lingeman, *Small Town America*.

32. James Madison, "The Federalist No. 10," p. 22.

33. John P. Roche, "We've Never Had More Freedom." The point is elaborated in John P. Roche, *Quest for the Dream*. See also Paul L. Murphy, "The Bill of Rights in Our Historical Development," in *The Future of Our Liberties*, ed. Stephen C. Halpern, pp. 26–28.

34. Paul L. Murphy, *The Meaning of Free Speech*, p. 17.

35. Barron v. Baltimore, 32 U.S. (7 Pet.) 243 (1833).

36. Tocqueville, *Democracy in America,* vol. 1, p. 275. The Victorian age's leading (and most obsessed) student and collector of pornography reached much the same conclusion: "America, as in other branches of industry, has made of late years great progress in the production of books, and not least those of an improper character. Until 1846 the Americans produced nothing, but merely imported such books" (Henry Spencer Ashbee, *Index Librorum Prohibitorum,* pp. xlix–l).

37. Wood, *Suburbia,* p. 274.

38. Sherwood Anderson, "Home Town," in *The Sherwood Anderson Reader,* p. 741. See also Lingeman, *Small Town America,* chap. 6.

39. As one historian of the American small town suggests, the succor and ordered life of that community may have been simply a more recent and democratic reflection of something much older: "The continuum stretched back unbroken through time. It was a great river of history that could be traced uninterruptedly back through the early American agricultural villages, back through the agricultural communes of Europe, back further in time, back to the living source—the primal village" (Richard Lingeman, *Small Town America,* p. 440).

40. Paul S. Boyer, *Purity in Print,* chaps. 1 and 2. See also Heywood Broun and Margaret Leech, *Anthony Comstock, Roundsman of the Lord.*

41. For summaries of early developments in antiobscenity law and litigation in the United States, see Frederick Schauer, *The Law of Obscenity,* pp. 8–29, 169–172; and Martha Alschuler, "Origins of the Law of Obscenity," pp. 73–80.

42. W. Cody Wilson, "Law Enforcement Officers' Perception of Pornography as a Social Issue."

43. Reported appellate cases, of course, represent only a small fraction of prosecutions undertaken. Yet except for a few contemporary ad hoc surveys of prosecutorial action directly (see, for example, "Project: An Empirical Inquiry into the Effects of *Miller v. California* on Control of Obscenity") they are still the chief systematic evidence of the invocation of the criminal process against erotic expression. Many legal writers have drawn conclusions from these appellate cases as though they represented the whole of prosecutorial reality on the issue.

44. The first such holding came in *Near v. Minnesota* (283 U.S. 697 [1931]).

45. These applications were made, respectively, in *Burstyn v. Wilson* (343 U.S. 495 [1952]) and *Roth v. United States* with *Alberts v. California* (354 U.S. 476 [1957]).

46. Richard J. Richardson and Kenneth N. Vines, *The Politics of the Federal Courts,* pp. 132–134.

47. See, for example, Henry P. Monaghan, "First Amendment 'Due Process,' " p. 518; J. Terrence Murphy, *Censorship, Government, and Obscenity,* pp. 217–218, 223.

48. See, for example, Kenneth M. Dolbeare, *Trial Courts in Urban Politics,* chap. 4.

49. See, for example, Richard S. Randall, *Censorship of the Movies,* pp. 149–158.

50. John P. Roche, "American Liberty: An Examination of the Tradition of Freedom," in *Aspects of Liberty,* ed. Milton Konvitz and Clinton Rossiter, pp. 129–162.

Chapter 7

1. Melvin L. De Fleur and Sandra Ball-Rokeach, *Theories of Mass Communication*, p. 22.
2. Figures in this paragraph and the one following are drawn mainly from U.S. Bureau of the Census, *Statistical Abstract of the United States, 1986,* and *Historical Statistics of the United States.* Extensive statistical information about the mass media is also conveniently compiled and coordinated in Christopher H. Sterling and Timothy R. Haight, *The Mass Media: Aspen Institute Guide to Communication Industry Trends.*
3. See generally Richard S. Randall, *Censorship of the Movies,* and Ira H. Carmen, *Movies, Censorship, and the Law.*
4. Albert Schneider, vice-president for policies and standards, American Broadcasting Corporation, New York *Times,* January 9, 1984, p. C-16.
5. New York *Times,* April 26, 1986, p. C-19.
6. Lee H. Smith, "Is Anything Printable?"
7. The *Times* substituted "an Anglo-Saxon word" and "a four-letter word," leaving unclear in the reader's mind exactly what word was involved. *Variety,* the show business weekly, which takes pride in a certain hard-boiled sophistication and which has few, if any, youthful readers, was only slightly more informative, describing the word as "the second most-tabooed in polite society" (Randall, *Censorship of the Movies,* p. 229).
8. See, for example, the Philadelphia *Evening Bulletin,* November 1, 1968, and the New York *Times,* December 30, 1973, both cited in Erving Goffman, *Frame Analysis: An Essay on Organization and Experience,* pp. 70–71.
9. Geoffrey Cowan, *See No Evil,* pp. 283–285.
10. U.S. Department of Justice, Attorney General's Commission on Pornography, *Final Report,* p. 1394.
11. These figures are quoted, respectively, in President's Commission on Obscenity and Pornography, *Report of the Commission on Obscenity and Pornography,* p. 7; James Cook, "The X-Rated Economy," p. 81; New York *Times,* February 9, 1981, p. 81; New York *Times,* July 3, 1984, p. A-8; and Attorney General's Commission, *Final Report,* p. 1353.
12. New York *Times,* February 9, 1981, p. 81.
13. Attorney General's Commission, *Final Report,* p. 1385.
14. Cook, "X-Rated Economy," p. 83.
15. Attorney General's Commission, *Final Report,* pp. 1390, 1393–1395.
16. Ibid., pp. 1413, 1451, and 1504.
17. Ibid., pp. 1430 and 1432.
18. Ibid., p. 1478.
19. Ibid., pp. 1471–1477.
20. Ibid., p. 409.
21. Ibid., pp. 1390–1395.
22. Cook, "X-Rated Economy," p. 84.
23. President's Commission, *Report,* p. 143; "Federal Bureau of Investigation

Report Regarding the Extent of Organized Crime Involvement in Pornography," cited in the Attorney General's Commission, *Final Report,* pp. 1070–1071.

24. Attorney General's Commission, *Final Report,* pp. 1042–1065. The commission found evidence that some of the profits of the movie *Deep Throat* may have been used to finance a base in Panama for smuggling drugs into the United States (p. 1060).

25. President's Commission on Obscenity and Pornography, *Technical Report,* vol. 6, pp. 56–57, 83–112; percentages from tables 108–110, 118, 127, 133, 135.

26. Douglas Wallace, Gerald Wehmer, and Edward Podany, "Contemporary Community Standards of Visual Erotica," pp. 75–79.

27. *Gallup Opinion Index,* Report no. 98 (August 1973), pp. 25–26.

28. Marvin A. Jolson, Gary T. Ford, and Rolph E. Anderson, "When Marketers Cope with Moral Pollution: The Case of Sex Content in Movies," p. 23.

29. Respectively, The Minnesota Poll, November 1973, reprinted in *Current Opinion,* vol. 2 (January 1974), p. 31; and Mid-Continent Surveys, 1977, reprinted in *Current Opinion,* vol. 5 (April 1977), p. 48.

30. *Gallup Opinion Index,* Report no. 142 (May 1977), p. 4.

31. *Newsweek,* March 18, 1985, p. 60.

32. The Roper Poll, May 1977, reprinted in *Current Opinion,* vol. 5 (August 1977), p. 88; *Gallup Reports,* no. 197 (February 1982), p. 5.

33. National Opinion Research Center (NORC), *General Social Surveys, 1972–1985,* Cumulative Codebook Annual, July 1985, pp. 147–228.

34. *Newsweek,* March 18, 1985, p. 60.

35. In one of the few referenda on pornography control, voters in Maine, in 1986, rejected by a margin of 2 to 1 a proposal that would have made selling or promoting obscene material a crime calling for a mandatory prison term of up to five years. Opponents of the measure, which had been placed on the ballot with 50,000 signatures, were able to turn attention away from pornography to the instrument of control itself, particularly the severity of its penalties and its failure to exempt libraries and individual magazine subscribers. That hard-core pornography had relatively little circulation in Maine may also have contributed to its defeat (New York *Times,* June 10, 11, and 12, 1986).

36. NORC, *General Social Surveys, 1972–1985,* Cumulative Codebook Annual, July 1985, pp. 147–228.

37. President's Commission, *Technical Report,* vol. 6, tables 120, 122, pp. 102–103.

38. President's Commission, *Technical Report,* vol. 9, app. L, pp. 82–84.

39. Extrapolated from President's Commission, *Technical Report,* vol. 6, tables 54, 55, pp. 54–55.

40. NORC, *General Social Surveys, 1972–1985,* Cumulative Codebook Annual, July 1985, pp. 147–228.

41. President's Commission, *Technical Report,* vol. 6, tables 54, 55, pp. 54–55.

42. Ibid., tables 57, 58, pp. 56–57.

43. Ibid., p. 56.

44. *Gallup Opinion Index,* Report no. 98 (August 1973), pp. 25, 26; Report no. 142 (May 1977), p. 4.

45. See also Howard D. White, "Library Censorship and Permissive Morality," p. 192.

46. President's Commission, *Technical Report,* vol. 6, pp. 83, 85.

47. President's Commission, *Technical Report,* vol. 9, p. 34; table 8, p. 47.

48. Jolson, Ford, and Anderson, "When Marketers Cope," table 1, pp. 18–21.

49. Harrell R. Rodgers, Jr., "Censorship Campaigns in Eighteen Cities," p. 383; Louis A. Zurcher, Jr., and R. George Kirkpatrick, *Citizens for Decency,* pp. 317–322.

50. Louis A. Zurcher, Jr., et al., "Ad Hoc Antipornography Organizations and Their Active Members: A Research Summary," pp. 81, 83.

51. White, "Library Censorship," p. 192.

52. Zurcher and Kirkpatrick, *Citizens for Decency,* p. 265.

53. Joseph Nocera, "The Big Book Banning Brawl," pp. 21–22.

54. Lee Burress, National Council of Teachers of English, personal communication with the author, December 22, 1982, and New York *Times,* November 28, 1982, p. 73.

55. See, for example, Harrell R. Rodgers, Jr., "Prelude to Conflict: The Evolution of Censorship Campaigns."

56. In urging citizens to form "community action organizations," the Attorney General's Commission on Pornography (*Final Report,* pp. 1321–1322) recommendations included the following:

solicitation of support from a broad spectrum of civic leaders and organizations;
gathering information about pornography in the community;
educating the public about the effect of pornography in the community;
communicating with law enforcement officials;
filing complaints with the Federal Communications Commission about obscene broadcasts;
creation of a "court watch" program;
lobbying legislatures for changes in obscenity laws;
offering private assistance and support to officials "in the performance of their duties";
grassroots efforts to express opposition to sexually explicit materials, including lawful picketing and store boycotts, contacting cable television companies and sponsors of television and radio programs, and using the media through letters to the editor and audience participation programs; and
patronizing businesses that demonstrate "responsible judgment" in the types of materials they offer for sale.

57. New York *Times,* April 16, 1977, p. 37; April 14, p. B-3.

58. One of the most ambitious of these was conducted by the Attorney General's Commission on Pornography in 1986, shortly before publication of its final report. Letters were written to a number of drugstore and convenience store chains informing them that they were identified with the "sale and distribution of pornography" and were to be listed in the commission's final report, and asking them to respond to the charges (New York *Times,* May 20, 1986, p. A-24). The commission was later enjoined from publishing the names in a suit by *Playboy* and the Magazine Publishers Association (New York *Times,* July 4, 1986, p. A-6).

59. See Randall, *Censorship of the Movies,* pp. 156–166; M. Marvin Finkelstein, "The Traffic in Sex-Oriented Materials in Boston," pp. 148–149; "Project: An Empirical Inquiry into the Effects of *Miller v. California* on the Control of Obscenity"; and *Time,* October 21, 1985, p. 81.

60. Examples of direct action gone awry may be found in Richard S. Randall, "Censorship: From *The Miracle* to *Deep Throat,*" in *The American Film Industry,* ed. Tino Balio, p. 452; and L. B. Woods, *A Decade of Censorship in America,* p. 15. The attack on Justice White was described in the New York *Times,* July 16, 1982, p. A-10; the self-immolation in New York *Times,* July 12, 1984, p. A-12.

61. See Randall, *Censorship of the Movies,* pp. 150–151; and "Censorship," pp. 450–454.

62. See Randall, *Censorship of the Movies,* pp. 156–158; Finkelstein, "Traffic in Sex-Oriented Materials," p. 147; Herold Price Fahringer and Paul J. Cambria, Jr., "Some New Weapons Being Used in Waging War Against Pornography"; New York *Times,* October 5, 1986, p. F-1; and Woods, "Library Censorship," p. 15.

63. In 1986, more than 8,000 drugstore and convenience store chain outlets discontinued sale of adult magazines. They represented about 5 percent of the 150,000 retail outlets selling magazines in the United States and about 10 percent of those stocking at least some adult publications. The chains had earlier received a letter from the Attorney General's Commission on Pornography saying they had been identified as selling pornographic materials. See note 58 above. Many of the stores had also been the target of local boycotts and picketing (New York *Times,* June 16, 1986, p. 1).

64. Rodgers, "Censorship Campaigns," pp. 378, 380–382. Findings in this paragraph are based on the study of campaigns in eighteen small and mid-size cities, one of the few systematic surveys we have of informal control.

65. Woods, "Library Censorship," p. 135.

66. New York *Times,* November 28, 1982, p. 73.

67. Rodgers, "Censorship Campaigns," pp. 375, 379, 387.

68. See, for example, Randall, *Censorship of the Movies,* pp. 171–172.

69. American Library Association, Office for Intellectual Freedom, *Intellectual Freedom Manual,* p. 173.

70. There are nearly 2,000 prosecuting jurisdictions in the country at city, county, and federal levels, but complete information on the volume of obscenity action is generally unavailable. The most extensive and systematic study to date, based on a questionnaire survey of local prosecutors in the mid-1970s, found that between 1,000 and 1,200 cases were brought each year in 500 jurisdictions that reported. These included about half the largest ones. See "Project: An Empirical Inquiry into the Effects of *Miller,*" p. 871.

71. W. Cody Wilson, Jane Friedman, and Bernard Horowitz, "Gravity of the Pornography Situation and Problems of Control," p. 5.

72. Attorney General's Commission, *Final Report,* pp. 370–371.

73. Smith v. California, 361 U.S. 147 (1959); Burt Pines, "The Obscenity Quagmire," p. 509.

74. Attorney General's Commission, *Final Report,* pp. 367, 505–506.

75. Young v. American Mini Theatres, 427 U.S. 50 (1976). The use of zoning

power was reaffirmed in City of Renton v. Playtime Theatres (475 U.S. 41 [1986]).

76. See generally Sharon Anne Watkins, "The Devil and the D.A.: The Civil Abatement of Obscenity," p. 1329; Fahringer and Cambria, "Some New Weapons," p. 553; and "Project: An Empirical Inquiry into the Effects of *Miller*," pp. 881–884.

77. Freedman v. Maryland, 380 U.S. 51 (1965).

78. An ordinance enacted in Indianapolis in 1984 has been a forerunner and model. See generally "The Indianapolis Pornography Ordinance: Does the Right to Free Speech Outweigh Pornography's Harm to Women?" and William Brigman, "Pornography as Group Libel: The Indianapolis Sex Discrimination Ordinance."

79. Hudnut v. American Booksellers Association, 475 U.S. 1002 (1986), affirming 771 F.2d. 323 (1986).

Chapter 8

1. Regina v. Hicklin [1868] L.R. 3 Q.B. 360.

2. Id. at 371.

3. Roth v. United States, Alberts v. California, decided together, 354 U.S. 476 (1957).

4. A few lower courts had already departed from various elements of the *Hicklin* rule, most notably in Judge Woolsey's celebrated opinion finding Joyce's *Ulysses* not obscene because, among other things, the book was a work of literary importance and thus had to be judged as whole rather than by isolated passages (United States v. One Book Called "Ulysses," 5 F. Supp. 182 [S.D.N.Y. 1933]). For examples of other departures from the *Hicklin* rule, see Frederick Schauer, *The Law of Obscenity*, p. 71 n12.

5. Roth v. United States, 354 U.S. at 484–485.

6. Even on this fundamental and enduring point—that the law might be used to control sexual expression qua expression—the Court was not unanimous. Justices Douglas and Black argued, in dissent, that sexual expression (of any sort) should be left unregulated unless a causal link were shown to *action* of the kind government had the power to prevent (id. at 514). For the Court, Justice Brennan pointed out that the legal proscription of obscenity was "mirrored in the universal judgment . . . reflected in the international agreement of over 50 nations, in the obscenity laws of all 48 states, and in 20 obscenity laws enacted by Congress from 1842 to 1956" (id. at 485).

7. Id. at 489.

8. Id. at 487 n.20.

9. Miller v. California, 413 U.S. 15 (1973).

10. Interstate Circuit, Inc. v. Dallas, 390 U.S. 676 (1968), at 704–705, and 704 n.1.

11. They are cited in Paris Adult Theatre I v. Slaton, 413 U.S. 49, 82 n.8 (1973) (Brennan, J., dissenting).

12. "Memoirs of a Woman of Pleasure" v. Massachusetts, 383 U.S. 413, 418 (1966).

13. See its citation of the American Law Institute's Model Penal Code, Jacobellis v. Ohio, 378 U.S. 184, 192 (1964) (Brennan, J., plurality opinion). Justice Brennan also referred to patent offensiveness synonymously as "a deviation from society's standards of decency." Id.

14. "Memoirs of a Woman of Pleasure" v. Massachusetts, 383 U.S. at 418.

15. Kingsley International Pictures v. Board of Regents, 360 U.S. 684 (1959).

16. For a listing of cases on both sides, see Schauer, *Law of Obscenity,* p. 11, nn.73, 74.

17. Ginzberg v. United States, 383 U.S. 463, 499 n.3 (1966) (Stewart, J., dissenting).

18. Id. at 467. In fact, the government admitted that the materials might not themselves be obscene. It is doubtful whether they could have been included in the emerging notion of hard-core pornography.

19. Id. at 475–476 (emphasis added).

20. See, for example, William B. Lockhart and Robert C. McClure, "Censorship of Obscenity: The Developing Constitutional Standards." See also Chief Justice Warren's concurring opinion in *Roth and Alberts* (354 U.S. at 494).

21. In Splawn v. California, for example, the Court held that "the circumstances of sale and distribution were relevant to determining whether the allegedly obscene material was without redeeming social importance," particularly where they indicated that "the matter was being commercially exploited for the sake of its prurient appeal" (431 U.S. 595, 597–598 [1977]).

22. Mishkin v. New York, 383 U.S. 502, 508 (1966).

23. The Court tried to deal with the matter by citing a standard psychiatric sourcebook (id. at 509 n.8, citing Silvano Arieti, ed., *American Handbook of Psychiatry,* vol. 1, pp. 593–604).

24. See the lower court decision in United States v. Thirty-One Photographs (156 F. Supp. 350 [S.D.N.Y 1957]), involving the U.S. Customs Department's seizure of hard-core pornographic materials imported by the Institute for Sex Research at Indiana University.

25. Butler v. Michigan, 352 U.S. 380 (1957); see also, for example, Prince v. Massachusetts, 321 U.S. 158 (1944).

26. Ginsberg v. New York, 390 U.S. 629 (1968).

27. Id. at 636.

28. Pinkus v. United States, 436 U.S. 293, 297–299 (1978).

29. Stanley v. Georgia, 394 U.S. 557, 565 (1969).

30. See, respectively, Paris Adult Theatre I v. Slaton, 413 U.S. 49 (1973); United States v. Twelve 200-Foot Reels of Film, 413 U.S. 123 (1973); United States v. Reidel, 402 U.S. 351 (1971); and United States v. Orito, 413 U.S. 139 (1973).

31. Rowan v. United States, 397 U.S. 728 (1970).

32. Kingsley International Pictures v. Board of Regents, 360 U.S. at 690–691.

33. Miller v. California, 413 U.S. at 25.

34. Id. at 24.

35. See Schauer, *Law of Obscenity,* 119 n.19.

36. Miller v. California, 413 U.S. at 30.

37. Though the Court spoke only of the state, later cases indicate that a state could "choose to define the standards in more precise geographic terms" (Jenkins v. Georgia, 418 U.S. 153, 157 [1974]. See also Smith v. United States, 431 U.S. 291 [1977]).

38. Chief Justice Burger expressly recognized the Court's inability since *Roth* to give definitional guidance and that this failure resulted not only in a large number of obscenity cases on the Court's docket but also in a great deal of tension within the judiciary (Miller v. California, 413 U.S. 15, 29 [1973]).

39. Id. at 26 n.9, quoting Roth v. United States, 354 U.S. 476, 492 (1957).

40. This review is sometimes said to involve legal as opposed to factual judgments or simply questions of "constitutional fact." These distinctions between fact and law actually mean that in jury cases there are two fact-finding agents on the designation issue—the jurors and the court. When the two disagree, the latter is likely to prevail and almost certainly will if the difference involves the redemptive part of the test.

41. Jenkins v. Georgia, 418 U.S. 153 (1974).

42. F.C.C. v. Pacifica Foundation, 438 U.S. 726, 747–748 (1978). Referring to Title 18 U.S.C., section 1464, the Court upheld the FCC's power to consider the offending broadcast when the station applied for renewal of its license.

43. New York v. Ferber, 458 U.S. 747 (1982).

44. Young v. American Mini Theatres, 427 U.S. 50 (1976).

45. Chief Justice Burger's comment in *Paris Adult Theatre* is the Court at its most forthcoming: "There are legitimate state interests at stake in stemming the tide of commercialized obscenity, even assuming it is feasible to enforce effective safeguards against exposure to juveniles and to passersby. Rights and interests 'other than those of the advocates are involved.' . . . These include the interest of the public in the quality of life and the total community environment, the tone of the commerce in the great city centers and, possibly, the public safety itself" (413 U.S. 49 [1973] at 57–58).

46. Most state antiobscenity statutes leave "prurient" undefined or adopt a definition using the words "shameful or morbid" (Brockett v. Spokane Arcades, 105 S. Ct. 2794, 2803 n.13 [1985]).

47. See, for example, Splawn v. California, 431 U.S. 595 (1977).

48. We may recall that few persons who object to pornography believe that they have themselves been harmed by it (Chap. 7, pp. 208–209). See President's Commission on Obscenity and Pornography, *Technical Report,* vol. 6, pp. 55–58.

49. Brockett v. Spokane Arcades, 105 S. Ct. 2794, 2802 (1985) (emphasis added).

50. Roth v. United States, 354 U.S. 476, 485 (1957), referring to Chaplinsky v. New Hampshire, 315 U.S. 568, 571–572 (1942).

51. Paris Adult Theatre I, 413 U.S. at 60–61.

52. Stanley v. Georgia, 394 U.S. 557 (1969).

53. Chapter 7, p. 209. See President's Commission, *Technical Report,* vol. 6, tables 54–55, 57, 58, pp. 54–57.

54. Miller v. California, 413 U.S. 15 at 34.

55. Pope v. Illinois, 107 S. Ct. 1918, 1919 (1987). The Court added in a footnote that "the mere fact that only a minority of a population may believe a work has serious value does not mean the 'reasonable person' standard would not be met."

56. Id.; Smith v. United States, 431 U.S. 291 (1977) at 301, 305.

57. See, for example, Chief Justice Burger's Opinion of the Court in *Miller* (413 U.S. 15 [1973] at 16–37). In *Smith* v. *United States* (431 U.S. 291 [1977] at 301, 303), the Court seemed to say that whether allegedly obscene expression depicted hard-core sexual conduct of the sort described in *Miller* was a prior question to whether the materials were patently offensive by contemporary community standards.

58. Although the Court provided some categorical description of hard-core pornography in *Miller*, it later held that sadomasochistic portrayals could be found obscene even though they did not fall into any of the *Miller* categories. The latter were merely offered as "examples and were not intended to be exhaustive" (Ward v. Illinois, 431 U.S. 767, 773 [1977]). Still, there is "a limit beyond which neither legislative draftsmen nor juries may go in concluding that particular material is 'patently offensive' " (Hamling v. United States, 418 U.S. 87, 114 [1974]).

59. Eric Barendt, *Freedom of Speech*, p. 275. Offensiveness was also the chief orienting consideration in the control reformulations of the Williams Committee in Britain. See Bernard Williams, ed., *Obscenity and Film Censorship*, esp. pp. 96–102.

60. Jenkins v. Georgia, 418 U.S. 153 (1974).

61. Mishkin v. New York, 383 U.S. 502 (1966); Stanley v. Georgia, 394 U.S. 557 (1969); Ginzberg v. United States, 383 U.S. 463 (1966). New York v. Ferber, 458 U.S. 747 (1982).

62. F.C.C. v. Pacifica Foundation, 438 U.S. 726 (1978).

63. See, for example, Times Film Corp. v. Chicago, 365 U.S. 43 (1960); and Freedman v. Maryland, 380 U.S. 51 (1965).

64. Smith v. United States, 431 U.S. 291 (1977) at 318–319 (dissenting opinion).

Bibliography

Abel, Gene G., and Edward B. Blanchard. "The Role of Fantasy in the Treatment of Sexual Deviation." *Archives of General Psychiatry* 30 (1974): 467–475.
———. "The Measurement and Generation of Sexual Arousal in Male Sexual Deviation." In *Progress in Behavior Modification*, vol. 2, edited by M. Herson, R. M. Eisler, and P. M. Miller. New York: Academic Press, 1976.
Abel, Gene G., David H. Barlow, Edward B. Blanchard, and Donald Guild. "The Components of Rapists' Sexual Arousal." *Archives of General Psychiatry* 34 (1977): 895–908.
Aberle, David F., Urie Bronfenbrenner, Eckhard H. Hess, Daniel R. Miller, David M. Schneider, and James N. Spuhler. "The Incest Taboo and the Mating Patterns of Animals." *American Anthropologist* 65 (1963): 253–265.
Abramson, Jeffrey B. *Liberation and Its Limits: The Moral and Political Thought of Freud.* Boston: Beacon Press, 1986.
Abse, D. W. "Psychodynamic Aspects of the Problem of Definition of Obscenity." *Law and Contemporary Problems* 20 (1955): 572–582.
American Library Association. Office for Intellectual Freedom. *Intellectual Freedom Manual.* 2d ed. Chicago: American Library Association, 1983.
Amoroso, Donald M., Marvin Brown, Manfred Pruesse, Edward E. Ware, and Dennis W. Pilkey. "An Investigation of Behavioral, Psychological, and Physiological Reactions to Pornographic Stimuli." In *Technical Report of the Commission on Obscenity and Pornography,* Vol. 8, pp. 1–40. Washington, D.C.: Government Printing Office, 1970.
Anderson, Sherwood. *The Sherwood Anderson Reader.* Boston: Houghton Mifflin, 1947.
Arieti, Silvano, ed. *American Handbook of Psychiatry.* Vol. 1. New York: Basic Books, 1959.
Arlow, Jacob. "Ego Psychology and the Study of Mythology." *Journal of American Psychoanalytic Association* 9 (1961): 371–393.
Arkes, Hadley. *The Philosopher in the City.* Princeton, N.J.: Princeton University Press, 1981.

Ashbee, Henry Spencer. *Index Librorum Prohibitorum*. 1877. Reprint. New York: J. Brussel, 1962.

Atkins, John. *Sex in Literature*. New York: Grove Press, 1972.

Bachrach, Peter. *The Theory of Democratic Elitism*. Boston: Little, Brown, 1967.

Bachy, Victor. "Danish 'Permissiveness' Revisited." *Journal of Communication* 26 (1976): 40–43.

Barbaree, H. E., W. L. Marshall, and R. D. Lanthier. "Deviant Sexual Arousal in Rapists." *Behavior Research and Therapy* 17 (1979): 215–222.

Barber, D. F. *Pornography and Society*. London: Charles Skilton, 1972.

Barendt, Eric. *Freedom of Speech*. Oxford: Clarendon Press, 1985.

Baron, Larry, and Murray A. Straus. "Sexual Stratification, Pornography, and Rape in the United States." In *Pornography and Sexual Aggression*, edited by Neil M. Malamuth and Edward Donnerstein, pp. 186–210. New York: Academic Press, 1984.

Baron, Robert A. "The Aggression-Inhibiting Influence of Heightened Sexual Arousal." *Journal of Personality and Social Psychology* 30 (1974): 318–322.

———. "Sexual Arousal and Physical Aggression: The Inhibiting Influence of 'Cheesecake' and Nudes." *Bulletin of the Psychonomic Society* 3 (1974): 337–339.

Baron, Robert A., and Paul A. Bell. "Effects of Heightened Sexual Arousal on Physical Aggression." *Proceedings of the 81st Annual Convention of the American Psychological Association* 8 (1973): 171–172.

———. "Sexual Arousal and Aggression by Males: Effects of Type of Erotic Stimuli and Prior Provocation." *Journal of Personality and Social Psychology* 35 (1977): 79–87.

Baron, Robert A., and Donn Byrne. *Social Psychology: Understanding Human Interaction*. Boston: Allyn & Bacon, 1977.

Bartell, Gilbert D. "Group Sex Among Mid-Americans." *Journal of Sex Research* 6 (1970): 113–130.

Bartlett, Francis H. "The Limitations of Freud." *Science and Society* 3 (1939): 64–105.

Bataille, Georges. *Death and Sensuality: A Study of Eroticism and the Taboo*. New York: Ballantine Books, 1959.

———. *Story of the Eye*. Translated by Joachim Neugroschel. New York: Urizen Books, 1977.

Beach, Frank A. "Cross-Species Comparisons and the Human Heritage." In *Human Sexuality in Four Perspectives*, edited by Frank A. Beach, pp. 296–316. Baltimore: Johns Hopkins University Press, 1976.

Bell, Roderick A. "Determining Community Standards." *American Bar Association Journal* 63 (1977): 1202–1207.

Ben-Veniste, Richard. "Pornography and Sex Crime—The Danish Experience." In *Technical Report of the Commission on Obscenity and Pornography*, vol. 7, pp. 245–262. Washington, D.C.: Government Printing Office, 1970.

Berger, Alan S., John H. Gagnon, and William Simon. "Pornography: High School and College Years." In *Technical Report of the Commission on Obscenity and Pornography*, vol. 9. Washington, D.C.: Government Printing Office, 1970.

———. "Urban Working-Class Adolescents and Sexually Explicit Media." In

Technical Report of the Commission on Obscenity and Pornography, vol. 9. Washington, D.C.: Government Printing Office, 1970.

——— . "Youth and Pornography in Social Context." *Archives of Sexual Behavior* 2 (1973): 279–308.

Berger, Fred R. "Pornography, Sex, and Censorship." *Social Theory and Practice* 4 (Spring 1977): 183–209.

Bergler, Edmund. "Obscene Words." *Psychoanalytic Quarterly* 5 (1935): 226–248.

Berns, Walter. *Freedom, Virtue and the First Amendment.* Baton Rouge: Louisiana State University Press, 1957.

——— . "Pornography vs. Democracy: The Case for Censorship." *The Public Interest* 22 (1971): 3–24.

Bettelheim, Bruno. *Symbolic Wounds: Puberty Rites and the Envious Male.* Rev. ed. New York: Collier Books, 1962.

——— . *The Uses of Enchantment: The Meaning and Importance of Fairy Tales.* New York: Alfred A. Knopf, 1975.

Bischof, Norbert. "The Biological Foundations of the Incest Taboo." *Social Science Information* 11 (1972): 7–36.

Bixler, Ray H. "The Incest Controversy." *Psychological Reports* 49 (1981): 276–277.

Black, Donald. *The Behavior of Law.* New York: Academic Press, 1976.

Blumler, Jay G., and Elihu Katz, eds. *The Uses of Mass Communications.* Beverly Hills, Calif.: Sage Publications, 1974.

Bollinger, Lee C. *The Tolerant Society: Freedom of Speech and Extremist Speech in America.* New York: Oxford University Press, 1986.

Bonnicksen, Andrea L. "Obscenity Reconsidered: Bringing Broadcasting into the Mainstream Commentary." *Valparaiso University Law Review* 14 (1980): 261–293.

Bowie, Theodore, and Cornelia V. Christenson, eds. *Studies in Erotic Art.* New York: Basic Books, 1970.

Boyer, L. Bryce. "On Aspects of the Mutual Influences Between Anthropology and Psychoanalysis." *Journal of Psychological Anthropology* 1 (1978): 265–296.

Boyer, Paul S. *Purity in Print: Book Censorship in America.* New York: Charles Scribner's Sons, 1968.

Brendel, Otto J. "The Scope and Temperament of Erotic Art in the Greco-Roman World." In *Studies in Erotic Art,* edited by Theodore Bowie and Cornelia V. Christenson, pp. 3–108. New York: Basic Books, 1970.

Brenner, Charles. *An Elementary Textbook of Psychoanalysis.* Rev. ed. New York: International University Press, 1973.

Briddell, D. W., et al. "Effects of Alcohol and Cognitive Set on Deviant Stimuli." *Journal of Abnormal Psychology* 87 (1978): 418–430.

Brigman, William E. "Pornography as Group Libel: The Indianapolis Sex Discrimination Ordinance." *Indiana Law Review* 18 (1985): 479–505.

Bristow, Edward J. *Vice and Vigilance: Purity Movements in Britain.* Totowa, N.J.: Rowman & Littlefield, 1977.

Broun, Heywood, and Margaret Leech. *Anthony Comstock: Roundsman of the Lord.* New York: Albert & Charles Boni, 1927.

Brown, Marvin, Donald M. Amoroso, and Edward E. Ware. "Behavioral Effects of Viewing Pornography." *Journal of Social Psychology* 98 (1976): 235–245.

Brown, Marvin, Donald M. Amoroso, Edward E. Ware, Manfred Pruesse, and Dennis W. Pilkey. "Factors Affecting Viewing Time of Pornography." *Journal of Social Psychology* 90 (1973): 125–135.

Brown, Norman O. *Life Against Death: The Psychoanalytic Meaning of History.* Middletown, Conn: Wesleyan University Press, 1959.

Brown, Richard Maxwell. "The American Vigilante Tradition." In the *History of Violence in America: Historical and Comparative Perspectives,* edited by Henry Davis Graham and Ted Robert Gurr, pp. 154–226. New York: Praeger Publishers, 1969.

Bryan, James. "Apprenticeships in Prostitution." *Social Problems* 12 (1965): 287–297.

Buchen, Irving, ed. *The Perverse Imagination: Sexuality and Literary Culture.* New York: New York University Press, 1970.

Bullough, Vern L. *Sexual Variance in Society and History.* New York: John Wiley & Sons, 1976.

Byrne, Donn. "Social Psychology and the Study of Sexual Behavior." *Personality and Social Psychology Bulletin* 3 (1977): 3–30.

Byrne, Donn, and John Lamberth. "The Effect of Erotic Stimuli on Sex Arousal, Evaluative Responses, and Subsequent Behavior." In *Technical Report of the Commission on Obscenity and Pornography,* vol. 8, pp. 41–67. Washington, D.C.: Government Printing Office, 1970.

Byrne, Donn, Jeffrey D. Fisher, John Lamberth, and Herman E. Mitchell. "Evaluations of Erotica: Facts or Feelings?" *Journal of Personality and Social Psychology* 29 (1974): 111–116.

Byrne, Donn, and John Sheffield. "Response to Sexually Arousing Stimuli as a Function of Repressing and Sensitizing Defenses." *Journal of Abnormal Psychology* 70 (1965): 114–118.

Cairns, Robert B., J. C. N. Paul, and J. Wishner. "Psychological Assumptions in Sex Censorship: An Evaluative Review of Recent Research." In *Technical Report of the Commission on Obscenity and Pornography,* vol. 1, pp. 5–22. Washington, D.C.: Government Printing Office, 1970.

Campbell, Joseph. *The Hero with a Thousand Faces.* Cleveland: World Publishing, 1949.

Canavan, Francis. *Freedom of Expression: Purpose as Limit.* Durham, N.C.: Carolina Academic Press, 1984.

Cantor, Joanne, Dolf Zillman, and Edna F. Einsiedel. "Female Responses to Provocation After Exposure to Aggressive and Erotic Films." *Communication Research* 4 (1978): 395–412.

Cantor, Norman F., and Michael B. Werthman. *The History of Popular Culture.* New York: Macmillan, 1968.

Carlin, John C. "The Rise and Fall of Topless Radio." *Journal of Communication* 26 (Winter 1976): 31–37.

Carmen, Ira H. *Movies, Censorship, and the Law.* Ann Arbor: University of Michigan Press, 1966.

Carter, Angela. *The Sadeian Woman and the Ideology of Pornography.* New York: Pantheon Books, 1978.

Chodorow, Nancy. *The Reproduction of Mothering: Psychoanalysis and the Sociology of Gender.* Berkeley and Los Angeles: University of California Press, 1978.

Cleland, John. *Fanny Hill, or Memoirs of a Woman of Pleasure.* Orig. pub. 1748–1749. New York: G. P. Putnam's Sons, 1963.

Cline, Victor B., ed. *Where Do You Draw the Line? An Exploration into Media Violence, Pornography, and Censorship.* Provo, Utah: Brigham Young University Press, 1974.

Clor, Harry M. *Obscenity and Public Morality: Censorship in a Liberal Society.* Chicago: University of Chicago Press, 1969.

———. "Obscenity and Freedom of Expression." In *Censorship and Freedom of Expression: Essays on Obscenity and the Law,* edited by Harry M. Clor, pp. 97–129. Chicago: Rand McNally, 1971.

———. "Public Morality and Free Expression." *Hastings Law Journal* 28 (1977): 1305–1313.

Chandos, John. *"To Deprave and Corrupt . . .": Original Studies in the Nature and Definition of Obscenity.* New York: Association Press, 1962.

"Colloquium. Violent Pornography: Degradation of Women Versus Right of Free Speech." *New York University Review of Law and Social Change* 7 (1978–1979): 181–308.

Conrad, Joseph. *Heart of Darkness.* Reprint ed. *Joseph Conrad: Tales of Land and Sea.* Garden City, N.Y.: Hanover House, 1953.

Cook, James. "The X-Rated Economy." *Forbes,* September 18, 1978, pp. 81–92.

Cook, Robert F., and Robert H. Fosen. "Pornography and the Sex Offender: Patterns of Exposure and Immediate Arousal Effects of Pornographic Stimuli." In *Technical Report of the Commission on Obscenity and Pornography,* vol. 7, pp. 149–162. Washington, D.C.: Government Printing Office, 1970.

Copp, David, and Susan Wendell, eds. *Pornography and Censorship.* Buffalo, N.Y.: Prometheus Books, 1983.

Corbett, Michael. *Political Tolerance in America: Freedom and Equality in Public Attitudes.* New York: Longman, 1982.

Coser, Lewis. "Some Functions of Deviant Behavior and Normative Flexibility." *American Journal of Sociology* 68 (1962): 172–181.

Court, John H. "Pornography and Sex Crimes: A Reevaluation in the Light of Recent Trends Around the World." *International Journal of Criminology and Penology* 5 (1977): 129–157.

———. "Pornography Update." *British Journal of Sexual Medicine* (1981): 28–30.

———. "Rape Trends in New South Wales: A Discussion of Conflicting Evidence." *Australian Journal of Social Issues* 17 (1982): 202–206.

———. "Sex and Violence: A Ripple Effect." In *Pornography and Sexual Aggression,* edited by Neil N. Malamuth and Edward Donnerstein, pp. 143–172. New York: Academic Press, 1984.

Cowan, Geoffrey. *See No Evil: The Backstage Battle over Sex and Violence in Television.* New York: Simon & Schuster, 1979.

Cox, M. "Dynamic Psychotherapy with Sex-Offenders." In *Sexual Deviation,* edited by Ismond Rosen. New York: Oxford University Press, 1979.

Craig, Alec. *Suppressed Books.* Cleveland: World Publishing, 1963.

Crewdson, John. *By Silence Betrayed: Sexual Abuse of Children in America.* Boston: Little, Brown, 1988.

Dahl, Robert A. *Dilemmas of Pluralist Democracy.* New Haven, Conn.: Yale University Press, 1982.

Davenport, William H. "Sex in Cross-Cultural Perspective." In *Human Sexuality in Four Perspectives,* edited by Frank A. Beach, pp. 115–163. Baltimore: Johns Hopkins University Press, 1976.

Davies, Christie. "How Our Rulers Argue About Censorship." In *Censorship and Obscenity,* edited by Rajeev Dhavan and Christie Davies, pp. 9–36. London: Macmillan, 1978.

Davis, Keith E., and George N. Braucht. "Exposure to Pornography, Character, and Sexual Deviance: A Retrospective Survey." In *Technical Report of the Commission on Obscenity and Pornography,* vol. 7, pp. 173–244. Washington, D.C.: Government Printing Office, 1970.

———. "Reactions to Viewing Films of Realistic Heterosexual Behavior." In *Technical Report of the Commission on Obscenity and Pornography,* vol. 8, pp. 68–96. Washington, D.C.: Government Printing Office, 1970.

Davis, Kingsley. "Sexual Behavior." In *Contemporary Social Problems,* edited by Robert K. Merton and Robert A. Nisbet, pp. 219–261. New York: Harcourt Brace Jovanovich, 1976.

Davis, Murray S. *Smut: Erotic Reality/Obscene Ideology.* Chicago: University of Chicago Press, 1983.

de Beauvoir, Simone. "Must We Burn de Sade?" In "Critical Introduction" to *The 120 Days of Sodom,* by Donatien-Alphonse-François de Sade. New York: Grove Press, 1966.

De Fleur, Melvin L., and Sandra Ball-Rokeach. *Theories of Mass Communication.* 3d ed. New York: David McKay, 1975.

Deforges, Régine. *Confessions of O: Conversations with Pauline Réage.* Translated by Sabine d'Estrée. New York: Viking Press, 1979.

de Grazia, Edward, and Roger K. Newman. *Banned Films: Movies, Censors, and the First Amendment.* New York: Bowker, 1982.

Dentler, Robert A., and Kai T. Erikson. "The Functions of Deviance in Groups." *Social Problems* 7 (1959): 98–107.

Devereux, George. *Reality and Dream.* New York: New York University Press, 1969.

———. *Ethnopsychoanalysis.* Berkeley and Los Angeles: University of California Press, 1978.

Devine, Donald. *The Political Culture of the United States.* Boston: Little, Brown, 1972.

Devlin, Patrick. *The Enforcement of Morals.* London: Oxford University Press, 1965.

Di Leo, Joseph H. *Children's Drawings as Diagnostic Aids.* New York: Brunner/Mazel, 1973.

Dolbeare, Kenneth M. *Trial Courts in Urban Politics: State Court Policy Impact and Functions in a Local Political System.* New York: John Wiley & Sons, 1967.

Donnelly, Peter. "Running the Gauntlet: The Moral Order of Pornographic Movie Theatres." *Urban Life* 10 (1981): 239–264.

Donnerstein, Edward. "Aggressive Erotica and Violence Against Women." *Journal of Personality and Social Psychology* 39 (1980): 269–277.

———. "Erotica and Human Aggression." In *Aggression: Theoretical and Empirical Views,* edited by Russell G. Geen and Edward Donnerstein, pp. 127–154. New York: Academic Press, 1983.

———. "Pornography: Its Effect on Violence Against Women." In *Pornography and Sexual Aggression,* edited by Neil M. Malamuth and Donnerstein, pp. 53–82. New York: Academic Press, 1984.

Donnerstein, Edward, and Leonard Berkowitz. "Victim Reactions in Aggressive Erotic Films as a Factor in Violence Against Women." *Journal of Personality and Social Psychology* 41 (1981): 710–724.

Donnerstein, Edward, Marcia Donnerstein, and Ronald Evans. "Erotic Stimuli and Aggression: Facilitation or Inhibition." *Journal of Social Psychology* 32 (1975): 237–244.

Donnerstein, Edward, Daniel Linz, and Steven Penrod. *The Question of Pornography: Research Findings and Policy Implications.* New York: Free Press, 1987.

Douglas, Mary. *Purity and Danger: An Analysis of Concepts of Pollution and Taboo.* Baltimore: Penguin, 1970.

Durkheim, Émile. *The Division of Labor in Society.* Translated by George Simpson. Glencoe, Ill.: Free Press, 1960.

Dworkin, Andrea. *Pornography: Men Possessing Women.* New York: G. P. Putnam's Sons, 1979.

Dworkin, Ronald. *Taking Rights Seriously.* London: Duckworth, 1977.

———. "Is There a Right to Pornography?" *Oxford Journal of Legal Studies* 1 (1981): 177–212.

Dye, Thomas R., and L. Harmon Zeigler. *The Irony of Democracy.* Belmont, Calif.: Duxbury Press, 1971.

Eisenstein, Elizabeth L. "Some Conjectures About the Impact of Printing on Western Society and Thought: A Preliminary Report." *Journal of Modern History* 40: 1–55.

Ellis, Albert. "Art and Sex." In *Encyclopedia of Sexual Behavior,* vol. 1, edited by Albert Ellis and Albert Abarbanel, pp. 161–179. New York: Hawthorn Books, 1961.

Ember, Melvin. "On the Origin and Extension of the Incest Taboo." *Behavior Science Research* 10 (1975): 249–281.

Emerson, Thomas I. *Toward a General Theory of the First Amendment.* New York: Random House, 1963.

———. *The System of Freedom of Expression.* New York: Random House, 1970.

Erikson, Kai T. "Notes on the Sociology of Deviance." *Social Problems* 9 (1962): 307–314.

———. *Wayward Puritans: A Study in the Sociology of Deviance.* New York: John Wiley & Sons, 1966.

Eysenck, H. J., and H. Nias. *Sex, Violence, and the Media.* London: Spector, 1978.

Fahringer, Herold Price, and Paul J. Cambria, Jr. "Some New Weapons Being Used in Waging War Against Pornography." *Capitol University Law Review* 7 (1978): 553–577.

Faust, Beatrice. *Women, Sex and Pornography.* New York: Macmillan, 1980.

Feinberg, Joel. " 'Harmless Immoralities' and Offensive Nuisances." In *Issues in Law and Morality,* edited by Norman S. Care and Thomas K. Trelogan, pp. 83–110. Cleveland: Case Western Reserve University Press, 1973.

———. "Pornography and the Criminal Law." *University of Pittsburgh Law Review* 40 (1979): 567–604.

Ferenczi, Sandor. *Sex and Psychoanalysis.* New York: Basic Books, 1950.

Findlater, Richard. *Banned! A Review of Theatrical Censorship in Britain.* London: MacGibbon & Kee, 1967.

Fine, Gary. "Obscene Joking Across Cultures." *Journal of Communication* 26 (1976): 138–139.

Finkelhor, David. "Sex Among Siblings: A Survey of Prevalence, Variety, and Effects." *Archives of Sexual Behavior* 9 (1980): 171–194.

Finkelstein, M. Marvin. "The Traffic in Sex-Oriented Materials in Boston." In *Technical Report of the Commission on Obscenity and Pornography,* vol. 4, pp. 99–154. Washington, D.C.: Government Printing Office, 1970.

Fischer, Heinz-Dietrich, and Stefan R. Melnick, eds. *Entertainment: A Cross-Cultural Examination.* New York: Hastings House, 1978.

Fisher, William A., and Donn Byrne. "Individual Differences in Affective, Evaluative, and Behavioral Responses to an Erotic Film." *Journal of Applied Social Psychology* 8 (1978): 355–365.

———. "Sex Differences in Response to Erotica? Love Versus Lust." *Journal of Personality and Social Psychology* 36 (1978): 117–125.

Flugel, J. C. *Man, Morals and Society.* Duckworth, 1945.

Ford, Clellan S. "Sex Offenses: An Anthropological Perspective." *Law and Contemporary Problems* 25 (1960): 225–241.

Forward, Susan, and Craig Buck. *Betrayal of Innocence.* Los Angeles: J. P. Tarcher, 1978.

Foucault, Michel. *The History of Sexuality.* Vol. 1, *An Introduction.* Translated by Robert Hurley. New York: Random House, 1980.

Foxon, David. *Libertine Literature in England, 1660–1745.* New Hyde Park, N.Y.: University Books, 1965.

Frankel, Charles. "Moral Environment of the Law." *Minnesota Law Review* 61 (1977): 921–960.

Freeman, Derek. "Totem and Taboo: A Reappraisal." In *Man and His Culture: Psychoanalytic Anthropology after "Totem and Taboo,"* edited by Warner Muensterberger, pp. 53–78. New York: Taplinger, 1970.

Freud, Anna. *The Ego and the Mechanisms of Defense.* Rev. ed. New York: International University Press, 1966.

Freud, Sigmund. *Totem and Taboo.* In *The Complete Psychological Works of Sigmund Freud,* standard ed., translated by James Strachey, vol. 13, pp. 1–161. London: Hogarth Press, 1953.

————. *Three Essays on Sexuality*. In *Complete Psychological Works*, standard ed., translated by James Strachey, vol. 7, pp. 135–243. London: Hogarth Press, 1956.

————. "Formulations on the Two Principles of Mental Functioning." In *Complete Psychological Works*, standard ed., translated by James Strachey, vol. 12, pp. 213–226. London: Hogarth Press, 1958.

————. *Jokes and Their Relation to the Unconscious*. In *Complete Psychological Works*, standard ed., translated by James Strachey, vol. 8. London: Hogarth Press, 1960.

————. *The Ego and the Id*. In *Complete Psychological Works*, standard ed., translated by James Strachey, vol. 19, pp. 13–66. London: Hogarth Press, 1961.

————. *Civilization and Its Discontents*. In *Complete Psychological Works*, standard ed., translated by James Strachey, vol. 21, pp. 59–148. London: Hogarth Press, 1964.

Friedman, Jane. "Zoning 'Adult' Movies." *Hastings Law Journal* 28 (1977): 1293–1304.

Frodi, Ann. "Sexual Arousal, Situational Restrictiveness, and Aggressive Behavior." *Journal of Research in Personality* 11 (1977): 48–58.

Gagnon, John H., and William Simon, eds. *Sexual Deviance*. New York: Harper & Row, 1967.

————. *Sexual Conduct: The Social Sources of Human Sexuality*. Chicago: Aldine, 1973.

Gans, Herbert J. "The Politics of Culture in America." In *Social Problems and Social Policy: Inequality and Injustice*, edited by Lee Rainwater, pp. 353–360. Chicago: Aldine, 1974.

————. *Popular Culture and High Culture: An Analysis and Evaluation of Taste*. New York: Basic Books, 1974.

————. "Democracy and the Arts: Adversary or Ally?" In *The Arts in a Democratic Community*, edited by Dennis Alan Mann. Bowling Green, Ohio: Popular Press, 1977.

Gardiner, Harold C. *Catholic Viewpoint on Censorship*. Garden City, N.Y.: Doubleday, 1958.

Gastil, Raymond. "The Moral Right of the Majority to Restrict Obscenity and Pornography." *Ethics* 3 (1976): 231–240.

Gay, Peter. *The Bourgeois Experience: Victoria to Freud*. Vol. 1, *Education of the Senses*. New York: Oxford University Press, 1984.

Gaylin, Willard. "Obscenity Is More Than a Four-Letter Word." In *Censorship and Freedom of Expression: Essays on Obscenity and the Law*, edited by Harry M. Clor, pp. 153–175. Chicago: Rand McNally, 1971.

Gebhard, Paul H., John H. Gagnon, Wardell B. Pomeroy, and Cornelia V. Christenson. *Sex Offenders: An Analysis of Types*. New York: Harper & Row, 1965.

Genet, Jean. *The Balcony*. New York: Grove Press, 1958.

Gibbons, Frederick X. "Sexual Standards and Reactions to Pornography: Enhancing Behavioral Consistency Through Self-Focused Attention." *Journal of Personality and Social Psychology* 36 (1978): 976–987.

Gibson, James L., and Richard D. Bingham. "On the Conceptualization and Measurement of Political Tolerance." *American Political Science Review* 76 (1982): 603–620.

Glassman, Marc A. "Community Standards of Patent Offensiveness: Public Opinion Data and Obscenity Law." *Public Opinion Quarterly* 42 (1978): 161–170.

Goffman, Erving. *Frame Analysis: An Essay in the Organization of Experience*. New York: Harper & Row, 1974.

Goldstein, Michael J., and Harold S. Kant. *Pornography and Sexual Deviance*. Berkeley and Los Angeles: University of California Press, 1973.

Goldstein, Michael J., Harold S. Kant, Lewis L. Judd, Clinton J. Rice, and Richard Green. "Exposure to Pornography and Sexual Behavior in Deviant and Normal Groups." In *Technical Report of the Commission on Obscenity and Pornography*, vol. 7, pp. 1–90. Washington, D.C.: Government Printing Office, 1970.

Goodman, Paul. *Utopian Essays and Practical Proposals*. New York: Random House, 1962.

Gordon, George N. *Erotic Communications: Studies in Sex, Sin and Censorship*. New York: Hastings House, 1980.

Gorer, Geoffrey. *The Life and Ideas of the Marquis de Sade*. London: Peter Owen, 1953.

Gosling, Robert. Untitled article. In *Does Pornography Matter?* edited by C. H. Rolph, pp. 55–79. London: Routledge & Kegan Paul, 1961.

Gregersen, Edgar. *Sexual Practices: The Story of Human Sexuality*. New York: Franklin Watts, 1983.

Griffin, Susan. *Pornography and Silence: Culture's Revenge Against Nature*. New York: Harper & Row, 1981.

Griffitt, William. "Sexual Stimulation and Sociosexual Behaviors." In *Love and Attraction,* edited by Mark Cook and Glenn Wilson. Oxford: Pergamon, 1979.

Griffitt, William, and Donn L. Kaiser. "Affect, Sex-Guilt, Gender, and the Rewarding-Punishing Effects of Erotic Stimuli." *Journal of Personality and Social Psychology* 36 (1978): 850–858.

Griffitt, William, James May, and Russell Veitch. "Sexual Stimulation and Interpersonal Behavior: Heterosexual Evaluative Responses, Visual Behavior, and Physical Proximity." *Journal of Personality and Social Psychology* 30 (1974): 367–377.

Grings, William W., and Michael E. Dawson. *Emotions and Bodily Responses: A Psychophysiological Approach*. New York: Academic Press, 1978.

Grosskurth, Phyllis. *Havelock Ellis*. New York: Alfred A. Knopf, 1980.

Grotjahn, Maurice. *Beyond Laughter: Humor and the Subconscious*. New York: McGraw-Hill, 1966.

Gusfield, Joseph R. *Symbolic Crusade: Status Politics and the American Temperance Movement*. Urbana: University of Illinois Press, 1963.

———. *Community: A Critical Response*. New York: Harper & Row, 1975.

Hacker, Andrew. "Liberal Democracy and Social Control." *American Political Science Review* 51 (1957): 1009–1026.

Haiman, Franklyn S. *Freedom of Speech*. Skokie, Ill.: National Textbook, 1976.

Hall, Stuart, and Paddy Whannel. *The Popular Arts*. New York: Pantheon Books, 1965.

Hammel, William M. *The Popular Arts in America*. New York: Harcourt Brace Jovanovich, 1972.

Hand, Learned. *The Spirit of Liberty*. New York: Alfred A. Knopf, 1960.

Hart, H. L. A. *Law, Liberty and Morality*. New York: Vintage Books, 1966.

Hart, Harold H. *Censorship: For and Against*. New York: Hart Publishing Co., 1971.

Hartogs, Renatus, with Hans Fantel. *Four-Letter Word Games: The Psychology of Obscenity*. New York: Dell, 1967.

Hartz, Louis. *The Liberal Tradition in America*. New York: Harcourt, Brace & World, 1955.

Hauser, Arnold. *The Social History of Art*. 4 vols. New York: Random House, Vintage Books, 1951.

Hausknecht, Murray, ed. "The Problem of Pornography." *Dissent* 27 (1978): 193–208.

Hayman, Ronald A. *De Sade: A Critical Biography*. New York: Thomas Crowell, 1978.

Heiby, E., and J. D. Becker. "Effect of Filmed Modeling on Self-Reported Frequency of Masturbation." *Archives of Sexual Behavior* 9 (1980): 115–121.

Heider, Karl G. "Anthropological Models of Incest Laws in the United States." *American Anthropologist* 71 (1969): 693–701.

Heiman, J. R. "A Psychophysiological Exploration of Sexual Arousal Patterns in Females and Males." *Psychophysiology* 14 (1977): 266–274.

Henkin, Louis. "Morals and the Constitution." *Columbia Law Review* 63 (1963): 391–414.

Herman, Judith Lewis. "Father-Daughter Incest." *Professional Psychology* 12 (1981): 76–80.

Hoggart, Richard. *Uses of Literacy*. New York: Oxford University Press, 1957.

Holbrook, David, ed. *The Case Against Pornography*. La Salle, Ill.: Library Press, 1973.

Holland, Norman N. *The Dynamics of Literary Response*. New York: Oxford University Press, 1968.

Hopkins, Keith. "Brother-Sister Marriage in Roman Egypt." *Comparative Studies in Society and History* 22 (1980): 303–354.

Howard, James L., Clifford B. Reifler, and Myron B. Liptzin. "Effects of Exposure to Pornography." In *Technical Report of the Commission on Obscenity and Pornography*, vol. 8, pp. 97–132. Washington, D.C.: Government Printing Office, 1970.

Hughes, Douglas A. *Perspectives on Pornography*. New York: St. Martin's Press, 1970.

Hughes, Everett C. *The Sociological Eye: Selected Papers*. New York: Aldine Atherton, 1971.

Hyde, H. Montgomery. *A History of Pornography*. New York: Farrar, Straus & Giroux, 1964.

"The Indianapolis Pornography Ordinance: Does the Right to Free Speech

Outweigh Pornography's Harm to Women?" *Cincinnati Law Review* 54 (1985): 249–269.

Jackman, Robert W. "Political Elites, Mass Publics, and Support for Democratic Principles." *Journal of Politics* 34 (1972): 753–773.

Johnson, Weldon T. "The Pornography Report: Epistemology, Methodology and Ideology." *Duquesne Law Review* 10 (1971): 190–218.

Johnson, Weldon T., Lenore R. Kupperstein, and Joseph J. Peters. "Sex Offenders' Experience with Erotica." In *Technical Report of the Commission on Obscenity and Pornography,* vol. 7, pp. 163–172. Washington, D.C.: Government Printing Office, 1970.

Jolson, Marvin A., Gary T. Ford, and Rolph E. Anderson. "When Marketers Cope with Moral Pollution: The Case of Sex Content in Movies." *Akron Business and Economic Review* 8 (1977): 16–25.

Jones, Ernest. "The Oedipus Complex as an Explanation of Hamlet's Mystery: A Study in Motive." *American Journal of Psychology* 21 (1910): 72–113.

————. *The Life and Work of Freud.* 3 vols. New York: Basic Books, 1955.

————. "Mother-Right and the Sexual Ignorance of Savages." In *Psycho-Myth, Psycho-History: Essays in Applied Psychoanalysis,* vol. 2, pp. 45–173. New York: Hillstone, 1964.

Joyce, James. *Ulysses.* 1922. Reprint ed. New York: Random House, 1961.

Justice, Blair, and Rita Justice. *The Broken Taboo.* New York: Human Sciences, 1979.

Kallich, Martin, Andrew MacLeish, and Gertrude Schoenbohm, eds. *Oedipus: Myth and Drama.* Indianapolis: Odyssey Press, 1968.

Kalven, Harry. "The Metaphysics of the Law of Obscenity." In *Supreme Court Review, 1959,* edited by Philip P. Kurland, pp. 1–45. Chicago: University of Chicago Press, 1960.

Kantorowicz, D. A. "Personality and Conditioning of Tumescence and Detumescence." *Behavior Research and Therapy* 16 (1978): 117–123.

Kaplan, Abraham. "Obscenity as an Esthetic Category." *Law and Contemporary Problems* 20 (1955): 544–559.

Kelley, Kathryn. "Variety Is the Spice of Erotica: Repeated Exposure, Novelty, and Sexual Attitudes." Paper read at the meeting of the Eastern Psychological Association, Baltimore, April 1982. Mimeographed.

Kendrick, Walter. *The Secret Museum: Pornography in Modern Culture.* New York: Viking Press, 1987.

Kilpatrick, James J. *The Smut Peddlers.* Garden City, N.Y.: Doubleday, 1960.

Kirkpatrick, R. George. "Collective Consciousness and Mass Hysteria: Collective Behavior and Anti-Pornography Crusades in Durkheimian Perspective." *Human Relations* 28 (1971): 63–84.

Kinsey, Alfred C., Wardell B. Pomeroy, and Clyde E. Martin. *Sexual Behavior in the Human Male.* Philadelphia: W. B. Saunders, 1948.

Klein, Melanie. *The Psycho-analysis of Children.* London: Hogarth Press, 1932.

Kline, Paul. *Fact and Fantasy in Freudian Theory.* 2d ed. London: Methuen, 1981.

Klossowski, Pierre. "Nature as Destructive Principle." In "Critical Introduction" to

The 120 Days of Sodom, by Donatien-Alphonse-François de Sade. New York: Grove Press, 1966.

Kluckhohn, Clyde. "Recurrent Themes in Myth and Mythmaking." *Daedalus* 88 (1959): 268–279.

Knowles, Lyle, and Houshong Poorkaj. "Attitudes and Behavior on Viewing Sexual Activities in Public Places." *Sociology and Social Research* 58 (1974): 130–135.

Kohen, Max. "The Venus of Willendorf." *American Imago* 3 (1946): 49–60.

Kornhauser, William. *The Politics of Mass Society.* Glencoe, Ill.: Free Press, 1959.

Kortmulder, K. "An Ethological Theory of the Incest Taboo and Exogamy." *Current Anthropology* 9 (1968): 437–449.

Kristol, Irving. "The Case for Liberal Censorship." *New York Times Magazine,* March 28, 1971, p. 24.

Kroeber, Alfred. "'Totem and Taboo' in Retrospect." In *Psychoanalysis and History,* edited by Bruce Mazlish, pp. 45–49. New York: Universal Library, 1971.

Kronhausen, Eberhard, and Phyllis Kronhausen. *Pornography and the Law.* New York: Ballantine Books, 1959.

Kuh, Richard. *Foolish Figleaves? Pornography in and out of Court.* New York: Macmillan, 1967.

Kupperstein, Lenore. "The Role of Pornography in the Etiology of Juvenile Delinquency: A Review of the Research Literature." In *Technical Report of the Commission on Obscenity and Pornography,* vol. 1, pp. 103–114. Washington, D.C.: Government Printing Office, 1970.

Kutchinsky, Berl. "The Effect of Pornography: A Pilot Experiment on Perception, Behavior, and Attitudes." In *Technical Report of the Commission on Obscenity and Pornography,* vol. 8, pp. 133–169. Washington, D.C.: Government Printing Office, 1970.

———. "Towards an Explanation of the Decrease in Registered Sex Crimes in Copenhagen." In *Technical Report of the Commission on Obscenity and Pornography,* vol. 7, pp. 263–310. Washington, D.C.: Government Printing Office, 1970.

———. "The Effect of Easy Availability of Pornography on the Incidence of Sex Crimes: The Danish Experience." *Journal of Social Issues* 29 (1973): 163–182.

———. "Eroticism Without Censorship." *International Journal of Criminology and Penology* 1 (1973): 217–225.

La Barre, Weston. "The Psychopathology of Drinking Songs." *Psychiatry* 2 (1939): 203–212.

———. "Kiowa Folk Sciences." *Journal of American Folklore* 60 (1947): 105–114.

———. "Folklore and Psychology." *Journal of American Folklore* 61 (1948): 382–390.

———. *The Human Animal.* Chicago: University of Chicago Press, 1954.

———. "Obscenity: An Anthropological Appraisal." *Law and Contemporary Problems* 20 (1955): 533–543.

———. "The Influence of Freud on Anthropology." *American Imago* 14 (1958): 275–328.

Lane, Robert E. *Political Ideology.* New York: Free Press, 1962.

———. "Individualism and the Market Society." In *NOMOS XXV: Liberal Democracy,* edited by J. Ronald Pennock and John W. Chapman, pp. 374–407. New York: New York University Press, 1983.

Laplanche, Jean, and J.-B. Pontalis. *The Language of Psychoanalysis.* Translated by Donald Nicholson-Smith. New York: W. W. Norton, 1973.

Laufe, Abe. *The Wicked Stage: A History of Theater Censorship and Harassment in the United States.* New York: Frederick Ungar, 1978.

Lawrence, D. H. *Lady Chatterley's Lover.* 1928. Reprint ed. New York: Grove Press, 1960.

———. *Sex, Literature, and Censorship.* New York: Viking Press, 1953.

Lawrence, David C. "Procedural Norms and Tolerance: A Reassessment." *American Political Science Review* 70 (1976): 80–100.

Laws, D. R., and J. A. O'Neil. "Variations on Masturbatory Conditioning." *Behavioural Psychotherapy* 9 (1981): 111–136.

Laws, D. R., and H. B. Rubin. "Instructional Control of an Autonomic Sexual Response." *Journal of Applied Behavior Analysis* 2 (1969): 93–99.

Lazersfeld, Paul F., and Robert K. Merton. "Mass Communication, Popular Taste, and Organized Social Action." In *The Process and Effects of Mass Communication,* edited by Wilbur Schramm and Donald F. Roberts, pp. 554–578. Urbana: University of Illinois Press, 1971.

League of Nations. *Records of the International Conference for the Suppression of the Circulation of Traffic in Obscene Publications.* C. 734. M. 299 (1923), chap. 4, pp. 21, 22. Geneva: 1923.

Lecky, W. H. *History of European Morals.* 3d ed. London: Longmans, Green, 1877.

Lederer, Laura, ed. *Take Back the Night: Women on Pornography.* New York: Bantam Books, 1980.

Legman, Gershon. *The Horn Book: Studies in Erotic Folklore and Bibliography.* New Hyde Park, N.Y.: University Books, 1964.

———. *Rationale of the Dirty Joke.* 2d ser. New York: Bell Publishing, 1975.

Lely, Gilbert. *The Marquis de Sade.* Translated by Alec Brown. New York: Grove Press, 1970.

Lerner, Daniel. "Toward a Communication Theory of Modernization: A Set of Considerations." In *Communications and Political Development,* edited by Lucien W. Pye, pp. 327–350. Princeton, N.J.: Princeton University Press, 1963.

Leroi-Gourhan, Arlette. *Treasures of Prehistoric Art.* New York: H. N. Abrams [1967].

Lesser, Simon O. *Fiction and the Unconscious.* Boston: Beacon Press, 1957.

Lester, David. "Incest." *Journal of Sex Research* 8 (1972): 268–285.

Lévi-Strauss, Claude. *The Elementary Structures of Kinship.* Translated by James H. Bell et al. Boston: Beacon Press, 1969.

Levy, Gertrude R. *The Gate of Horn.* London: Faber & Faber, 1948.

Levy, Leonard W. *The Emergence of a Free Press.* New York: Oxford University Press, 1985.

Lewis, Felice Flannery. *Literature, Obscenity, and the Law.* Carbondale: Southern Illinois University Press, 1976.

Lewittes, Don J., and William L. Simmons. "Impression Management of Sexually Motivated Behavior." *Journal of Social Psychology* 96 (1975): 39–44.

Lindzey, Gardner. "Some Remarks Concerning Incest, the Incest Taboo, and Psychoanalytic Theory." *American Psychologist* 22 (1967): 1051–1059.

Lingeman, Richard. *Small Town America: A Narrative History, 1620–the Present.* Boston: Houghton Mifflin, 1980.

Lipset, Seymour M. *The First New Nation: The United States in Historical and Comparative Perspective.* New York: Basic Books, 1963.

Little, Graham. *Political Ensembles: A Psychosocial Approach to Politics and Leadership.* New York: Oxford University Press, 1985.

Livingston, Frank B. "Genetics, Ecology, and the Origins of Incest and Exogamy." *Current Anthropology* 10 (1969): 45–49.

Lockhart, William B., and Robert C. McClure. "Censorship of Obscenity: The Developing Constitutional Standards." *Minnesota Law Review* 45 (1960): 5–121.

Longford Committee Investigating Pornography. *Pornography: The Longford Report.* London: Coronet Books, 1972.

Loth, David. *The Erotic in Literature.* New York: MacFadden Books, 1962.

McClosky, Herbert. "Consensus and Ideology in American Politics." *American Political Science Review* 58 (1964): 361–382.

McClosky, Herbert, and Alida Brill. *Dimensions of Tolerance: What Americans Believe About Civil Liberties.* New York: Russell Sage Foundation, 1983.

Machlup, Fritz. *Knowledge and Knowledge Production.* Vol. 1. Princeton, N.J.: Princeton University Press, 1980.

Madison, James. "The Federalist No. 10." In *The Federalist,* by Alexander Hamilton, John Jay, and James Madison. Garden City, N.Y.: Doubleday, Anchor, 1961.

Malamuth, Neil M. "Rape Fantasies as a Function of Exposure to Violent Sexual Stimuli." *Archives of Sexual Behavior* 10 (1981): 33–47.

———. "Aggression Against Women: Cultural and Individual Causes." In *Pornography and Sexual Aggression,* edited by Neil M. Malamuth and Edward Donnerstein, pp. 19–52. New York: Academic Press, 1984.

Malamuth, Neil M., and James V. P. Check. "Penile Tumescence and Perceptual Responses to Rape as a Function of the Victim's Perceived Reactions." *Journal of Applied Social Psychology* 10 (1980): 528–547.

———. "Sexual Arousal to Rape and Consenting Depictions: The Importance of the Woman's Arousal." *Journal of Abnormal Psychology* 89 (1980): 763–766.

———. "Effects of Mass Media Exposure on Acceptance of Violence Against Women: A Field Experiment." *Journal of Research in Personality* 15 (1981): 436–446.

———. "Sexual Arousal in Rape Depictions: Individual Differences." *Journal of Abnormal Psychology* 92 (1983): 55–67.

———. "Effects of Aggressive Pornography on Beliefs in Rape Myths: Individual Differences." *Journal of Research in Personality* 19 (1985): 299–320.

Malamuth, Neil M., Seymour Feshbach, and Yoram Jaffe. "Sexual Arousal and

Aggression: Recent Experiments and Theoretical Issues." *Journal of Social Issues* 33 (1977): 110–133.

Malamuth, Neil M., Scott Haber, and Seymour Feshbach. "Testing Hypotheses Regarding Rape: Exposure to Sexual Violence, Sex Differences, and the 'Normality' of Rapists." *Journal of Research in Personality* 14 (1980): 121–147.

Malamuth, Neil M., Maggie Heim, and Seymour Feshbach. "Sexual Responsiveness of College Students to Rape Depictions: Inhibitory and Disinhibitory Effects." *Journal of Personality and Social Psychology* 38 (1980): 399–408.

Malinowski, Bronislaw. *Sex and Repression in Savage Society*. London: Harcourt, Brace, 1937.

Mann, Jay. "Experimental Induction of Human Sexual Arousal." In *Technical Report of the Commission on Obscenity and Pornography*, vol. 1, pp. 23–60. Washington, D.C.: Government Printing Office, 1970.

Mann, Jay, Leonard Berkowitz, Jack Sidman, Sheldon Starr, and Stephen West. "Satiation of the Transient Stimulating Effect of Erotic Films." *Journal of Personality and Social Psychology* 30 (1974): 729–735.

Marcus, Steven. *The Other Victorians: A Study of Sexuality and Pornography in Mid-Nineteenth-Century England*. New York: New American Library, 1974.

Marcuse, Herbert. *Eros and Civilization: A Philosophical Inquiry into Freud*. New York: Random House, 1962.

———. *One-Dimensional Man: Studies in the Ideology of Advanced Industrial Society*. Boston: Beacon Press, 1964.

———. "Repressive Tolerance." In *A Critique of Pure Tolerance*, edited by Robert Paul Wolff, Barrington Moore, and Herbert Marcuse, pp. 81–118. Boston: Beacon Press, 1969.

Massey, Morris E. "A Marketing Analysis of Sex-Oriented Materials in Denver." In *Technical Report of the Commission on Obscenity and Pornography*, vol. 4, pp. 3–98. Washington, D.C.: Government Printing Office, 1970.

Mead, George Herbert. "The Psychology of Punitive Justice." *American Journal of Sociology* 23 (1918): 577–602.

Mead, Margaret. "Sex and Censorship in Contemporary Society." In *New World Writing*. New York: New American Library of World Literature, 1953.

Meiklejohn, Alexander. *Political Freedom: The Constitutional Powers of the People*. New York: Oxford University Press, 1960.

Mendelsohn, Harold. *Mass Entertainment*. New Haven, Conn.: Yale University Press, 1966.

Merton, Robert. *Social Theory and Social Structure*. Rev. ed. Glencoe, Ill.: Free Press, 1957.

Michelson, Peter. *The Aesthetics of Pornography*. New York: Herder & Herder, 1971.

Middleton, Russell. "Brother-Sister and Father-Daughter Marriage in Ancient Egypt." *American Sociological Review* 27 (1962): 603–611.

Mill, John Stuart. *On Liberty*. 1859. Reprint ed. New York: Liberal Arts Press, 1956.

Monaghan, Henry P. "First Amendment 'Due Process.' " *Harvard Law Review* 83 (1970): 518–581.

Money, John. "Pornography in the Home: A Topic in Medical Education." In *Contemporary Sexual Behavior: Critical Issues in the 1970's,* edited by Joseph Zubin and John Money, pp. 409–440. Baltimore: Johns Hopkins University Press, 1973.

Morton, Newton E. "Morbidity of Children from Consanguineous Marriages." In *Progress in Medical Genetics,* edited by Arthur G. Steinberg, vol. 1, pp. 261–291. New York: Grune & Stratton, 1961.

Mosher, Donald L. "Psychological Reactions to Pornographic Films." In *Technical Report of the Commission on Obscenity and Pornography,* vol. 8, pp. 255–312. Washington, D.C.: Government Printing Office, 1970.

———. "Sex Callousness Toward Women." In *Technical Report of the Commission on Obscenity and Pornography,* vol. 8, pp. 313–325. Washington, D.C.: Government Printing Office, 1970.

Mosher, Donald L., and I. Greenberg. "Females' Affective Responses to Reading Erotic Literature." *Journal of Consulting and Clinical Psychology* 33 (1969): 472–477.

Mosher, Donald L., and Kevin O'Grady. "Homosexual Threat, Negative Attitudes Toward Masturbation, Sex Guilt, and Males' Sexual and Affective Reactions to Explicit Sexual Films." *Journal of Consulting and Clinical Psychology* 47 (1979): 860–873.

Muldoon, Linda, ed. *Incest: Confronting the Silent Crime.* St. Paul: Minnesota Program for Victims of Sexual Assault, 1979.

Murdock, George P. *Social Structure.* New York: Macmillan, 1949.

Murphy, Earl Finbar. "The Value of Pornography." *Wayne Law Review* 10 (1964): 655–680.

Murphy, Paul L. "The Bill of Rights in Our Historical Development." In *The Future of Our Liberties,* edited by Stephen C. Halpern, pp. 19–37. Westport, Conn.: Greenwood Publishing, 1972.

———. *The Meaning of Free Speech.* Westport, Conn.: Greenwood Publishing, 1972.

Murphy, Terrence J. *Censorship: Government and Obscenity.* Baltimore: Helicon, 1963.

Murray, R. D. "The Evolution and Functional Significance of Incest Avoidance." *Journal of Human Evolution* 9 (1980): 173–178.

Murtagh, John, and Sara Harris. *Cast the First Stone.* New York: McGraw-Hill, 1957.

Musaph, Herman. "Introduction." In *Handbook of Sexology,* edited by John Money and Herman Musaph. New York: Elsevier/North-Holland Biomedical Press, 1977.

National Institute of Mental Health. *Television and Behavior: Ten Years of Scientific Progress and Implications for the Eighties.* Vol. 1, *Summary Report.* Rockville, Md.: National Institute of Mental Health, 1982.

National Opinion Research Center. *General Social Surveys, 1972–1985.* Cumulative Codebook Annual. Chicago: National Opinion Research Center, July 1985.

Nawy, Harold. "The San Francisco Erotic Marketplace." In *Technical Report of the*

Commission on Obscenity and Pornography, vol. 4, pp. 155–224. Washington, D.C.: Government Printing Office, 1970.

Nelson, Edward C. "Pornography and Sexual Aggression." In *The Influence of Pornography on Behavior,* edited by Maurice Yaffe and Edward C. Nelson, pp. 171–248. New York: Academic Press, 1982.

New York Public Library. *Censorship: 500 Years of Conflict.* New York: New York Public Library, 1984.

Nisbet, Robert. *The Quest for Community.* New York: Oxford University Press, 1953.

Nocera, Joseph. "The Big Book Banning Brawl." *New Republic,* September 13, 1982, pp. 21–23.

Nunn, Clyde A., Harry J. Crockett, Jr., and J. Allen Williams, Jr. *Tolerance for Nonconformity.* San Francisco: Jossey-Bass, 1978.

Nye, Russel. *The Unembarrassed Muse.* New York: Dial Press, 1970.

"Obscenity and the Arts." *Law and Contemporary Problems* 20 (Autumn 1955): 531–688.

O'Higgins, Paul. *Censorship in Britain.* London: Nelson, 1972.

Paletz, David, and William F. Harris. "Four-Letter Threats to Authority." *Journal of Politics* 37 (November 1975): 955–979.

"Panel on Folk Literature and the Obscene." *Journal of American Folklore* 75 (1963): 189–265.

Parens, Henri, Leafy Pollock, Joan Stern, and Selma Kramer. "On the Girl's Entry into the Oedipus Complex." In *Female Psychology,* edited by Harold P. Blum, pp. 79–107. New York: International University Press, 1978.

Parker, Seymour. "The Pre-Cultural Basis of the Incest Taboo: Toward a Biosocial Theory." *American Anthropologist* 78 (1976): 285–305.

Parsons, Talcott. "The Incest Taboo in Relation to Social Structure." *British Journal of Sociology* 5 (1954): 101–117.

———. "Social Structure and Development of Personality: Freud's Contribution to the Integration of Psychology and Sociology." *Psychiatry* 21 (1958): 321–340.

Paul, James C. N., and Murray L. Schwartz. *Federal Censorship: Obscenity in the Mail.* New York: Free Press, 1961.

Pearsall, Ronald. *The Worm in the Bud: The World of Victorian Sexuality.* New York: Macmillan, 1969.

Peckham, Morse. *Art and Pornography.* New York: Basic Books, 1969.

Perrin, Noel. *Dr. Bowdler's Legacy.* New York: Atheneum, 1969.

Piaget, Jean, and Barbel Inhelder. *The Psychology of the Child.* New York: Basic Books, 1969.

Pines, Burt. "The Obscenity Quagmire." *California State Bar Journal* 49 (November-December 1974).

Plato. *The Republic.* Translated by Benjamin Jowett. New York: Random House, Modern Library, 1941.

Polsky, Ned. *Hustlers, Beats, and Others.* New York: Doubleday, Anchor Books, 1969.

Pool, Ithiel de Sola. *On Free Speech in the Electronic Age: Technologies of Freedom.* Cambridge, Mass.: Harvard University Press, 1983.

Potter, David M. *People of Plenty: Economic Abundance and the American Character.* Chicago: University of Chicago Press, 1954.

────── ."The Quest for the National Character." In *The Reconstruction of American History,* edited by John Higham. New York: Harper & Row, 1962.

────── . "Changing Patterns of Social Cohesion and the Crisis of Law Under a System of Government by Consent." In *Is Law Dead?* edited by Eugene V. Rostow, pp. 260–285. New York: Simon & Schuster, 1971.

Praz, Mario. *The Romantic Agony.* Translated by Angus Davidson. New York: Oxford University Press, 1970.

President's Commission on Obscenity and Pornography. *Report of the Commission on Obscenity and Pornography.* New York: Bantam Books, 1970.

────── . *Technical Reports.* 9 vols. Washington, D.C.: Government Printing Office, 1970.

"Project: An Empirical Inquiry into the Effects of *Miller v. California* on the Control of Obscenity." *New York University Law Review* 52 (October 1977): 810–939.

Prothro, James W., and Charles M. Grigg. "Fundamental Principles of Democracy: Bases of Agreement and Disagreement." *Journal of Politics* 22 (1960): 276–294.

Provizer, Norman W. "Of Lines and Men: The Supreme Court, Obscenity, and the Issue of the Avertable Eye." *Tulsa Law Journal* 13 (1977): 52–81.

Raglan, FitzRoy James Richard Somerset. *The Hero: A Study in Tradition, Myth, and Drama.* London: Watts, 1949.

Randall, Richard S. *Censorship of the Movies: The Social and Political Control of a Mass Medium.* Madison: University of Wisconsin Press, 1968.

────── . "Censorship: From 'The Miracle' to 'Deep Throat.' " In *The American Film Industry,* edited by Tino Balio, pp. 432–457. Madison: University of Wisconsin Press, 1976.

────── . "Erotica and Community Standards: The Conflicts of Elite and Democratic Values." In *Civil Liberties: Policy and Policy Making,* edited by Stephen L. Wasby, pp. 169–178. Lexington, Mass.: D.C. Heath, 1976.

Rank, Otto. *The Myth and the Birth of the Hero.* Translated by F. Robbins and S. E. Jellife. New York: Robert Brunner, 1952.

Ray, Rose E., and Walker, C. Eugene. "Biographical and Self-Report Correlates of Female Guilt Responses to Visual Erotic Stimuli." *Journal of Consulting and Clinical Psychology* 41 (1973): 93–96.

Read, Alan. "An Obscenity Symbol." *American Speech* 9 (1934): 264–278.

Réage, Pauline. *Story of O.* Translated by Sabine d'Estrée. New York: Grove Press, 1965.

Reich, Wilhelm. *The Sexual Revolution.* New York: Farrar, Straus & Giroux, 1945.

────── . *The Mass Psychology of Fascism.* 1946. 3d ed. Translated by Vincent R. Carfagno. New York: Farrar, Straus & Giroux, 1970.

Reifler, Clifford B., James L. Howard, M. A. Lipton, Myron B. Liptzin, and D. E. Widman. "Pornography: An Experimental Study of Effects." *American Journal of Psychiatry* 128 (1971): 575–582.

Reisner, Robert. *Graffiti: Two Thousand Years of Wall Writing.* Chicago: Henry Regnery, 1971.

Rembar, Charles. *The End of Obscenity: The Trials of Lady Chatterley, Tropic of Cancer and Fanny Hill.* New York: Random House, 1968.

Richards, David. "Free Speech and Obscenity Law: Toward a Moral Theory of the First Amendment." *University of Pennsylvania Law Review* 123 (1974): 45–91.

———. *Moral Criticism of Law.* Belmont, Calif.: Dickenson, 1977.

Richardson, Richard J., and Kenneth N. Vines. *The Politics of the Federal Courts.* Boston: Little, Brown, 1970.

Rieff, Philip. *The Triumph of the Therapeutic: Uses of Faith after Freud.* New York: Harper & Row, 1966.

Rist, Ray C. *The Pornography Controversy.* New Brunswick, N.J.: Transaction Books, 1975.

Roazen, Paul. *Freud: Political and Social Thought.* New York: Alfred A. Knopf, 1968.

Roche, John P. "We've Never Had More Freedom." *New Republic,* January 23, 1956.

———. "American Liberty: An Examination of the Tradition of Freedom." In *Aspects of Liberty,* edited by Milton Konvitz and Clinton Rossiter, pp. 129–163. Ithaca, N.Y.: Cornell University Press, 1958.

———. *Quest for the Dream: The Development of Civil Rights and Human Relations in Modern America.* New York: Macmillan, 1963.

Rodgers, Harrell R., Jr. "Censorship Campaigns in Eighteen Cities." *American Politics Quarterly* 2 (1974): 371–392.

———. "Prelude to Conflict: The Evolution of Censorship Campaigns." *Pacific Sociological Review* 18 (1975): 194–205.

Roheim, Geza. *Psychoanalysis and Anthropology.* New York: International University Press, 1950.

———. "The Psychoanalytic Interpretation of Culture." In *Man and His Culture: Psychoanalytic Anthropology after "Totem and Taboo,"* edited by Warner Muensterberger, pp. 31–51. New York: Taplinger Publishing, 1970.

Rolph, C. H., ed. *Does Pornography Matter?* London: Routledge & Kegan Paul, 1961.

———. *The Trial of Lady Chatterley.* Baltimore: Penguin, 1961.

Rosten, Leo. "The Intellectual and the Mass Media." *Daedalus* 92 (1963): 333–346.

Rubin, Rick, and Gregg Byerly. *Incest: The Last Taboo, An Annotated Bibliography.* New York: Garland Publishing, 1983.

Rugoff, Milton. *Prudery and Passion: Sexuality in Victorian America.* New York: G. P. Putnam's Sons, 1971.

Sachs, Wulf. *Black Hamlet: The Mind of an African Negro Revealed by Psychoanalysis.* London: G. Bles, 1937.

Sade, Donatien-Alphonse-François de. *Crimes of Passion.* Edited and translated by Wade Baskin. New York: Philosophical Library, 1965.

———. *Juliette.* Translated by Austryn Wainhouse. New York: Grove Press, 1976.

————. *Justine and Other Writings*. Translated by Richard Seaver and Austryn Wainhouse. New York: Grove Press, 1966.

————. *The 120 Days of Sodom and Other Writings*. Translated by Austryn Wainhouse and Richard Seaver. New York: Grove Press, 1967.

Sagarin, Edward. *The Anatomy of Dirty Words*. New York: Lyle Stuart, 1962.

St. John-Stevas, Norman. *Obscenity and the Law*. London: Secker & Warburg, 1956.

Sargent, Helen Child, and George L. Kittridge. *English and Scottish Popular Ballads*. Boston: Houghton Mifflin, 1932.

Sarnoff, Charles. *Latency*. New York: Jason Aronson, 1976.

Scanlon, Thomas. "Freedom of Expression and Categories of Expression." *University of Pittsburgh Law Review* 40 (1979): 519–550.

Schaefer, Helmuth H., and Aloma H. Colgan. "The Effect of Pornography on Penile Tumescence as a Function of Reinforcement and Novelty." *Behavior Therapy* 8 (1977): 938–946.

Schaefer, Helmuth H., G. J. Tregerthan, and Aloma H. Colgan. "Measured and Self-Estimated Penile Erection." *Behavior Therapy* 7 (1976): 1–7.

Schauer, Frederick. *The Law of Obscenity*. Washington, D.C.: Bureau of National Affairs, 1976.

————. "The Return to Variable Obscenity?" *Hastings Law Journal* 28 (1977): 1275–1291.

————. "Reflections on 'Contemporary Community Standards': The Perpetuation of an Irrelevant Concept in the Law of Obscenity." *North Carolina Law Review* 56 (1978): 1–28.

————. "Speech and 'Speech'—Obscenity and 'Obscenity': An Exercise in the Interpretation of Constitutional Language." *Georgetown Law Journal* 67 (1979): 899–933.

————. *Free Speech: A Philosophical Inquiry*. New York: Cambridge University Press, 1982.

Schechner, Richard. "Incest and Culture: A Reflection on Claude Lévi-Strauss." *Psychoanalytic Review* 58 (1971): 563–572.

Schill, Thomas, Mark Van Tuinen, and Don Doty. "Repeated Exposure to Pornography and Arousal Levels of Subjects Varying in Guilt." *Psychological Reports* 46 (1980): 467–471.

Schmidt, Gunter. "Male-Female Differences in Sexual Arousal and Behavior During and After Exposure to Sexually Explicit Stimuli." *Archives of Sexual Behavior* 4 (1975): 353–365.

Schmidt, Gunter, and Volkmar Sigusch. "Sex Differences in Response to Psychosexual Stimulation by Films and Slides." *Journal of Sex Research* 6 (1970): 268–283.

Schramm, Wilbur, and Donald F. Roberts, eds. *The Process and Effects of Mass Communication*. Rev. ed. Urbana: University of Illinois Press, 1971.

Schull, William. J., and James V. Neel. *The Effects of Inbreeding on Japanese Children*. New York: Harper & Row, 1965.

Schur, Edwin M. *The Politics of Deviance*. Englewood Cliffs, N.J.: Prentice-Hall, 1980.

Schwartz, Joel. "Freud and Freedom of Speech." *American Political Science Review* 80 (1986): 1227–1248.

Scott, Joseph E. "An Updated Longitudinal Content Analysis of Sex References in Mass Circulation Magazines." *Journal of Sex Research* 20 (1986): 385–392.

Scott, Joseph E., and Jack L. Franklin. "Sex References in the Mass Media." *Journal of Sex Research* 9 (1973): 196–209.

Seligman, Brenda Z. "The Problem of Incest and Exogamy." *American Anthropologist* 52 (1950): 305–316.

Selznick, Philip. "Legal Institutions and Social Control." *Vanderbilt Law Review* 17 (1963): 79–90.

Shils, Edward. "The Theory of Mass Society." *Diogenes* 39 (1962): 45–66.

Simari, C. Georgia, and David Baskin. "Incest: No Longer a Family Affair." *Child Psychiatry Quarterly* 13 (1980): 36–51.

Simons, G. L. *Pornography Without Prejudice*. London: Abelard–Schuman, 1972.

Simpson, A. W. B. *Politics and Pornography: A Look Back to the Williams Committee*. London: Waterlow Publishers, 1983.

Slade, Joseph P. "Pornographic Theatres Off Times Square." *trans-action* (now *Society*) 9, nos. 1–2 (November–December 1971): 35–43.

Smith, Lee H. "Is Anything Printable?" *Columbia Journalism Review* (1968): 19–23.

Soble, Alan. *Pornography: Marxism, Feminism, and the Future of Sexuality*. New Haven, Conn.: Yale University Press, 1986.

Sontag, Susan. "On Pornography." *Partisan Review* 34 (1967): 181–212.

————. *Styles of Radical Will*. New York: Delta, 1970.

Sorokin, Pitirim. *The American Sex Revolution*. Boston: P. Sargeant, 1956.

Spencer, Joyce. "Father-Daughter Incest: A Clinical View from the Corrections Field." *Child Welfare* 57 (1978): 581–590.

Spitz, David. *Democracy and the Challenge of Power*. New York: Columbia University Press, 1958.

Spitzer, Matthew L. *Seven Dirty Words and Six Other Stories*. New Haven, Conn.: Yale University Press, 1986.

Steiner, George. "Night Words: High Pornography and Human Privacy." *Encounter* 25 (1965): 14–19.

————. *Language and Silence: Essays on Language, Literature, and the Inhuman*. New York: Atheneum, 1967.

Stephens, William M. *The Oedipus Complex: Cross-Cultural Evidence*. New York: Free Press, 1962.

————. "A Cross-Cultural Study of Modesty and Obscenity." In *Technical Report of the Commission on Obscenity and Pornography*, vol. 9, pp. 405–452. Washington, D.C.: Government Printing Office, 1970.

Stephenson, William. *The Play Theory of Mass Communication*. Chicago: University of Chicago Press, 1967.

Sterling, Christopher H., and Timothy R. Haight. *The Mass Media: Aspen Institute Guide to Communication Industry Trends*. New York: Praeger Publishers, 1978.

Stern, Mikhail, with August Stern. *Sex in the U.S.S.R.* New York: New York Times Books, 1980.

Stoller, Robert J. *Perversion: The Erotic Form of Hatred.* New York: Delta, 1975.
————. *Sexual Excitement: Dynamics of Erotic Life.* New York: Pantheon Books, 1979.
Stone, Leo. "On the Principal Obscene Word in the English Language." *International Journal of Psychoanalysis* 35 (1954): 30–56.
Sullivan, John L., James Piereson, and George E. Marcus. "An Alternative Conceptualization of Political Tolerance: Illusory Increases, 1950s–1970s." *American Political Science Review* 73 (1979): 781–794.
————. *Political Tolerance and American Democracy.* Chicago: University of Chicago Press, 1982.
Sundholm, Charles A. "The Pornographic Arcade: Ethnographic Notes on Moral Men in Immoral Places." *Urban Life and Culture* 2 (1973): 85–104.
Sussman, Norman. "Sex and Sexuality in History." In *The Sexual Experience,* edited by Benjamin J. Sadock, Harold I. Kaplan, and Alfred M. Freedman. Baltimore: Williams & Wilkins, 1976.
Sykes, Gresham M., and Donald Matza. "Techniques of Neutralization: A Theory of Delinquency." *American Sociological Review* 22 (1957): 664–670.
Symons, Donald. *The Evolution of Human Sexuality.* New York: Oxford University Press, 1979.
Tannahill, Reay. *Sex in History.* New York: Stein & Day, 1980.
Taylor, G. Rattray. *Sex in History.* New York: Vanguard Press, 1954.
Teachout, Peter R. "Chains of Tradition, Instruments of Freedom: Contours of the Emerging Right to Community in Obscenity Law." *Capital University Law Review* 7 (1978): 683–731.
Tennent, Gavin, John H. J. Bancroft, and James Cass. "The Control of Deviant Sexual Behavior by Drugs: A Double-Blind Controlled Study of Benperidol, Chlorpromazine, and Placebo." *Archives of Sexual Behavior* 3 (1974): 261–271.
Thomas, D. M. *The White Hotel.* New York: Viking Press, 1981.
Thomas, Donald. *A Long Time Burning: The History of Literary Censorship in England.* New York: Praeger Publishers, 1969.
————. *The Marquis de Sade.* Boston: Little, Brown, 1976.
Thornberry, Terrence P., and Robert A. Silverman. "Exposure to Pornography and Juvenile Delinquency: The Relationship as Indicated by Juvenile Court Records." In *Technical Report of the Commission on Obscenity and Pornography,* vol. 1, pp. 175–180. Washington, D.C.: Government Printing Office, 1970.
Tighe, Thomas J., and Robert N. Leaton, eds. *Habituation: Perspectives from Child Development, Animal Behavior, and Neurophysiology.* Hillsdale, N.J.: Lawrence Erlbaum Associates, 1976.
Tocqueville, Alexis de. *Democracy in America.* Vol. 2. New York: Alfred A. Knopf, Vintage Books, 1954.
Toffler, Alvin. *The Culture Consumers.* Baltimore: Penguin, 1965.
Tribe, David. *Questions of Censorship.* London: George Allen & Unwin, 1973.
Tucker, D. F. B. *Law, Liberalism, and Free Speech.* Totowa, N.J.: Rowman & Allenheld, 1985.
Turnbull, Debi, and Marvin Brown. "Attitudes Toward Homosexuality and Male

and Female Reactions to Homosexual and Heterosexual Slides." *Canadian Journal of Behavioural Science* 9 (1977): 68–80.

United Kingdom. Parliament. *Report of the Committee on Obscenity and Film Censorship.* Cmnd 7772. London: HMSO, 1979.

U.S. Bureau of the Census. *Historical Statistics of the United States.* Washington, D.C.: Government Printing Office, 1975.

U.S. Bureau of the Census. *Statistical Abstract of the United States, 1986.* Washington, D.C.: Government Printing Office, 1985.

U.S. Congress. Senate. Subcommittee of the Committee on the Judiciary. *Hearings, Juvenile Delinquency: Obscene and Pornographic Materials.* 84th Cong., 1st sess., 1955, p. 313.

U.S. Department of Justice. Attorney General's Commission on Pornography. *Final Report.* Washington, D.C.: 1986.

Unwin, J. D. *Sex and Culture.* London: Oxford University Press, 1934.

Van den Berghe, Pierre L., and Gene M. Mesher. "Royal Incest and Inclusive Fitness." *American Ethnologist* 7 (1980): 300–317.

van den Haag, Ernest. "Quia Ineptum." In *"To Deprave and Corrupt. . . ,"* edited by John Chandos, pp. 109–124. New York: Association Press, 1962.

———. "Democracy and Pornography." In *Where Do You Draw the Line?* edited by Victor B. Cline, pp. 257–270. Provo, Utah: Brigham Young University Press, 1974.

———. "Pornography and Censorship." *Policy Review* 13 (1980): 73–81.

Waelder, Robert. *Basic Theory of Psychoanalysis.* New York: Schocken, 1964.

Wagner, Peter. "Pornography in the Courtroom: Trial Reports About Cases of Sexual Crimes and Delinquencies as a Genre of Eighteenth-Century Erotica." In *Sexuality in Eighteenth-Century Britain,* edited by Paul-Gabriel Bouce, pp. 120–140. Manchester: Manchester University Press, 1982.

Wahl, Charles William. "Psychodynamics of Consummated Maternal Incest." *Archives of General Psychiatry* 3 (1960): 188–197.

Walker, C. Eugene. "Erotic Stimuli and the Aggressive Offender." In *Technical Report of the Commission on Obscenity and Pornography,* vol. 7, pp. 91–148. Washington, D.C.: Government Printing Office, 1970.

Walker, Jack. "A Critique of the Elitist Theory of Democracy." *American Political Science Review* 60 (1966): 285–295.

Wallace, Douglas, and Gerald Wehmer. "Pornography and Attitude Change." *Journal of Sex Research* 7 (1971): 116–125.

Wallace, Douglas, Gerald Wehmer, and Edward Podany. "Contemporary Community Standards of Visual Erotica." In *Technical Report of the Commission on Obscenity and Pornography,* vol. 9, pp. 27–88. Washington, D.C.: Government Printing Office, 1970.

Wallace, Edwin R. *Freud and Anthropology.* New York: International University Press, 1983.

Watkins, Sharon Anne. "The Devil and the D.A: The Civil Abatement of Obscenity." *Hastings Law Journal* 28 (1977): 1329–1358.

Webb, Peter. *The Erotic Arts.* Boston: New York Graphic Society, 1975.

Weeks, Jeffrey. *Sex, Politics, and Society: The Regulation of Sexuality Since 1800*. New York and London: Longman, 1981.

Werner, Heinz, and Bernard Kaplan. *Symbol Formation: An Organismic-Developmental Approach to Language and the Expression of Thought*. New York: John Wiley & Sons, 1963.

White, Howard D. "Library Censorship and Permissive Morality." *Library Quarterly* 51 (1981): 192–207.

White, Leonard A. "Erotica and Aggression: The Influence of Sexual Arousal, Positive Affect, and Negative Affect on Aggressive Behavior." *Journal of Personality and Social Psychology* 37 (1979): 591–601.

White, Leslie A. *The Evolution of Culture: The Development of Civilization to the Fall of Rome*. New York: McGraw-Hill, 1959.

Wilensky, Harold. "Mass Society and Mass Culture." *American Sociological Review* 29 (1964): 173–197.

Williams, Bernard, ed. *Obscenity and Film Censorship*. Cambridge: Cambridge University Press, 1981.

Williams, Raymond. *The Long Revolution*. Westport, Conn.: Greenwood Press, 1961.

Williams, Robin. *American Society: A Sociological Interpretation*. New York: 1966.

Wilson, Edmund. "The Vogue of the Marquis de Sade." *Eight Essays*. Garden City, N.Y.: Doubleday, 1954.

Wilson, Edward O. *On Human Nature*. New York: Bantam Books, 1979.

Wilson, James Q. "Violence, Pornography, and Social Science." *The Public Interest*, no. 22 (Winter 1971): 45–61.

Wilson, W. Cody. "Law Enforcement Officers' Perception of Pornography as a Social Issue." *Journal of Social Issues* 29 (1973): 44–50.

Wilson, W. Cody, Jane Friedman, and Bernard Horowitz. "Gravity of the Pornography Situation and Problems of Control." In *Technical Report of the Commission on Obscenity and Pornography*, vol. 5, pp. 5–14. Washington, D.C.: Government Printing Office, 1970.

Winnick, Charles. "Clients' Perceptions of Prostitutes and of Themselves." *International Journal of Social Psychiatry* 8 (1961–1962): 289–297.

———. "Some Observations of Characteristics of Patrons of Adult Bookstores." In *Technical Report of the Commission on Obscenity and Pornography*, vol. 4, pp. 225–244. Washington, D.C.: Government Printing Office, 1970.

Wolchik, Sharlene A., Sanford L. Braver, and Karen Jensen. "Volunteer Bias in Erotica Research: Effects of Intrusiveness of Measure and Sexual Background." *Archives of Sexual Behavior* 14 (1985): 93–107.

Wolchik, Sharlene A., S. Lee Spencer, and Iris S. Lisi. "Volunteer Bias in Research Employing Vaginal Measures of Sexual Arousal." *Archives of Sexual Behavior* 12 (1983): 339–408.

Wood, Robert C. *Suburbia*. Boston: Houghton Mifflin, 1958.

Woods, L. B. *A Decade of Censorship in America*. Metuchen, N.J.: Scarecrow Press, 1979.

Wright, Charles F. *Mass Communication: A Sociological Perspective*. New York: Random House, 1959.

Yaffe, Maurice, and Edward C. Nelson. *The Influence of Pornography on Behavior.* New York: Academic Press, 1982.

Young, Wayland. *Eros Denied.* New York: Grove Press, 1966.

Zetterberg, Hans L. "The Consumers of Pornography Where It Is Easily Available: The Swedish Experience." In *Technical Report of the Commission on Obscenity and Pornography,* vol. 9, pp. 453–468. Washington, D.C.: Government Printing Office, 1970.

Zillman, Dolf. *Connections Between Sex and Aggression.* Hillsdale, N.J.: Lawrence Erlbaum Associates, 1984.

Zillman, Dolf, and Jennings Bryant. "Effects of Massive Exposure to Pornography." In *Pornography and Sexual Aggression,* edited by Neil M. Malamuth and Edward Donnerstein, pp. 115–138. New York: Academic Press, 1984.

Zillman, Dolf, Jennings Bryant, and R. A. Carveth. "The Effect of Erotica Featuring Sado-Masochism and Bestiality on Motivated Intermale Aggression." *Personality and Social Psychology Bulletin* 7 (1981): 153–159.

Zillman, Dolf, Jennings Bryant, Paul W. Comisky, and Norman J. Medoff. "Excitation and Hedonic Valence in the Effect of Erotica on Motivated Intermale Aggression." *European Journal of Social Psychology* 2 (1981): 231–252.

Zurcher, Louis A., and R. George Kirkpatrick. *Citizens for Decency.* Austin: University of Texas Press, 1976.

Zurcher, Louis A., Jr., R. George Kirkpatrick, Robert Cushing, and Charles K. Bowman. "Ad Hoc Antipornography Organizations and Their Active Members: A Research Summary." *Journal of Social Issues* 29 (1973): 69–94.

Legal Cases

Alberts v. California, 354 U.S. 476 (1957).

Barron v. Baltimore, 32 U.S. (7 Pet.) 243 (1833).

Brockett v. Spokane Arcades, 472 U.S. 491 (1985).

Burstyn v. Wilson, 343 U.S. 495 (1952).

Butler v. Michigan, 352 U.S. 380 (1957). '

Chaplinsky v. New Hampshire, 315 U.S. 568 (1942).

F.C.C. v. Pacifica Foundation, 438 U.S. 726 (1978).

Freedman v. Maryland, 380 U.S. 51 (1965).

Ginsberg v. New York, 390 U.S. 629 (1968).

Ginzberg v. United States, 383 U.S. 463 (1966).

Hamling v. United States, 418 U.S. 87 (1974).

Hudnut v. American Booksellers Association, 475 U.S. 1002 (1986).

Interstate Circuit, Inc. v. Dallas, 390 U.S. 676 (1968).

Jacobellis v. Ohio, 378 U.S. 184 (1964).

Jenkins v. Georgia, 418 U.S. 153 (1974).

Kingsley International Pictures v. Board of Regents, 360 U.S. 684 (1959).

Manual Enterprises v. Day, 370 U.S. 478 (1962).

"Memoirs of a Woman of Pleasure" v. Massachusetts, 383 U.S. 418 (1966).

Miller v. California, 413 U.S. 15 (1973).

Near v. Minnesota, 283 U.S. 697 (1931).

New York v. Ferber, 458 U.S. 747 (1982).
Paris Adult Theatre I v. Slaton, 413 U.S. 49 (1973).
Pinkus v. United States, 436 U.S. 293 (1978).
Pope v. Illinois, 107 S. Ct. 1918 (1987).
Prince v. Massachusetts, 321 U.S. 158 (1944).
Regina v. Hicklin [1868] L.R. 3 Q.B. 360.
Renton v. Playtime Theatres, 475 U.S. 41 (1986).
Roth v. United States, 354 U.S. 476 (1957).
Rowan v. United States, 397 U.S. 728 (1970).
Smith v. California, 361 U.S. 147 (1959).
Smith v. United States, 431 U.S. 291 (1977).
Splawn v. California, 431 U.S. 595 (1977).
Stanley v. Georgia, 394 U.S. 557 (1969).
Times Film Corp. v. Chicago, 365 U.S. 43 (1960).
United States v. One Book Called "Ulysses," 5 F. Supp. 182 (S.D.N.Y. 1933).
United States v. Orito, 413 U.S. 139 (1973).
United States v. Reidel, 402 U.S. 351 (1971).
United States v. Thirty-One Photographs, 156 F. Supp. 350 (S.D.N.Y. 1957).
United States v. Twelve 200-Foot Reels of Film, 413 U.S. 123 (1973).
Ward v. Illinois, 431 U.S. 767 (1977).
Winters v. New York, 333 U.S. 507 (1948).
Young v. American Mini Theatres, 427 U.S. 50 (1976).

Index

327

Compositor:	ICC
Printer:	Maple-Vail Book Mfg. Group
Binder:	Maple-Vail Book Mfg. Group
Text:	10/13 Galliard
Display:	Galliard